Michelangelo Red Antonioni Blue

The publisher gratefully acknowledges the generous support of the Eric Papenfuse and Catherine Lawrence Endowment Fund in Film and Media Studies of the University of California Press Foundation.

Michelangelo Red Antonioni Blue

Eight Reflections on Cinema

Murray Pomerance

UNIVERSITY OF CALIFORNIA PRESS
Berkeley · Los Angeles · London

University of California Press, one of the most distinguished university presses in the United States, enriches lives around the world by advancing scholarship in the humanities, social sciences, and natural sciences. Its activities are supported by the UC Press Foundation and by philanthropic contributions from individuals and institutions. For more information, visit www.ucpress.edu.

University of California Press
Berkeley and Los Angeles, California

University of California Press, Ltd.
London, England

Library of Congress Cataloging-in-Publication Data

Pomerance, Murray, 1946–.
Michelangelo red Antonioni blue : eight reflections on cinema / Murray Pomerance.
p. cm.
Includes bibliographical references and index.
ISBN 978-0-520-25870-9 (cloth)
ISBN 978-0-520-26686-5 (pbk.)
1. Antonioni, Michelangelo—Criticism and interpretation. I. Title.
PN1998.3.A58P66 2011
791.4302'33092—dc22 2010038908

19 18 17 16 15 14 13 12 11
10 9 8 7 6 5 4 3 2 1

To Bill Rothman, true line of sight

We need always to be returning to the fact of how mysterious these objects called movies are, unlike anything else on earth.

—Stanley Cavell, *Themes Out of School*

The new library building, which in both its entire layout and its near-ludicrous internal regulation seeks to exclude the reader as a potential enemy, might be described, so Lemoine thought, said Austerlitz, as the official manifestation of the increasingly importunate urge to break with everything which still has some living connection to the past.

—W. G. Sebald, *Austerlitz*

For in spite of tricks which we shall presently describe and which created the image which we shall always have of him, he knew very well that his famous look was identical with the thing at which he was looking, that he would never attain true possession of himself, but simply that listless sampling of himself which is characteristic of reflective knowledge.

—Jean-Paul Sartre, *Baudelaire*

Contents

Plates

Acknowledgments

Any writer of passages such as these gets by with a little help from his friends, but in this case I have received generous support, encouragement, and aid over more than two decades from a number of people who began by loving Antonioni as much as I do and came eventually to smile upon me far more than I deserved. While the flaws and faults herein are entirely my own, I do wish to express my sincerest gratitude to those who have illuminated my path: Patricia Albanese (Toronto), Enrica Antonioni (Italy), Stephen P. Arkle (Technicolor, Los Angeles), Michal Bardecki (Toronto), Nikesh Bhagat (Toronto), Judy Boals (New York), Joseph John Cooke Esq. M.B.E. (Lincoln, England), Terry and Bob Dale (Los Angeles), Brett Davidson (Margaret Herrick Library, Beverly Hills), David Desser (Collegeville, Pa.), Rufus Dickinson (Toronto), Eugene Di Sante (Toronto), Michael Doleschell (Toronto), the late Slobodan Drakulic (Toronto), Julie Duxbury (Lincoln, England), David Edgar (BFI, London), Kris Erickson (Toronto), Megan Follows (Toronto), Lester Friedman (Bethesda, Md.), Linda Gerth (*The New Republic,* Washington), Terry Gillin (Toronto), Fernando Gómez Hervis (Toronto), Assheton Gorton (Montgomery, Wales), Chris Graeber (Local 600 Publicists, Los Angeles), Don Guest (Tours, France), Paul Hadian (Toronto), Benjamin Halligan (Manchester), Daria Halprin (Marin County, Calif.), J.J. Hoffman (Los Angeles), Nathan Holmes (Chicago), Andrew Hunter (Toronto), Paul Jeremias (Toronto), Trevor Johnston (London), Daniel Kasman (New York), Glenn Kenny (New York), Anastasia Kerameos (BFI, London),

Mark Kermode (Southampton), Leonard Klady (Los Angeles), Kristine Krueger, (Margaret Herrick Library, Beverly Hills), Bill Krohn (Los Angeles), Local 600 Publicists (Los Angeles), Mark Lubell (New York), Danny Lyon (Clintondale, N.Y.), Jill McConkey (University of Toronto Press, Toronto), Andrew McGovern (PhotoFest, New York), Douglas Messerli (Los Angeles), Tamara Micner (Google), Will Mills (Toronto), Janet Moat (BFI, London), Paul S. Moore (Toronto), Nigel Morris (Lincoln, England), Mike Munson (Technicolor, North Hollywood), Steven Muzzatti (Toronto), Hiro Narita (Petaluma, Calif.), Matt O'Casey (Manchester), Ronan O'Casey (Los Angeles), Bob Olson (Technicolor, North Hollywood), Christopher Porter (Nova Scotia), Taira Restar (Kentfield, Calif.), Ned Rifkin (The Smithsonian Institution, Washington, D.C.), Ken Robbins (Springs, N.Y.), Erik Rocca (New York), William Rothman (Miami), Bob Rubin (Tulsa), Don Snyder (Toronto), Vivian Sobchack (Los Angeles), Harrison Starr (Los Angeles), Alison Stawarz and John McAslan (John McAslan and Associates, London), Michael Sugar (Los Angeles), Richard Summers (Toronto), Dean Tavoularis (Los Angeles), Carol Tavris (Los Angeles), Jamie Thompson (Toronto), Matthew Thompson (Toronto), Charles Warren (Boston), Bruce Winstein (Chicago), and Joshua Yumibe (Dundee, Scotland).

Exceptionally gracious in contributing to my understanding of 35 mm color processes has been Richard Haines (Croton-on-Hudson, N.Y.), an artist and scholar of astounding knowledge and a warm and patient teacher. Further, I have been touched by help far beyond the call of duty from Ned Comstock at the Cinema-Television Library of the University of Southern California and Jenny Romero at the Margaret Herrick Library of the Academy of Motion Picture Arts and Sciences, Beverly Hills. And Beverly Walker (Los Angeles) has worked hard and eagerly on my behalf, even while suffering the flu, out of a respect and love for Michelangelo which are undying. To James Daley (Wheaton, Ill.) for his assistance with photographic reproduction, and for still being there after all these years, my heartfelt thanks. My assistant Ian Dahlman was a whirling dervish of a researcher, or at least a supersleuth, able to leap tall reference stacks in a single bound and never less than a perfectly cheery ideal reader. And my friend and colleague John Oslansky (Perugia) has been an inspiration for the thoughts contained here.

To Mary Francis, Suzanne Knott, Caroline Knapp, Kalicia Pivirotto, and Eric Schmidt at University of California Press go my sincere thanks for a sweet collaboration. And to Nellie Perret and Ariel Pomerance, who have made many helpful comments and been my support through thick and thin, not to say the craft for my craft, a special thank you for keeping home lights burning.

Toronto, Los Angeles, Dooagh, Dublin, London
October 2010

On the Images in This Book

Acknowledging the splendid frontispieces made for all the volumes of that edition by Mr. Alvin Langdon Coburn, in his preface to the 1909 Scribner's edition of *The Golden Bowl,* Henry James argued for the sort of image that might "plead its case with some shyness." My desire in finding a way to illustrate this book was to go still further, with images that might each, in an idiosyncratic way, summon up the whole tenor or tension evoked by the poetry of a film while at the same time drawing into recollection the unfolding argument of this writer's prose. Michelangelo Antonioni's color films are complex and monumental structures, and finding the "right" image for each was a project with problems. Conventional publicity stills, for example, are made to highlight either action—not always at the heart of my analysis—or principal actors in character (so as to publicize their work quite as much as the film itself). These shots are therefore typically repetitive for any film, inspirations for my fear that the reader would in most cases have come across them, or very similar images, before. The canonical reading of Antonioni's works tends toward gender relations in a time of modernist alienation, and one will have trouble scouting through publicity stills if one wishes to find brilliant and evocative images that do not bark this now worn (if not, indeed, misconstrued) theme. Further, many publicity shots are technically altered for color, in order to reproduce well in newsprint. And still worse, many of the shots typify filmic moments vaguely but do not actually represent what we ever precisely see onscreen. To make matters more painful, if more painful they can be: with some of the films included in this book there are virtually no usable publicity images in existence.

Thus I have turned to digital frame enlargements, which permit a very precise selection of moments and a sharply focused attention to the exact nuances of color and composition in any image. Our decisions in printing the images as they are to be found here were made with a view to heightening their sense of color and form, and to getting the best possible reproduction given the necessarily variant and restrictive limits of the originating materials. One image is worth a special word, and that is the illustration for *The Mystery of Oberwald*, plate 8. This film was produced originally for Radiotelevisione Italiana using an electronic—not a cinematic—recording process, and the resultant film was later transferred to celluloid in Los Angeles, through the now rather outdated process of kinescoping, in which a camera records on film the image that is broadcast in front of its lens on a television screen. Given that Italian television uses a different screen resolution than American television in the first place, even watching the film on TV here would have been a visually degraded experience; but a kinescope makes for a picture that is even softer and imprecise as to color. It is therefore the case that the picture I include, for all its lack of sharpness, really does represent *Oberwald* as closely as is possible now (there are no sharper publicity stills)—really does hint at the muted and subtly transformational color Antonioni had in mind.

Introduction

Where does violet end and lilac begin?
—Kandinsky, *Concerning the Spiritual in Art*

In one of Antonioni's films that I discuss in these pages, two characters meet by chance outside a theater after watching the same film. They talk about one another, about the chance of their encounter, but of the film they have not a word to say. A film can enter us and reside there, turning and changing through our biography and our fortune. To evoke a film, speak of it, try to write its long and ghostly presence: and especially an Antonioni film, one of the eight major works in color that he produced starting in 1964, after it became hopelessly apparent that color was his world: to face the growing fact of a film, honest as to its structure, its repetitions, its allusions and elusions, its tones, the way something suddenly becomes obvious that was invisible before, to address a film not only as subject material but as form, is my challenge here. That a story does not mean everything, indeed sometimes means nothing. That a revelation can be charged through the turn of a face from shadow into light, colored shadow into colored light. Colors, after all, are more than facts, more than indications. Color has resonance, descends into a past, causes us to remember and fall. To find—not the theme, not the statement, but—the song of the films, what they intimate and how they intimate it, not their formula but their personality.

"There are, indeed, things that cannot be put into words," wrote Wittgenstein (*Tractatus* 6.522). So, these eight meditations might have been a string of silences. It is always difficult to use language for coming to terms with a cinematic image, especially Antonioni's images, brilliant, provocative, fugitive. Stanley Cavell said the problem beautifully of another book: "Its difficulty lies as much in the obscurity of its promptings as in its particular surfacings of expression" (162). The Antonionian surface is complicated by delicacy, pain, rhythm, distance, time, urgency, body, the perils of sound. Cavell also suggests that in color films, "the world created is neither a world just past nor a world of make-believe. It is a world of an immediate future" (82). Antonioni always has his eye on the future: What is this? That is, what is this becoming?

Things to remember:

1. What people—that is, characters—say in film is not the same as what we see.
2. There is no proper treatise for elucidating or unlocking the puzzles Antonioni has left us. The puzzle, the mystery, is a quintessentially serious form.
3. What James Agee wrote of Charles Chaplin's *Monsieur Verdoux:* "Disregard virtually everything you may have read about the film. It is of interest, but chiefly as a definitive measure of the difference between the thing a man of genius puts before the world and the things the world is equipped to see in it" (253).

Also three caveats:

First, I do not deal with the very lengthy *Chung Kuo—Cina* (1972), or the rather brief *Il provino* (1965); *Ritorno a Lisca Bianca* (1984); *Roma* (1989); *Kumbha Mela* (1989); *Noto, Mandorli, Vulcano, Stromboli, Carnevale* (1993); *Sicilia* (1997); or *Lo sguardo di Michelangelo* (2004). This book is about the major color narratives, only.

Next, there is no attempt here to work out or exercise a color theory, nor should there reasonably be, since color as Antonioni uses it is not a rigid language nor a set of tools but part of the sense of the world at any moment. For children, wrote Benjamin, "picture books are paradise"; and "children learn in the memory of their first intuition." Also, "For adults, the yearning for paradise is the yearning of yearnings" ("Notes" 264, 265).

What we know as a vocabulary of color is only a shallow abstraction suffered through the bureaucratic press of social organization in the modern world, but with color we always see more than we know how to say. "Color," say Morgan Russell and Stanton Macdonald-Wright, "is just as capable as music of providing us with the highest ecstasies and delights" (Levin 129; qtd. in Gage, *Culture* 241). As to the technology of his color—among the fans of which was Alfred Hitchcock (Robertson, Letter to Ascarelli)—we would do well to remember that no matter who shoots a film and how, it is the producer who arranges for the printing (Pomerance, "Notes on Some Limits"). Antonioni had the luck to find producers who trusted his poetry.

Lastly, stories and story analysis absorb the attention of the vast majority of scholars and writers who take up cinema. But films are events in themselves, not packages for stories. There are only happenings in film, and happenings are everywhere. A purple coat, a pink cottage. Here, I often jump around, neglect "narrative continuities." The reader is encouraged to find a happy way of balancing all this.

Viewing is balancing, at any rate.

In *Cahiers du cinéma* of May 1980, we find a little note from Antonioni to Roland Barthes, including this (in my translation): "Thank you for *Camera Lucida,* which is at once luminous and very beautiful. It astonishes me that in chapter three you describe yourself as being 'a subject torn between two languages, one expressive and the other critical' . . . But what is an artist if not also a subject torn between two languages, one language that expresses and another that does not?" Immediately after this, the maestro added, "I was in the middle of writing this letter when news came to me by telephone that Roland Barthes had died."

On the morning of July 31, 2007 when I learned that Antonioni had died—he had been debilitated for some long while—I was stunned, because that night I had dreamed of him. And I thought how wonderful it was that we still had his films. The more I watch them now, the more I feel affected by the language that does not express.

Beyond the Clouds

We all know that memory offers no guarantees.

—Antonioni

The origins of modernity are obscure, notwithstanding scholarly attempts to fix as key dates the Industrial Revolution, around 1750; the institution of railroad time and invention of the daguerreotype around 1839; the demonstration of vitreous construction and the new visible interior at the Crystal Palace in 1850; or the demonstration at the Eiffel Tower in 1895 of the efficacy of iron replacing wood in construction—a "nonrenewable resource [replacing] a renewable one" (Billington 29). Looking backward through history, it is less taxing to determine certain harbingers that prefigured the conditions we now call "modern," such as the trial, in 1560, of the man called Martin Guerre. Having come to the Pyrenean village of Artigat four years previously, he gave himself out as a person who had run away from the place years before, soon after his marriage in fact; and then returned to live with the wife he had taken and the son she had borne him until it came to seem, for various reasons, that he was, perhaps, an imposter. He was subjected to judicial authority in Rieux, some thirteen miles away, this in front of a jury of strangers before whom his accusers needed to produce a claim entirely unattached to the folk and communal knowledge of neighbors whose understanding of the man had grown in the deeply committed, agriculturally based matrix of everyday life: a claim which, by contrast, stood upon the sorts of facts one needed no history to grasp nor any particular familiarity to clearly discern. The man, whose name was found to be Pansette, was found guilty, condemned, and burned at the stake, an early victim, historically speaking, to the faux pas and misconstructions that are always present in impression management (see Natalie Zeman Davis). To present oneself to strangers is a rigorous task, demanding the most constant vigilance not of what one senses oneself to be and hopes to become but of what one is projecting to the surveillers who form one's social surround. And modernity, indeed, can be seen to develop in late Feudalism as a form in which strangers proliferate, mingle, interact, and structure a world where private knowledge, traditionalism, family history, and intimacy play a relatively marginal part. Modernity also opens gender, a favorite subject of Michelangelo Antonioni, to new perspectives and understandings, being, as Susan Sontag has said, "the only culture that makes possible the emancipation of women" (*Time* 114).

Beyond the Clouds is, in a way, an extended essay on the symptoms and possibilities of modern life, certainly insofar as modernity both cultures and bounds people's ability to become intimate and engaged with, or sensitive and attuned to, the increasingly distant others who move past and around them in an incessant flux. A boy and girl cannot quite get together; crime does not sit comfortably in the seat of habitual behavior and friendship; a man and woman cannot quite speak the same language; religious passion hovers uncertainly in the precincts of an ancient city, whose stones reverberate with a sense of the deep past. It is superficial to say that this film is about love.

Antonioni's project was to cull some of the substantial material he had written over several years (and ultimately published in *That Bowling Alley on the Tiber*) and fashion it for the screen as a quartet of episodes, each running a little under half an hour and each following the story of characters occupying different social settings. The first gives the story of a young fellow who meets a girl in Ferrara, but then loses her, and then finds her again. The second, set in Portofino, puts a film director into the presence of a girl who draws him out of his meditations with a chilling story of having committed a killing. The third begins with a marriage in trouble in Paris, and continues with a strange and perhaps fortuitous meeting over a problem with real estate. The last, in Aix-en-Provence, has a young man meet a young woman who should love him, and who perhaps does, except that she has plans he cannot interrupt. In these episodes, we see the interwoven and dominant presence of movement counterpoised against tranquility; strangeness challenging the desire for contact; urbanity in the face of traditionalism; etiquette interplaying with urgency; communication either broken or made painfully ambiguous; seasonless merchandising; and the deeply horrifying possibility that our unitary relations have been slowly, methodically exploded over time so that it is only as fragments and with fragmentation of spirit that we may be condemned to lead our lives.

For aficionados of Antonioni and devotées of this particular film, a brief apology, because there are parts of it I studiously avoid addressing here:

Having suffered a massive stroke in 1985, Antonioni was exhausted and partly debilitated when it came time to shoot *Beyond the Clouds*. The insurers insisted on the presence behind the camera of a healthy and competent director. Out of friendship, Wim Wenders agreed to play this role, and eventually himself directed certain introductory, transitional, and concluding narrative passages or bridges involving John Malkovich in the film-director role of episode two: a scene in an airplane "above the clouds"; a scene at a windy lonely beach; a scene on a train heading into France; meditative scenes in the streets of Ferrara; scenes at the Hotel Cardinal in Aix-en-Provence; and a hilltop scene involving Marcello Mastroianni conversing with Jeanne Moreau as, painting Mont Sainte-Victoire, he attempts to recapture the inspiration that had seized Cézanne (and also the inspiration of Borges's Pierre Menard, whose "admirable intention was to produce a few pages which would coincide—word for word and line for line—with those of Miguel de Cervantes" [66]). I work around these insertions by Wenders—which were photographed by Robby Müller (exquisitely, but not, I think, as Antonioni would have had them photographed) and written with a view to perhaps making more explicit the connections I cannot help but feel Antonioni would wish us to tease out on our own. That Wenders is paying homage to Antonioni is without question—in his diary of the shoot, for March 9, 1995, he writes of a particular shot, "He shoots it again and again, with tiny variations, as though to put off the end for as long as possible" (138)—nor can there be any doubt that the younger man held the older with the greatest of esteem and bore him a profound love. Yet for all this, he is not and was not Antonioni, and the interludes are distinct in every important way. In a proposed edit, writes Wenders, Antonioni sliced out almost all of the additions. "'Leave my film alone! My stories don't need any framing, they can stand by themselves.' What he wasn't capable of saying in words, he's just told me in the form of his edit" (181). So I leave them to the reader's pleasure, just as Cézanne's mountain is left to the painter who must now find a way to regard it through another man's eyes.

CARMEN AND SILVANO

Portico

Stone and stones. Receding from the camera, a long straight portico, with matched rows of cement columns topped by white plaster arches and a vaulted ceiling. A cobblestone walkway. Beside this to screen left, a road, bordering the modest green of what looks like a rugby pitch. Dense fog. Comacchio, the little Venice, town of more than a hundred arcades, near Ferrara, city of the House of Este; probably the Portico of Capuccini, in that late part of fall where winter can almost be seen.

We are peering at the single, advancing lamp of a bicycle—a typically Antonionian view, recalling immediately how in his cinema we are given what Gilberto Perez calls "partial views of arresting partiality" (368); certainly a view that tends to "render the uncertainty of modern life with elegant exactness" (369). Then, on the road, a car (with two lamps) advances. "Gendered" vehicles, then, one showing twice the light of the other. The car stops and a young man (Kim Rossi-Stuart) jumps out, excusing himself rather gracefully just as the cyclist, a girl perhaps not quite as young as he (Inès Sastre), stops pedaling and turns to face him in the stillness. He needs directions to a good hotel: expensive or cheap, he trusts her. Just there—she points behind. As he walks back to his car she regards him carefully, then rides on, and with a quick turn he discovers that she is gone.

Tall, thin as a whooping crane, expensively dressed in slate gray, he has long hair stylishly cut. Her long hair was neatly tied, and she had taken care to make up her face primly and cleanly. We will learn that he is an engineer, out here in the country on a job; that she is a teacher, cloistered until school closes, but under these measured, shady columns they were only a boy and a girl, a stranger and someone who knew the territory, someone who drove a car through the fog and someone who kept inside a portico making circles in the air with her feet. One searched only what he needed to know, the other was happy to be margined and marked, to guide herself in the columnar shade of art and civilization.

There is no *reason* why we should wish or expect these two to meet again, except perhaps the intoxication of their beauty, which suffuses us with a desire they perhaps do not feel. Yet it seems instantly true that when these two are in one another's presence they are (even lightly) bonded, a single twosome, not two solitudes, and that they work in a sensitive negotiation to produce what has been called a "togethering" (Ryave and Schenkein 269ff). Watching them as, tentatively, they hold this coupling, it is not difficult to be reminded a little of the conversation in *Vertigo* between Scottie Ferguson and Madeleine Elster outside his house near Telegraph Hill, the day after he has pulled her out of San Francisco Bay, when, reading her thank-you note he smiles and says, "I hope we will, too." She waits a moment. "What?" He waits half a moment. "Meet again sometime." And she says, very matter-of-factly, "We have," I think to underline that there is no reason for us to hope they will have another encounter. "Only one is a wanderer," Madeleine tells Scottie, "Two together are always going somewhere." That strange voice does seem to be echoing from the depths of Carmen (we will see that the subtle invocation of *Vertigo* is no accident.) Silvano and Carmen are distinctly *not* going somewhere, yet there lingers the idea that they ought to be, will be, must be—a connection born in a thought.

He turns his car around, at any rate, and drives back the way he came.

Etiquettes

In a strange little scene Silvano checks in at the hotel: a scene that is strange in the way that only Antonioni's scenes can be strange, seeming to go forward and backward in time and space at once. We are lingering in the forecourt as he enters a hazelnut green atrium and speaks to the innkeeper, a stocky man who gesticulates in a wearied, businesslike way. There are fancy iron bars over the door panes, such that our view is a little obstructed, and outside where we are positioned there is no telltale sign that proclaims this rather squat building a hotel. Room number 4, says the innkeeper, do you have any bags? The boy says they're outside, then fluidly emerges to get them. The innkeeper gazes through the door but, losing this moment, we suddenly dissolve to the same lobby later on, our young man entering from outside as though from another world. The innkeeper is gone.

"Time in Antonioni," Perez notes, "is a time of the moment" (370). With a real ferocity, one can think to pass by way of a memory into a history long decayed, or, in the magical spasm of *déjà vu,* think to have spied in a faraway past a secret event that has only just now transpired. Outside, it is quite as bright as when the boy checked in. Have only a few seconds elapsed? Where has Silvano been that he should now be returning as though steeped in the traces of some exploration? And why did we not accompany him? This transition that signals a change of time and attitude conveys a sufficient instigation to believe something is different about the boy, something we cannot see (and that is therefore catching).

He enters the breakfast room, where a man—one of those mushroom-colored souls who always fill the background when we travel to strange places—is devouring something with a glass of water near a window. In a second room, Carmen is seated alone, modestly finishing her meal. She gets up as though instinctually and joins him at the window, says ciao. Something of a Narcissus, he is surprised. The beautiful thing, says he, gloating a little because he finds her attractive and is tickled that she is paying attention to him, is that he came here by chance. When, formally enough, she asks why it's beautiful—since in her perfect *pudeur* she does not leap to the conclusion that she could be found attractive—he rattles on about how he was supposed to go somewhere else and at one point let the car drive him, a car that we may like to believe had a personality and will of its own. One can recall Fred Astaire captivated by Cyd Charisse in *The Band Wagon,* taking her for an evening's ride in a hackney cab and letting the horse decide where they should go. Fate enters human affairs through the body of a substitute: a horse or else a car so attached to one's person that one has no consciousness of guiding it. Silvano's car is a spirit blown by the wind, and so his meeting with Carmen is ordained by the gods.

Silvano makes to nuzzle against Carmen's tawny neck and, charmed and a little excited, she moves off, her lips and sweater red as berries. Turning her head away from him, she reveals a light smile of satisfaction. They sit down at her table and smile into one another's eyes. He thinks he has caught her. She knows she has caught him. But Antonioni will show, here and elsewhere in this film, what it means to catch, and how equivocal experience can be.

Meanwhile, what universe do we inhabit with these two adventurers, the modern one? A girl behaves in a courtly fashion, conscious of her own demureness as though it is a garment tailored to her form, while a boy gives the impression, perhaps without affectation, of having come on a quest, while on the highway behind them, that through its echoes and its racing flashes seems to dominate their space, those modern symptoms, movement and mechanism, are indicated forcefully with every speeding cipher. A man in blue punts down a little canal near the road, an emphasizing contradiction, medieval in every effortless stretch of his arms as he plies his pole. And is Silvano not a knight, with his invisible baggage and his air of privilege? The architecture was built in the twentieth century no doubt, but on a Romanesque model. The walls of the breakfast room are chrysalis green. What imago, we have to wonder, is waiting here to be born?

Once again they stroll along that portico beside their road, sunlight streaming through the archways. Their pace is casual but relentless, as though a riddle is to be worked out. He speaks of sunsets (in what one irked reviewer calls a "witheringly silly" line [Atkinson]). (Young people always want to have something to say.) They look up and see an icon of the Mother and Child appearing to bless them. Carmen talks about voices, suggesting that the voice is a creature, nervous, secretive. It's strange, he muses, we always want to live in someone's imagination; I like your eyes, completely empty of everything except sweetness. They kiss one another hungrily, and—oddly, because there is nothing of presence or intimacy that is not already given in the touch of these lips that have so artfully held back from intercourse with one another while still entreating and invoking so much with their hints of discourse—we approach, approach and judiciously examine, approach with hunger to see or know more. Then the scene fades, a conventional love story: that is, a story in which appetites are subject to etiquettes, in which conventions themselves are loved.

The Kiss

That we should approach, lean toward, that kiss! We have seen kisses onscreen before. For decades, they constituted the royal icons of cinema. Plainly enough, this one comes from passion, is erotic for both partners, surprises, and deeply pleasures. It escorts us to a new, or apparently new, depth. Yet, to learn this we need not dolly in. Does the camera movement perhaps provide explanation for—thus cover—our lingering interest in a sight that should normally seduce just a passing glance, for to let the shot run long with a steady camera might embarrassingly reflect a viewer's attention back upon himself (even in the dark, where it cannot be optical relish for others, the rush of blood to the face is a palpable experience)? But the movement inward (or outward, away from ourselves, into ecstasy) produces in itself an interest and a payoff: not that something might be detected in the kiss with a closer view but as though the smooth gliding form of our fascination is a direct biophysical response to the kiss's solicitation. We take leave of ourselves to kiss the subject matter of the film just as, smoothly and effortlessly, Silvano draws Carmen toward him in this kiss.

"HOTEL"

Dissolve. We discover our duo walking into the upstairs hallway of the hotel. She is leading him to her door. Centered in the frame is a pair of French doors giving out into the night, presumably over the forecourt, and through them we can see a bright turquoise neon sign, possibly "HOTEL"—it is visible only as a fragment—eerily agleam. (Only from *inside,* that is, do we see a sign that this is a hotel!) A shimmering reflection of this colored light is behind the boy's back, around the doorframe of the room opposite Carmen's. While she waits, he goes over to the French doors, opens them, steps out into the turquoise night, turning his face momentarily so that it is bathed in the rich undersea color. Then he steps back in, closes the doors behind him, says good night. Before going into her room, she follows him with her eyes, and we can see plainly enough that she is hungry for him. This is no dance of suspension and titillation for holding off the pleasure of a sexual encounter, for winding up the audience, but a careful and ritualized outplaying of fruitful ambiguity and doubt, the commonplace etiquette of modern life, when anticipations need not lead to resolution, when invitations need not lead to happiness.

In his pale green room, with its comforting vaguely Scandinavian lacquered wooden furniture and brown wooden doors, Silvano stands undecided. In her pale green room, Carmen slowly undresses after turning on her television. Having doffed his overcoat, Silvano mops his face with a towel, muses for a moment, quickly turns and opens his door to scan her territory—maybe she has left her door open a little, a hint. Nothing. He closes his door and turns off the light. Carmen is pulling on a prim pink nightgown, oblivious to some drawings made by her very young students taped to the wall behind her next to a small framed landscape and the television. She sits on her bed thinking (presumably of Silvano): "What is he doing? When will he come? What will he look like when we are warm together, when his neutral gray skins are slivered off?" She is certainly not thinking, "Curious, unappetizing man." Antonioni's skill is to give us what feels like certainty about the most intrinsic and private realities—what they are musing, each of them, alone—while also showing these realities to be unimportant, insubstantial. Silvano is sitting on his bed fully clothed while we hear a car pass by outside. He stretches out, pulls a blanket over himself, shows some anxiety as the scene slowly fades. In the morning, from above, we look down on him still asleep as cars pass one another on the busy road outside and someone sounds a horn. He rises in a trance but while tying his shoes seems suddenly to remember a girl . . . a girl who spoke of voices and kissed him. He moves out quickly to check for her. She has gone.

He asks the concierge to buy her some flowers. But it's too late. Carmen and Silvano do not find one another again.

Two or three years go by.

In the modern world, which is the world in which yesterday has no hold upon tomorrow, the constant and enervating circulation that throws strangers against one another without introducing them produces a situation described by Georg Simmel, in which we experience a particular fear or perplexity that comes with seeing people we cannot hear ("Visual Interaction"). Carmen had told her knight earlier, "Voices never become part of you like other sounds." She says you end up not hearing the sea, for instance, but "a voice you can't help listening to." Yet at the same time, these two say very little to one another, afford one another only briefly and superficially the opportunity to hear and know each other's voice. They seem continually to pass like cars on a road, in a reflex that materially embodies our modern experience of social relationship: we see others without knowing them, relate to them only in a specific and particular way, applying ourselves to only a slice of their capacity and being. These two have no grounding beyond the hotel in which they spent the night, a dazed, neutral experience of the cars speeding by on the road outside, the soothing green walls that presumably relax and comfort them (as they do us) but that have been designed explicitly to soothe strangers who can be presumed to require soothing. No childhood memories in common, no labor, no plan for the future. Their lives are structured and scheduled according to different principles, on different tracks as it were, and once the night has passed there is little possibility—little reason—for them to connect again.

Two questions present themselves:

Why in the middle of the night does the boy not steal into the girl's room? No one else is around to disturb them, she is directly across the hall, there is no reason to doubt that she has desire but in any event she would extend him every grace and gentility even if she refused. Is he afraid of sex? The nature of the kiss shows he is not. This question becomes increasingly perturbing when we note how slowly and self-pleasingly she slips off her underwear and her stockings, how she moves upon the bed in the silk nightgown, conscious of her body and its sensitivities, and when we reflect that as a schoolteacher devoted to her students (the drawings on the wall) she might not have many opportunities for meeting men, especially young and attractive men such as this one. As to him: without getting directions from her, he would never have found this hotel. Why does he hesitate? Could it be that he is thinking of making love to her, imagining the sensation of her body against his, wandering through the corners of a pleasure that has not yet been his, anticipating it with such concentration that the imagined pleasure, swollen, overwhelms him? Could the etiquette and shyness which is holding him back, coupled with the beauty of the anticipation, not produce a state of affairs in which, for him, the thought of romance is more pregnant than the act?

That is one. Another:

Why should Alfred Hitchcock's *Vertigo* be invoked, as, surely, it is? Scottie Ferguson has followed the salesgirl Judy Barton to her home in the Empire Hotel on Sutter Street, a shabby environment with a turquoise neon sign outside the window. Having cajoled her into allowing him to dress and style her (so that through her he may invoke Madeleine Elster, his former object of fascination and obsession taken too early in death), Scottie is waiting in her hotel room for Judy to return from the hairdresser, and as he stands to look out her window he is bathed in the light of the turquoise sign. It is the same "hotel" light that bathes Silvano for a moment as, standing outside her room, he contemplates the possibility of love with Carmen. Might it be that there was another woman for Silvano, before, in another life, and that she is dead or vanished; that Carmen has animated pungent memories of her, and that through Carmen the woman is haunting him? Amazed that he has found her, he fears that if he comes to her in the night he will be able to detect how she is different from the other, detect that she is only herself. Or he knows that if he comes to her, the actuality of the love will fail to match the anticipation. More chilling still: if he comes to her, he will learn that she is the other one, reborn. That the dead live. That he is making love to a ghost.

(Antonioni knew and often reflected the work of Hitchcock, who was also charmed by memory in this way.)

The green light may suggest that every love is a haunting, that every man at each moment with a woman is haunted by his memories of other women, by their persistence and reflection; or if not of other women then by his memories of this woman at some moment before, as she was when first he realized her. Every man looks backward, at any rate, while every woman looks to the future, and even though they seem to be staring into one another's eyes they see at cross purposes.

The green love in the green room, next to the green sign, has chilled him with remorse and fear, with deep need, to such a degree that he must hide from it in a pocket of selfishness. Or else, riddled with memories of loves gone awry, he must patiently make plans, think things over, decide whether he may permit himself to admit the feelings that possess him, as we can see, as we have already seen.

The turquoise light that now bathes—if not his body—the thought of his thoughts: glyphs, parts of a word, something primordial. Frame lines of the French windows slice and interrupt the sign: interruption is modern. This sign is also reminiscent of another turquoise neon sign, in no known language, that illuminates the magical park setting in *Blow-Up*. In both cases, illumination emanates from, and constitutes, meaning itself: no message is conveyed but conveyance, a meaning that is meaning, the process of metaphor which is bringing (the fire) across the chasm. Not *a particular* metaphor, but metaphor: the possibility that one thing can be another. The fact that every thing already is what it is not.

After a Film

Two years later in another town. In a public hall a film screening is concluding. The film may be difficult for some viewers to identify, given that we see only the end credits and that these name only actors involved in an Italian dubbing, but Jonathan Rosenbaum gives it as Nikita Mikhalkov's *Urga* (1991), a story of cultural and experiential tension between a shepherd and a truck driver. A single smokestack is seen in a long shot, rather similar to what is shown at the end of *The Red Desert,* where "birds learn that the smoke is toxic, and do not fly there anymore." Carmen and a girlfriend are leaving, and so is Silvano, who discovers them in the courtyard, as if by "miracle." "Nothing," says Carmen a little archly, "happens by chance." She is pointing to the force of modernity that guides and guards our lives, notwithstanding our innocent conviction that we are blown by the winds of fate. The two walk off, and find her apartment in a building that strikes him—wrongly, it turns out—as expensive. She makes it plain that a woman needs to hear words, and, in a more mundane light, that a boyfriend has recently broken off with her. For his part, Silvano walks around her simple apartment, gazes out the kitchen window, tries to nuzzle against her neck as he did in Ferrara. Once again, swiftly, she withdraws. Now, of course, it is impossible for him to gauge whether she is teasing or rebuffing and he chooses the conservative path, courteously taking his leave.

We observe him walking down the echoing stone staircase outside her door. He stops and takes a beat: not an actor taking a beat, but a character taking a beat. "Maybe I misinterpreted." Slowly he returns. Inside with her, he becomes passionate. They are unclothed. He is running his hands over her skin, yet not in such a way as actually to touch. His fingers explore, but remain a quarter of an inch away. When she jumps forward to take his lips he pulls back a little so that the *delice* of contact must remain a hope, an imagination. He dresses, walks out, passes through the colonnade downstairs and into the street, looking up and backward as from her window she follows him with her eyes. The tale of Carmen and Silvano is over.

Why—how—does he *not* touch her? She is ready, she desires him. She is ripe. For one staggering moment she hesitated and held him off, but now it is evident she has made up her mind to forget that past, embrace the present as a road to some blissful, or at least stable, future. Silvano, however, lives in his reflections, nourishing himself with not desire but memory of desire. Also, he is unable to say his need, to make the utterance that constitutes a voice. Or: mute, his voice is only in his hands. How alone we are when we cannot speak across the incalculable void that separates us from alluring strangers, how imprisoned we are by our world when we cannot depict it. Perhaps, however, Silvano's entire world has taken the shape of Carmen's hungry body. Her body and his understanding have the same boundaries. In running his hands over her with such precision, such delicacy—Rosenbaum suggests that this scene "paradoxically makes one more acutely aware of the warmth of both their bodies than any conventional coupling would"—he is engaged exactly in speaking his world to her; and she cannot grasp what he is "saying" because she does not take herself seriously enough to presume she could be so much for him.

At any rate, time has run out for them. ("Their diffident natures and the idealization of their romances prevent them from actually consummating and, thus extending their encounter," wrote *The Hollywood Reporter,* coolly, as if without remorse [Byrge].)

Yet it is also true that, failing to possess Carmen, Silvano nevertheless inhabits her, and she him. It is remarkable how intimate these two become, between glances, between phrases, in these quiet places, given that they basically do not unite. Perhaps they will not forget one another, but they are on the move, he onward and out of her life, she, at her window, to the destination of all those unknown folk whom we meet through a glance as they shuttle toward something we will never see.

A DIRECTOR IN PORTOFINO

Before

A film director (John Malkovich), who talks to himself rather articulately about a film he is thinking of making, goes to Portofino with a character in mind, and one morning in a little shop by the water, where the choppy green Ligurian sea is slopping onto a quay, and when the shutter has been lifted and the door unlocked, he finds a young woman (Sophie Marceau). She is, we must say, "perfect." Her eyes are hazel, her hair long and evanescent; she wears a taupe suit, she looks at him looking at her and shows anticipation, as though his gaze has made her catch her breath. Later, they talk at a pink café spread with green-and-white chairs under lush green trees, and it's misty. She's arrived in blue slacks and a beige coat over a fisherman's sweater, having told an English boyfriend in a yellow slicker to get lost. "It's better that I speak to you plainly. Whatever you have in mind, I'd better tell you who I am," says she, announcing a little sententiously that she stabbed her father twelve times. She holds her breath some, speaks without any particular expression. We hear the water splashing in. She is looking out to sea. She walks away a few paces, and a cat sits and placidly watches her. "When?—" he asks calmly. Far too calmly. Only John Malkovich ever exhibits this calm in the face of horror, onscreen. For three months, she replies, they kept her in prison, and then she was acquitted. She will not say why she did it, but he surmises that he knows, and also that twelve times is "more domestic" and "more familiar" than two or three would have been. All the while we see the charming little village, its houses piled vertically up the lush green hill all the way out of this world, the crisp but at the same time overcast sky, the jiggling sailboats at anchor. He cannot get over the magnitude of her crime, the *twelve* stabs: "You counted them?" "*They* did," says she. She runs off and dances on a pier beside the jade green water: "Are you going or staying? Do you want to see me tonight?" She almost touches his face. He reaches out and almost touches hers, but playfully, like a cat, she runs off. Slowly, thoughtfully, he follows, as only John Malkovich does. "You remind me of . . . somebody," she teases. He wants to know whom. "I'm not sure yet," she answers, in a riddling and slightly pretentious voice.

During

At prodigious length they make love—"the body never lies" (Feeney)—twisting and coiling and groping for something in one another that no one ever has a real hope of finding, a lovemaking that recalls the *Alexandria Quartet* in its hunger and its hopelessness. "It was never in the *lover* that I really met her" (Durrell 63).

After

Without much satisfaction they part, and for a moment he looks back at her through the window of her cottage, unable to get out of his mind that she stabbed her father *twelve* times. The sun is shining, they wave to one another amicably, she leaps up and stands naked looking after him. The fact that she stabbed her father does not, alone, intrigue him, but again, and still: why twelve times? No doubt the father raped her, and thrust himself into her twelve times before finishing. Or: he raped her, month after month, every month in the year. Or: twelve different times she was raped by this man. Or: she did not count and did not know. Since it was the police who determined and made it public, she learned as everyone else learned what it was that she had done. We do not know what it is that we do, we are apprised by listening and watching. When in modern life we do something, we are lost in the panic of our action, and in this way she was lost.

There is no signal that the girl's life is changed by her meeting with this director, no signal that his is changed by meeting her, except in this one respect, that, having come to this place in search of a character, he found a story, and now "the story let me think of nothing else, not even of my own." The *familiarity* of that chilling number twelve! He sits thinking/talking beside a turquoise swimming pool—a turquoise that one can taste!—bitterly minty—sliced by the camera so that we see only a triangle of it, stretching away from him. There is no point staying in this place.

Stories wait everywhere to speak through the voices of their characters, and we can have no idea when one of them will speak to us.

CARLO, PATRIZIA, HER HUSBAND, AND HIS LOVER

Un Café

On the Right Bank of Paris, in a plush little café, a young woman in pink (Chiara Caselli) introduces herself to a man who is caught up in a newspaper (Peter Weller) by saying that she has just been reading something fascinating in her magazine and wants to talk with someone about it. "*J'avais envie d'en parler avec quelqu'un*"—very polite, sweet, formal. He is American, she is Italian, so they speak in a deliciously awkward French that makes it easy for us to understand. "*C'est moi que vous avez choisi*?" he asks: "And you chose me?" She tells him a story of how in Mexico some scientists hired porters to carry bags for them to an Incan city in the mountains. At one point the porters suddenly stopped in their places and wouldn't move. The scientists got angry and tried to rouse them, unable to understand the delay. After some hours, the porters started up again. The leader decided to explain. (She looks at the American, and he smiles, now beginning to be engaged.) He said they had been "marching too fast. They'd left their souls behind." It's terrific, says she, because the way we run through our affairs we are in peril of losing our own souls. "We should wait for them." Now the man is skeptical. "To do what?" And she pauses before answering, letting a modest smile, an embarrassed smile, itself a little pink, creep into her face. "Everything that is pointless." Surely this is a come-on, an approach? She is so young, suffused with such an air of innocence that covers her like a talc. Or, she is acting out of civility and a little loneliness, the quintessentially withdrawn European. Given that in this bustling world attraction is based on what is presented immediately to the eye, there is probably little difference between civility and flirting: either way the impression will not, cannot, last.

The man comes home to his (much less effervescent) wife, Patrizia (Fanny Ardant), who is strained with both boredom and anxiety in their lavish modern apartment. Tall and wraithlike, she sits in a dove-gray dress with her legs crossed nervously, in front of a painting of a ballerina standing in second position and bending over to massage her shin. Have you been with *her* again?, she asks wearily: it's been three years since that story in the café about the souls. Some things, says he in irritation, can't be called off overnight: the old, old story. Patrizia strides away, the tails of her swank garment fluttering like those of an undertaker's tuxedo. "It's her or me."

Since at least in cinema we have come to accept interactions like this as commonplace, the torn, desiccated marriages of the monied class, we can move quickly through the chess that these two play, his breathless expressions of ennui, her increasingly taut fear of loss, his swelling apathy, her anger, all reactions to the central fact of impermanence (or that blurry prospect visible from a moving train), which is what the experience of life amounts to for these movers and shakers. Swiftly now, after a cut, the young lover pulls him into her apartment with a voluptuous (and starved) kiss. "We have to talk," says he: the old, old story. He wears gray, she wears red: cardinal red, poppy red. On her kelp green velvet sofa she straddles him. "Talk . . . but caress me." He closes his eyes: "I forget . . ."

It is telling the way we bounce back and forth between the different habitats that seem to occupy a single cultural and experiential space, without observing (engaging in) the transportation that leads from one to the other, as though locomotion is so prevalent as to be invisible. Did he walk to the lover's place, did he drive, did he take the Métro or bus N° 72? Now, we look down from a balcony in their foyer as, coming home, the husband calls out for Patrizia, plays a few bars of something vaguely baroque on his jet black grand piano, and methodically climbs the stairs, a man in motion but without prospect. In the bedroom she is happily, drunkenly smashing a celadon vase. He finds her standing on the other side of a plate glass shower partition in the bathroom, leans forward to press his lips against the glass where hers are. Gently their lips peck at one another by way of the thick glass. Although he's been phoning for days, she won't say much. "*Vase . . . fleurs . . . couleurs . . . beauté . . .*" And we all fall into the trap, she adds: the old, old story. There is such a resignation in her voice, as though being trapped is the main preoccupation in life (the philosophy of Norman Bates: trap as modern condition). He says (in English) that it's sad to see her like this, "drinking, drunk, desperate." They're on the vanilla-cream bed. He protests that he was on a trip. (Didn't you take *her?*) He didn't take *anyone.* She bites him, then laughs. "Last night," says he—this would be a confession in virtually any other circumstance, but here it seems a banality and a ploy—"Last night, I realized how much I miss making love to you." A difficult admission, since it implies and invokes nostalgia, the ability to carry traces of an experience across time and space and a dangerous state of affairs when mobility is at stake. She climbs on top. "I'll come back if you leave *her.*" "Today," says he, surrendering, "This morning, *now,* right now." As they kiss, she murmurs, "Don't leave me. Don't leave me," again and again, through tears, "*Ne me laisse pas*," a mantra but also a child's song. "*Ne me laisse pas, ne me laisse pas. Ne me laisse pas.*" Traffic is moving on a boulevard, people leaving people, even as the echo of her plea wears thin. Indoors again, watching the (same?) cars, the man turns to his lover, who, in a silver slip against a blue wall and next to a painting of a blue man hanging upside-down in agony, pouts, "Do you still make love behind my back?"

He is both alluring and lured. She wants to know if he has told the wife he will leave her. Today I pitied her, says he and she stamps her foot on the ground breaking into a bitter and impatient sob. As he moves across the room in a long shot we notice that in the painting there is a second figure, a line sketch, sitting on the ground and staring out at the viewer. "For three years you've been bringing her smell here," she barks, "the stale smell of a cheated wife!" They fight, and he throws her onto her bed (a tangerine-and-white checkerboard duvet), tears off her panties and her platinum slip to reveal her tiny, pert breasts and hungry thighs, brings himself toward her belly and then her crotch as her legs spread and the scene fades. Desire is not only a fuel, it is a vehicle.

A car. It pulls up outside a decidedly modern apartment building on the Right Bank, and Carlo (Jean Réno) is delivered with an expensive black valise. Tall, purposeful, maybe a pilot. He enters, takes the lift upstairs (in the company of a girl who cannot take her eyes off him), lets himself into his pied-à-terre with a blasé sense of ease. But: the place has been cleaned out, almost every piece of furniture removed, and the gleaming parquet floors are an accusation. The huge plate glass windows all round present Paris as a bleak mist. In a closer shot, we see the man's seriousness, his well-tanned but perturbed visage. Outside, the city is brighter, white and domed, rather like Durrell's Alexandria—"A camel has collapsed from exhaustion in the street outside the house. It is too heavy to transport to the slaughter-house so a couple of men come with axes and cut it up there and then in the open street, alive" (Durrell 54). Jars and boxes of food have been arranged neatly—too neatly—on the floor. The phone rings, rather persistently. When he answers, we hear the voice of his wife remonstrating with him for being so long away. "You emptied the place?" says he. "You could have left a note!" she answers. "It's because of my work!" he explodes. She says, "Don't try to find me." This is the title of the story from which Antonioni made this section of his film. "One afternoon she comes home with a truck, loads it with some furniture and two suitcases, and leaves. Without a whisper, almost stealthily. An hour later on the telephone she tells him why. At any other moment he would have known what to answer" (*Tiber* 204). Furious, Carlo stands by the window and we hear a steady rain falling. He throws himself disconsolately onto a black leather chair. We cut to a shot looking down on him in his midnight blue suit and black t-shirt as he rises from the chair after his nap, paces around to the sound of a siren in the street, *Ee-or ee-or ee-or ee-or,* finds a torn photograph on the floor of beautiful Claire, naked, trailing a pepper red scarf over her crotch, staring languidly or haughtily into the camera. She's a peppery one, and this is how she had the guts to pick up and vamoose. He's assembled the pieces of the picture, gashes in the photographic paper slashing across her mouth and breast, but now the doorbell sounds. When he opens, he finds Patrizia in a chocolate ganache overcoat and with her oxblood leather bags. "*Madame est là*?—" Next to her feet a framed orange print has been standing on his floor: the black shape of a woman's head, closely shorn, looking away. "—I spoke to her about renting the place." Carlo is nothing if not confused, says it was undoubtedly his wife's idea, that personally he is not sure he agrees. She walks in anyway, rather as though, at this moment, he suddenly does not exist, looks around, puts her bags next to his black chair, sits to appreciate the space, the view: "Don't say that or I'll go crazy." She tells him the story of her marriage. The door again, this time probably it's the furniture movers, bringing her husband's furniture. She has taken off her coat and stands in a vanilla-white suit. She walks around the stripped bed, goes into the bathroom, turns, stares back at him through a thick plate glass partition. "I guess I'll have to go away again," says he, "I was planning to stay put . . . Maybe that's why she went to live with *him*." She recognizes that he, too, is in a precarious position. He shows her the torn photograph. The phone rings, not so persistently. This time it's for her. She listens for a moment, then says into the receiver, "Don't try to find me." Looks around, a cat establishing its territory. "There's a cure for everything," says he, and she tells him it's this that disturbs her. They hold each other's hands. The rain has stopped.

Change proceeds at such a pace that adults are disconnected from the sentiments of their own childhood. One is continually meeting people, continually thrust into the close proximity that makes possible readings of human intent and alignment. If the universe has not yet been evacuated of its aesthetic qualities—in Antonioni the universe is invariably such a place—the proximity invokes a kind of erotic studiousness, with the result that people are often, if swiftly, appraising one another and presenting themselves as possible partners in physical adventure. The contract, constraint, and discipline of marriage are a contradiction of the speeding allure of the world, and the characters we meet in this episode are all, to some degree or other—Carlo perhaps least, yet still appreciably—projected into the air that surrounds things, caught in transit as they move through the social space that supports their commitments and perceptions. The constant movement leaves emotion behind, replaces it with promise. Thus it is that we can be said to be marching ahead too quickly, to have left our souls behind, if our souls are our capacities for feeling and wonder. However, there is no practical way to stop and wait "until the souls catch up," since territory itself has gained a new complexion as a space through which advancement can be achieved rather than a place of habitation. Locomotion has replaced habitation, anticipation has replaced experience.

When Patrizia moans "*Ne me laisse pas!*" she is surely already imagining a number of possible future considerations, that the American might disappear, as for three years now he has been threatening to; that she might be the one who does the leaving (as turns out to be the case). The "don't leave me" is an utterance in regard to future possibility, not an outgrowth of present experience, a prayer not an observation, since at the moment he is comfortably wrapped in her arms and she in his. Even in warmth she can imagine the chill of motion. The chill of motion dominates her life. She and her husband are culturally, emotionally, and psychologically passengers, "human parcels who dispatched themselves to their destination" (Schivelbusch, *Journey* 38–39).

Everyone in this tale possesses or regards framed paintings or lithographs, and the artwork bespeaks the condition of those who exhibit it at the moment we see them. Perhaps the reflection is of a permanent or enduring condition. Carlo is perennially confronted with the back of a woman, a woman receding, a woman in departure, and this is why, although he is perturbed and angry, he is neither impossibly confused nor shocked. The young lover is perpetually in the presence of an inverted figure in agony or a watcher, perhaps always herself suspended in hunger or staring uncomprehendingly at the world. And Patrizia is to some degree always haunted by the specter of an artful, tasteful woman, a woman of style, who bends to take care of herself. Do the images predict the behavior that we see, or have the characters, living long with these images, learned to imitate them? Film, however, passes by and does not linger to haunt us as these framed pictures and forms do. We move through film much as these characters move through the city, through their time with one another. Time is "nothing but a disquiet of the soul" (Sebald, *Emigrants* 181).

Un Feu

It is not so much that feeling is impossible during the rush of modern experience, as that only feeling is possible, feeling but not the awareness of feeling, feeling but not the ability to speak of it. So, Carlo, Patrizia, her husband, and his lover make utterances that are notoriously practical—"I have come about renting the apartment"—or feverishly displaced—"For three years you have been bringing her smell here"—but in any event inarticulate about the true state of affairs overwhelming the inner world. Patrizia and her American husband straining to kiss through the plate glass partition of the shower stall, the partition that distends the lips and darkens the faces: what is this doomed project but an icon of the separation of men from their gods (who reside, of course, inside the creatures they serve)? Eager to negotiate and map territory, identity, position, possibility, miscalculation, the modern personality cannot connect with its own primitive hunger. The second glass partition in Carlo's apartment: through it, a sighting takes place of moving personalities one and the other, a vacancy and an image where there might be a fire.

Let us imagine as we see them on both sides of this thick glass that Carlo and Patrizia will finally meet—meet, that is, after the few moments of preamble we have been entitled to see—and that they will remain in one another's company, perhaps married, but certainly together in life, for a long time, a very long time by comparison with the abbreviated sentences which have filled the scenes so far, so that in the end, looking at the gross field of their lives and experiences, everything in this little filmed story will turn out to constitute only a caesura, a pause, a pit stop. Perez notes that *L'eclisse* begins at the end (367), so why might not this story, in an equally adumbrated fashion, present only the beginning, a beginning that is like an end? It becoming necessary for Carlo to explain to friends how he met Patrizia, he recounts this whole story, all of it given, no doubt, by her recountings to him of what she remembers—the twisting urgencies upon the bed, the smashed celadon, the repeated questions never answered—and her traumatic, exaggerated imaginations of the scenes she cannot possibly have witnessed. In the event, Carlo and Patrizia are a perfect couple, handsome, professional, businesslike, matter-of-fact, attuned to the moment, well-balanced (if precariously positioned), sane if not happy in their matching expensive suits—his the blue of midnight, hers the color of ice cream in the Tuileries—standing face to expressionless face, his darkness absorbing her brightness, his hopeless calm drinking in her sad frenzy. He speaks, this Carlo of the future, of what she recounted to him, but it is all a vision: the craven little mistress who dresses for seduction, invents improbable stories, desires endlessly, enacts jealousy with a fury in her blue apartment upon her green sofa in her red chemise; and the husband who plays something not quite Bach on the dark polished piano, who says almost nothing when the moment for speaking has come.

Each of these persons is a stranger to the others even—perhaps especially—during lovemaking. Modern life brings us close to distance, surrounds us with people we recognize but do not know. "Was [Antonioni] just fashion?" Michael Atkinson wondered with youthful irritation in *The Village Voice,* describing the film's episodes as "dreamy, pretentious fickle-finger-of-fate mini-tales" containing "preposterously casual . . . sex" that "seems only to invoke an itch the 83-year-old filmmaker can perhaps no longer scratch" ("Snoozes"). Antonioni is showing how lovemaking is the most distant act of all, a fact the young are too distracted by the promise of pleasure to apprehend.

On the Boulevard

That cozy, colorful, well-lit café (the clean, well-lighted place) in which at the beginning of this episode the husband meets the girl who will become his lover (the prowler, the mover), is on or near one of the great boulevards of Paris, magnificent post-Haussmannian thoroughfares that through the nineteenth century, as Hazel Hahn writes, housed those sententious organs, the newspapers and were thus made into "a centre for news and communications that reached its peak at the fin de siècle":

> The newspapers themselves not only reported in minute detail on events on the Boulevards, but were read in the cafés along the street so that much of what was advertised was available just around the corner. The proximity of the places where newspapers were read to the boutiques, department stores, theatres and café-concerts advertised in their pages underscored the centrality of information and consumption to life on the Boulevards. (156)

A particular urbaneness must have characterized the denizens of the café, an openness to advertisement as a mode of speech and a vulnerability to strangeness and the exotic. Not only is the habitué of the café continually on the make, shuffling along beside the traffic, meandering through the crowds, entering and exiting shops for a relatively brief sojourn and experience; but he is also continually prone to being influenced by a world brought from afar, an imported universe, for that is what the newspaper offered on a consistent basis. While the girl's reaction to the story of the Mexican porters is surprise, the fact that she is surprised does not surprise her, since surprise is precisely the fruit of the sort of casual encounter one has through reading in a spot like this.

Nor can her surprise at the punch line of the story—that the porters felt they were moving so fast their souls had not caught up with them—fail to indicate the intensive degree to which, as an inheritor of the culture of the nineteenth century and an inhabitant of Paris in its stage of hypermodernization, she casually takes her own motion for granted and does not quite see in her own jittery dispensation the same tendency to displace an inner and more ancient world, even though she points, with a certain slack liberalism, to the "peril" of losing her own soul. It is clear if we look carefully at her open, but also modulated and articulately controlled, features when she speaks to the man; and at his guarded, but also unreservedly eager, features when he responds, that more than experiencing interest and fascination, these two are advertising availability to one another, playing skillfully where the presentation of a claim is an expected immediate feature of the environment. They are like posters for a pretense, and, like what is reproduced upon the typical French poster of the fin de siècle, neither face, as it will turn out, has a "direct link" with the "announced object" (Hahn 169). That here and throughout the episode the girl wears relatively bright colors hardly mitigates against our interpretation of her as a spectacle offering itself to a view.

The same publishing industry that brings the husband and his lover together at the beginning has the responsibility for linking Patrizia and Carlo at the end, since she discovers him only because in the want ads she has discovered the apartment in which he lives (and from which he, apparently with too much frequency, travels). No less than the other two, Patrizia and Carlo are thus gullible to advertisement and committed to a lifestyle in which claims and presentations, traveling at the speed of newsprint, take precedence over feelings. The intent of the Haussmannian boulevard, first and finally, was to make possible a great urban fluidity, to let the masses shift position from one neighborhood, horizon, and perspective to another; it worked to link—as Wolfgang Schivelbusch shows in *The Railway Journey*—the new railroad transportation with the transactional domain of the department store. The café in which this tale begins is suffused with the atmosphere of the boulevard, designed to facilitate this motion and structured as a business enterprise to encourage both the quick conversations that epitomize rational calculation and the quick transactions that make for uncontaminating profit. Movement was inexorably bound with shopping, and shopping bound with the glance. What the characters are engaged in here: a shopping spree.

NICCOLO IN AIX
The Pathway

A young hopeful, Niccolo (Vincent Perez), emerges from an architect's office in an apartment building in Aix-en-Provence and holds the door for a young woman emerging behind him (Irène Jacob). He catches up with her and they walk together, speaking of religion because she is going to mass. He tells her it is evident to him she is in love, and insists she is like a cherry tree he read about in a newspaper, that eats its own cherries. The word "aloof," originating as it does in military taxonomy, does not do justice to her abstractness, which is like that of a nurse ready to give an injection, or to the boldness with which she demands to know whether he believes in God, the humility in which she retracts that question, and the renewed boldness in which she withdraws the retraction. He makes it plain he's interested in her but she tells him he would do well to abjure physical desires, using the tone of a moral guide, quite as though she recognizes that his search is for truths and goodness, not architecture. The church, finally opening at the end of a narrow street, is the Église Saint-Jean-de-Malte, from the thirteenth century. She sits apart from him and loses herself in prayer—"Throughout the entire mass she remains on her knees," Antonioni had written originally (*Tiber* 33), though we do not see her do this—and having wandered among the columns, observing the choir, he sits and falls asleep. When he wakes the church is empty and he must run to find her, but she has disappeared. He scours the glistening nocturnal streets. Then, blocks away at a little fountain, there she is, innocently chalking flowers onto the pavement. He tells her he does not find flowers beautiful because they last a few days and then die (and that is why the Japanese do not grow them). "You are afraid of death," says she, "I am afraid of life"—meaning, the life that people are leading nowadays. It is night. Rain begins to fall. He continues to follow her, admitting that he could love her, and she slips on the pavement and gets her coat wet. Rather than crying, however, she laughs. Back at her apartment, she enters by way of great wooden doors. He races after her. The stairwell is painted a vivid angelica green and pale Béarnaise yellow, and the carpet is deep Beaujolais red. Outside her door he stands awkwardly, until their eyes meet.

Both of these people voyage without awareness, in a way. She was going to mass, and did not expect to encounter this young man. Now she has fallen into something of a relationship with him, so that before she can make the transition she is planning for the morrow—the culminating moment of her life at this time—she must first account to him for it, must experience his reaction either directly or in her imagination. For his part, he was on point of delivering a portfolio, perhaps opening the door to a future, with no thought of meeting a young woman he might wish to accompany. "I *should* accompany you," he proclaimed at one point. Heading toward a mass, as he surmises, he cannot know that he will fall asleep and awaken lost, disturbed, dislocated in time and space, or that he will be desperate to find her, or that in finding her he will continue a journey upward to a summit that brings, instead of perspective, a riddling fog. "Mental suffering is effectively without end" (Sebald, *Emigrants* 170).

Cézanne

Sebald writes that there is no past or future. I was given one day, as a boy, by a gentle piano teacher, a small book containing black-and-white reproductions of paintings by Paul Cézanne. I had no idea who Cézanne was, or why it was this that I was given, or why, for that matter, I was given anything, but certainly there was a mystery to this book of all possible books, and I found many of the pictures ungainly and aggressive without being convincing and also what a boy's mind would think disorganized. But the fact that I had been made the gift, and with no pretext and on no particular occasion, haunted me for years, and I treasured the book and bore it with me wherever I went, off to school at a big city in Ontario, then to a small Midwestern college town and afterward, as the 1960s wound to a close, circulating through the cities of the East, still, in all this time, not a particular admirer of the painter whose shadows filled its pages. It was only many years later that I saw his canvasses unmediated by printer's ink and my own limited imagination—freed possibly by having heard Debussy's *L'îsle joyeuse* but also entrapped by a swelling galaxy of curiosities—and found that they constitute the epitome of order and beauty. I was helped some in appreciating Cézanne by Guy Davenport's four Alexander Lectures at the University of Toronto in 1982, "Objects on a Table: Still Life in Literature and Painting," lectures soon enough invoked—yet only invoked—in a charming publication called *Apples and Pears* but not, as it happens, to appear in print themselves for some sixteen years—a depressingly long time, since I had been smitten by them and much of what I wished to read was only hanging in the mist. He had graciously given me a moment to say hello before one of these talks and had seemed delighted that anyone in his audience might have been genuinely stimulated by the connections he was so rapidly and voraciously making as he spoke. So stunned had I been by the range of his scholarship and the mystery of his attachments to paintings, paragraphs, poems, colors, and ideas—his personal warmth in the pewter chill of Toronto's November seemed to augment and color my already rich experience of listening to him at his podium—that years later, when I mounted four groups of Polaroid SX-70 photographs as an address to Debussy's Bergamasque Suite, and included for one of the movements a series of still lifes of apples, it seemed obvious to me that I should dedicate the show to him. Accordingly, I sent him slides and he was most grateful, but that was the end of our tangential and charged contact. When sometime after his death in January 2005 I learned that he had arranged for the donation of his organs to medical science, I remember being both struck by the nobility and simplicity of this gesture and deeply confused to realize that the person I had met was in fact now divided; or had always been quite remote from the body he inhabited and was thus more than the eyes smiling at mine or the voice gently but disconnectedly encouraging me or the gracile penmanship—a skill retained from the early twentieth-century days when personality and conviction had to live in markings upon paper—that characterized his little note of thanks. The recurrence of the female form of the apple and the male form of the pear in literature particularly interested him—he spoke of apples and pears as being "married" (*Objects* 55)—as did the Sherlock Holmes stories of Arthur Conan Doyle, and much painting. Cézanne's still lifes, Van Gogh's 1888 picture of his bedroom in Arles, and Monet's work on the waterways around Paris occupied the central position in these 1982 talks, which ranged over a tremendous amount of material—to me at the time, an entire world—and made a chain of startling connections that I could not now reassemble without the help of a notebook I have stowed away somewhere, or lost, I cannot be sure, a notebook that was red, apple red. At any rate, I came to adore the still lifes of Cézanne, and to marvel at how he had accomplished giving the fruit bulk but also weightlessness, and of course at the shockingly simple and complex ways in which he positioned the peaches and oranges and apples around one another to make compositions that echoed Bach. Cézanne, at any rate, lived in Aix as Niccolo does, and, like Antonioni, was deeply moved by color. In late Cézanne "the sketch is the painting" (Davenport, *Gracchus* 275).

Color, for Cézanne and for Antonioni and also for Davenport, was a reverberation of past events, an echo of echoes, and it occupied time, that same color that Picasso said "is a distraction in a painting" (qtd. in *Gracchus* 183).

Aix—old Aix, at least—is a city of sandstone buildings, tiny streets, and a thousand fountains, with the grand, confrontational Mont Sainte-Victoire on its eastern edge among modest, shady groves of pine. It is a place—at least the Aix that Antonioni photographs in *Beyond the Clouds* is a place—that offers itself to the spirit of the wanderer without making any imposition. As we follow Niccolo and the girl, as we listen to them address one another in an extended dolly that moves down blocks and turns corners and crosses little squares, we have no anticipation of arriving at a summary destination but only, with each of their steps, contentment at the experience of penetrating and then relinquishing a space. Satisfaction is beyond consideration. "Are you satisfied, madame?" the young man asks a middle-aged woman who is passing by, and she smiles indulgently at the ridiculousness of the question; yet we see that she is entirely pleased with her condition, even though it is not a condition of satisfaction. She is hardly bored, or irritated, or even displaced by her lack of satisfaction. Aix removes the question of satisfaction from the equation.

To experience art is an act of faith. To make art, to paint a canvas, is innocent, an abandonment while also a consumption of the self. Everything is the subject, its distance, its roundness, proportion, history, implication, its weight—which is to say, in Cézanne, its lack of weight, its light. (Color *is* light, and that is why color is everywhere.) But to look at a painting is an affirmation of the self, because in this act we struggle to believe in the existence of the qualities we admire. We elevate art, but not without the expenditure of effort that also produces an elevation of the self. To see the world clearly, as Cézanne saw it, is to diminish the self to a point, but in order to admire someone else's vision of the world one lifts it onto one's shoulders. One is working, after all, to convince oneself that this is an Original—special, worthy of considered attention—but then suddenly, as though on the opening of a door into a grand arena, one sees or hears all of it with a new and surprising clarity, and it is all present and accounted for, effortless, pristine, full, in a flash, and then originality disappears as a consideration, becomes trivial in the face of what the work actually *is*. Yet is this vision or this audition not something like what occurred for and to the artist at work? For an instant we have the opportunity to share that vision or audition by performing it again, by repeating history. (In the brief interlude directed by Wenders, when Mastroianni painting the Mont Sainte-Victoire is interrupted by Moreau stepping up to converse with him, this is what he tells her, too: that the meaning for him in copying the original Cézanne resides in trying to experience what the painter experienced, *and this is not copying.*) The artist, it is certain, labors with the conviction that such an audition, such a perception, is possible, surely for the artist who regards the world but also for those who come to the work of art. He shows or perhaps sings the world in such a way that others can know how he saw it, or heard it open itself and sing to him, through the obstruction of daily life—and not just obstruction but continual obstruction and darkness, that rent to be paid, the paint dry upon the palette, the *bon mot* slipping away into those moist blue recesses of the absurd and the undiscovered. Or the opinions of the strangers standing next to one's elbow, always too informed. The world must finally vibrate so that it rises off the map: Mont Sainte-Victoire ceases to be that stalwart lump at 43° 32' N, 05° 39' E and becomes an ineffable presence. If one listens carefully to a choir in a church, if one gives oneself entirely to each voice and the combination of voices, one can also hear the stones from which the vibrations of these voices are recoiling. It is the stones, as much as the music, that have the power to put one to sleep, since by way of those who sing the stones themselves have voice, just as by way of the painter the mountain speaks or as by way of the filmmaker the space of the urban intérieur (which Walter Benjamin described, "furnished and familiar" [Gunning 106]), its cherished objects or its lack of things, its paintings even standing upon the floor, its plate glass partitions, is permitted to enunciate the world.

Voices

It is rather evident to the eye, even disturbingly so as we watch, that as they walk through the city, the girl almost never looks at the young man. Speaking through the voice of an off-camera narrator in *To Make a Film Is to Be Alive,* a documentary about the making of *Beyond the Clouds* that is published on the DVD, Antonioni explicitly draws attention to the fact. She needs, says this narrator, "no reassurance from him. Security is not what she needs. A serenity verging on indifference seems to pervade her." This is surely difficult, if only because serenity is sacred while indifference is mundane. The girl is unruffled, but she is also a little stiff, as though the force of attraction exercised by his hungry ministrations and gaze has made her capable of falling from a kind of pedestal that is gliding beneath her. The boy certainly thinks she occupies a higher plane, perhaps because her lips are the precise Iranian pink of a Gloire de Guilan rose. She tells him she wants to escape from her body, and at that he pauses to slake his thirst. By easily satisfying his body, has he escaped from it? Is she trapped in the fact that she insists on denying herself? What Antonioni typically wishes to escape from is the prison of rationality, the abject quotidian use of intelligence, or at least the use of words that, "more than anything else, serve to hide our thoughts" (Cottino-Jones 21). Her self-contentment, her private love—these are not rational. Later, this narrative voice that is both Antonioni and not-Antonioni mentions the sound of the water running in the fountains as a voice, gives evidence that he hears voices everywhere, a voice but not mere words. "The voice is a 'noise' which emerges with other noises in a rapport" (Cottino-Jones 49). The voice is the expression of the spirit of the moment through the fact of the body, and what is said, the message to which words are tantamount, does not summarize the voice but merely localizes it. The voice, indeed, is presence and fullness of the act of speaking itself. Goodman says, "When speaking intervenes in the world and shapes experience, it often is, or is taken as, a direct action in the environment, an energy or even a physical thing, rather than the use of the common code for communication" (19). Speaking itself is the voice. In this part of the film, for example, the boy and girl speak to one another, from the moment of their meeting until the moment of their parting, rather as though at cross purposes, and certainly following two apparently discreet lines of intent that do not promise to intersect. Yet here, as in the story of Carmen and Silvano, the voices of two human beings gradually approximate to one another, just as the rationales upon which they insist on basing their lives move apart. Does one follow the voice or the message?

"This Body of Filth" is the name of the little story from which this segment of the film is taken. It has an interesting ending:

> Only now does he notice her strong sensuous figure. It seems to him that he's never felt so intense a desire to possess a woman. But it's a different desire, with a certain tenderness and respect. It's ridiculous, he thinks. And yet there's a quaver in his voice, and he can't help it, when he says,
>
> "Can I see you tomorrow?"
>
> She keeps on smiling in the few seconds of silence that precede her reply. And her voice is devoid of all emotion when she speaks.
>
> "I'm entering a cloistered convent tomorrow."
>
> What a stunning opening for a film. But for me it's a film that ends here. (Tiber 35)

And we can imagine it, indeed, ending precisely there. On that top landing of the flat of apartments in which she lives. The angelica green, so dense and sweetly gummy one feels the color warping through one's flesh, and the wine red carpet, red as sacrificial blood, transubstantial, interior. She at her door, looking directly into him, then the door closing. Fade to black.

But onscreen this is not how Antonioni ends his story at all.

We cut to Niccolo frozen in place, his mouth open in shock or amazement, in disappointment or incomprehension, his eyes trained upon her door. Then clumsily he turns, makes his way to the stairwell, and we look down the opening to see him pass all the way to the bottom level—Orfeo searching for Eurydice in the nightmarish bureaucracy in *Orfeu Negro* (1959), where papers fall down such a stairwell like snow, or Antoine Doinel running away from Fabienne Tabard in *Baisers volés* (1968)—and stride out of the building. Down the golden street he goes, golden after the rains have washed the sandstone buildings, the street studded with golden light, and walks faster, and breaks into a run. Perhaps, stunningly, he has decided that she is altogether not the person he hoped she would be, that the voice she had kept hidden deep inside, the voice of all truths, the voice he hears only at the end, is a radically strange, even inimical, voice. He is running to save himself. Or he has accepted the impossibility of his love in the face of the definitiveness of hers for something beyond the mortal, and he runs now in freedom, having released—perhaps not her but—the hope of her that he has cherished and targeted. Or else that hope of her has chained him to the rocks, his gaping wound open to the sky.

It doesn't matter, because also possible is that she has not yet spoken with her truest voice, that she has only made a little speech to fill in the map of her days, to put him off a little, to suspend him. She may well be bypassing both her feelings and what she wants. And this boy: perhaps at her doorway he could have stepped forward instead of remaining in place, extended himself across the gap. So it is that the final moment of Antonioni's film, in which Niccolo scampers down the street, perhaps singin' in the rain, is full of optimism and hope, not a moment of closure at all, since both of them may yet find the voice that speaks a companionship. He may stop, just after we can no longer watch, and reconsider: "Maybe I misinterpreted."

BEYOND THE CLOUDS

Beyond the Clouds, a "box-office smash" in Italy (Rosenbaum), found a more rational appreciation among the American critics. Jonathan Rosenbaum noted "a lot of beautiful things" in the film, saying that it "isn't so much sexy as erotic . . . every bit as involved with the erotics of place as with the erotics of flesh" yet does not manage to get beyond desire ("Return"). In *The New York Times,* Michael Holden wrote—enthusiastically but also without the clarity that comes with conviction—that "you are all but transported through the screen to a place where the physical and emotional weather fuse into a palpable sadness" and also that the vignettes "portray characters caught up in romantic obsessions presented as metaphors for the artist's pursuit of an elusive truth" ("Transformed"). But the central glory of Antonioni, after all, is that in his films truth is not elusive, that he depicts a truth quite clearly, although it is perhaps a far more complex truth than we crave in an era of uncommitted movement, promise, pulse, and surface.

Much as when we fly above the clouds we sense ourselves to be "beyond" the society churning below, out of touch and in fact hopelessly, if also deliriously, unable to make contact; and sense that our movement is dependent on our status as outsiders; so all of the characters in the four stories Antonioni has filmed for *Beyond the Clouds* are separated from one another and, thus, from shared direct presence and experience. All of them are, in some deep and evocative sense, alone. It is perhaps the case that in this, they resemble and even mirror the condition of every person, always, trapped on one or the other side of some barely substantial essence that keeps people away from the human race. We cannot fully know the world, even though we can recognize its surfaces, and so the surfaces become the world: a thematic that Seymour Chatman attributes to Antonioni's filmmaking. Gilberto Perez very perceptively writes of a kind of *separation* in Antonioni's camera's vision, to the extent that "we observe the man and the woman from the point of view of a stranger who somehow has come upon them" (367). But it is not this that I have in mind when I invoke separation, since strangers, too, have homes, and all strangers can imagine a country in which they are neither separated from those they watch nor set apart from the rituals of the flow of life. I have in mind, much more, a kind of nostalgia for an irrevocable but unforgettable past, such as was felt by a diarist Sebald quotes, who is remembering a "distinctly creepy" house to which her family moved: there, she writes, "I leafed through a page or two of the blue velvet postcard album which had its place on the shelf of the smoking table, and felt like a visitor" (*Emigrants* 210). In *Beyond the Clouds,* it is exactly as though, in some "distinctly creepy" place, and looking at images of some irrevocable but unforgettable past, we have become visitors, arbitrarily and knowingly accelerating out of that familiar orbit from which we might see a world presented in its telling details, so that, moving more quickly than our souls can move, we stand outside ourselves and look back with the eyes of some well-meaning *inconnu*. All this horribly sweet turmoil is artfully measured and evidenced in Silvano almost touching Carmen while not touching her; in the director and the girl making love with movement and tension, with drive and hunger, while yet seeming to be on different planets, their bodies unaware that they are gliding against one another in our view as we busily note (to quote Durrell again) not them exactly but the act in which they are engaged; in Carlo and Patrizia navigating through the waters of the memory of their marriages, their lost furniture, their betrayed dreams; in Niccolo running away from someone who is also running away, in Aix. In all of this, the relation of touch, which is the oldest relation, and the one that confers upon objects their identity as "things" (see Ortega) has long dissipated in favor of promise, which is also that glint in the eye with which we detect the periphery of a world in its continual unfolding and a voice that rushes like water and says, "I search."

. . .

Al di là delle nuvole (1995), photographed by Alfio Contini (and, for sequences by Wim Wenders, by Robby Müller) in the 1.66: 1 format at Ferrara, Aix-en-Provence, and Portofino and printed as an Eastmancolor positive; 104 m. Released in the United States as *Beyond the Clouds,* October 8, 1999.

Identification of a Woman

The investigation proceeded with vigor, if not always with judgment, and numerous individuals were examined to no purpose.

—Poe, "The Mystery of Marie Rogêt"

LOVE STORY

I wonder what kind of love story can possibly have meaning in our corrupt society today.

—Mario, Niccolò's collaborator and friend

In Federico Fellini's *8½* (1963), the celebrated filmmaker Guido Anselmi (Marcello Mastroianni), having had an enormous screen success, has entered a kind of creative crisis as he searches for the subject of his new film, a crisis in which his producer, his writer, the stars he has worked with, his wife, and the remembered salient figures from his childhood who now seem to have returned to populate his consciousness all swirl around him, suddenly sweep forward, and then ebb into the recesses of his thought without being able to leave behind the trace of an inspiration. Everywhere are women, each one a special magnificence, teasing, enchanting, cleansing, reproving, adoring Guido, but to no avail. He is tormented by possibilities. He cannot see what is coming next.

In Antonioni's *Identification of a Woman,* the celebrated filmmaker Niccolò Farra (Tomas Milian) is searching, too: if not exactly for the subject of a new film then for the female presence around which such a film might take shape, perhaps in the way a crystal takes shape when it forms around a single vital granule or the way that from a material speck a pearl takes shape within an oyster. Niccolò, at any rate, has been cutting out photographs of women and tacking them on his board, patiently, a little peremptorily, a little hopelessly, in his capacious apartment that looks upon a pine-lined Roman street and outside of which a bird's nest sits empty in an evergreen branch. He wants to make a film about "a feeling in female form." It is this feeling for which he seems to be searching—his wife having left him, and he now frequently being in the company of a young woman named Mavi Luppis (Daniela Silverio) whom he presumes (correctly) to come from the class of the aristocracy, although she denies it. A feeling in female form. He has a sister, a modest gynecologist looking for a promotion at the hospital, whose little boy has been leaving phone messages about some special postage stamps Niccolò promised him. Mavi takes him to a party where everyone knows her, especially an older man who stops her for a private conversation on the staircase. Niccolò is uncomfortable there, and also, in a way, in his relationship with Mavi altogether, until and unless he is making love to her, which he does furiously and with a great hunger while she writhes in an agony of pleasure (but also shifts position during orgasm to watch herself in a mirror). She spent time at a college in Wales, says she, where with the other girls she practiced lifesaving in their canoes and where there was no sex. (Quickly we are shown the canoes in the splashing navy blue waters crested with creamy foam, and the sedate stone college in its green lawn.)

Niccolò has a rather vexing and mundane problem that is overwhelming him, transcending even his creative block. At home one night he received a telephone call from a strange man and an invitation to an encounter in a café the next morning. There, the bloke, sitting presumptuously with a dish of ice cream, told him that someone else was interested in "the girl" he was seeing; and that he should be "careful." In outrage Niccolò left, but still cannot get this conversation and its implications out of his mind. Who is watching him? Who has hired this thug? Who is trying to come between Mavi and him and for what reasons? At the party with Mavi he therefore scans every face, even considers one genteel man, who is quickly retreating out of view, to be the culprit. Mavi is a little impatient with his continuing fears. At home, reading the newspaper—an article about the dangers of the sun expanding—he is discomforted, ill at ease. Learning from his sister that her application for promotion was unsuccessful, he is immediately certain his mysterious pursuer has arranged this defeat and is punishing him by hurting someone he loves. He feels that in general he is being watched. Indeed, one night, a man is outside his apartment eyeing him from the street. He escapes in his car, picks Mavi up, and flees with her into the country, where they are caught in a dense fog. She is frightened, and he is unsympathetic. She confesses her fear that she is being pursued by her mother's lover, the man who spoke with her at the party, but in a flashback we learn that the man's true purpose in drawing Mavi aside was to announce the shocking news that he is her father. Mavi and Niccolò drive to a villa he rented once, and to which he still has the key. But the place frightens her even more and she wants to leave. They make love. In the morning, he sees that two young women have in fact rented the place, and also that Mavi is gone. Back in Rome he searches for her, to no avail. He phones her mother's house and the butler announces, "Niccolò Farra is on the telephone, searching for Maria Vittoria." "Let him search," the old lady replies. Mavi has gone off the map.

Still, Niccolò thinks he is being haunted by a mysterious force that is drawing Mavi away. His sister comes with her son to visit, but is insufficiently sympathetic to suit Niccolò's needs. The boy gets his postage stamps and is especially fond of a pair that show astronauts. "You should make a science fiction film!" says he. Niccolò hunts Mavi at a swimming pool, where he meets a young woman (Lara Wendel) whose sexual preference is masturbation, especially with someone who knows how to help her; and who admits to having slept with Mavi one night when the men they were with wanted to talk about soccer. Then Niccolò meets an old girlfriend, who agrees to spend a pleasant evening with him in town. She needs to find a place to pee, so they head toward a theater, where a young woman, one of the cast of the play, is disappearing inside. "Sexy," says Niccolò's friend. Later the same night, the old friend having left, Niccolò returns to the theater and meets this actress, Ida (Christine Boisson). They spend time together, especially at her villa on the outskirts of town where she keeps horses. He becomes her lover, and tells her all about Mavi and the strange case of being followed. A huge bouquet of red chrysanthemums is delivered for Mavi at Niccolò's apartment; he sends them away. He goes off with Ida to her place, but soon she must go into town, only to return after several hours with the news that she has "found" Mavi, via an article in an issue of *Time*. How did she come by it? She went to the florist whose name was on the chrysanthemums, and found that they had been sent by a woman, probably the secretary of the person who had hired the man to follow Niccolò. And oddly, a copy of the magazine was at the flower shop. From an old contact, one of the editors of *Time* in Rome, Niccolò secures Mavi's address, and drives there in his car. It is an apartment building with a marvelous curling staircase. He goes up and knocks on doors, one by one, but no one knows of Mavi. In one of the apartments he meets a young woman who regards him closely. He drives away but comes back in the late afternoon, this time climbing to the top of the stairs and waiting. Mavi enters the building and goes to the young woman's door, but cannot find her key. He hears them conversing. "Niccolò is here, he came into the building," says the voice from behind the door. Mavi looks up and sees him. She goes into the apartment and shuts the door.

He becomes closer and closer to Ida, takes her to see the empty lagoon at Venice in the winter. In their skiff, on the waters which are as gray as dust and as sleek as silver, they embrace. Returned to their hotel, she gets a telephone call and comes to him elated. She is pregnant, has been since before they met. He responds coolly, it becoming clear immediately that for him this relationship has no future.

Niccolò, finally, has made his film, about space explorers using an asteroid-ship to voyage near the sun in order to make calibrations. This ship is made of "a rare mineral, that resists a million degrees." The little nephew's voice asks why we go to the sun? "To study it," Niccolò explains off-camera as we watch the asteroid approaching the great ball of fire. "The day mankind understands what the sun is made of . . . and the source of its power . . . perhaps we'll understand the entire universe . . . and the reason for so many things." "And after that?" asks the boy, with perfect composure.

Identification of a Woman is over.

A CHANGE OF LIGHT

> Nothing is ever lost in space: toss out a cigarette lighter, and all you have to do is to plot its trajectory and be in the right place at the right time, and the lighter, following its own orbital path, will with astronomical precision plop into your hand at the designated second. The fact that in space a body will orbit about another to infinity means that sooner or later the wreckage of any spaceship is almost always bound to turn up.
>
> —Stanislaw Lem, *Tales of Pirx the Pilot*

But in the middle of this, there comes upon us an astonishing transition, one of those movements by which Antonioni (in various films) shows us that space is time. (Film is all transition, all continuity.) Space exists to be moved into, moved away from, moved through. When we care about people, we are curious about space because they exist in it: visiting Niccolò's apartment, Ida says it's him in this place she wants to see, not merely this place. When, like Niccolò, we are not so capable of caring about people (Mavi makes it clear to him that he needs her, but does not love her), it is objects moving through space that enchant us, and perhaps people become objects in this regard: the clay-pale asteroid-spaceship in Niccolò's movie gliding through the dark intergalactic void toward the sun. Niccolò has been hunting for Mavi and has driven to the address that his friend at *Time* has provided. A narrow street, with old stone facades in front of which he can draw up his vehicle near the doorway to Mavi's apartment building. After he has investigated the apartments, we see him leave the building, check out the neighborhood a little, get into his car, and drive away, off-left.

Now, the scene does not change by so much as the tiniest fraction of a degree, compositionally. The light fades some. He drives in from the right, and parks exactly where he had parked before.

This is a strange and delicious infusion of dimensions. The camera has been locked down, so that the frames match precisely. The road has undoubtedly been marked for the car's position. And the cutting has been managed securely because the lighting conditions in the two parts of the shot are not so very different that a splice would be noticed; yet, at the same time, the day has clearly waned, hours have passed, between Niccolò's departure and his return.

And between this departure and this return what seems a whole world is eclipsed. In the first sequence he is desperate, hopeful, eager, filled with the feeling that at last he has found her again and can at least expect an explanation for her sudden termination of their affair. When the occupants of the various apartments offer their various portrayals of ignorance about Mavi, he is increasingly doubtful, not so much about her presence in this place as about these agents. In the second sequence he seems possessed of a sad certainty, a knowledge he would rather not have but which, like a recurring melody, must be played out to its finale. In this transitional shot in the street, which has a magical quality because the editing is so seamless and because we cannot imagine how in so brief a spate of time a man who has just driven offscreen left can possibly be driving onscreen from the right, there is a sense in which time has a palpable essence, the same essence as that of light, and that as the light slowly drops away, time does the same, yet visibly. And in this tiny hiatus, of course, Niccolò travels the entire universe.

The evidence that lies before Niccolò before he drives away from Mavi's building and the evidence when he returns are precisely the same: (a) a vague, rather ugly warning to "be careful"; (b) a fact: that someone else apparently has designs on Mavi; (c) another fact: this someone is at least connected to the voice of a woman who ordered the chrysanthemums; (d) the strange tale of the girl at the swimming pool; (e) Mavi's curious self-regard during lovemaking, her libidinous passion, her general lack of interest in Niccolò and recognition that he lacks interest in her. The rest of what Niccolò is worried about is pure supposition: that the mysterious enemy has taken steps to disenfranchise his sister at the hospital; that this stranger attended the soirée and had an eye out for Niccolò, then fled; that the stranger means to do Niccolò, or for that matter anyone, harm. If his vanity were ripe, after all, he might well assume that the comment, "Be careful," meant, "You are about to be endangered," but that is not all it can mean.

Further, we are given direct reason to query the strength and fidelity of Niccolò's troubled suppositions and fears. In that dense fog, when pacing outside the car he hears that there has been an incident at the river, with shooting, with the police, he leaps immediately to the conclusion—it is really astonishing how Antonioni leads us to be able to see this, by the expressions on his face, by his movements—that Mavi has jumped to her death, or been shot, or that she is involved in something horrific and indescribable. But Mavi has nothing to do with this, and is already—as we very soon discover—sitting back in the car, waiting for him with her cigarette. (Her cigarette that she does not really want to smoke, like all the cigarettes she asks for, and begs help in lighting, then quickly stubs out.) His terror, then, is rather like a fog that descends in an instant out of nowhere. For Mavi, if we look objectively rather than through Niccolò's analysis, we can see that Niccolò has certain attractive qualities: he is well known and intelligent, if neurotic; he is a fine lover; he knows how to treat her to a pleasant time. Nor need any of this dislodge a certain trepidation she seems to feel in his presence throughout, as though, tasting gingerly from his cup of pleasure she is nevertheless always like a bird on point of flight, a bird ready to leave a nest. His attempts to frame her departure as a conspiracy are overdrawn: she is fragile and flighty in the first place. When finally she does disappear, in that morning at the country villa, it is not really alarming or surprising except to Niccolò, who—she was correct the night before in pronouncing—needs her more than he loves her.

If the evidence available objectively to Niccolò rests the same before and after his departure that afternoon from the precincts of Mavi's apartment block, what accounts for the change in his view, his attitude, his expectation? How does his hopefulness become acceptance and detachment? He is not simply a man who returns for a second look to a scene where a lost article has not been found; he is another man altogether on his return, come to see a world he previously could not imagine. It can only be time itself that has changed him, or light, both of which signal the voyage around the universe that Niccolò makes in his little car while we wait, calmly, arms outstretched as it were, for the object that he is, having finished its revealing orbit, to return.

What, in the end, is this universe in which Niccolò has made his circuit as the scene subtly changes? One, clearly, in which if he orbits, he is yet a kind of sun, with creatures circling him like planets obedient to his pull. His sister has had her career either ruined or seriously interrupted, for all intents and purposes, yet his sole response is to see some reflection upon himself: that a nefarious stranger pulled strings in order to hurt him by hurting her. The thug eating ice cream in the café: it does not occur to Niccolò to actually listen to him, even though in all his utterances so far, in person and on the telephone, the man has been the soul of courtesy. He is only a brute, employed by another brute, who brings menace Niccolò's way. The writing partner and chum Mario (Marcel Bozzuffi), who cannot imagine what kind of love story could possibly make sense in a corrupt world: for him Niccolò has little time or conviction, since only his own desire occupies him. "Corruption is what unites our country," Niccolò says rather glibly, "and corrupt people are the first to want love stories." Yet Niccolò does not see that his own immense attractiveness to others is a form of corruption, and that he is among those who are first to seek love. The women with whom he surrounds himself are certainly parts of his universe more than he is a part of theirs. Mavi, Ida, the girl at the pool, his former girlfriend, all of them exist in order to function, and function as potential subjects for his characterization. "Looking for a character means looking for contexts, facts," claims he, but he does not look for the reality of their experience. Mavi becomes more and more important to him, though she has disappeared, because the riddle of her pursuer has not been solved, not because of anything intrinsically interesting to him about her.

In the end, Niccolò treats himself as the glowing orb being approached by the exploratory probe (who inhabits that asteroid-ship, what their intentions for the knowledge they will surely amass, he does not know), but it is the ship, in truth, that is his. Well protected against harmful radiation, he seeks proximity to a sun that we may imagine as the quintessence of feeling in female form.

The former girlfriend has a lesson of sorts that Niccolò is unable to apprehend when, wanting to find a place to pee, she walks with him up the steep dark steps toward the theater. "I think you're happy," says she, "when your body is in tune with your thoughts. Mine is used to being near fields, rivers, trees, frost. Thoughts are different there from thoughts in the city. The laws of nature don't count here, and I feel . . . empty." The body, then, is part of a physical world, subject to temperatures, winds, visions, colors, textures, waves, obstructions, objects. But Niccolò is an obsessive, persistently unaffected by the physical scene, persistently concentrating on locating his "woman," a character with whom he can be "silent" and "have with her the kind of relationship one has with nature." Underneath that villa he imagines is still his, to which he brings Mavi out of the fog, is a Roman atrium, and when he takes her down there, coolly disinterested in history and locale, he is moving to another universe, but without consciousness. She is terrified by a flying creature—perhaps a giant bat, more likely an owl. He seems not to have noticed.

BLIND KNOWLEDGE

Our words become increasingly impenetrable.
—Niccolò to Mario

As Alain Bergala points out, Mavi and Ida both keep secrets, and so identifying them is a matter of difficulty (part of what makes this film, for John Powers, merely "another evaporating detective story"). In this they typify any "other," who is unknowable because in possession of an inaccessible inner life: Niccolò's struggle to know them, for the purposes of either love or characterization, represents any person's work at intersubjectivity. Mavi knows, but does not reveal, the shape of her desire. Ida does not know she is pregnant when she takes up with Niccolò, but she suspects it, and has clearly planned going for the test the results of which are announced in Venice. (Mavi is the one who makes an appointment to see a gynecologist, Niccolò's sister.) Nor does their secrecy exhaust the impenetrability of the film. Barriers to understanding are everywhere around, especially for Niccolò, so that he must send out interrogatory probes into social space to investigate the foreign bodies that hover before him in order to have any hope of increasing his knowledge, rounding off his understanding. Niccolò himself does not grasp his own working method, except to say he wishes to find a certain kind of woman. He certainly does not understand the confusions that beset him as he searches for this ideal character.

Every action is something of a question for Niccolò, every step a possible augmentation of experience. Yet at the same time, every presentation is a riddle. Mavi has bathed and is drying herself with a carmine red towel. She notices, high on her thigh, cellulite, and comments that a woman her age shouldn't have that, yet she does. How to interpret this? Does she, for instance, have knowledge about the cause of cellulite, and is she suggesting that something in the way life is lived today favors women developing this—in short, telling us that she is like many young women, all different than their mothers were at their age? Or is she puzzled, because all her friends have smooth skin and she cannot imagine how this happened to her? Is she concerned about herself, or is she thinking that perhaps Niccolò will notice and find the ripples unattractive? Is she making a light-hearted comment, or a humorous reflection on her own condition—saying she is older than she feels? Niccolò is listening carefully to her, perhaps too carefully. Indeed, at the party scene he chides her at one point for not taking seriously something he's said and gives a tiny lecture: "Mavi, we must listen to one another." As he listens, what does—what could—he apprehend that is of any use to him in deciding where he will go next, or what he will do? To be extremely sensitive to one's universe is a kind of (delicious) passivity, a force that makes one stand in a doorway with eyes wide open drinking in the pleasures of a soirée but unable to move. Situated human action, after all, shares with other instances of organized production a reliance not only on appropriate materials, available spaces, and talented performers but also on knowledge, or at least what simulacrum of knowledge seems sufficient and credible. And just as being able to go somewhere or do something—something complex, for example, like making a film—hangs upon knowing one's world in a certain way; so, too, does knowing one's world hang upon motive and reason.

Yet—and this is the central thrust of *Identification*—Niccolò does make his way forward. What this film suggests about human action, then, is that we commit ourselves ongoingly, without having real knowledge at all. One could say that knowledge is a dramatization, and thus that a film is a way of knowing the world or a demonstration and collection of knowledge, a library. Unable to access the world, cut off from contact, from direct perception, and restricted to the apprehension of surfaces and our conventions for guessing what surfaces may cover, we know by picturing, and the act of picturing is always an attempt, always fallible. Niccolò is trying to get a "picture" of Mavi, and later of Ida, and in both cases it could be said that he fails, yet it is also true that he makes—that Antonioni, acting for him, makes—a sufficient picture for us to believe we have seen them and can come to know them. He makes way.

For each of us, understanding is beyond. This is why at the end of *Identification,* we must imagine that Niccolò is aboard that asteroid-craft. Somewhere, near the sun or near some other part of the universe, he will find what he needs.

SCIENCE

To observe attentively is to remember distinctly.
—Poe, "The Murders in the Rue Morgue"

The argument can be made—is often made, in fact, in the most commonplace ways as well as the most sophisticated ones—that the right and proper approach toward expanding human knowledge is science, which to most people means a system of methods with its history, its taxonomy, its devotions, its rigors, and, to be sure, its enemies. We think of scientific progress, scientific revolutions, scientific laboratories, mad scientists, and so on, following more or less from Francis Bacon's theorizing at the end of the sixteenth century. For him, the world had previously been accepted as a completed creation with its laws implicit and open to deduction, but now and henceforth it was to be seen instead as an aggregation of facts which were open to discreet observation. Just as the laws according to which nature moved had to be induced from an accretion of suppositions based upon clearly observed facts, so, too, was the power of the observer now held paramount in the formation of knowledge. Seeing clearly, discerning with refinement, measuring with assiduity—these were the powers involved in learning the world. And such a world, structured so as to be learnable, shone in its special visibility, its openness to measurement and observation. In this enlightenment, as Jean Starobinski described it, the processes of the reasoning mind "appear to have been closely akin to those of the seeing eye" (*Invention* 210; qtd. in Jay 85). Martin Jay describes the difficulties of apperception as they applied to politics: the court of the Sun King (Louis XIV) "at once theater and spectacle, was a dazzling display of superficial brilliance, bewildering to outsiders but legible to those who knew how to read its meaning. Here courtiers learned to decode the signs of power, distinction, and hierarchy in the gestures and accoutrements of bodies semaphorically on view" (87)—a type of situation handily described again and again by Dumas, of course, in *Le Comte de Monte Cristo.*

Science understood in this (limited) way involves calibration, measurement, recording, publication, testing and retesting, doubt, hypothesis, experiment, controlled variables, and so on. The observation upon which it stands is very old as a process. "All early natural philosophers acknowledged that vision is man's most noble and dependable sense," claims David Lindberg (qtd. in Jay 39). In the Enlightenment, writes Patricia Fara, "seeing was closely allied with knowing. Progressive thinkers often claimed that they were living in an enlightened age, when the bright flame of reason would dispel the dark clouds of ignorance and superstition" (15). Scientific experiments became rationalized as a superior avenue to the truth, even though they weren't always successful, even though "people make mistakes, ignore results that later seem significant, or persuade themselves—and others—to adopt theories that turn out to be false" (Fara 10). Beyond wanting to understand the world, "Enlightenment philosophers wanted . . . to promote themselves by displaying their command of apparently inexplicable phenomena" (20–21), and "hoped to gain authority over society by proving their dominion over nature" (22), ultimately beginning to professionalize themselves as did Joseph Priestley, the "electrician." What comes to be constituted in this shaping of "science" is a particular institutionalization of the more general process of human science, which has always been the human quest for knowledge of the world, or the repository of knowledge that any person may possess. Jay gives one illustration of the warping quality of such institutionalization, for example, when he writes that "space was robbed of its substantive meaningfulness to become an ordered, uniform system of abstract linear coordinates. As such, it was less the stage for a narrative to be developed over time than the eternal container of objective processes. It was not until the time of Darwin that narrative regained a significant place in the self-understanding of science" (53). And Michel Foucault gives another, as he discusses the pre-Freudian discourse on sex, wherein "we could take all these things that were said, the painstaking precautions and detailed analyses, as so many procedures meant to evade the unbearable, too hazardous truth . . . and the mere fact that one claimed to be speaking about it from the rarefied and neutral viewpoint of a science is in itself significant" (53). That "rarefied and neutral" viewpoint couched and covered, among other things, "a refusal to speak" and in this way bolstered "a science made up of evasions" (53). This "science" of sexuality, Foucault says, is "geared to a form of knowledge-power" (58), that is, it connects knowledge with control, mastery, superascendency, discipline, and, ultimately, class.

By contrast, Vincentio opens *Measure for Measure* by reflecting to Escalus upon a different and broader way of knowing, suggesting that as to the properties of government "your own science/Exceeds, in that, the lists of all advice/My strength can give you" (I.i.7–9). For Shakespeare, science exceeded observation and data collection, exceeded the amassing of "facts," and included any and all aspects of knowing and apperceiving. The more limited "science" of white-coated technicians heavily equipped and wrapped in secrecy, that largely informs our view of this process today, valorizes certain professionalizations and class restrictions, accredits and sanctions some seekers as "legitimate" and "authoritative" while others are relegated to the marginalia of history as charlatans, dilettantes, skeptics, and so on. We may think of the sacred tasks of scientific philosophers touted in Mary Shelley's *Frankenstein:* "They penetrate into the recesses of nature, and show how she works in her hiding-places. They ascend into the heavens: they have discovered how the blood circulates, and the nature of the air we breathe. They have acquired new and almost unlimited powers; they can command the thunders of heaven, mimic the earthquake, and even mock the invisible world with its own shadows" (47). And for a "would-be science which could never even step within the threshold of real knowledge" one would reasonably have "the greatest disdain" (41).

But all thinking creatures have their respective scientiae, and working upon our relation to the world we *do* scientia routinely, if unevenly and unrepeatably; even and especially is this the case for those whose science is articulated as an art. Auteurism is something of an equivalent to science, utilizing different methods and rigors and with an altogether separate history and taxonomy. For example, if David Bordwell suggests that the credits of an art film "can tease us with fragmentary, indecipherable images that announce the power of the author to control what we know" (43), it remains true as well that the author is being teased by his world, and is responding in kind. The artist explores the world, searching with a different kind of eye than our typical "scientist" uses; what the artist sees must be accepted as though others can also see and understand it, but this acceptance, this recognition, must be immediate and does not depend upon careful replication of experimental technique and comparison of results. The artist must speak in a language that is instantly apprehendable.

Is Niccolò autobiographical, Antonioni was asked by *Cahiers du cinéma;* "What happened to him never happened to me. . . . A film is autobiographical to the extent that it is authentic and, in order to be that, it has to be sincere" (Cottino-Jones 368). Our attention is being directed to Niccolò as a filmmaker, and to the process not of forming an artistic crystal but of finding the seed around which, if conditions are right, the crystal will unavoidably form. The "seed" in this case is a certain female sensibility that seems open to some form of continuance (sadly lacking in both Mavi and Ida). To the extent that we may view the filmmaker's quest as his science, *Identification of a Woman* turns out to be, actually, the sci-fi film that the little boy asks for; a sci-fi film, indeed, about the ultimate making of a sci-fi film, that "new mysticism" (Kelly 42). Serge Daney and Serge Toubiana said to Antonioni, "The little boy asks Niccolò, 'Why don't you make a sci-fi film?' We ask the same question of you." And he replied to them, "It's a question a little boy like that can ask, but not you!" (5)

Niccolò's search for his character is a voyage with, but also around, women who constitute not only his alien "other" but also his universe, a universe, in the filmmaker's view, of startling moral discontinuity:

> Today the world is endangered by an extremely serious split between a science that is totally and consciously projected into the future, and a rigid and stereotyped morality which all of us recognize as such and yet sustain out of cowardice or sheer laziness. . . . Science has never been more humble and less dogmatic than it is today. Whereas our moral attitudes are governed by an absolute sense of stultification. . . . we have not been capable of finding new ones, we have not been capable of making any head-way whatsoever towards a solution of this problem, of this ever-increasing split between moral man and scientific man, a split which is becoming more and more serious and more and more accentuated. (*Film Culture* 31–32)

Niccolò's is likewise a universe that is sure to be changed: "In the future—not soon, perhaps by the twenty-fifth century—these concepts will have lost their relevance. I can never understand how we have been able to follow these worn-out tracks, which have been laid down by panic in the face of nature. When man becomes reconciled to nature, when space becomes his true background, these words and concepts will have lost their meaning, and we will no longer have to use them" (Samuels 82). Antonioni admitted to Seymour Chatman that he had begun to read more and more about science: "As soon as you talk about the universe, everything is involved" (Chatman, "Interview" 156).

In the last scene of the film, this link between science fiction, the filmmaker, his world, and his women is apparent. Coming home, he stops to listen through the door of his apartment. Who can he be listening for? What is he thinking? That she is inside. *She?* Not Mavi, to be sure, because Mavi is with her lover, Mavi has forgotten him. Not Ida, because he has abandoned Ida. He is listening for the sounds—female sounds absolutely—that will identify his world and connect him with it, the sounds of his truest nature, indeed a sound, distinct, that will address specifically and only him. Then we go inside. Jauntily he tosses his coat away. A landscape hangs restfully upon a wall, seen from an acute angle. The door to his study—it is marked with a Greek key—he steps past it, places his hand upon the wall, lets his fingers creep toward the handle. Quickly, without a reflective pause, he opens. No one is in there, but through a beautiful vertical rectangle the window light spreads in, and, far off, a rolling hill is covered with cushions of trees. "In each of Antonioni's films, especially those in color, there exists a proportionate relationship between the sheer beauty of the images and the terrible reality contained in them" (Kelly 42). He grabs some sunglasses and positions himself in the window. We cut to a close-up of his face as, shielding his eyes a little, he peers outward. Delicate sounds of exploratory music. The sun, informing and blinding, floods in upon him as his voice is heard narrating the story of the asteroid-ship that is his film. Indeed, as his image dissolves away, certain hot spots linger on the screen and become dark green, parts of the space void that the ship haunts. "Individual time accords mysteriously with that of the cosmos" (Antonioni; qtd. in Cardullo 154).

ATTENTION

> The facial features and eyes, said Ferber, remained ultimately unknowable for him.
>
> —W. G. Sebald, *The Emigrants*

Seymour Chatman is neither at ease with *Identification of a Woman* nor able to escape the temptation to imagine how it could have been improved, when he writes,

> There is no discernable answer to the question that Niccolò writes in the steam on a window of his apartment (in the treatment only): "But why am I so attracted to this woman whom I cannot manage to respect?" It might have been well if the question had been asked in the film. At least it would have helped focus the issue a little more clearly. Whether Milian was not quite up to the subtleties of the role or Antonioni did not provide him with sufficiently explanatory lines and action, the basis for Niccolò's absorption with Mavi remains unclear. (*Surface* 225–226)

Nor when he suggests that "Part of the problem with Mavi's characterization may lie with the actress who plays her. It is all very well to depict a character whose psyche is chaotic, incompletely formed, *inachevée*. But clearly the role must be played by someone who is herself clear about what she is doing" (227). Nor when, discussing the notable wordiness of this film in the director's oeuvre, he remarks, "Too many lines are spent establishing the believability of Niccolò's erotic charm" (233). Nor when, in regards to the finale, he chides, "It is sad that Antonioni's budget did not permit him to end the film with the kind of finale that he wanted (and that it seems to need). For if the science fiction sequence had been realized with effects of the caliber of *2001*, *Star Wars*, or *Blade Runner*, one's feelings about Niccolò and his situation as an artist might be entirely different" (237). There is never much sense in reconfiguring an artist's motion picture along the lines of one's own tastes and predilections—of pretending to be the filmmaker oneself. The only film ever worth studying is the one the filmmaker has put upon the screen—worth studying only because it is in our desire to study it—and our challenge is to understand how all of its aspects cohere beautifully and meaningfully into a statement that might not at first be intelligible to our limited reception. There is no doubt that we can be wrong, in myriad ways, but any other project of the self is ultimately an evasion of the facts. Rather than squabble with a film, we must adjust ourselves to it; and that adjustment is the true adventure of cinema-going. Antonioni told Pierre Billard, "Mistakes are always sincere, absolutely sincere" (Cardullo 51).

What kind of science—what kind of eroticized science—is Niccolò doing, that we should understand his charm? And his science fiction film, which is certainly not *Star Wars* or *Blade Runner* but which offers a stunning, if abrupt, vision and draws the film to a profound conclusion—what about its significance exactly and wholly in its own terms? When Antonioni spoke with Daney and Toubiana, he did not regret that he lacked the funds for making extravaganzas like those American ones, he merely indicated that in Italy filmmaking was done in radically different terms than in Hollywood. Moreover, the asteroid-ship isn't the true sci-fi figure in this film, Niccolò is. And the glowing sun only signifies the mysterious universe that is thrown up more concretely in the presences that Niccolò confronts.

Two fascinating features of the film are indeed valuably invoked in Chatman's critique: the incomprehensibility and vagueness of the world that fascinates our protagonist (to such an extent that one might question the merit of that fascination); and the nexus between fascination and erotic appeal. The world's incomprehensibility is one thing as regards knowledge and another as regards perception. We have a long history of seeking to apprehend structures and relations that are not immediately given to the senses, and in this respect it can be argued that the quest for knowledge is a continual negotiation with the world's mystery or incomprehensibility. After the Enlightenment, science of any sort attempts to illuminate, thus to make experience more understandable and to dissipate the darkness: where id was, there shall ego be. But the world as an incomprehensible datum changed at the end of the nineteenth century, with William James's theory of active perception. Prior to this, philosophers had posited "the mere presence to the senses of an outward order" (James, vol. 1, 402), which in the case of perceptual difficulty implied either a damaged or an improperly attentive perceptual apparatus, absent which the apparent (and complete) structure of the world would have been directly perceivable. For James, early writers were "bent on showing how the higher faculties of the mind are pure products of 'experience'; and experience is supposed to be of something simply *given*" (402). James suggests that perception is bound up with attention, and attention is "the taking possession by the mind, in clear and vivid form, of one out of what seem several simultaneously possible objects or trains of thought" (403–404). He goes on to stipulate that in paying attention, we must accomplish "withdrawal from some things in order to deal effectively with others" (404). Part of what is troubling Niccolò, seen through a Jamesian lens, is the decision, in regard to both Mavi and Ida, as to what he should attend to and what he should disregard. In causing him this trouble these women also spark his concern about other aspects of the world and the decision he must make, always, in seeing. This is why the title of the film is so appropriate. As much as the problem is women, it is also identification, and, indeed, identification of a woman, that spirit so ineluctable and enticing: woman as the motive of science (not in the crass way that scientists, who are frequently men, objectify women and try to control them through knowledge; but in the spiritual way that scientists, who are humans, seek the ineffable knowledge of their own origin, the place of no return).

One signal consequence of the shift to thinking of active perception, writes Jonathan Crary, "was that the functioning of vision became dependent on the complex and contingent physiological makeup of the observer, rendering vision faulty, unreliable, and, it was sometimes argued, arbitrary. Even before the middle of the [nineteenth] century, an extensive amount of work in science, philosophy, psychology, and art involved a coming to terms in various ways with the understanding that vision, or any of the senses, could no longer claim an essential objectivity or certainty" (12).

Niccolò can err in his calculations and estimations; as can every other character in the film. Language can seem ambiguous. For example, when the girl at the swimming pool acknowledges that on one occasion she and Mavi slept together, it can be totally unclear what, ultimately, she is saying: that Mavi is a lesbian? That circumstances led to a fortuitous experience, once? That Niccolò has no hope with Mavi? That men tend to misunderstand and misrepresent women? The world's ostensible "incomprehensibility" can result not simply from inaccurate or faulty (that is, correctible) sight of an object that is fully given, but from a biased observer's position or attitude in the face of an object that takes its form only in being apprehended. But, suggests Crary, the independence of subjective perception comes to be challenged in further ways: "The rapid accumulation of knowledge about the workings of a fully embodied observer disclosed possible ways that vision was open to procedures of normalization, of quantification, of discipline. Once the empirical truth of vision was determined to lie in the body, vision (and similarly the other senses) could be annexed and controlled by external techniques of manipulation and stimulation" (12). The vision of the discrete observer is thus measurable and quantifiable, and can be schematized, so that perception can be fitted into a broader calculus of hegemonic control and knowledge. Vision could be instrumentalized "as a component of machinic arrangements" (13). To the extent, then, that the visionary act was externalized as a social entity (through the action that eventuated from it), even as a public resource, any act of identification or discrimination could stand obediently to order within a matrix of predictable and exploitable observations and thus gain its place among what Crary calls "the delirious operations of modernization" (13). A move was induced culturally to "discover what faculties, operations, or organs produced or allowed the complex coherence of conscious thought" (15). Perception and knowledge became rationalized as a system of control.

Looking at attention as "an inevitable fragmentation of a visual field," Crary cites John Dewey to the effect that the mind is concentrated "in a point of great light and heat. So the mind, instead of diffusing consciousness over all the elements presented to it, brings it all to bear upon some one selected point, which stands out with unusual brilliancy and distinctness" (24). In bringing consciousness to bear this way, moreover, we come to accept the reality of the thing observed, engaging in "belief in a thing for no other reason than that we conceive it with passion," which commitment of attention and conviction, writes James, Charles Renouvier calls "mental vertigo" (James, vol. 2, 309). In showing Niccolò's visual field with sharpness and precise illumination, and in showing him wrestling with the problem of attaining focus upon any such "thing," Antonioni produces a Deweyan escapade, offering us a chance at each moment to see that the selected field of vision is arbitrary and potentially hopeless even as he shows that it is stunning and alluring.

Erotic sensibility is a potential escape route from the controlling uniformity of rational vision. Crary argues, for example, that socially organized perceptual schemes develop and shift through time, and that "film, photography, and television are transient elements within an accelerating sequence" of changing visual forms (13); this very regularity in perception tends to couch and motivate the sort of critique one finds in Chatman, who bemoans the fact that Antonioni's Niccolò didn't have the production funds for a (presumably) authentic—and regular—science fiction film. Filmic forms, such as the science fiction type to which *Blade Runner* so handily conforms, are only part of the rationalization of public perception, only a result of the operations of measuring, tabulating, regularizing, constraining, filtering, and emphasizing conventional modes of perception. Niccolò's film, a piece of which we see in a sequence that links the footage directly to his gazing eye—and thus to the personal quality of this vision (its eros)—is his attempt to see independently of the controlling system. Chatman is merely pointing out how deviant Antonioni is. Oddly, writing about the sex in *Identification of a Woman,* Chatman has no trouble spelling out this same revolutionary stance, noting that Mavi reveals her personal sexual attitude (keeping her underpants on until the last possible moment) "with the confidence of one instructed by her society that every person's sex is his or her own affair, not subject to moral or psychological evaluation. She is simply explaining her preferences, not excusing herself for having them" (220). (It could also be argued that society did not instruct Mavi, but simply failed to provide instruction in this vital area of experience.) Our society also "instructs" us that the artist's vision is problematically beyond social instruction: Niccolò's way of filming is a part of his own erotic life, a part of what he endures that cannot be fully calibrated and regimented through the system. He is scrupulously personal (as is Antonioni), more so than the Ridley Scott who made

Blade Runner or the George Lucas who made *Star Wars* or even the Stanley Kubrick who made *2001*, all of whom finally sacrificed their own inner tensions and lacunae, doubts and interruptions to the grammar of a system that could rationalize their address to a diffuse and hungry public.

It is not because he has taken a vow to maintain principles of searching, labeling, knowing, and illuminating that Niccolò seeks to "identify" a woman as the center of his creative operation. He is neither monk nor bureaucrat. He is not committed a priori to a dispassionate and (officially) scientific gaze. Every step he takes in this film is tied to breathing, hopefulness, anticipation, disappointment, reawakened desire, and movement toward a resolution, and so there is an eros implicit in his very act of looking: not as though he gazes to find a sexual object, but as though his gazing is an absolute form of his sexuality. In his science fiction film Niccolò is finally divorced even from himself, not in the way that Crary, following Deleuze—and also a little eagerly—suggests the perceiver must ultimately be after cinema: "It is precisely the nonselectivity of the cinema eye that distinguishes it from the texture of a human attentiveness" (344), but through a careful and devoted selectivity, an all-absorbing selectivity, that throws him out toward a universe. This, too, is why Niccolò—a human, but also a maker of cinema—is continually ill at ease with the fact of his own gazing, since although he attempts to see the world around the core of a woman's experience, to focus on a "point of great light and heat," he knows at the same time that ultimately his film will produce a field, not a point, a field that is bounded, to be sure, yet one in which the depth of his concentration will not find a marker. Baudelaire, writes Sartre, had a similar obsession, with infinity, "something which is, without being given; something which today defines me and which nevertheless will not exist until tomorrow" (37–38).

NEITHER NIGHT NOR DAY

A feeling, for which I have no name, has taken possession of my soul—a sensation which will admit of no analysis, to which the lessons of by-gone time are inadequate, and for which I fear futurity itself will offer me no key.

—Poe, "MS. Found in a Bottle"

At the soirée, Mavi and Niccolò are standing in conversation while in an adjacent room (that is painted avocado green) well-dressed aristocrats, some of whom have lots of money and some of whom haven't a bean, chat the night away. "We don't have one single idea of a society," complains Mavi. We cut to another room (also avocado green, that soothing but also alarming color) where the voice of a woman praises François Mitterand as a "nice man" whom she hopes "will do well." (I stood once in the lobby of a hotel while Mitterand padded from the elevators to the door, a silent gentle little gnome, it seemed, surrounded by gruff security men who did not appear to recognize him.) At one point an old man escorts a much younger woman through the frame, gloating to her in a whisper, "One of my ancestors invented the double-bass!" (This is perhaps an invitation to rest awhile upon his lap, since the earliest bass was a violone da gamba and the speaker may be referring to a certain familial "expertise" [See Stiller, 462]. It is also, most surely, a genealogical claim dating back at least four hundred years.) Standing in front of a massive canvas (Tiepolo? Caravaggio?), Niccolò and Mavi are discovered by a doyenne:

MAVI: Niccolò is trying to find someone.

DOYENNE: What has the poor man done?

MAVI: Nothing.

DOYENNE (taking her leave): Why look for him then?

What is this polite disengagement, this attitude of lethargy that permeates the upper class—a class that has nothing to do but consider itself? Mavi "moves like in a ballet within this world made up of counts, dukes, princes, and the black aristocracy, where there isn't a single object that isn't authentic. She moves at ease within these walls made up of ancient leather wallpaper" (Antonioni; qtd. in Bachmann, "Love" 172). "The Aristocrat devours nature," writes Sartre. "The exquisite imperfection of forms and a discreet blurring of colours are the best guarantees of authenticity" (Masturbation 115–6).

Niccolò is in a doorway next to a young man in a tux, who gazes forward, past the camera, at someone or something, yet with an empty regard that betokens neither comprehension nor involvement. "Is there always this sectarian atmosphere at your parties, cocktails, and dinners?" the director asks the boy, "Are you afraid of being spied upon?" The kid drops his eyes: "Many of us have escaped already." As if a comment were in order, Niccolò rejoins, "Once it was the poor who emigrated from Italy. Now it's this lot." Need we be told that the poor who emigrated had nothing to hope for, and therefore nothing to lose? But these rich: clearly they have everything and are still destitute. They have escaped in order to have more than everything. We can suddenly read the slightly pouting, pampered expression on the boy's face. The eyes glazed, observant but uncaring; the lips, fulsome but pursed with possessiveness; the dark curly hair cut as though to impress Donatello, the shoulders artfully slouched. Nothing in his world appeals to this boy, has merit for him, holds his commitment. As Niccolò was told by Mavi, this is a society in which there is no orientation, no sense of duty or obligation, no agreement on higher principles that can guide everyone in a unifying way. It's a world of personality and disconnection, in which the social life has dried up and everyone who can afford to escape has jumped to richer pastures.

In a party like this, one should be able to find the greatest lights of a society, the repositories and voices of its most supreme values. The paintings should be inspiring and beautiful, both classical and futurist: Guercino, Miró, Boccioni, Ensor, Crivelli, Duchamp, Canaletto, De Heem, Malevich. The language should be poetry, not the garble of the marketplace or the voting booth. Instead of talking about the double-bass, one should be invoking music. Meanwhile, a paid lutist is playing something inoffensive, popularly Mediterranean, vacuous, when he could be playing Bach or Vivaldi. And, given all the meaningless chatter, it is difficult for the personality who searches for light to locate a source of inspiration. All the guests are interchangeable, all the rooms interchangeable, the conversations all forgettable if indeed they are not full of lies or dissemblings: for instance, Mavi invites a man and his wife to dinner at her house, but soon makes it clear to Niccolò she hopes to borrow *his* place for this cultural adventure.

What sort of an aristocracy or managerial class works without a principle upon which to base its designs? "In fairly populous societies," wrote Gaetano Mosca in the 1930s,

> ruling classes do not justify their power exclusively by de facto possession of it, but try to find a moral and legal basis for it, representing it as the logical and necessary consequence of doctrines and beliefs that are generally recognized and accepted. So if a society is deeply imbued with the Christian spirit the political class will govern by the will of the sovereign, who, in turn, will reign because he is God's anointed. . . . And yet that does not mean that political formulas are mere quackeries aptly invented to trick the masses into obedience. Anyone who viewed them in that light would fall into grave error. The truth is that they answer a real need in man's social nature; and this need, so universally felt, of governing and knowing that one is governed not on the basis of mere material or intellectual force, but on the basis of a moral principle, has beyond any doubt a practical and a real importance. (207–208)

No chance here of satisfying that need. Mavi and Niccolò have invaded a den of lotos-eaters. In their presence it is difficult if not utterly impossible to discern value, truth, or loyalty to an idea. The "idea," as it were, is the momentary self and nothing more.

As the bourgeois revolution continues, writes Marx, the distinctions between people are diminished and also exaggerated, so that only two great classes—"two great hostile camps" (103)—remain. Among the slaving workers, "machinery obliterates all distinctions of labor" (110), a phenomenon illustrated again and again, to be sure, in the factory scenes of *The Red Desert,* but we can also understand this obliteration as an enhancement and reflection of a greater and more diffuse social change, in which distinction itself loses importance. As the bourgeoisie retreats further and further from the proletariat—"escaping already"—contrasting lifestyle and value are nowhere to be detected. The principle social value is selling and buying, a value broadly diffused through the population, coming to define freedom itself (as Marx writes), and supplanting a central feudal value, "the most heavenly ecstasies of religious fervour, of chivalrous enthusiasm, of philistine sentimentalism" (105). What eventuates is a condition in which people progressively lack the ability to gain true purchase on experience, because experience has been degraded into an exchangeable commodity that merely fluctuates around and shuttles between those who pay for and those who profit by it (see Pomerance, "Gesture"). Every experience is a quick fix, a snatch, a detachable, accountable, and expendable waste. Baudelaire describes modern bourgeois life as a "moving chaos where death strikes from every side at once" (*Spleen* 94), and Marshall Berman suggests that

> the man in the modern street, thrown into this maelstrom, is driven back on his own resources—often on resources he never knew he had—and forced to stretch them desperately in order to survive. In order to cross the moving chaos, he must attune and adapt himself to its moves, must learn to not merely keep up with it but to stay at least a step ahead. He must become adept at *soubresauts* and *mouvements brusques,* at sudden, abrupt, jagged twists and shifts—and not only with his legs and his body, but with his mind and his sensibility as well. (159)

In experience—which is the zone of interest for an artist, or at least for an artist such as Niccolò—the somersaults and brusque movements required in the modern flux are vague and insensible to the degree that no solid world resists them, no fixed forms or established values, even revolutionary values, linger and persist as frictionable surfaces against which one can sense, thus find, oneself in motion. One is continually twisting and turning in modern life—just as Antonioni's camera twists and turns in its Brownian motion through this soirée—without particularly feeling the stress of motion. "All that is solid," says Marx, "melts into air" (106).

Corresponding to the loss of material stability implied by the relentless motion of bourgeois life under capitalism, is a sharp discontinuity with classical visual forms, in which the "proximate vision" that Ortega places at the center of optical experience in the Quattrocento finally submits to revolution, as it were. Whereas in Giotto, for example, we had seen "'in bulk,' convexly," by the time of the Impressionists an object "placed farther away, for distant vision, loses this corporeality, this solidity and plenitude. Now it is no longer a compact mass, clearly rotund, with its protuberance and curving flanks; it has lost 'bulk,' and become, rather, an insubstantial surface, an unbodied spectre composed only of light. . . . In passing from proximate to distant vision an object becomes illusory" (*Point of View* 111). Thus, by the time he had come to a thorough repudiation of classical techniques through which space and material bodies were rendered with discreteness and depth, the painter of "Un dimanche après-midi à l'Île de la Grande Jatte" (1884) found himself giving "an illusion of deep space" by placing the spectator "in a foreground of deep shadow" and by drawing the eye into the picture "stage by stage, in a dark-light progression that gradually leads into a light, bright distance" (Thomson 108); all this using his pixillating brushstrokes that laid upon the canvas not the lines and planes that were elements of a classical form but a vast field of explosive luminous punctuations, an atomic theory of vision. Nor did Georges Seurat stand alone in his fascination with light, its play, its changes, and the way it affected color and surface when examined for itself. Louis Émile Edmond Duranty remarks with delight on a sort of social abrasiveness the impressionists manifested as, following the likes of Whistler, they began to use a "highly personal palette," and to produce "the most daring innovations" as they worked "with color variations of infinite delicacy—dusky, diffused, and vaporous tints that belong to neither night nor day" (42). Indeed, Duranty reveals that for the impressionists, who were at the center of modern life, a particular use of paint could have one particularly astonishing effect on our observation of the world as objective and corporeal, namely to fragment and dissipate it: "They are not merely preoccupied by the refined and supple play of color that emerges when they observe the way the most delicate ranges of tone either contrast or intermingle with each other. Rather, the real discovery of these painters lies in their realization that *strong light mitigates color,* and that sunlight reflected by objects tends, by its very brightness, to restore that luminous unity that merges all seven prismatic rays into one single colorless beam—light itself" (42, italics mine). "*La grande lumière* décolore *les tons*." Invoked in impressionism, then, is the potentiality for a disintegration of objective reality, for that limiting condition in which bourgeois existence, riddled with motion and substantiated by glancing visions—Ortega notes that in impressionism one sees out of the corner of the eye, as though seizing a vision while moving through space—comes to make the world of experience an ultimate challenge for the now outdated sensibility that wishes to seize and fix objects, find a center, penetrate an interest, develop for things and places a history and biography that is unique.

THE MODERN SELF

> Mirrors are subject to the defects of the individual substances of which they are made and react the way they really and truly want to.
>
> —Julio Cortázar, "The Behavior of Mirrors on Easter Island"

Much of the relatively meager critical appreciation of *Identification of a Woman* concentrates seriously on Mavi and Ida, even debunking Niccolò as merely an "absent-minded fellow" (Chatman, *Surface* 216), as a "zombie-like" male who must constitute "a critique of the modern world" (Sarris), or as "the most ethically disoriented of the film's major characters" (Kelly 38). Andrew Sarris finds the film revolting if not nonsensical: "Antonioni has always been up there on the screen, but we tended to mistake his reflection for a portrait of Modern Man with all his wires disconnected. Yet now that the director stands at last nakedly before us, the absence of a plausibly compelling narrative drains his confessional film of the necessary tension to sustain our interest. And the cryptic intimations of rampant feminism, lesbianism, and even masturbatory solipsism seem overly tentative and dilettantish." Narrational penis too small, in other words: doesn't "sustain our interest." A serious viewer of the film might well disagree, since serious viewing recapitulates that "naked" director as a field in which multiple engagements and intentionalities intersect and work to blossom. As to the solipsism of masturbation: the young woman at the swimming pool who discusses her fondness for self-manipulation doesn't strike the eye or the intelligence as solipsistic at all, especially given her extremely civil, even modest, reactions to Niccolò; nor, in her desperate self-reflections alternated with pregnant philosophical comments, does Mavi. In Sarris's rejection, we can see a persistence of Enlightenment assumptions about the masturbatory act, as summarized by Thomas Laqueur:

> Three things made solitary sex unnatural. First, it was motivated not by a real object of desire but by a phantasm; masturbation threatened to overwhelm the most protean and potentially creative of the mind's faculties—the imagination—and drive it over a cliff. Second, while all other sex was social, masturbation was private, or, when it was not done alone, it was social in all the wrong ways: wicked servants taught it to children; wicked older boys taught it to innocent younger ones; girls and boys in school taught it to each other away from adult supervision. Sex was naturally done *with* someone; solitary sex was not. And third, unlike other appetites, the urge to masturbate could be neither sated nor moderated. Done alone, driven only by the mind's own creations, it was a primal, irremediable, and seductively, even addictively, easy transgression. Every man, woman, and child suddenly seemed to have access to the boundless excess of gratification that had once been the privilege of Roman emperors.
>
> Masturbation thus became the vice of individuation for a world in which the old ramparts against desire had crumbled; it pointed to an abyss of solipsism, anomie, and socially meaningless freedom that seemed to belie the ideal of moral autonomy. It was the vice born of an age that valued desire, pleasure, and privacy but was fundamentally worried about how, or if, society could mobilize them. It is the sexuality of the modern self. (210)

And the feminism—by which Sarris must mean the presence of women—is hardly rampant, the lesbianism indeed virtually enshrouded. At any rate, Sarris's comment is a beautiful example of the denigration of Niccolò. And the descriptions of Seymour Chatman give an equally pointed elevation to the principal females. "Mavi, a trendsetter, tends to represent the attitudes of an entire generation," writes he, "She has a restless need to experiment" (219, 220). As her masseur—in one scene, after she accuses him of needing her rather than loving her, he offers an extended pudendal friction through her underwear—"Niccolò . . . is very much the servant of Mavi's imperious sexual needs. And her 'right' to so elaborate a sexual life seems guaranteed in some sense by her membership in the leisured class" (226). Some, following D.H. Lawrence, would postulate that the poor experience an authentic, vigorous, bawdy sexuality while the etiolated rich are too self-conscious even for the depths of pleasure. Ida, for her part, "is fresh, frank, and, though young, level-headed and warm" (215); "healthy, down-to-earth, direct, sincere, in every way estimable, indeed to a fault: one cannot imagine why Niccolò would want to give her up" (227). Perhaps Niccolò does not *want* to give her up; mercifully, this issue doesn't get explored. Vincent Canby waved the film off as "excruciatingly empty," but could not forbear from finding Mavi an "enigmatic young woman . . . who makes love with a furious abandon that is about the only thing in the film that works."

Niccolò does give Ida up, however, it being a repeated truth that he looks for a creature he has not found. That fact is central to the film's structure. He gives up Mavi, too, once it becomes clear to him she does not wish to be found, will not permit it. In the end, he has given everyone up.

The way Sam Rohdie sees the film, the camera "is always with Niccolò . . . beside him as it were, looking as he looks, encountering as he encounters, like him facing the exact same problems of identification, of sorting out reality from its simulacrum, desire from the other" (188). Here is presented once again, this time in the context of an Antonioni work, one of those delicious Baudrillardian gauntlets, the crippling challenge of the simulacral world; and one of those piquant Lacanian projections, too, the problem of knowing the beloved apart from love itself, seeing the line between one's conceits and the objective strangeness that confounds them. These are interesting riddles, but they do not describe Niccolò in this film as much, perhaps, as the viewer who is obsessed with them. The camera surely is beside Niccolò throughout, and we see the world as he sees it, a place without sharp discriminations. There is a tasteful, but also dulling harmony to colors and forms, as though everything has been managed into shape and all objects contrived to join one another in neat arrangements (the bed is always where Niccolò would like it to be, or better, where he expects it to be, because he is past finding sexuality an act worth appreciating). His friends, his family, his lovers, his business contacts, strangers he has never met before: with all of these he maintains a calm and even disinterested tone, quite as though they have been subjected to a ray that equalizes their statuses in his regard.

As to that regard: it moves lethargically, like the monster from the black lagoon, yet also methodically, so that he can maintain clarity without interruption as he searches in all directions for a central feature, a sacred object upon which to fasten the fascination. Daily life is a chain of obstacles, weeds entangled around him as he strokes his way forward: the ineffable, unretrievable beeper that will disarm his apartment's warning system; his sister's complaints about her troubles at work; his little nephew's innocent but also incessant demands for additions to his stamp collection; the inexorably stringent demand of Mavi's secret lover—demand or provocation; Ida's very fluidity, her ability to do everything, to sense everywhere, to love without hesitation. At a certain point "*nel mezzo del cammin di nostra vita,*" the world can become a locus of events, sensations, and encounters that are all—that are each—precisely and only matters of fact. Its romantic patina worn away, its charming gleam dissipated by a movement of the light, the wine glass is merely a vesicle, its contents merely a calculated distillation from grapes that endured a particular winter upon a particular slope. What had seemed sacred and mysterious, overwhelming, even irritable—the genitalia of the lover—become anatomical parts in an array; just as, with a subtle change of light, the mundane becomes evanescent. As Camus wrote, "What wells up in me is not the hope of better days but a serene and primitive indifference to everything and to myself" (39). Sitting in his window in the finale, Niccolò is bathed in an ethereal, holy light—light from the sun; yet at the same time he is merely illuminated, with more illumination than some objects (like the stars of Hollywood's golden age, upon whom, says cinematographer William Daniels in *Visions of Light* [1992], a few extra foot candles were expended to make them "pop") and less than others. He exists on a kind of scalpel blade between perfunctoriness and salvation, corruption and purity, the everyday and the unworldly. Because each term implies the other, every special instant invoking and requiring the mundane, it is also true that neither term is true. Neither mundanity nor sanctity survive outside the arbitrary judgments through which we mandate and create them. In the end, what confronts us is light.

All things are connectable. Niccolò searches for his woman not as the center of his narrative but as the starting point from which he can join together the various threads that bind all things to all things. In that apartment building where Mavi has been hiding away with her girlfriend—her cool, even supercilious girlfriend; her brutish girlfriend (because it is this girlfriend who has hired the thug)—there appear to be a number of discreet apartments, but actually all of these spaces exist together, simultaneously, and each footstep taken by any person in any one of them echoes or contradicts a footstep taken above or below. Moral stricture, ethical suasion, aesthetic form, political mandate, economic imperative: all of these, at once, are ways of formulating and predicting the sorts of events that Niccolò is moving toward and away from, observing carefully, thinking through as possible additions to the story he wishes to make. When one has adopted a certain state of readiness, every discernable nuance is potentially raw material. It is not so much that Niccolò is apathetic, that he does not feel his relations with Mavi and Ida, as that he is obsessively devoted to the work at hand. He is continually, and inextinguishably, burning with the motive to narrate.

And what is this story, this supreme construction? That a few dozen red chrysanthemums are delivered by hand. That one drives off into the night to escape from Rome. That a collaborator wonders about what kind of love story can be written in a corrupt world. That the swimmers move through a pool, while a strange girl watches them in self-absorption. That outside one's window, in a pine tree, there is a birds' nest, but no birds. The human presence, a ghost of sorts, inhabits this world and circulates among objects, caressing them with its intent. As Ida and Niccolò leave his apartment, they pass the concierge's cubby and see half the chrysanthemums scattered on the floor: some ghost dropped them, the red flowers, perhaps it is me.

BORED

We no longer know how to see the real faces of those around us.
—Camus, "The Desert"

One difficulty that has beset viewers of this film, and confounded critics—"When it hit New York in 1982," moans John Powers, "this elusive, challenging work received the kind of dismissive reviews more appropriate to Claude Lelouch than to one of the century's great artists"—stems from the expectation that one should be watching vital, healthy people—especially if they are neurotic—who struggle ardently, even nobly, to make achievements we can detect and applaud: a transformation of the social arrangements that imprison the powerless, a transformation of space according to a new aesthetic, a transformation of the self. A film, then, about a personality who meanders and turns in circles, who stares out the window, whose encounters are systematically, repeatedly, emphatically fruitless? No. A man should be looking for a love partner, and find one. He should be solving a mystery. He should be erecting a pyramid. But Camus put it best: "Everyone wants the man who is still searching to have already reached his conclusions. A thousand voices are already telling him what he has found, and yet he knows that he hasn't found anything" (155). Niccolò has not reached his conclusions, and his search, which we must accompany, is exhausting, overwhelming. "You have found me," says Mavi, in effect, and Ida echoes; as we presume the wife echoed, too, earlier, in another life. But he never finds Mavi, we only want him to. Never finds Ida. This film is not about the result or motive of a search, but about the search itself, its vertigo, sloppiness, unpredictability, passionate yet hopeless intensity. Given the incessant movement and complexity of the world in and through which Niccolò searches, it is perhaps obvious to say that he is bored. He experiences, that is to say, boredom in the most exquisite and high-minded sense of the term, a "nagging desire for *something*, the nature of which is forever hidden" (Healy 48; qtd. in Winter 28).

It is not that Niccolò feels a yearning but does not know what it is that he yearns for. It is that he experiences desire, but *cannot* know its object. "In an instant," he knows, with Vladimir and Estragon, "all will vanish and we'll be alone once more, in the midst of nothingness." This is what it is to be searching for form, reaching into the ether in every posture one assumes, combating that gravity, straining against convention and history, trying through the unilluminated void to see shape, not *any* shape but the singular shape that will give to one's sensibility and memory, placement and purpose and potentiality. As Tennessee Williams's poet Nonno writes in *The Night of the Iguana:*

> Sometime while night obscures the tree
> The zenith of its life will be
> Gone past forever, and from thence
> A second history will commence. (123)

Niccolò is like this poet, but his mutterings are gazes; and the tone of his voice is in the way he stretches out his arm, the way he enters a room. The opposite of this boredom, this relentless but evenhanded search, is commonplace action: the partygoers, for example, carrying on trivial little conversations at the soirée as though it mattered what one said, as though one were actually being informative in adjoining oneself genealogically to the inventor of the double-bass; or a shopgirl fiddling with a male mannequin in her vitrine, as though to give a signal, as though to embody a daydream; or an actress giving a performance, or circling an enclosure on her steed; or a woman giggling with excitement because she has to find a place to pee; or the noxious mundanity of trying to get into one's apartment through the burglar alarm one has forgotten to disable; all these and a myriad more commonplaces, the stuff of daily life but poison to the soul (poison like the ice cream the thug is slurping in the café while he tells Niccolò that he should give Mavi up), poison because the soul is looking for the phrase to complete the line, the line through which to move the object through space.

. . . The parabolic line that Niccolò's filmic space-asteroid takes as it moves off toward the sun (the same as the parabolic line of David Locke's Land Rover hurtling off into the desert in *The Passenger* and the parabolic line of the Jeep curving away into the park with the shouting revelers in *Blow-Up*). In the universe, there are no straight lines.

The soul is breathing and cannot tolerate that obstructive garbage, matter, clogging every passageway to every horizon. To be bored with the commonplace is to strive to outlast and outdistance it, to work at escape. Boredom is the true vitality. Continually and everlastingly, in its commonplace fashion, the earth orbits around the sun. To break with this, Niccolò strikes up the idea of voyaging *to* the sun, coming to know it. We have used the sun only as a vehicle for knowing ourselves, and we have come to the end of the line. A "Charlie Bubbles-ish ending" is what John Powers deprecatingly calls this snippet of science fiction footage, which is so challenging and exciting to watch. The color of deep space is not only green but a vivid and forestial green, chlorophyll green, and there is nothing but a superfluity of optimism in the passage of the platinum colored asteroid, which wobbles a little insecurely with the perils of its voyage and thus attracts our sympathy.

IMPOSSIBLE EXPERIENCE

The art of storytelling is coming to an end.
—Walter Benjamin, "The Storyteller"

"The earliest symptom of a process whose end is the decline of storytelling," writes Benjamin, "is the rise of the novel at the beginning of modern times" ("Storyteller" 87): the novel, we might add, that has so often become the film. The novel, dependent upon the form of the book, abjures the storyteller's idiosyncratic speech, tactile experience, direct unmediated relation to his nature and his world. For a man to be able to find and tell a story, he must relax, withdraw himself from the mechanical pressure and rhythm of the modern world; and, Benjamin sadly observes, such a state of relaxation "is becoming rarer and rarer" (91). Niccolò is in search of a story, very like his creator, who felt himself to be searching for "a new kind of story" (Samuels 92). He believes in storytelling. Perhaps, as Benjamin says of the storyteller, "he has borrowed his authority from death . . . it is natural history to which his stories refer back" (94), but at any rate there is something morbid about his gaze, his flaccidity, his patience.

Although Benjamin does not put it this way, for him boredom is a thoroughly appropriate response to modernism, one that symptomatizes the healthy spirit at war with a condition in which we prefer to validate information over intelligence. Information "lays claim to prompt verifiability," and the "dissemination of information has had a decisive share" in a state of affairs that has seen storytelling decline (89). We may consider the distinction that Patricia Meyer Spacks makes between two usages of the word "interesting" in the history of the novel. The word can apply to the spirits and tastes of the individual: bored, one declines to find things "interesting," appealing to the self; or it can apply to a social and cultural importance "inherent in the old meaning of *interesting*" and involving "reliance on communal values" (115). One usage of "interesting" applies to the public realm, then, and the other to "private tastes" (117). For Spacks, a reader can be bored by privileging the private, indeed by denying that public interest might adhere to certain texts or situations. Niccolò is appropriately bored with the quotidian trivia of the world in which he moves with Mavi, and the slow turning of the film and of its protagonist's movements in searching for her depths is itself a calculated statement about the boredom he experiences in his life. As the modern world of mercantile, journalistic, superficially social, and professional experience seems to tumble by, his boredom is a way of withdrawing in order to be attuned to the voice of an "artisan form of communication" of an earlier, and richer, day (Benjamin, "Storyteller" 91). And the fact that he experiences boredom—a sense of the undifferentiated equality of events and contingencies, a flatness of affect, a constant hunger and readiness for something richer—may lead us to expect that Niccolò will find his story in the end. "Boredom," says Benjamin, "is the dream bird that hatches the egg of experience" (91).

But Adam Phillips more neatly strikes the chord when he reflects, "Boredom, I think, protects the individual, *makes tolerable for him the impossible experience of waiting for something without knowing what it could be.* So the paradox of the waiting that goes on in boredom is that the individual does not know what he was waiting for until he finds it, and that often he does not know that he is waiting" (77–78; my emphasis). We must understand that Niccolò himself is the central character of the science fiction film he eventually makes: he is floating through space on an exploration, slowly approximating himself to the brilliant center of things. What he can know about himself is his own hunger to travel and search, but not precisely what he is searching for, and often—because the search is relentless and occupies every aspect of his existence—not even that he searches. He experiences a "determination of the present by the future, of what already exists by what does not yet exist . . . which philosophers today call transcendence" (Sartre, "Baudelaire" 38).

When we are bored the world taxes us by lacking nodes worth special focus. Objects do not stand out as either central or peripheral, light does not assist us by flattering surfaces or points. All of the optical field makes itself accessible uniformly, so that Ortega's "luminous hero" (of the Quattrocento) is merely a trace memory or a vague hope ("Point of View"). Direction impossible, pathways are indistinct and unnavigable, the lights of the heavens are inaccessible through their very profusion and constant motion, philosophy is a riddle. We move in a fog.

The eloquent and magnificent fog sequence in this film:

Niccolò, certain that his house is being watched, escaping through the back door and racing in his silver car to Mavi's house; fetching her and driving into the country, because he knows that villa he rented once. But on the way they encounter a field of mists, or rather what seems a cloud that has given up its immortality and dropped to earth. The suddenness of this manifestation, its impenetrability, the feeling we must have that Niccolò and Mavi have been waylaid in their life journey by an obstacle that is at once material and insubstantial, practical and ephemeral. As Niccolò advances, the cloud swallows them. "Drive slowly," says Mavi. A close shot of the white lines slowly slipping under the wheels. "I can't see," she says, and he promises to just follow the white line. Directional placards loom up out of the whiteness. Swerving left and right, they hope they are on the right road. A gray sheen of darkness doesn't quite illuminate them in the car as, through the rear window, we see the papery surface of the fog. A cigarette for Mavi. She offers it to him, and another car's lights swing up from behind. They kiss. The vehicle behind has gone, but Niccolò sees a traffic light blinking lazily. He stops and gets out, a dark shadow against the swirling mists. The road is glistening. His footsteps as he walks away are crisp and clear, a metrical voice.

After a few steps he stops and looks around. A dog is barking somewhere. A car, its headlamps blazing into the fog and turning it to pearls. Niccolò watches a man approach a bush, turn, walk away. The sound of another car revving up. The low ticking sound of steps—no, the mechanism of the traffic light, and a whistle as of a train. He backs away as a car approaches going the other way, passes him, turns offscreen. Mavi strains to see through the windshield and confronts nothing in the mist but the headlamps of a parked car blinking on and off into her face. She becomes anxious, opens her door, stands up. Hazy amber light floods her face from the traffic light. "Nic—where are you?"

Out of the depths of the cloud: "I'm here."

His body approaches.

"Don't disappear, please. Someone's spying on us even here." Not a logical deduction, but a sensible fear. She is so caught up with the idea of being exceptionally visible, of being watched, evaluated, judged, that it does not seem to occur to her no observer would see her in this cloud. "—What makes you say that?" he wonders, and she says she feels it. "I'll bet we can shake them off." They get back into the car, he guns it, they pull off into the cloud. We cannot see a thing as the motor races on.

He tries to wipe the window, narrowly missing another vehicle. She is panicking: "You're crazy. Please stop." Darkness outside, the motor racing. "I'm frightened. Stop!" She is screaming hysterically. Trying to open her door. Trying to bite his hand. They fight. He stops, pulls on the emergency brake, gets out, slams his door, strides around to her side, opens the door for her angrily. She is on the road, his headlamps burning into her distrustful face. He closes himself in the car. She runs off into the cloud, and for a long moment we hear the sound of her footsteps on the pavement, the slow diminuendo, then nothing.

He buries his face in his hands.

Fog all around. He gets out and walks after her, calling her name, louder, louder. Dimly at first, then more discernable, the sound of footsteps—by the tread, a man's. Niccolò in the woods at the side of the road, behind a tree. The camera on the road, slowly searching for the walker but discovering only the fog, pans a little as the steps move left across the screen, stop, turn, head off in a different direction. He emerges, looks around. Sits on the metallic road barrier. Hears a horn and sees the shape of a lorry pass by. Takes a few steps back and forth. Walks into the cloud. An approaching car, with another man and woman sitting in their brittle shroud of darkness:

"Did you see a girl?"

"No one can see anything . . . there's a mess down there. Shots were fired, didn't you hear?"

"No"—in a flat voice, the voice of fog.

"I think someone fell in the river . . . gang of hooligans . . . steal cars and assault passengers . . ." Not Mavi, the muscles of his face seem to pray without a voice. Not Mavi!

How could Niccolò not have heard them ringing the bells, or the ambulance? Is he deaf? "No." Now in close-up, more concerned, he's gazing into the fog, then stepping back to his car where Mavi sits in the glow of a match as she lights up.

"Don't you feel well?" he asks gently. Tense, she has been gripping the cigarette, has snapped it out in the ashtray with a sullen face. He turns, lowers his window, looks out, and the camera, directly outside his window, catches his reflective, hopeless expression as he sits with chin on hands and Mavi's suspicious stare behind him. The white cloud still hovers all round. "Still angry with me?"

She makes no answer.

This fog, this cloud, this evanescence, this uniformity, this blindness, this caesura is not meant to be understood as climatological, historical, geographical, or psychological. It is a precise statement of a certain condition which can be thought and imagined, a stalemate in a game one does not cease to play. Niccolò is always and continually in this cloud, unable to frame a world but at the same time hungry and passionate in his move toward framing. Finally by film's end, the cloud has transformed itself. He is in an elegant hotel in Venezia with Ida, and has learned that she is with child, not by him. He walks calmly to some French doors looking out upon a canal, where a flock of white gulls, happily cawing, swoop and circle above the water. The convictions, the pathways of these birds, taken together, would spin a blinding cocoon. "Beautifully enough but not too beautifully" (Winstein), and also with enough pedal that the notes become watery, a pianist offscreen in the lobby plays the Poème in F#, Op. 32, No. 1 by Alexander Scriabin, a composer who thought of tones as colors (and of F#, specifically, as lavender). "You are my love," Ida weeps, "my celebration, my New Year, my cocaine. . . . But you don't bring order to my life."

He stares outward, inhabiting the space of those birds. A launch chugs slowly by on the bright canal.

• • •

Identificazione di una donna (1982), photographed by Carlo di Palma in the 1.85: 1 format at Rome and Venice and printed by Technicolor (Rome) as an Eastmancolor positive; 128 m. Released in the United States as *Identification of a Woman,* September 30, 1982.

The Red Desert

To you is left (unspeakably confused)
your life, gigantic, ripening, full of fears,
so that it, now hemmed in, now grasping all,
is changed in you by turns to stone and stars.

—Rilke, "Evening"

RENT

Upon images of a strange and wonderful "oasis" floating at some incalculable distance in a leaden red haze, the opening credits of *The Red Desert* are superimposed: an oasis that is a city but also a geological residuum, with a horizon backed by a cloudless sky, a sky cut with forms, fumes, connectors, spaces, positions, industrial artifacts, pure-hewn geometrical shapes, pillars, trees, sheds. In this quasi-terrestrial geography, the roaming camera discovers no living creatures. We hear, first, electronic, vaguely mechanical or vaguely extraterrestrial statics and tattoos by Vittorio Gelmetti and then a haunting sub-Saharan ululation written by Giovanni Fusco and sung by Cecilia Fusco, evidence that everything in sight emerged at some long forgotten moment from stone and sands. Emerged and remains. The past is with us, pretechnological, precapitalist, awkward, and beautiful in a posttechnological, postcapitalist, gracile, and problematic universe. R. Bruce Elder suggests interestingly that the protagonist of this film shows a "human impulse towards unity" (5). To me it seems that she lives upon a recognition more than an impulse: that the world is one, that—at least for her—unity is already and eternally present. At the same time, the world of others is divided. "We have been rent," writes Norman O. Brown, "there is no health in us. We must acknowledge the rents, the tears, the splits, the divisions; and then we can pray" (*Love's Body* 80). Also he remembers "His Fall into Division & his Resurrection to Unity" (84), but for Giuliana (Monica Vitti), unity is a torment, not a resurrection.

This early theme—Arcady invaded by technology, or, the technological arcadia—will resound throughout the film. We are caught in a hybridized time that is at once ancient, poetic, coherent, and incomprehensible; and technical, modern, brutalized, and wrecked. In the opening shot, a hot yellow flame spurts with an urgent rhythm from the top of a smokestack, not only evidence of the investment of capital and the excresence of industrialization but also, in its rhythmic persistence and its proportions, the ejaculation of some mammoth, angered prefeudal dragon. Then a group of figures is to be seen standing beside what seems a long, straight, silver canal, until the camera shuffles a little and we detect instead a glistening road: not water, but asphalt being rained upon. Some of the people have cheap transparent plastic sheaths over their heads. They are engaged in a strike action (a division of labor), outside a factory or a prison, we cannot tell. Someone, a lowly criminal, is apparently being marched to his cell, or to his terminus, between two soldiers, abrupt, erect; but these are only police agents escorting a worker who does not sympathize with his colleagues (another division of labor) through the factory gates. A little car pulls up with loudspeakers on its roof, and a man hops out to announce, in a rather sharp but also quite amicable voice, "Romeo Salviati. What are you doing in there? You're not a manager. You work to support your family! Come out! Join us out here! Your wife's too ashamed of you to leave the house!" (A woman locked to a man's fate.) We see this Romeo walking up a pathway toward some factory structures that emit white steam against the pewter sky, and at his side is a brilliant emerald green lawn. Outside again, Giuliana, in an overcoat about the same color as this lawn, is escorting her son Valerio (Valerio Bartoleschi) among the men; that loden coat beautifully sets off her rust-colored hair while the boy tramps along in a beige duffel coat and high rubber boots, a perfect scamp. Giuliana's hair has a rusty, metallic quality, like parts of the factory buildings, yet it is also wild and supple, and Valerio's boots of black rubber also echo the industrial context, but their coats, green and brown, bespeak nature, the moist primeval forest. (Many scholars, including Gerald L. O'Grady in a lecture I heard recently, cling to a theory of color coding for this film, in which yellow indicates toxicity, red danger, green or brown the natural world, and blue recuperation.) Ravenous, Giuliana buys a partially eaten sandwich from a worker while Valerio watches sheepishly; she then goes off behind a mound of detritus to devour it—in secrecy, like a beast, or like a person whose animal instincts are healthy and intense. All around: the dirty brown earth, dark twigs, and dark leafless shrubbery (it is winter), and that puffing dragon flame, dark brown broken pipes and packages all muddied over on the ground, unidentifiable silver fabric like a long-abandoned parachute, tin cans set upon dark piles of steaming powdery matter, the monstrous factory, angry men, the gray sky. Giuliana, a little embarrassed at her hunger, seems perfectly at home in this wasteland. She takes Valerio by the hand and they walk off.

As she devours that sandwich, it is hard not to detect in Giuliana a certain reticence—even frenzy—of regard, as though she is in some sort of danger. Yet at the same time, wearing heels and a dress coat, she carries herself with surety and apparent comfort in this post-urban nowhere, this "*terrain vague* site of industrial passage" (Conley 258ff). It is not precisely the physical environment that threatens her, not the earth, its vapors, its rot, its liquids, its darkness. Is she afraid of people? . . . men? . . . herself? Not men: she would rather buy a worker's sandwich, partially eaten, than take a few steps to get herself a fresh one (in supplication to the brittle rigor of the marketplace), as though contact with his person and personality through food gives her a kind of safety. Nor, by her casual regard as she walks into the scene, is it people in groups who frighten her. Something more abstract (and therefore more painful): the social. Not sociability itself, which is to say, the gathering of souls in nature, but a particular social form that has emerged and taken over the world, a type of organization through which, enslaved in its meshes, people live out their purposes. While Giuliana's intelligence realizes and grasps modern conventions—industrialized employment, tangential relationships, momentary commitments, bourgeois prudery—her emotional life lags far behind in a long forgotten state where objects, places, movements, forms, whispers, breezes, colors, growths, scents, coatings, surfaces, lyrics are blended and powerful and true.

Giuliana is around thirty. The grace in her posture and movement utterly belies her relative youth and inexperience, the saturation of her desire. It is as though she has always been here, in this toxic precinct of Ravenna, always and for all time. Elder labels her "depressive" (9) and other writers, equally serious, who have discussed this film, agree that she suffers from "neurosis" of one type or another. This certainly appears true, yet Giuliana's problem lies outside her personality, is, as it were, circumstantial. Her trouble lies in her lack of fit with the world in which she must live—and thus in her resemblance to anyone, man or woman, who fully senses his or her humanity, animality, and linkage to what is around. In this film, she is the most explicitly drawn version of this type. Others lean toward the sensibilities Giuliana exhibits, yet do not commit themselves as fully, as comprehensively, as she does: a wife who admits that she trembled with fear when her husband went off on business trips (Lili Rheims); a friend (Xenia Valderi) who hides her observations and sensations so as to accommodate the patrician needs of an aggressive mate (Aldo Grotti); Corrado Zeller (Richard Harris), a visiting entrepreneur on the hunt for men to work his property in Patagonia—in certain moments he is almost sensitive to Giuliana's predicament, but always he draws back prudently into a closed-mouthed professional distance.

Because the question of Giuliana's fate is central to the film—for her, Rilke's words seem to ring true: "there is no place/that does not see you" ("Archaic Torso of Apollo")—we must also ask, is Antonioni criticizing modern life? The steam towers we see at the factory are symptoms of modernity, but at the same time they are part of the ineffable beauty of the scene. (How often, in our contact with factories and industrial processes, do we fly past without gazing!) Reality, said Antonioni, "is steadily becoming more colored": "Think of what factories were like, especially in Italy at the beginning of the nineteenth century, when industrialization was just beginning: gray, brown, and smoky. Color didn't exist. Today, instead, almost everything is colored. The pipe running from the basement to the twelfth floor is green because it carries steam. The one carrying electricity is red, and that with water is purple. Also, plastic colors have filled our homes, even revolutionized our taste" (Billard 65).

Antonioni does not regard modernity with nostalgia for the primitive past, or with remoteness from the world of today. His camera glides past the towers, the myriad input and output pipes of the factory, with an insatiable hunger to arrange the planes and perspectives in a colorful harmony, even if, as O'Grady has argued, shot after shot presents a kind of "breaking" of the frame with railings, chains, ropes, window frames, and so on. If the frame, or world depicted in the frame, is not "broken," it is surely divided. A world of parts and pieces that did fit together once. For Giuliana, perhaps, the pieces fit together still, have never been separated, and in this lies her denial of—her misfit with—this separated world. That she has ingested (but cannot digest) this world, that she lives it out of herself while simultaneously holding it together (against its principles), is her agony. And if her steps, her expressions, her experiences are her life—she says at one point, "Everything that happens to me is my life"—the world in which she struggles constitutes not only her universe but her case (see Davenport *Objects* 32). Davenport describes a "stagnant selfishness into which a habitual introversion must deteriorate" (46) and quotes a diagnosis of Robert Burton: "the Scene alters upon a sudden, Fear and Sorrow supplant those pleasing thoughts, suspicion, discontent and perpetual anxiety succeed in their places; so little by little, that shoeing-horn of idleness, and voluntary solitariness, Melancholy, this feral fiend, is drawn on" (47).

Giuliana holds our interest exactly because she must find a way to live, and live fully, under conditions that do not support her. It is an error, I suppose, to leap to the conclusion that her conditions are tragic, as much as it is to surmise that her life is merely mundane. She faces a supreme challenge, and stands for us all in doing so: the world has changed around her, abandoned her, but she may go on without acquiescence and without obliviousness, in a continual erosive struggle.

MONSTROUS SCENERY

The high chimneys had the sky to themselves.
—Charles Dickens, *Hard Times*

Around 1850, the black moths that came to dominate the industrial areas of England gained scientific notice for the first time, as the lighter gray-speckled moths, increasingly visible to predators against the background of soot-darkened trees, began consequently to vanish. Here it can be seen how industrialism was so intensive and far-reaching as to transcend the human sphere altogether and insinuate itself into nature. "I do not believe there is anything inherently and unavoidably ugly about industrialism," George Orwell wrote in *The Road to Wigan Pier* (1937), framing his critical gaze with delicious precision on the blunt social and political fact that "a factory or even a gasworks is not obliged of its own nature to be ugly, any more than a palace or a dog-kennel or a cathedral. It all depends on the architectural tradition of the period. The industrial towns of the North are ugly because they happen to have been built at a time when modern methods of steel-construction and smoke-abatement were unknown, and when everyone was too busy making money to think about anything else" (100).

Further, looked at "from a purely aesthetic standpoint," says he, the factory—for Antonioni, directly or in principle the setting of *The Red Desert*—"may have a certain macabre appeal" (99–100). In the industrial era, the factory was first an assembly point for workers who would ply their skills with commonly shared materials in a common space, but soon came to be occupied more principally by machinery. Henry Mayhew wrote of the Great Exposition of 1850 that machinery was "from first to last the grand focus of attraction" and also "the most peculiar sight of the whole": "Here every other man you rub against is habited in a corduroy jacket, or a blouse, or leathern gaiters; and round every object more wonderful than the rest, the people press, two or three deep, with their heads stretched out, watching intently the operations of the moving mechanism" (qtd. in Pike 32). The factory was a *mysterium,* a secret trove of wonders, inhabited by the elected few who could understand, who could cohabit with, machines.

It is difficult not to be awed a little by Orwell's meticulous descriptions of the industrial wasteland he was visiting at the behest of Victor Gollancz, awed, perhaps, as one is by Picasso's "Guernica" or by a stunning De Chirico with its towering smokestacks against a polluted teal green sky. Like the territory in and around Ravenna that we see in *The Red Desert,* England's northern pottery and mining towns presented "monstrous scenery": a rolling array of "slag-heaps, chimneys, piled scrap-iron, foul canals, paths of cindery mud criss-crossed by the prints of clogs" (Orwell 15); "'dirt-heaps', like hideous grey mountains" (27–28); with houses that are "poky and ugly, and insanitary and comfortless, . . . distributed in incredibly filthy slums round belching foundries and stinking canals and slag-heaps that deluge them with sulphurous smoke" (47); altogether "an ugliness so frightful and so arresting that you are obliged, as it were, to come to terms with it" (97). Monstrosity of any kind is forever and altogether stunning to the eye, a way of querying our convictions about proportion, form, godliness, and truth. In the industrial tracts, men have brought their amassed knowledge, capability, machinery, and strength toward (a kind of Nietzschean) superhuman creation with its all-enveloping furnaces and towers, its half-mechanical slaves, its fires of doom, its ruination of nature.

Orwell describes slag-heaps of the sort Giuliana is wandering through early in this film:

> A slag-heap is at best a hideous thing, because it is so planless and functionless. It is something just dumped on the earth, like the emptying of a giant's

> dust-bin. On the outskirts of the mining towns there are frightful landscapes where your horizon is ringed completely round by jagged grey mountains, and underfoot is mud and ashes and overhead the steel cables where tubs of dirt travel slowly across miles of country. Often the slag-heaps are on fire, and at night you can see the red rivulets of fire winding this way and that, and also the slow-moving blue flames of sulphur, which always seem on the point of expiring and always spring out again. Even when a slag-heap sinks, as it does ultimately, only an evil brown grass grows on it, and it retains its hummocky surface. (97)

Water figured largely in factory development (and so it is little wonder that *The Red Desert* should depict a factory that sits near a canal, or that in the opening sequence we should immediately be convinced we are looking at a silver stream). Wigan, the principal site of Orwell's observations of the living conditions of the working poor, was an important node on the Leeds and Liverpool Canal, a late eighteenth-century construction (completed, after some forty years' work, in 1816) that serviced heavy industry along its banks. The canal made it possible to supply the factory with machinery and materials, and to remove finished product. But water had other purposes and not all factories concerned themselves with massive machinery. While the Industrial Revolution initially favored the development and agglomeration of manufactories, where expertise and energy could be amassed, organized, and disciplined as workforce—and where resistance could be mounted to the restrictive craft guilds, as mercantilism was made a dominant economic system—these new working environments were not automatically associated with heavy machinery and cumbersome materials. Between 1760 and 1792, for example, Christophe-Philippe Oberkampf's toile works at Jouy-en-Josas (outside Paris) expanded significantly along the banks of the Bièvre. Rather than machinery, this factory contained principally dye vats and woodblocking facilities for cloth, design and etching rooms, and fields in which the printed toile could be sun baked; the river's principal utility inhered in the freshness of its water, which could be used again and again for the multiple washes the fabric required (Riffel 18). Nevertheless such developments as the canal made feasible the input of large masses of material and the transportation of heavy product, and led the way to an increased demand that would be satisfied, after the middle of the nineteenth century, by the development of railroads and the incursion of railroad tracks into the precincts of the factory.

W. G. Sebald reflects on the early importance of the canal for factory industrialization in Manchester, "the city from which industrialization had spread across the entire world" (*Emigrants* 156). The canal here, "begun in 1887 and completed in 1894" (165), came relatively late as an industrial development, given that the railroads were by that time fairly well expanded across England: "The work was mainly done by a continuously reinforced army of Irish navvies, who shifted some sixty million cubic metres of earth in that period and built the gigantic locks that would make it possible to raise or lower ocean-going steamers up to 150 metres long by five or six metres. Manchester was then the industrial Jerusalem" (165). Thanks to this canal, ships from around the world gathered in its port, and "the loading and unloading never stopped: wheat, nitre, construction timber, cotton, rubber, jute, train oil, tobacco, tea, coffee, cane sugar, exotic fruits, copper and iron ore, steel, machinery, marble and mahogany—everything" (165). We can imagine, but not actually see, the raw materials and products moving to and from the factory zone in *The Red Desert,* in huge steamers that glide silently among the trees, or that approach a long pier where in a private hut Giuliana, her husband, and their friends take time for an erotic little picnic (calling up Manet's "Déjeuner sur l'herbe"). Sebald could be imagining Antonioni, in fact, when he recalls an observation made by his painter friend Ferber:

> Given the motionlessness and deathly silence that lay upon the canal now, it was difficult to imagine, said Ferber, as we gazed back at the city sinking into the twilight, that he himself, in the postwar years, had seen the most enormous freighters on this water. They would slip slowly by, and as they approached the port they passed amidst houses, looming high above the black slate roofs. And in the winter, said Ferber, if a ship suddenly appeared out of the mist when one least expected it, passed by soundlessly, and vanished once more in the white air, then for me, every time, it was an utterly incomprehensible spectacle which moved me deeply. (166)

If the water we see around Giuliana in this film lies in stagnant, chemically infused pools, if fishing is impossible and swimming undesirable, yet still there is something magical about the pollution as Antonioni sees it. His camera (influenced by Walker Evans's *American Photographs*) never seems to linger long enough.

A certain romantic spirit, adduced by Ortega in a discussion of primitivism and history, underlies much thought about industrialization. "The romantics of every period," he writes, "have found a . . . subtly indecent spectacle in the landscape with ruins, where the civilized, geometric stone is stifled beneath the embrace of wild vegetation. When your good romantic catches sight of a building, the first thing his eyes seek is the yellow hedge-mustard on cornice and roof. This proclaims, that in the long run, everything is earth, that the jungle springs up everywhere anew" (*Revolt* 88–89).

With this romantic spirit in its breast, the dominant critical approach to *The Red Desert* has posited a foundation upon rape or debauchery. The force of industrialism represented by the factory, that fount of brutality, which amasses only the darkest and most profane of human resources toward the exploitative ends of capital, has overtaken the hitherto untrammeled, "civilized" soul of Giuliana, sullied and "stifled" her, so that she is left, at the moment the film begins, as little more than a filthy spoil. As Orwell's miners were so coated with grime they could never get it off parts of their bodies, Giuliana is coated and besmirched, but on the inside. The ugly residue of modernity has marred her essential immaculateness. Through its apotheosis the factory, industrialization has poisoned and degraded her, and for that we disparage industrialism, as though before and without it people like Giuliana lived in a fecund, perfect, blissful world.

Chatman, for example, sees Giuliana reflecting "a Pandora's box of seething emotions." Displaced, wounded, she "clings to walls, expresses terror," and engages in "testing reality" (121). And the film as a whole announces "the aridity of the emotional life," with its "disturbed" antiheroine married to a "cool" man (Chatman and Duncan 88). For O'Grady she is "unstable." Sam Rohdie detects Giuliana's "twisting, turning, seeking hands . . . her fingers spread in pain and in ecstasy, searching for something solid, on the bed, in the body of Corrado" (133); she is without support, in other words. Presumably, her placement against the fogs and steaming pits of industrialism suggests its role in sapping her of orientation and solidity. René Prédal sees her threatened by, wanting protection from, her dismal environment, so omnipresent (that is, so intensively institutionalized) is the inhospitable world: "Notwithstanding that color is fundamental to our humanity: 'Did you know there are animals who live in black and white?' says Corrado to Giuliana. Doubtless this is why she is afraid of all that gray: the façades of a street painted over in dark gray, the dull gray of clothing, the steely gray of a vendor's fruits and vegetables, a black isolate house, a meadow burned with a flame-thrower, oil poured on water . . ."(149).

Peter Brunette is concerned with Giuliana's "neurotic, even suicidal mind," wondering "if the out-of-focusness and the (often clashing) colors are to be read as a projection" (95). In a fabular sequence set on a desert isle, shot in intensively saturated "natural colors" and illustrating a little tale Giuliana recounts to her ostensibly paralyzed child, there is, suspects he, a telling of "human experience" and a demonstration of reality "as Giuliana wishes it were—that is, different from the world that appears to her as transformed, alienated, obsessive to the point of being *monstrously deformed*" (95; emphasis mine). Transformed, that world has been touched by the force epitomized in factories: industrial development. Development for the romantic is disease. In *The New York Times,* Jeanne Molli reported that, "Due to the love scene with Monica Vitti, members of the crew are already convinced that one result is certain. Every Italian spectator worth his salt as a male—and there are no Italian males who think they are not—will leave the theater in hot pursuit of the nearest neurotic woman he can find." Even William Arrowsmith, taking pains to stress the inappropriateness of a "kind of lazy, McLuhanite" glossing of Antonioni's films, and urging viewers to appreciate that Antonioni, with the "complexity of his composition, the coherence of his structure implicit in every scene, the functional beauty of his detail, and his unmistakable effort to think and feel in genuinely cinematic terms, has taken the great risk of demanding from his audience the kind of intellectual respect or attention it would willingly give to a poem, a play, or a painting," proceeds to find in *The Red Desert,* if not a story of neurosis, at least "an account of individuation, a story of the emergence of the psyche in a time when individuation has become exceptionally difficult" (85–86). "A time" suggests much less a mythical moment than a historical era, in which the factory and its dictates shape and constrain social life.

And that natural world we are to imagine Giuliana as having once inhabited, perhaps as ruler, before industry brought her down, was apparently nothing less than an Arcadia: its "river against the sun was a sheet of dull silver on which a jet black duck moved noiselessly, a swan silhouetted as if cut in black paper, swam with his neck beneath the water, a wind came fretting the river blowing a handful of pale blossoms into the grass," as the besotted travel writer H.V. Morton rhapsodized in his rather purple *In Search of England* (1927) (qtd. in Schama 472). The romantic reading has Antonioni's desert isle sequence configuring that utopia, with its sweeping vistas of fleshy pink sands; its rocks shaped like (tranquil, pensive) faces; its limpid greeny waters which, bathed in sunshine all day long, warmly lure; its beautifully tanned and healthy little girl; the intrusive ship that makes to invade her world but then suddenly disappears. Through fluid, even hypnotic traveling shots (mostly long pans) we follow the action here—not through the static, if profoundly elegant, compositions set in Ravenna and its surround—and that movement is accompanied by a gentle, treble ululation that, like the desert itself, is deliciously incomprehensible, continuing, unprovoked. This is the same sound that is manifested over the concluding part of the opening credits, suggesting not only something outside of this industrial world to which we are about to be introduced but something prior and definitive: something allied tightly with Giuliana, what she remembers, what she dreams, who she is. And one can find in this sound a precise indication of the antitechnology that seems to be Giuliana's emblem. When in voiceover her little boy asks where the sound is coming from, who is singing, she answers, "*Tutti,*" meaning, in one sense, "Everybody is singing," but also indicating, in musical parlance, "the entire ensemble." In a tutti passage, every member of the orchestra (and chorus) participates in making music at once. If Giuliana believes "everyone" is singing, this "everyone" is figuratively the rocks, the beach, the rabbit, the waters, the boat, the sky; yet what we hear is a female soprano *solo,* as though perhaps to indicate that Giuliana sees herself as "everyone," and sees "everyone" as herself. On an oil rig, chatting with Corrado about his travels to South America, she mentions that if she were going away she would take "everything," and yet we must wonder, does she mean by this, only herself?

The romanticism of readings that contrast the primary and utopian beauty of the desert isle with the too-present and hideous wreck of the industrial landscape denies what is onscreen in this film: first, the astonishing matter-of-factness that characterizes the presentation of the scene (the harmonies of color, the gentleness of the luminosity), a matter-of-factness that does not accept the sundering world of the factory as utopian but nonetheless pronounces it real, present, total, the world in which we find ourselves; then, the evident troubles that face Giuliana in her attempts to relate to other people, coupled with her notable comfort in her surround (suggesting that it is the social relation that is bothering her, not geography or topology); then, the fact that it is not only Giuliana who seems removed from social intercourse, from communal feeling, but everyone she knows, even the child; and finally, the intensive focus on labor relations pointed to by Matthew Gandy:

> The environs of modern Ravenna provide a vivid portrayal of a new and unfamiliar landscape emerging under the post-war *miracolo* of Italian economic prosperity. . . . The abstract dynamics of industrial change are emphasized by the detached and technical terms used to explain the future of the factory. We observe the pensive faces of workers gathered to hear details of

> their relocation, but their experience does not become the focal point for the film. Antonioni's exploration of social change develops not from the vantage point of the industrial workers, but through an intense exploration of the alienation felt by the upwardly mobile workers of the new Italy. (221)

The Red Desert seems to emerge, as though in science fiction, from a new world at once discernable and unfamiliar. Its happenings and locales point to a race of aliens who only appear to be human, only appear to be living life as we know it, all the while also seeming to be doubles of creatures we might recognize, if we could awake.

RED

> Neo-Gothicism and functionalism, Symbolism and industrialism, have the same enemy. They all denounce the relationship that obtains between the soulless production of the world of commodities and the ersatz soul imparted to objects by their pseudo-artistic prettification.
>
> —Jacques Rancière, "The Surface of Design"

We enter the factory. A few workers are at their posts in a control room of sorts. Ugo (Carlo Chionetti) and Corrado are discussing the difficulty of acquiring some workers for a project in South America; Ugo gets on the phone unsuccessfully trying to get various of his contacts—in a refinery, in another factory, in a government department—to help. This control room is futuristic, with dark slate gray walls and tasteful—that is, modest—recessed ceiling lighting. Along the back wall, dozens of meters and clocks are arranged, with switches and levers: this array is being manned by two men in identical dark blue jumpsuits (shades of an early James Bond movie!). A third man, casually dressed in a green windbreaker, sits in the foreground, talking on the phone at his desk. In Fred McLeod Wilcox's *Forbidden Planet* (1956), an aged scientist on the distant planet Altair IV demonstrates to the captain and officers of a visiting spacecraft a secret control facility (designed by Irving Clock and Mentor Huebner) built, as the story has it, eons earlier by the extinct and super-brilliant race of the Krell. It has the same look as this: gray walls, dozens upon dozens of levers and illuminated meters that glow in succession when the power level becomes high enough. Power as transparent, omnipresent, controllable, obedient. The Krell world powered by this control station is later revealed in all its technological glory: a limitless expanse of space punctuated by lean bridges, spasmodically arcing electricity, the cold blueness of distance and magnificence. Similar in volume and tone is the New York of the future envisioned by Rummel in 1911 (see Caramel and Longatti 29), with its skyscrapers and street channels receding to an infinite distance, its colossal bridgeworks for multi-level electric trains, and its aircraft frozen in place as they head in every direction within the vault of a grisly, hopeless sky. One imagines that the control room in Ugo's factory is marshalling, metering, and manipulating the sorts of forces that build such a world, somewhere else, beyond these limiting walls. Or that, as a result of the constraints and channelings of force and energy these controls direct with the help of human hands, such a state will exist tomorrow (a Metropolis!), a topos wherein mankind can aspire to experience the delirium of release and meditative fulfillment that such bold designs always tend to promise. "The decorative must be abolished," wrote the futurist architect Antonio Sant'Elia in his manifesto: "Just as the ancients drew inspiration for their art from the elements of nature, we—materially and spiritually artificial—must find that inspiration in the elements of the absolutely new mechanical world that we have created" (qtd. in Caramel and Longatti 303). This was a reflection of Boccioni's call for "dynamic sensation" in an art that would sweep aside "all subject previously used" in order "to express our whirling life of steel, of pride, of fever and of speed" (149, 152).

At once, Ugo is in the foreground, looking off and holding that phone to his ear. He wears a fawn-colored leather jacket and a tie with his black, checked, v-neck shirt. This place is no repository of filth. His colleague at the other end of the line is in an oil refinery, comfortably ensconced at his gray futuristic desk, wearing a gray suit with matching tie; beside him, through a huge picture window framed in silver within a creamy wall, pose a pair of gray spherical tanks against a white sky, testicles of industry perhaps, but more likely twin moons of some far-off constellation hinting at possibilities undreamed-of on earth. Again: streamlined, even minimalist efficiency, politesse, silence, puissance. Ugo calls another comrade, who is managing in a dark cavernous factory with massive steel beams and huge pieces of machinery, and this gentleman, in a silver safety hat, dark shirt, and gray sports coat, seems relaxed and self-assured, even good-humored, as though he has been interrupted reading the newspaper at his club on a Sunday afternoon. The space in which our story takes place, then, is energized by and produced through an interlocking chain of sedate and fundamentally hygienic factory locales, managed rationally by intelligent men of expertise and grace. A government cipher speaks on his phone adjacent yet another picture window, this one showing a rosy factory with conveyors and chimneys nestled comfortably behind a row of ancient trees. (Modernity is a fait accompli. The modern process has received its accommodations. Modern men are comfortable with their world, and even Giuliana has learned how to circle through it.) We are back with Ugo and Corrado, the former apologetic about failing to find workers, the latter pensive in the trenchcoat he almost never takes off (like Lemme Caution in Godard's *Alphaville*). They move into a large chamber with white tanks and silver connecting pipes, in which a black and mustard yellow mosaic has been set into one of the walls: a star or two, large amoebic colored forms, modern art. In this factory, *die Kunst* and *das Techne,* the two great divisions of art, are united to the throbbing sound of ongoing eventfulness (production) and ease (consumption).

Giuliana has entered and Ugo introduces her to Corrado. She strides through this place with perfect composure, yet also with a touch of sadness: past poppy-red pipes, silvered vats, an olive green tank or enclosure, a massive ceiling-mounted orange conduit, a pale lavender air intake that blows her coppery red hair and makes her twist in her loden overcoat. "By assembling words or forms," writes Rancière (and Antonioni is here assembling forms as words), "people define not merely various forms of art, but certain configurations of what can be seen and what can be thought, certain forms of inhabiting the material world" (91). Antonioni is producing what Rancière would call a "transformation of the graphic signifier into visual volume" (99). The brutality of work neither alarms Giuliana nor distances her, and the factory is merely a scene. Ugo will lead Corrado outside for a little tour, and also for the purpose of telling him about Giuliana (she had an accident with a car, she was in a hospital, she's not—Ugo gestures with rigid fingers—quite in the right gear. Certainly we will join them, but first:

Why in this factory is there so much color? It is something of a playground. "The chief aim of color should be to serve expression as well as possible," claimed Matisse (qtd. in Ball 303).

Perhaps the most obvious *riposte* to such a question is another, why indeed should color be absent? Who could imagine that the worker felt alienated from the natural world, or from art; and that the worker did not envision for himself an ideal environment filled with the same beautiful forms as delight his masters every day? Must there not of course be vivid murals on the walls within which tanks and pistons do their work? Hans Ulrich Gumbrecht recalls a July 1926 speech from the German

Foreign Secretary, Gustav Stresemann, to the effect that "taking an arrogant, superior attitude toward the working class is a dangerous legacy from prewar times" (220). And a little later, Orwell derides the "traditional upper-class attitude towards 'common' people," which is "an attitude of sniggering superiority punctuated by bursts of vicious hatred" (*Pier* 116). It stands to reason that beauty should be anywhere and everywhere. If beauty has a part to play in the work space, indeed a principal part, how can it be divorced from color? "'Red' and 'beautiful,'" Walter Benjamin reminds us, are *one* word in [old] Russian" ("Moscow" 33); and also, "Even inside a factory, everyone is as if surrounded by colored posters all exorcising the terrors of the machine" (40).

Antonioni has his own reasons. "Colors have always thrilled me. I always see in color. I mean that I realize they are there, always." In his view, "color has, in modern life, a significance and a function that it had not in the past"; the "outside world" is a colored one, and colored in a purely contemporary way (pressbook for *Red Desert*). The mystery of color is not as simple as why or how it has been applied—why, for instance, the suspended venting system here in this Ravenna factory is tangerine orange. The issue is not a set of symbolic codes, a language, but a mystery, since every color is essentially impenetrable. "There was not a word in the language of the inner man which could describe the distinctive quality which attracted the attention of other people" (Sartre, "Baudelaire" 24). The mystery of color, the mystery of sight, lies in its fondness for surfaces and thus in its happy inability to leech into a world that is unmistakably, but ineluctably, interior.

To look at the colors of the factory is to be struck with allures and retreats, matches and clashes, ambiguous forms in complex relation, delicate balances, propitious densities, stunning heats: Kandinsky. Watching the fluid stream of color and tension that is produced as Giuliana walks down a metallic stairway in her rich green coat, it becomes simplistic to speak merely of the film's "metaphoric colors" *(Village Voice)* or to suggest that Antonioni succeeds at "linking alienation and the breakdown of identity to the industrial rape of the environment" (UCLA Archive), or to consider hyperbolically, with the *New York Times,* that these images create "a haunting conception of the vaporous nature of the lives of the lonely, isolated people who grope so barrenly and pitifully for—call it love" (Crowther, "Red Desert").

Still other modes of dismissal are possible in the face of all this color. Ann Guerin was ravished, and accounted for her sentimentality by elevating both the status of the film and her own appreciative ego:

"Its producers could quite possibly earn back their entire investment by taking a scissors, cutting up a print and selling it frame by frame—any frame—to museums and collectors of modern painting. It is one of the most breathtakingly lovely color films ever made." Pauline Kael, by contrast, thought the whole project a "red herring" and complained, "I found the movie deadly: a hazy poetic illustration of emotional chaos" (*Off-Beat* 45).

To look carefully at the screen is to bypass these summative glyphs. One is suddenly, and profoundly, aware that because there is color in the world and objects reflect color, light exists. Ugo's fawn brown jacket, Corrado's vanilla trenchcoat and rusty hair: by that hair alone we can see in an instant that he has more in common with Giuliana than dark Ugo does. The play of colors is an avenue whereby we may use our eyes to see light itself (not just the perceptible array of objects it offers).

Gandy interestingly suggests about Antonioni's chromatics that "colour in *Red Desert* is used to . . . heighten our identification with the visual acuity of the main protagonist Giuliana," who "is convalescing after a car accident which has left her psychologically damaged. One of the consequences of her accident is that she has become much more aware of the aesthetic characteristics of her surroundings" (225). Surely she has been wounded, at least physically, and she is healing. There is a fine and taut style Vitti has of holding her arms stiff at the shoulder, as though locking herself in, afraid of the possibility of being hurt. "With her modern and nervous acting she has rendered this character with extraordinary sincerity," Antonioni wrote (pressbook for *Red Desert*). Let it be said that she is in recuperative mode. For Gandy, this leads to the conclusion that "Antonioni has deployed an established romantic trope of illness and suffering as a means towards heightened states of creative insight" (225), a trope, we might add, straight out of Poe. In "The Man of the Crowd," the observer has been gravely ill but now has his health again, and for him the play of movement and form in the streets is especially distinct, even hyperreal. "I . . . found myself," says he, "in one of those happy moods which are so precisely the converse of *ennui*—moods of the keenest appetency, when the film from the mental vision departs . . . and the intellect, electrified, surpasses as greatly its every-day condition, as does the vivid yet candid reason of Leibniz, the mad and flimsy rhetoric of Gorgias. Merely to breathe was enjoyment; and I derived positive pleasure even from many of the legitimate sources of pain. I felt a calm but inquisitive interest in every thing" (84).

This prototype resembles the photographer hero of Hitchcock's *Rear Window* in his intensive, recuperative perception (see Pomerance, "Recuperation"). "At first," explains Poe's narrator, but he could be describing Jeff Jefferies's experience or Giuliana's, "my observations took an abstract and generalizing turn. . . . Soon, however, I descended to details, and regarded with minute interest the innumerable varieties of figure, dress, air, gait, visage, and expression of countenance" (85). What is it all for, where to grasp it, how are the movements linked, what summation do the arrangements indicate? These are the sorts of mysteries with which the eye is confronted.

"How should I use my eyes?" Giuliana begs to know, echoing the problem of the viewer who is confronted with a devastated but also delirious world, a group of disaffected but also hungry characters, a woman trying to survive, at each instant, with each step, in every twisted gaze and agonized extension of the hand. Disconnected from modernity—as each individual person is—she has not given up hope of finding a way to live with it. Yet she has not yet found a way.

This is Antonioni's first color film. He had had extraordinary success using black and white (with *L'eclisse, L'avventura, La notte*), and could have continued to do so. The factory must be colored so that we will see it. Not see *in* it, not focus on some narrative crux, some singular telltale instant out of a flow, but see the factory itself, for what it is in every dimension. See the territory containing the factory. See not objects, not persons, not nodes, but the entire field of the screen. Like Giuliana, we will see all of what is given, all of every form, all of the surface beneath which we cannot presume to extend our touch, and be struck dumb by the question that has been plaguing her: "How should we use our eyes?"

GUILT

This is the lower sling swivel. And this
Is the upper sling swivel, whose use you will see,
When you are given your slings. And this is the piling swivel,
Which in your case you have not got. The branches
Hold in the gardens their silent, eloquent gestures,
    Which in our case we have not got.

—Henry Reed, "Lessons of the War"

Fragments, fractures. Edward Dimendberg notes how in modernity "police identification technologies divide the body of the criminal subject into progressively smaller distinctive features (facial characteristics, fingerprints, and today DNA sequences) through which it becomes parcelized, surveyed, and 'screened' in ever more diminutive and precise fragments for investigation" (27). It is modernity that Antonioni is filming, with its divisions and displacements, expert dissociations, perceptual fogs. Yet characters in *The Red Desert* seem to bear traces of an earlier memory, something wholer and more generically integrated, call it the classical world—or to have forgotten. Whatever completeness Giuliana possessed before her accident—or before marrying Ugo, perhaps they are the same—she can now only dimly recall, and yet she knows she has lost *something* because her every step, every regard, is tentative, as though social gravity has failed and negativity is pulling her through. The factory operates through fragmentation of labor, which requires the fracture of objects into manageable pieces (pieces that can be handled under the requisites of management). The colors assist us in seeing how the space of manufacture is not homogeneous. Corrado escorts Giuliana to the apartment of an aerial worker whose services he would very much like to contract. The worker is not home, but his wife offers hospitality. Giuliana used to live in this apartment, it turns out, but her consciousness has been severed from what it was then, so that, standing in her own space, as it were, she is nowhere. The worker, an expert of sorts, is out of town servicing radio telescopes. Giuliana and Corrado go to meet him (the man refuses the contract) and we are treated to a panoramic display of gargantuan scarlet discs set to receive radio signals from the stars. All of this nicely dramatizes what every earthling knows, yet rarely heeds, the fact that we spin through space in a kind of isolation, cut off from everything else by a dark vacuum. Giuliana is intensely conscious that the vacuum penetrates between human beings as well. Agonized, she strives to reach through its obstructive essence until she can establish some extension of herself through others.

She is not resigned that such an extension is impossible. We could say she is in love with everyone. If this is not naturally a debility, it has become one under social arrangements that depend upon separation, discreetness, identity, and choreography. Giuliana does not move gracefully, but as though the world moves with her. Of course it does not, so she seems clumsy, out of touch with herself.

"Capitalism," writes Benjamin, "is perhaps the first instance of a cult that creates guilt" ("Religion" 288).

FIT

We live, in fact, through a succession of crises and resolutions.
—Wayne Barker, *Brain Storms*

As they stroll outside the factory, Ugo is telling Corrado that even though Giuliana is home from the hospital, something still isn't well about her, he doesn't know what. (This is the way she feels about the world.) She wants to open a shop in the Via Alighieri (a street named after the poet who voyaged to the Inferno). Ugo has been smoking casually, and now he tosses away the cigarette and exhales a little cloud, at the same time as a vent is opened in the factory wall and a monstrous bubble of white steam pours out, hissing, expanding, filling the frame. In a second shot we stand behind the two men as they gaze at this dragon's breath fulminating and evaporating. Then in a longer shot, as they march away, the cloud seems to dominate the surround. A reverse angle shows the steam enveloping a cluster of red drums. For several more shots, from various angles, the emission continues, with the steam expanding and disappearing into the air as it envelops the space, sweeps across the flat cold ground. The sound fades, the steam subsides. The place is as it always was. To see Ugo blowing out smoke immediately before the building does is to establish a sort of relation. We may think that the factory is "exhaling," and in technical terms, that is precisely what is happening, since the steam represents the waste product of an internal biochemical process. The factory is imitating Ugo, who controls it. But it is also clear that Ugo is imitating the factory, in that he carelessly ejects his waste "steam" without regard for its effect on the surround. The information he passes to Corrado about his wife is just such "steam," steam Ugo is "blowing off," as we can see from the distressed, slightly irritated expression on his face: it is hardly Corrado's place, after all, to know that in her husband's opinion Giuliana did not leave the hospital totally healed, or to see Ugo's reaction to this state of affairs. Ugo has now become the sort of man who fits perfectly into this world of blind systematicity, this production line. Whatever he is making—order in the factory, increased efficiency—requires a build-up of steam that must once in a while be vented. So we see him venting. But it is the factory's emission of steam that draws our attention: in other circumstances, we would take Ugo and his confessions for granted as the stuff of modern life, without concentration or regard.

At this point we must discover Giuliana's secret. Waking in the middle of the night, she slips a thermometer under her arm, whimpers to herself, then detects the sound of something mechanical grinding in the distance. She slides out of bed, while Ugo sleeps. In another room, its walls painted as blue as the sea, back and forth beside a blue folding chair a blue robot is relentlessly gliding. It is made of Meccano construction pieces: its gleaming electric eyes suggest eternal vigilance and its seemingly interminable back and forth movement, profound stupidity. In bed near the robot is Valerio, asleep. She catches the device, lifts it off the floor, fiddles at its base where four wheels spin crazily, turns it off. There is something Giacomettian about this robot: slender and graceful, it seems human enough, but human for a world in which presence is more important than experience. Tenderly, hesitantly, she fondles the boy's hair, then turns and walks offscreen and out of the room, shutting the door. We remain at the bedside, where in the pitch darkness the two gleaming robot eyes continue to watch. The robot is not watching the boy, it is watching us.

Now Giuliana hears whirring sounds and goes into a panicky fugue, finally throwing herself onto a wooden seat (built for function, not comfort). In his pajamas—clinical and white—Ugo approaches, reassures her she's not running a fever. She falls into his arms, sobbing. The wall behind him, the railing behind her, are dark sea blue. She dreamt that her bed was on quicksand, sinking "deeper and deeper." She seems in pain, or at least engorged with feeling, perhaps still living the dream, although she knows she is awake. Is she afraid? Is Ugo the enemy? He kisses her and she moves hungrily toward him, but then pulls away, moves against a white wall in her white nightgown. He embraces her again and she tenses, full of need, her fingers taut and curled. "No," she whimpers when he kisses her again, and their heads are together with an abstract painting, perhaps the child's painting, on the blue wall behind them.

Let us consider that this scene is shot in blue and white—the child's blue room and robot, the blue chair, the blue wall and railing in the vestibule; Giuliana and Ugo in white. "Blue is for distance, distance is blue," as Tennessee Williams has Sancho Panzo call out to Don Quixote in *Camino Real,* and white suggests unity and presence, immediacy, since it is at once a fulmination and a retreat of color: all colors, in scientific truth, and yet white seems to hide the intensities of its colors beneath the brilliant abstraction which envelops and melds, but also deindividualizes, them all. Distance and presence. Blue is also depth, of course, and inexplicability, and change and intoxication and loss. With Giuliana, much is going on, many contradictions, all at the same time. She is intensely aware but also emotional; her body is in movement in many directions. It seems that she moves jerkily from thought to thought, or from fragment to fragment, her body a nexus at which multiple pathways cross and press for resolution. Is it possible that here, emphatically—in this scene designed to emphasize it—but also throughout the film in various ways, Giuliana is having a "fit"?

Here is how a major scholar of epilepsy describes that condition:

> A fit, even the grossest major convulsive fit of epilepsy, is many things happening at once. Fits are patterns of awareness and action, combinations of knowing, feeling, and doing. They are episodes of behavior and experience put together by the brain during crises in the continuity of living. Such crises are characterized by a sudden coming together of a complex of conflicting and disparate ideas, images, and impulses; fits are syntheses of such complexes that both resolve and represent their otherwise unthinkable contradictions and ambiguities. By providing more or less fitting resolutions of crises, fits serve to maintain or restore the crisis-disrupted continuity of transactions between organism and environment. (Barker 14)

Giuliana is a paradigmatic example of the person in conflict (indeed, the *creative* person in conflict, given her tasteful ideas for the coloration of her store on the Via Alighieri, although she hasn't figured out yet what she will sell in it). "If we can endure confrontation with the unthinkable," writes Barker, "we may be able to fit together new patterns of awareness and action" (15). The "fit," indeed, is symptomatic of a kind of bad fit, that is, an incompatibility or disalignment between a person and her circumstances. People who do *not* experience "fits" in fact fit their social scene perfectly, they conform and go along, nothing jars them. Ugo has no "fits." The world has become technical, yet he is a technical man (he is a man!), and so he "belongs." When he demonstrates a yellow plastic gyroscope to Valerio, the device could be torn from his own interior—it *is* the stability it produces, a stability in motion that characterizes those whose modern experience is painless.

As to Giuliana's apparent illness: it is easy to see *The Red Desert* as the story of a neurotic woman caught in an industrial environment that painfully and unceasingly oppresses her, and to see her behavior as evidence of that pain and oppression, just as one can see the bleak, threatening environment against which she reacts. The protagonist of the film, in other words, is merely neurotic from the start, and in her special, disabled condition she is unable to muster an adequate response to the factory world and the social relations it implies and demands.

Modernity is not for the weak of spirit; they flag there, they wilt; and eventually they are replaced by types—like Ugo and Corrado—who are better suited to the conditions: a pretty, neat, Darwinian speculation. But let us take another, equally plausible, view. Giuliana is not inherently, generically, "naturally" neurotic; it is not by accident or fatality that she cannot get through the day without "fits." She is perfectly adjusted to another world altogether, an environment we might describe as being "whole" and "unfractured," certainly a premodern and pretechnological state of things, existing now, perhaps, only in her dim imagination, where people have not been split apart into functions, where bodies are united, where the outside and the inside are merged, singular, indistinct. Say that she has not yet been born into Ugo's world, or not yet adjusted to the shock of birth. Say that she is Wagnerian, demanding a synaesthetic response to an array of indiscriminate stimuli. Say that she is pastoral, attuned to the seasons and to fecundity, to mystery and fear, to surprise and feeling. The factory as a vivid material world does not bother her. But the factory as a social organization, with its amalgamated, interlocking pieces and its bounded, surveilled job tasks; and the wider universe built around the premise of the factory, with its emphasis on—obsession for—product, profit, systematization, and reduction: all this is poison. She has come to terms with the alienness, regardless of the fact that sometimes it is excruciating. This is her life, and her pain. Not mechanics, but brutality, excludes her.

"Some people," writes Barker, "seem to have an affinity for unthinkable situations but lack the ability to resolve them" (15). Affinity: she is in love with Ugo (and also, in her way, with Corrado), and she loves her child, who is perfectly at home in this scientific universe. She is enmeshed in "some kind and degree of uncanny experience" (Barker 6), which leads to a sense of incongruousness, obscenity, impracticality of movements in relation to one another. "Even momentary shakings of the ongoing integration of one's 'self' with its permanent and changing frames of reference are felt as peculiarly unusual activities of body, mind, or person—as, for example, nausea, giddiness, and shivering; intimations of ecstasy or uneasiness; feelings of falling apart or coming together; losing and finding one's self; and so on" (6).

It is not that a neurotic has bumped up against the logic of industrialism, but rather that the obscenity of industrialism has bumped up against the logic of the poet. Bruce Elder has commented very usefully on the fact that in the early 1960s, when this film was initially released, traditional psychiatric diagnostic practices were increasingly coming into question as a result of the work of thinkers such as Thomas Szasz and R.D. Laing (personal conversation). Giuliana is not really neurotic at all. But she is living in a world that is entirely and utterly hostile to her true interests, a world that makes "neurotics" out of people like her.

ABSTRACT

I picture thinking as a stream of which only the surface is visible.
—Wilhelm Stekel

Corrado has come to the Via Alighieri, a gray lane between gray rows of buildings curving off under a gray sky: something of an Utrillo. He sees one particular building, lets himself in, then quickly retreats. Giuliana emerges. He says he was passing by, but then corrects himself: "I don't want to start with a lie." She is in a mulberry purple dress and black scarf, at once self-protective and tasteful. She cuts to the heart of something that he would prefer to turn away from: "—Start what?" Relationship is instantaneously present for her, though for him it is something to hide away or dream about. Like a good planner, he pretends he wants "to talk," and so now, trapped in his pretenses, she must civilly go along with conversation, with hypothesis, with conjecture, with proposition. Already she has turned and is leading him (hopelessly?) inside.

It was a shawl, not a scarf, and now she opens it around her (because, as we can see, already she needs protection: he attracts her but alarms her, innocent as he is of his true power or of what she knows, that they are together *already*). She will use blue, says she, for the walls, and green for the ceiling (making a world upside-down?). The camera tilts up and we see a magnificent construction of whitewashed walls, a sienna strip, an umber ceiling. Originally the film was to be titled, in fact, *Blue and Green* (*Observer* 24 February 1963). The conversation between them is maddening. He has no advice as to what she should sell; she likes ceramics but knows nothing about them. Faenza is nearby, says he, and they have lots of ceramics (meaning, "Don't go into competition") but she races to her notebook to write it down. "Write what?" "Faenza," says she, "I'll go there," but then she sees phone numbers she must call back and is put off, runs out of frame. The standard critical response to Antonioni is that his films are light on dialogue, indeed that often people do not speak (as though garrulousness is or should be a natural state of affairs and silence is noteworthy). Certainly for Antonioni, silence is natural and speech is noteworthy. Corrado has come to the Via Alighieri (far from the factory); she is there; there is nothing they need to say to one another. Or, silence is what they need to say. Now she's dialing, but she hangs up. Suddenly: "Did Ugo tell you about me?" "No," he lies. Did he find a hotel? Where does he live? He tells where he was born, what he's done with his life. (He's done a considerable amount of moving around.) She keeps him talking. He paces, in his butterscotch brown necktie and blue overcoat. She leads him outside. A piece of newspaper drifts down from above, and she steps on it, lets it curl around her legs and blow off. It is "today's paper," literally, a rectangle of inked, pressed pulp blowing here, floating there, given importance by the arbitrary weight of definition, nothing more: "It hardly stays alone a minute . . . , the pile of printed sheets is converted into a newspaper again when a young boy sees it, reads it, and leaves it converted into a pile of printed sheets. . . . an old woman finds it, reads it, and leaves it changed into a pile of printed sheets. But then she carries it home and on the way home uses it to wrap up a pound of beets, which is what newspapers are fit for after all these exciting metamorphoses" (Cortázar, "Daily" 67).

Giuliana has wrapped the shawl into a scarf again, and uses it to cover her nose and mouth. Then she walks to a fruit vendor's cart—gray cart, fruit vendor dressed all in gray, the cart covered with baskets of gray fruit, like clay—and sits in a chair. "Tired?" he asks. The vendor gazes at her, with an exceptionally sour sneer. "No," says she, but she is hearing voices, a choir. The vendor looks at her askance. A train whistle in the distance. A whirring electronic sound. The empty street. Corrado looks down at her. "Giuliana, are you tired?" She nods her head: "Yes, always. No, not always, sometimes." What is the difference between sometimes and always? She walks away, then turns back. She is going home, he is going to Ferrara. She walks away again, hugging the left wall, as though without its comforting regularity the task of finding a path out of this maze would be insurmountable (like Midge, after visiting Scottie in the sanitarium, in *Vertigo*).

By afternoon it is sunnier, there are lush colors in the environment. They are near a fish market. He begins to tell her how remarkable are some fish, that some are even transparent, but she finds this terrifying. Is he dismayed by her reaction? "Do you have to love an animal to eat it?" he asks, as they walk past some pink roses growing in a large green lawn bordering a yellow shed. He teases her about eating kittens, cute little kittens, as we watch, with those roses out of focus in the foreground. "Until *Red Desert,*" Antonioni told Pierre Billard, "I always filmed with a single camera, and thus from a single angle. But from *Red Desert* on, I began using several cameras with different lenses, but always from the same angle. I did so because the story demanded shots of a reality that had become abstract, of a subject that had become color" (52). A quick *riposte,* as they enter an apartment block and she climbs the stairs: "Would you eat me?" What can be terrifying about the idea of transparent fish? Here there are no fish, transparent or otherwise. The idea—its invocation—is a pure abstraction. Abstract conversation is modern (also urban), implying unrelenting movement and change of scene as well as the disconnection of action and setting: that far from waters one can discuss fish. Thought and language become tools one carries from circumstance to circumstance, applying them *in situ* to the best effect. What one says is always fluid (in relation to what one has already said), but has no continuity with the situation, does not spring from roots in the situation, is instead imported and imposed. Thus is the human severed from the scene, in that meaning has no direct relation to place, but is portable, essentially *motive*. We mean *by* going, *through* going, and meaning is a way *of* going, a function of an overall focus on locomotion and development. Writing on the denaturalization of the industrial era, Schivelbusch informs us that the birth of the railway in the middle of the nineteenth century depended on the "destruction of animal power" and quotes James Adamson to the effect that transportation had earlier involved the "sort of irregular hobbling" of an animal, "which raises and sinks its body at every alternate motion of the limbs" (*Journey* 8); one did not move regularly forward, in a way that steam power would allow rail-bound vehicles to do, and indeed horse-and-carriage transit had been characterized by passengers' much more direct experience of motion: "We heard our speed, we saw it, we felt it as a thrilling; and this speed was not the product of blind insensate agencies, that had no sympathy to give, but was incarnated in the fiery eyeballs of the noblest among brutes, in his dilated nostril, spasmodic muscles, thunder-beating hoofs" (De Quincey; qtd. in Schivelbusch *Journey* 11–12).

Giuliana's reality is brutal by comparison with Corrado's more streamlined experience: when she talks of fish, fish are present, immediate, real; he can talk of fish in the absence of fish and while thinking of something else. We may recollect that he was born in one town, moved to another and then another, and that he is on his way across the seas, but always he has words at his disposal and speaks without hesitation. Giuliana is far less garrulous. For her, language is presence, position, perspective. Corrado has the spirit of the railway traveler of the nineteenth century, who "saw the objects, landscapes, etc. *through* the apparatus which moved him through the world. . . . he could only see things in motion" (Schivelbusch *Journey* 64).

It should not strike us as particularly surprising, then, that she cannot quite come to terms with him, or comprehend him, that she cannot quite subsist in the world that supports his continual movement. "When we cannot find a word for a thing or an event," writes Barker, "our experience of it is incomplete; we cannot think about it as a 'real' phenomenon without a defining center of relevance or circumference of reference. . . . When the right or 'right' word fails to come to us (or we fail to find it because we can't conceive it, or it has lost meaning for us), we can be stuck in an 'intention to say' (or in similar circumstances with an 'intention to do'). Then we find ourselves truly at a loss for words (or action)" (232).

To speak of transparent fish while walking past a tiny implantation of roses into a cool apartment complex is the height of abstraction. Modernity, mass society, rapid mobility, and industrialism all favor the abstract relation, but Giuliana is trying hard, against considerable odds, to be *here* in what she thinks, what she says, and what she does, and so the "transparent fish" are terrifying. Not the fish themselves but the invocation, which is itself transparent, slippery, always evading the real.

DOWN

Hallucinations compete with perception. Imagery doesn't.

—Oliver Sacks

In the aerial worker's apartment, his wife gone to fetch some wine, Corrado is alone with Giuliana. She sits on the sofa, which is covered with a blanket woven with a scene of snow-laden winter branches. Dark blue, dark forest green, dark brown, white. She wants to know if honestly Ugo didn't tell him about her accident and he says, now, "Yes. You were in a hospital, for stress." She says she met a girl. "Where?" The answer is, "There," but Giuliana has bent over and is running her finger in the space between the trees designed on that blanket. He takes her to mean in the hospital, of course. The girl was "very sick" because she "wanted everything" and the doctor told her to love someone or something: her husband, her son, a job, a dog. She gets up and runs to the vestibule. "—But not," says she, "husband, son, job, dog, tree, river." Her hand is on her chest. She is trapped in a corner, the walls painted soft encroaching olive green, her sweater unprotective dove gray, her hair the color of olive bark in the spring, her face rosy with its fine-lined nose and perfect, helpless persimmon lips. It is impossible not to cherish everything about this vision, the hair against the wall, the wall against the sweater, the hand upon the sweater not quite grasping, not searching, the cold mechanical intercom on the wall against the gentle, troubled expression on her hopeful face, the play of light in the green paint and upon her torso. Situated thought and situated language are not necessarily rational, but linkages abound between foreground and background, surface and depth, memory and insight. Rationality is a way of restricting experience for utilitarian purposes. She knows Corrado is rational, yet she is fascinated by him. And she fears what he will make of the information she is giving out, fears any evaluation that might lead to rational conclusions, fears that he has diagnostic power at all.

He persists in clinical interrogation, always and forever asking the wrong question: "Did she tell what she was feeling?" Giuliana has taken a step or two and is framed against the back lighting that illuminates the glass pane of the door. "The ground seemed to give way," says she in perfect honesty, describing, too, what she must be experiencing now with him, the ground giving way because she is swept up by his presence. The girl, Giuliana says, had a feeling of sliding down, of being always "about to drown." (The girl was aware, then, of her presence within a string of contingencies.) Again, the problem here is not a failure to focus on a thought or an act but that the world demands focus, and shifting focus, compels those who love generally to love only specifically. Returned with the wine now, the aerial worker's wife is not at all sanguine about her husband being offered a high-paying job far away. She would live in terror at his absence and would not be prepared to join him. But Corrado is interested in manning his factory, not preserving the family. Industrialism proceeds by neglecting the family bond, by shattering it or allowing it slowly to crumble. Orwell stood with one family in a "dreadful room in Wigan," for instance, "where all the furniture seemed to be made of packing cases and barrel staves and was coming to pieces at that; and an old woman with a blackened neck and her hair coming down denouncing her landlord in a Lancashire-Irish accent; and her mother, aged well over ninety, sitting in the background on the barrel that served her as a commode and regarding us blankly with a yellow, cretinous face. I could fill up pages with memories of similar interiors" (55). A purposive man, Corrado decides to find the worker at the Medicina radar station and use all his powers of persuasion, and Giuliana goes with him.

At Medicina, the camera, at a distance, frames the horizon just above the bottom of the screen, so that the golden grasses, a black house, and the figures of Corrado and Giuliana, not to mention the chain of radar towers, are set against a vast expanse of colorless sky. The red towers say nothing, hear nothing. They form an antenna for "listening to the stars." Given that they beckon meaning, but offer none, they constitute a kind of "desert," a vast and empty, but magnificent, potentiality. It is in this "desert" setting, a place purified of all bias, that we see Giuliana, briefly, in conversation with the worker and recognize that they share something deep and personal. There is a friendly directness to her smile that she never has for Ugo or Corrado, as though the worker understands something about her that no one else will ever understand. She claims that he used to be a "neighbor."

With Ugo, and waiting for friends, they are now at the lip of a swamp that the factory uses for drainage. Black soil and water, shapeless, yawning endlessly away from the camera. From above we see Giuliana in a black coat, standing upon the black earth, as we hear from Ugo that there is no longer any fishing here. (A pause to examine this image. She may be the fisher who can fish no longer, someone who once felt at home in this spot where land and water meet, but for whom the water must now be forbidden. She fished perhaps for special fish—if not "transparent fish" then unique fish—but those times are gone. We see the jagged line of the land against the stagnant water, and contrast it with the soft line of her shoulders. We wonder if being alone like this at the water's edge may bring her peace. Every shot in this film is a poem riddled with such suppositions and possibilities and we must tear ourselves away from the shots to follow the "story," such as it is.) Ugo confides to Corrado that on the day of Giuliana's accident he was in London, and that no, he didn't come back, because the doctors said he didn't have to. The camera pans. A landscape at once astonishingly beautiful and terrifyingly bleak: in the distance, against a paper-gray sky, a receding line of dark trees, each like a dark ball upon a stick; then, closer, a row of steel towers, only the bottoms of which can be seen (what are they for?); and in the foreground a pool bordered by denuded shrubbery, with its surface turned acid yellow-green—the green of putrefied Chartreuse—due to the influence of some chemical waste, and in the water the shrubs mirrored upside down. She wants to know if Corrado is a Leftist or a Rightist and he says these are big words, that it is difficult to say what one believes in, but he believes in humanity, in justice "a little less," in progress "a little more" and that the important thing is to "act in a way one believes right for oneself and for others. With a clear conscience!" (It seems impossible to take him quite seriously.) All the while as he speaks, a few birds, somewhere offscreen, converse incessantly, *beep cheep deep deep,* perhaps defining political reality for themselves but certainly, whatever they are "saying," managing conversation with less hesitation and self-consciousness than Corrado. The problem with rationalization is that every selection of thesis and posture is a negation of something else, a guilty sin. Every manifesto is a denial. "A nice group of words," she says to him, with a humoring smile. Max and his wife Linda have showed up, a tedious bourgeois pair from the start, and they will all go to Max's cabin on the pier for some fish he has prepared. Giuliana turns away. After bellowing with its foghorn, a freighter is silently gliding among the trees.

The cabin. A fire is burning low in the grate and Mili (Rita Renoir), another friend, is trying to warm her feet. Max is assuring people that the quail eggs he is serving are aphrodisiacs! Mili goes into a red room and stretches out on the mattress with her head on Linda's back. The women joke about Max's "eggs." The walls are so red it is as though they have been daubed with blood. The talk is sex, sex, and sex. Writes René Prédal, "The malady of eroticism thoroughly poisons the relationships" (79, my translation). Ugo comes in a little decorously, loosening his tie. Corrado fits himself modestly into a corner and Mili uses her hand on his knee to see if she can stimulate him, while Ugo and Linda watch like scientists: he doesn't feel much. Giuliana leans up against Corrado, who shrinks away a little—modesty? propriety? distaste?—but then she hears, from somewhere outside, what at first sounds like a baby's cry and then becomes a man screaming. No one else seems to hear a thing. In her fist she has one of Max's quail eggs, peeled, and now, slowly, in a little vaudeville routine, she nibbles it. "Eat them all!" chortles Max, and she goes out to help herself to another. Mili and Linda cannot take their eyes from her as she seems to be getting warmed up. "I want to make love!" Everyone collapses in laughter. Max's hand is well up Mili's green skirt. Young Orlando, who works in Max's factory, has interrupted now with his chubby girlfriend. The conversation quickly turns to aphrodisiac unguents that can be applied to extend pleasure, "crocodile fat with spices," "shark fins." For Prédal, this is "a strange verbal exchange between the two social classes strictly on the level of erotic allusion" (79), but it is also, it seems, a rationalization and commodification of cultural practices that begin with natural relations and sensitivities. Soon, however, with the youngsters gone off, and the shack tightly wrapped in a blue fog, the cold has set in. There isn't enough wood so at Mili's instigation they demolish the red room, using the boards of the wall to feed the stove. In the fog outside the window, Giuliana has seen a huge ship gliding past the pier. Corrado takes advantage of the moment: the ships, which unload here, go back empty, and so he could load them up and do his shipping straight from the factory zone rather than moving materials to a distant port. Mili lets Linda know that she loathes Max, always ready to pounce on a factory in trouble or on a lonely woman (chauvinist capitalism). Giuliana draws Ugo close and whispers to him that it's true she wants to make love, and he chuckles appreciatively, and also defensively, because his modesty (his bourgeois propriety) controls him: "How can we?" Prédal: "The game is cut short because the husband is there to stifle it" (79). Like a good modernist, Corrado explains to Max that he's traveling because it makes sense, because it's good to change one's life and work. Giuliana, however, "can't look at the sea for long and not lose interest in what happened on land." For these technocrats, sex is a contest, and it works perfectly well as hypothesis and metaphor. Talking about sex is sex. The red room has less symbolic meaning for them than it does for us; they can tear it down to feed the fire just as effortlessly as they can gather there for word games.

What is that bloody chamber, a womb of sorts? A coliseum? Now with a wall torn down, it radiates at one side of the hut, its interior a messy shambles of pillows and mattresses where these bizarre siblings had lain and out of which they were born. "What should I use my eyes for? What should I look at?" Giuliana asks Corrado, as he stands with the red room behind him. His response says everything about his need to wander. For him the question is how to live, but it's the same. Yet, he's wrong: it's not at all the same. For Corrado, how to live means where to go, what to buy, what to make, who to employ—it's all progress. For Giuliana, what to look at means where to stand, how to make boundaries, how to arrange surfaces, how to lose interest in the land when one gazes at the sea.

Now they see a doctor arrive on the quay. He climbs up a ladder onto the ship's deck, awkwardly. The ship is being quarantined, yellow flag. Giuliana urgently wants to go. The men argue, but she takes her coat and leaves. The shack is sky blue, its chimney smoking against the gray sky. All of them run along the pier, as the fog draws away from the boat. Giuliana has left her purse behind and Corrado offers to fetch it but she adamantly refuses, clinging to his sleeve (a little too evidently). An ambulance arrives. The fog swirls around as one by one the friends and husband judgmentally watch her holding Corrado, the fog swallowing them so that alternately they seem to evanesce and become embodied again. She gets into her car and drives, but down a jetty instead of the pier. At the very end, next to the foghorn at water's edge, she brakes, as the others scramble up to the car. Another inch and there would have been a reprise of her "accident," yet the car is completely safe, Giuliana is intact. No no, I made a mistake!, she insists. Ugo seems not to believe her. She is crying, "I'm sorry, I'm sorry, I didn't see." To the engineer it seems clear—and the others have the same view—that Giuliana was trying to end herself.

Our understanding of the film, of course, hangs upon whether or not we agree with his view.

ONE

Thinking inevitably culminates in a crisis.
—Wayne Barker, *Brain Storms*

Ugo has taught Valerio a cute little game to play on Giuliana. "What is one and one?" The answer, apparently, is "one." The kid drops a bubble of blue-tinted water onto a slide, and then puts a second. We watch them merge. Elder sensibly hopes that Giuliana's smile at this moment is a recognition of the boy's having discovered "an important human truth concerning the human impulse towards unity, a truth far more satisfying than those scientific truths based on division and separation whose effect has been to rend the world asunder"; and notes, with appreciable sensitivity, that as she leans over to kiss the boy, "the camera frames the kiss so that, like the two drops of water, his hair and hers become one fused mass" (5). Yet it is Ugo's engineering that has put this little science into action, not the spirit of Giuliana's more poetic world. Valerio means his demonstration as a kind of masterly play: Look how I can control liquid, thought, perception. Ugo is going away for five or six nights and she has packed his shirts. We can see them in the suitcase, slightly overlapping. One plus one. Do they merge? Do all his nights away from her become one long agonizing night? Ugo has a yellow plastic gyroscope and Valerio sets it spinning erect on the floor. "Ships have them, to steady them in heavy seas."

We will go immediately to a ship on the sea, where the need for a gyroscope is paramount, but: why this little word game about the number one? Because it is important that we should understand Ugo and his influence on Giuliana, understand that it is Ugo's professional and religious commitment to scientific process, industrialism, and technocratic division that make him the kind of man whose presence is confounding to Giuliana. It is not his personality. Under all this garb, Ugo has something of a feminine approach to the world (and indeed, compared with Corrado, there is a slightly feminine, polished look about him, throughout). Our ideas of "I" and of "thinking," claims Barker,

> are acquired in a masculine-oriented, Western civilization that distrusts Eastern or "womanly" intuition and is overcommitted to ideas of stepwise logical deduction as the only real thinking. Our distrust of the nonrational merges with our fear of the irrational. And to our sex- and geography-based bias, we add our "scientific" hostility to the spontaneous nonrational, which we misconceive as irrational or supernatural. For we are still, many generations after the Enlightenment, vigorously defending an impossibly constricted concept of the personal against any, even momentary, takeover by forces in the vast realm of the nonpersonal . . . as if we might otherwise become possessed by the demons and demonology that plagued our ancestors. (207)

Two characteristics of Ugo:

First, he is professionalized man, who has created, or succumbed to, a work personality distinct from his everyday self. He plays a role in the factory and in his business commitments. That ego, a "proper" self, he bears with him as he jaunts outside town with Corrado, as he muses and cavorts with his friends in the shack, as he jabbers on the phone in his office. There is a private Ugo quite different from this persona, perhaps even in conflict with it, the Ugo that built that blue robot for his son—a mechanical device, yes, but also something of a creature, and with a kind of weird personality; the Ugo that winds up the gyroscope, with hope and excitement. Here with Valerio, we see that personal, nonprofessional Ugo. At Giuliana's side—except in that one moment in the shack when she tells him she would like to make love—we see the professional one. Being committed to his bureaucratic status, Ugo preserves his dignity by standing at a certain remove from the "'womanly' intuition" that is otherwise his forte (as it is Giuliana's). Perhaps it is her "accident" that forced him to become stiff and professional with her, that split their marriage; we do not know, any more than we ever know what is made in Ugo's factory.

Secondly, as a person fundamentally susceptible to and close to feminine insight, Ugo understands the basic unity of the world prior to its division (in this case through capitalism and industrialization). He knows the secret of how one and one make one, just as by a reverse process Giuliana, having accommodated herself to her husband over the years, knows to adopt the "mentality" of the professional when it is called for and admit that one plus one equals two. She kisses the little boy as she sees that Ugo is offering him a poetic riddle, but this is the same Ugo who must now leave on a business trip, the same Ugo who did not return home from London when she had her accident because the doctors said it wasn't necessary. Given that he can marvel at the blending of water drops, it is hardly Ugo the man, Ugo the personality who troubles Giuliana. It is Ugo the professional. The man she married was swallowed up by the factory as he controlled it.

An oil rig is tied to a tanker. As gulls swoop and caw in the air, Giuliana looks at the heavy piping, frequently painted red, that feeds into the yellow-painted ship. Corrado has made a shipping deal. She wants to know what he'll take along and he lists some factory equipment. Of his own things, virtually nothing, a few bags. "If I were to leave, I'd take everything," she confides. "All I see and have at hand every day, even ashtrays." The rig emits a relentless hum as they speak. For her, travel "seems an excuse to abandon everything." They have walked to the railing, where the pale blue-gray sea flickers under the misty white horizon, and where red and white poles and tanks back them. She needs to know whether things and people will be there when he returns, and whether they'll be the same. He suggests that he might not come back. "Were I to leave not to return," says she, "I'd take you, too. Because you're part of me." Corrado stands doubtfully against the seascape, squinting a little. "Had Ugo looked at me the way you do, he'd have found out a lot." Corrado closes his eyes: "About the accident? . . ." She nods. ". . . And the girl in the hospital?" She nods again. "It was you!" Not even Ugo knows that she tried to kill herself. The worker at Medicina was in the hospital with her, very sick. The wind is blowing through her hair, throwing it in a thousand directions, as behind her the yellow deckwork of the adjacent ship shines against the greeny blue of the sea.

Her hair is fully alive. We look down upon them (in a Hitchcockian remove) as she strides past him. She's fine now, everything's fine. (It is only a bureaucratic logic that sees her as continually hovering on the verge of suicide.) She steps away, past red boilers, down a cherry red gangway, to a waiting skiff. Corrado comprehends her but comprehension isn't the solution to the riddle. It isn't comprehension that she needs. In fact, there is altogether too much comprehension, and, at the same time, motion, dispersal, the changing and naming of parts, codes and coding, attraction and distraction. Everything in every shot is wonderful, and Giuliana sees the world the way Antonioni does. She is less a figure who intrigues his thought than a stand-in, a way for him to figure himself ecstatically.

As, in a subsequent scene, Corrado briefs potential workers for their trip to Patagonia, a huge map hangs on the wall behind him. This map, hardly a reference point for his discussion with the men, stands as a figuration of Giuliana's consciousness. Before print culture, that is, before the modernity that has eclipsed her and back in the eco-cultural space that is her true domain, "maps were few and far between," writes Tom Conley: "Often a manuscript or an object of veneration in a sacred space, a *mappamundi* did not provide its users with information about their location or about the physical nature of the world. The map, often found in churches or manuscripts, was iconic rather than locational. An object for contemplation, the map tended not to tell the spectators who gazed upon it exactly where they were but to encourage reflection on the ordered immensity of the world within the watery surround of its *ecoumène,* or ocean sea" (253).

As is emphasized on the oil rig, Giuliana is a character surrounded by an "ocean sea." Exact geographical location is pointless for her. Corrado will exist in that map of Patagonia: he will be memory and anticipation, comment and gaze, always having perceived, and perduringly perceiving, what she "really is" in a way that Ugo cannot, but also to no effect.

TUTTI

On the few occasions that I dream, I dream in colour.

—Antonioni

It is suddenly the case that young Valerio cannot stand or walk, but collapses in a heap into his mother's arms. She finds him in bed. What happened? He is silent. Does it hurt (she squeezes his thighs)? He shakes his head. She bends his leg at the knee, taps his knee. "I don't feel anything," he says. Her face clouds over. "What do you mean, you don't feel it?" She taps again. "No." She smiles: he is having her on, he wants to skip school. She goes to the window and coos over a great ship outside. He turns away. She bends and kisses him. Her maid picks him up and releases him, and the boy crumples to the floor. "Love, please tell me," she kisses his foot with some desperation, "how I can help!" She sits him on the maid's lap and taps his knees again, with no result. "How can this be!" Cradling the child in her arms—a pietà—she whimpers, "How did it start?" Did he wake up like this, did it start last night? (We could ask similar questions about Giuliana.) Linda has come to help, they are talking about polio. Linda flips through a magazine with photographs of crippled children. Giuliana sits on the floor against Valerio's gray chalkboard, chewing her fingers, while behind her, through a plate glass window, we see a ship cruising down the canal and hear it sound a horn. "I'm tired of this game," says the boy, off-camera, "Draw me a new picture." She moves to the chalkboard, takes a piece of purple chalk, uses the side of it to make a huge circle. He is playing with a helicopter, throws it to the floor, makes as though to get out of bed but curbs himself. He wants her to tell him a story.

The narrative now moves into the story Giuliana tells. A little girl, with tanned skin, swimming in turquoise water off her island. "She was bored with grownups, who scared her." The girl smiles, frolics in the water, splashes with her feet, all this among the twittering birds. We see a cormorant swimming near her, a gull on a rock, a wild rabbit scampering along the waterline and dipping in for a bath. Green rills run among soft rocks, and the camera tilts up to the girl in her turquoise lagoon. On her "little isolated beach" the sea is transparent, the sand pink. "The reasons for the painfulness of Giuliana's existence are all to be found in this scene," writes Elder, "She is bound by the recollection of this paradisiacal experience and so her constant effort is to reconstruct the blissful experience of undifferentiation. Accordingly, she refuses to accept the more limited gratification offered by a world composed of discrete particulars" (20). We pull back for a panorama traveling shot of the inlet, the blue waters, the delicate promontories, the splashing sounds. "Nature's colors were so lovely . . . and there was no sound." (We may recollect that the artificial colors of industry were also lovely, in their way, but who could prefer the factory to this!) The girl steps out of the water, lies on the sand in the hot sun. The waves trickle in. She leaves as the sun goes down.

(How can Giuliana invent this tale, some will ask? Did she vacation in such a spot at one time? Was she once a little girl, taken away from such a paradise to be with Ugo in Ravenna?)

"One morning a boat appeared." Running to the beach, the girl sees a white sail on the horizon. "A real sailing ship, one of those that braved the seas and the storms of this world and, who knows . . . of other worlds." A closer shot of the ship approaching, splendid from afar but mysterious—a ghost ship—as it nears. No one aboard. Masts, sails, a slender prow. This vehicle as much represents and results from technology as any of the freighters gliding up the canal outside Ugo and Giuliana's house; but it bespeaks a technology in tune with the wind, the tide, the moment—a premodern technology. The boat stops, veers, then "silently, just as it had come," sails off. As soon as the girl comes back to shore there is a haunting treble voice (her voice?), singing in magnificent ululation, without words. The camera moves around her as she gazes off. "Who was singing? The beach was deserted." For a moment the voice seems here, then there. In the sea. She goes to the water, swims gracefully past clusters of rocks, as the voice lures her. "Many rocks that, she had never realized, looked like flesh." More than just flesh, too: the rocks are severely eroded, and so they look like the flesh of others like her, who have long walked against the wind.

"Who was singing?" Valerio asks.

"Everybody. Everything."

This can only mean a loss of personal discreteness, a dissolution of the individual self in the surrounding objects and situations of life. One *is* one's perceptions.

Later, she returns to Valerio's room and sees through his open door that he is standing. She draws him to her, kisses him furiously all over. But then, as a cloud seems to cover her: "Why? Why did you tell me that . . . ?"

The boy's sham may constitute a kind of "fit" in itself, may be an indication that like his mother, Valerio is out of tune with the mechanical world (of his toys, of his father's labor); or that, like Ugo, he is out of tune with her. Barker describes a case of an astute pupil who, to test a mentor's claim that he could always distinguish between an authentic symptom and a false one, faked a seizure by collapsing during the teacher's lecture. ("In considering the tendency for individuals to oscillate between being off guard and being on guard, . . . " writes Erving Goffman, noteworthy is a "difference in capacity to respond to alarming signs effectively with a minimum of disturbance to routine," and this involves, among other capabilities, "the quick discounting of false alarms" [*Relations* 242–243]). The idea for the student's performance, Barker suggests, "no doubt came to him in a flash, like any other great idea. Perhaps he was stimulated by the authoritative assertions of the master, and his great idea may well have been hatched in an incubation period of contrary-mindedness. The suddenness of his inspiration, the speed with which he acted upon it, and the apparent spontaneity of his performance are characteristics of other fits" (103–104). Valerio is certainly putting on a little performance—what is for him a little performance but for Giuliana a monstrous one—and is doing so with apparent spontaneity, thoroughness, and meticulous control. What is most important about the performance cinematically, of course, is that even when it is dispelled, even when we can see that the paralysis was a kind of game for the child and nothing more—a game, moreover, in which while no real cry of distress was emitted, a mother "heard" the pain—the residuum for us is that magical tale of the little girl by the sea. The child's distress evaporates, as does Giuliana's concern: but the ability of that girl to hear that voice among those rocks (a voice we cannot but remember) when there was no one there to emit it, is haunting.

The voice is haunting. But the story of the voice is more haunting still.

Giuliana hears the world because she is invested in it; her investment produces her sensations. She is not an inventor, she is an observer. At the shack by the pier, her friends denied the presence of that voice crying out in pain (a strange, primitive voice). She attends to things, and is then plagued by their effects, so multitudinous are they, circling all round in every dimension, waxing and waning. Antonioni is pointing out her perspective: if the rocks in the island tale are like flesh, why might everything in the film not represent life? All the machines are human constructs, every pipe was molded and soldered by someone, every ship chugs up the canal under the fingers of a navigator at a wheel. The world is a cacophony of forces, intentions, purposes, schemes: the steam flowing out of the factory, Ugo playing with Valerio, the radar towers at Medicina, Corrado's corralling of the workers for Patagonia (where there will be television, and they can phone home on a regular schedule).

Barker also shows that in performing a sham death (or sham paralysis), a creature can be saying, "I am uninteresting," "I am inedible." Valerio is terrified of being devoured alive. But also: to the extent that Giuliana is persisting in her own symptoms, she may be shamming too, effecting to defend herself from the spontaneous aggressions of the variegated social universe. And a mother may play wounded to lure a threat away from the nest (Barker 205). Valerio's "play illness" raises for us the prospect that Giuliana's performance attracts Ugo and his minions away from the little boy, at least to some degree.

Valerio's ploy may well have been intended to attract his mother's attention, to draw her out of herself. But what is interesting is that she could have been attractable. That he explicitly played the game means that she has been explicitly self-involved, and to the degree that he can detect it, resent it, wish to alter it, Valerio can see she must be drawn out of her bubble. For Giuliana, that "bubble" is no mere protective shell, it is a response in all genuineness to the horrifying improbability of the new world. She takes everything seriously, and takes her son most seriously of all—a fact he cannot appreciate, since like his father he has learned to focus and detach himself. That is why now, even Valerio becomes a threat, and she must run—as perhaps she imagines it—into that island world where the sun is always shining.

NOTHING HAPPENED

Complete silence reigned.

—Virginia Woolf, describing a failed dinner party

Giuliana goes to Corrado's hotel room. Mahogany brown wood paneling, brown carpet. She's cold, takes off her coat. A mechanical whirring sound—the air conditioning? "You don't love me, do you?" Silence, then: "Why do you ask?" She needs to know why she always needs other people. She'd like all the people who ever loved her to be here around her, like a wall. He wants to know what happened. "Nothing." She falls to the floor, hugs his brown chair. The whirring sound. "I'm not well. I'll never get well." A higher-pitched whine. "We all suffer from it, more or less," says he, "We all need help." The whine again, diminishing, persistent. She pulls a folded map from his bedside table, they look at it together. South America. Perhaps there's a place in this world where we could be safe? "It's go, go, go, only to come back to where we started," he says, paraphrasing Eliot. He holds her head, she wraps into him, gets up. She tears off her sweater, sits on the bed, picks up a book. The whine again. He looks around. She has one shoe off. She lies on the pillow. He looks down at her. "Help me. I'm afraid I won't make it." She is afraid of the factory, the streets, colors, people, everything. They embrace, he pulls off her shirt, they are on the bed, she is panting and twisting, we see her legs. A whirring sound interrupts. She leaps up. Outside in the street there is only an old man walking slowly home. In a frenzy of desire she struggles with withdrawal. They lie naked, out of focus. She awakens to the sound of a high-pitched chiming, and everything is white. She runs through the streets. He follows. She retreats from him, then comes back and gets into his car. Back in her store on the Via Alighieri she paces against a white wall and tells him, "There's something terrible about reality, and I don't know what."

She is beside an old ship on the wharf, at night. She ascends the gangway, her steps echoing. A sailor in a blue and black striped watch cap comes down to meet her, and says something unintelligible. "Tell me . . ." says she. He says something unintelligible. "Does this ship take passengers? . . ." What he says is unintelligible. ". . . I haven't decided yet . . ." What he says is unintelligible. She walks away and he follows. "I can't decide. I'm not a single woman. But at times I feel separated. . . . The bodies . . . are . . . separated. If you pinch me, you don't suffer. . . . I have to think that all that happens to me, is my life. Forgive me." He stands and watches silently as she backs away. He says something unintelligible. It is clear to Giuliana that she is not human in the way that others are. When the world reacts, she does suffer. She is, in fact, the world that happens to her.

Morning. She and Valerio are outside the factory. He points up. Why is that smoke yellow? Because, says she, it's poisonous. But then, he worries, the little birds who fly through it will die. She takes him by the hand. By now the birds know, and they don't fly through it anymore. This is hardly an optimistic statement about Giuliana's future. She is not announcing, in our "presence," that finally she has adjusted to "normality," even though she has had an extramarital affair. She is pointing out the incontrovertible fact that the people around her, her community, have adjusted even though she has not. (We owe gratitude, since it is through her separation that we have experienced the film.) Does this recognition mean that perhaps someday soon she will be able to adjust, too? "The only possible outcomes now are convulsive or creative," Barker concludes (253). Something, after all, will have to fill that shop on the Via Alighieri, and she will color its walls.

PROGRESS

The film was born on the spot.
—Antonioni

A pair of brief concluding observations, both about Giuliana as a woman:

First, we do not see Corrado and Giuliana in their lovemaking, except out of focus, shoulders up, and for only two or three seconds. What we see, with great concentration, is Giuliana's legs twisting and moving, groping and calling, in their nylon sheaths on his bed. ("The end of *Red Desert,*" said Antonioni to a questioner in San Francisco, in November 1968, "was invented in one night, because Richard Harris walked out with a third of the film unfinished. The love scene in *Red Desert* has 47 shots in it, but only seven have Harris in them" [Setlowe]). This is not mere culminating, historical sexuality, this is undulating ahistorical perduring eros. Her desire is not a shallow pool to be dried, a matter-of-fact query to be addressed, a physical need to find the terminus of satisfaction. It is life, the ride up and the ride down, the quest which is also a memory of a quest and a hope for a quest, a unity of time. She is entirely desire, trying to live in a world that is masculinist and purposive. The men are going somewhere, doing something, achieving, accomplishing, fulfilling, enriching, ennobling, yet also aggrandizing. Although with Giuliana we can gaze at the vistas Antonioni presents and find each of them stunning, evocative, deliciously unresolved (for example, the ship sailing toward us up the canal, seen through the window behind her as she worries about Valerio's "paralysis"), a more industrial focus than hers would find directions, engagements, and expansions (the ship is delivering a cargo which will enrich someone; it can be hired to return a cargo elsewhere, to enrich someone else; in the same way the film will deliver a plot, a turn, a resolution). If we neglect poverty—and the managerial class we are watching here would argue that, in general, we should—what we see in this film is a play of a preindustrial, and potently female, sensibility against a constraining masculinist modern culture.

Secondly, it is not strange that inside the little fairy tale, as Giuliana tells it, the beautiful girl on the beach, sticking her copper head out of the turquoise waters, "didn't like boys, all pretending to be grownups" and "so, she was always alone." Pretending to be grownups means, explicitly, capitalizing on resources, mobilizing the economy, producing wealth, exploiting nature, abandoning or utilizing art, wanting femininity with a desperation that can only lead to losing it. Boys are all around in this film, most strikingly in the fog upon the wharf, where they seem to form a gang. This world is boys' work, Giuliana the price boys are paying for their progress.

. . .

Il deserto rosso (1964), photographed by Carlo di Palma in the 1.85:1 format at Ravenna, Sardinia, and Incir de Paolis Studios (Rome), and printed by Technicolor (Rome); 120 m. Released in the United States as *The Red Desert,* February 8, 1965.

Plates

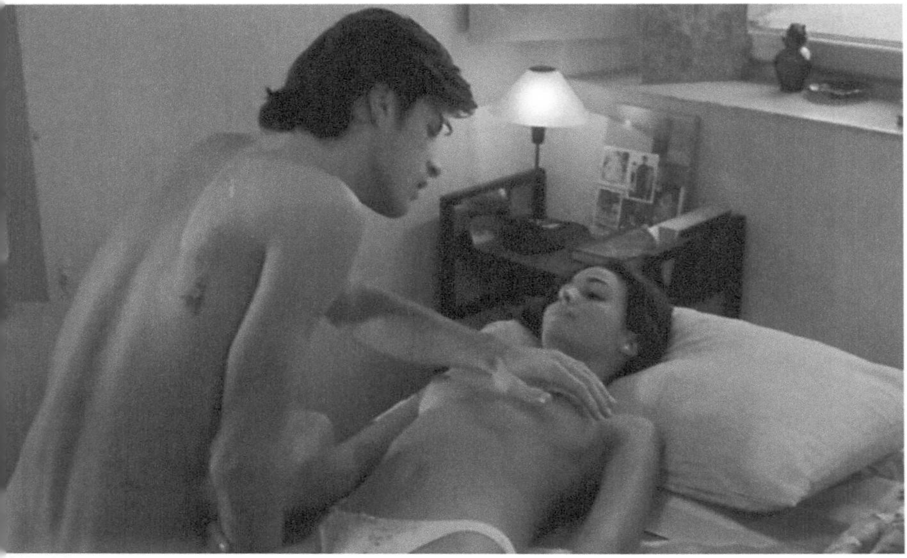

ATE 1. *Beyond the Clouds:* Carmen and Silvano

PLATE 2. *Beyond the Clouds:* A Director in Portofino

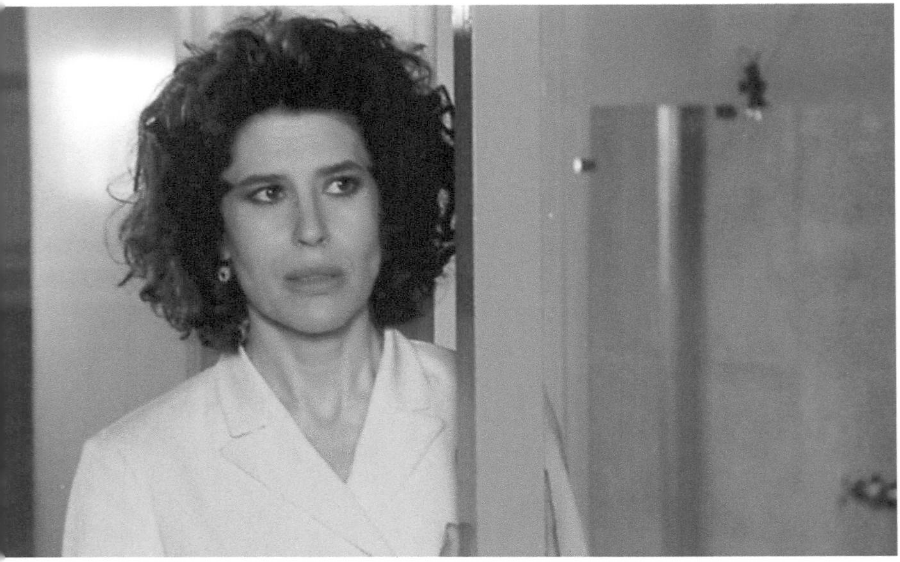

TE 3. *Beyond the Clouds:* Carlo, Patrizia, Her Husband, and His Lover

PLATE 4. *Beyond the Clouds:* Niccolo in Aix

ATE 5. *Identification of a Woman*

PLATE 6. *The Red Desert*

TE 7. *The Dangerous Thread of Things*

PLATE 8. *The Mystery of Oberwald*

ATE 9. *Zabriskie Point*

PLATE 10. *The Passenger*

E 11. *Blow-Up*

The Dangerous Thread of Things

He who listens hard does not see.

—Walter Benjamin, "Some Reflections on Kafka"

I
Oblivion

There is, for example, no such thing as the memory; there are only specific facts and ideas which have become available for recall because we have found use for them.

—Richard J. Hofstadter

Given the enchanting swirl of pointers and places that stretches as far as we can imagine, all at once in every direction, the placards, the plastic luminous baubles, the pages of books foxed and torn, the tedious tortillas, the splintering sounds of harmonies and cacophonies, the formulae for calculating arterial pressure and rocket thrust, the mathematics of nonfinite numbers, the worn fabric upon the beloved furniture, the mechanics of the triple-head projector with its golden mirrors and water-cooled lamp; given melodrama, given fear and lust, given the top hat and white tie and tails, given limousine service with pink champagne and also the cardboard shelters of the homeless, given penicillin and its discontents, given the submarine, given oxygen masks and advertisements for singing golf tees; given all the arrangements and relationships, interlinkages, and intercalations, the unfoldings and encasements it is possible to see, or at least to conceive, in an explosion of concentration . . . given ferns and facilities, fractures and fables, fiddlers and funiculars: given what can be given of the vortex, what an intensive commitment we also persist in making to the linear and continuous! We are fabricators of history, investors in capital development, organizers according to projective rhythms, fixated upon probability and its embeddedness (in fiction and in what we call fact), convinced that causality is temporal.

As to causality, "And is not human life in many parts of the earth governed to this day less by time than by the weather," writes Sebald, "and thus by an unquantifiable dimension which disregards linear regularity, does not progress constantly forward but moves in eddies, is marked by episodes of congestion and irruption, recurs in ever-changing form, and evolves in no one knows what direction?" (*Austerlitz* 100–101).

We link our expectations to our memories, our memories to expectations; and also to the belief that human life progresses or develops as time rolls by, with the result that our understandings are founded upon the conceits of immaturity and maturity, ripeness, senescence, blossoming, and decay. We are always going, always cherishing and vitiating promise. Life is pictured as a journey through time, and because of this deep affinity between the conditions of our existence and the idea of the voyage, voyages themselves come to seem adventurous, time-bound, throwing us back into memory and forward into prospect. The young, we surmise, have promise, potential, something to look forward to. The old, having gradually expended their promise and potential, have something to look back upon. Enthusiasm and melancholy. With our belief in longitudinal reality—that is, in reality as a longitudinal phenomenon—we see expertise as the bounty of experience and growth; yet even as we admire it (sometimes to the point of jealousy), we hesitate to trust it or place reliance in its vision. The old master, apparently past his prime, degenerates toward a grave, his powers diluted, his gestures febrile and weak, his impulses thin, his ideas barmy, while at the same time a promising young spirit is heralded with the gravest seriousness precisely because of the capacity he holds in reserve, his vault of possibility, what we can predict (and wager) he will do before the sun shines tomorrow.

Age is at once venerated and disregarded. We pass by our elders with a respectful (or a disdainful) silence. Our greatest enthusiasms are for youth, and our sense of the boundless Fountain of Possibility is that youth guards and maintains it. This idea, entrenched now in the marketplace of mass culture, is hardly new. At the turn of the twentieth century, G. Stanley Hall wrote, "The guardians of the young should strive first of all to keep out of nature's way. . . . They should feel profoundly that childhood, as it comes fresh from the hands of God, is not corrupt, but illustrates the survival of the most consummate thing in the world" (qtd. in Hofstadter 367). John Dewey and the developmentalists had a commitment to the education of the natural child who was threatened by societal artifice. "For them," writes Hofstadter, "the child came into this world trailing clouds of glory, and it was the holy office of the teacher to see that he remained free, instead of assisting in the imposition of alien codes upon him" (368). The teacher or *magister,* or the artist, mature in career and perspective, is either denigrated or given the shabbiest reward. No one who can be a movie star or a heart surgeon stoops to being a teacher. In Frank Oz's *In & Out* (1997), when the hot young movie star Cameron Drake (Matt Dillon) reveals during his Oscar acceptance speech a certain lingering admiration for a high school teacher, the moment is structured as the centerpiece of a grand comedy. In the late nineteenth century, writes Hofstadter, school readers centered on "not the aesthetic content of an artist's work but his career as evidence of the virtues of assiduous application" (308); the career was a successful voyage, in which the energies and curiosities of bounteous youth were concentrated upon substantial and continuous production, production that redounded to the economic credit of the producer rather than only offering illumination and insight to those who sought it. And by the middle of the twentieth century, it was possible to report that "the status of schoolteaching as an occupation is lower in this country than elsewhere, and it is far lower than that of the professions in the United States" (Hofstadter 311). Philosophy is—has to be—its own reward, and this to the degree that those who might openly profess devotion to it fall into a kind of solicitous disrepute: "American students have more sympathy than admiration for their teachers" (312). By 2008, conditions deteriorated to the point where a film called *No Country for Old Men* could top the Academy Awards, celebrating, as it does, the silent, hopeless impotence of an aging Texas sheriff faced with consummate depravity and violence. In a café, with another old sheriff from another county, he sits in the silence of the resigned. The old have nothing serious to contribute, nothing provocative to say.

In such light as this, Antonioni's final film, *The Dangerous Thread of Things,* a contribution to the trilogy *Eros* (which also has short works by Wong Kar-Wai and Steven Soderbergh), has the striking potential to ring as a hollow and pathetic reminder of a career gone stale. And this is precisely what we find in the popular reviews. "Antonioni is the author of several masterpieces," wrote Carina Chocano in the *Los Angeles*

Times, "His major contributions to cinema don't need the grief of sharing space on a filmography with this." For David Rooney in *Daily Variety,* "'The Dangerous Thread of Things' has no thread to speak of. . . . Contrived enigma follows bored couple . . . who speak exclusively in non sequiturs rendered even more risible by their stilted English dialogue." Finally, denigrating its maker, the film "unintentionally but cruelly parodies the vintage work and violates the dignity of a once-significant filmmaker." In the *New York Times,* the culturally learned A. O. Scott finds it "somewhere between a Mad magazine satire and a Maxim photo spread." Yet, we are surely forced to admit that our belief in development, our wholesale addiction to the idea of progress, inevitably renders all mature careers stale. In order to be convinced that Antonioni's work was (once) of sufficient value to inspire fresh (and inspiring) work in (younger) others, it must at its close be made to seem vitiated and empty, precisely, some would claim, as empty as this film. In *Sight & Sound,* Philip Kemp complains that the effect of the film "is of a geriatric fantasy, in which all females are large-breasted and shed their clothes without hesitation." A film, then, which betokens the arrival of the shrunk shank, and sounds the once manly voice turned childish treble, piping and whistling. Then, winding down that dangerous thread:

> Last scene of all,
> That ends this strange eventful history,
> Is second childishness and mere oblivion,
> Sans teeth, sans eyes, sans taste, sans everything.
> (*As You Like It* II.vii.1061–1064)

The Dangerous Thread of Things (Il filo pericoloso delle cose)—or, as it might as well be named, *The Dangerous Thread of Events,* since the Italian word *cosa* also means matters of fact—tells a story that is, in a way, simple enough. Christopher (Christopher Buchholz) has been living with Cloe (Regina Nemni) in an abandoned tower, apparently one of two such structures, beside an estuary. They fight, and clearly she is tired of him. At lunch in a restaurant nearby, sitting in silence as a rowdy group takes pleasure at the next table, they see a young woman riding her horse on the beach. "She is the girl who lives in the other tower," says Cloe. She goes off for a walk with him, continuing their squabble, and finally he seems to break off from her. Sometime later, Christopher takes himself to Linda's (Luisa Ranieri) tower. They make love. Sometime afterward, Cloe is off to the water's edge again. On the beach she strips and dances in the breeze, lies down to bask in the sun.

Linda appears, also strips and dances, and comes upon Cloe. We see her standing next to Cloe's shadow, peaceful, meditative. Nothing more.

Where is the thread, the dangerous thread? It may be what binds discreet events into a drama, that propulsive and always impending sense of motive and target. In narrative terms alone, we are perhaps used to thinking of this connective, this binder, in terms of probability, attitude, and action. Cloe and Christopher have a bitter squabble, then he is clearly disenchanted, then he goes with the other woman; and there are other possibilities as well. But Antonioni is a visual artist principally, not an enchainer of emotional or geopolitical facts. Everything for him has a look, indeed a cultured look. Having parked near the beach restaurant, walking along the path that leads to the water, Cloe and Christopher pass by a sign that reads VIETATO INTRODURRI ANIMALI (No Animals), which will soon take on a double meaning: that Linda does not read, or does not feel obligated by, rules posted in this way (Linda is not the same sort of creature that Christopher and Cloe are); and that in going to the restaurant, for all its promise of gaiety and sensuality, Christopher and Cloe leave their animal selves behind. They become utterly rational, methodical, even contriving. But how is all this visible? We are stepping behind them, and see a swath of green trees against a white sky. The eye is led to a field of low grasses, among them ruddy grasses, which connect with the red shirt Cloe wears and the ruddiness evident in her sunlit hair. Matching her form is the partnering Christopher, dark and pensive as he walks. Because of the camera's close position, the muscular movements of these two become exaggerated in the frame, and the natural harmony suggested by the complementarities of color is broken apart by Cloe's springy step, her arms thrown out, and Christopher's mechanical pacing. The landscape is merely a substance these two navigate through, and the state of affairs for them, their pique, their energy, takes precedence over their placement. They are operating a plan, not inhabiting a space, as animals would do. As they move on the path, the camera picks up slender wooden fence posts passing by, as though to measure out and calculate their progress toward some impending summation. The "dangerous thread" thus begins with green trees against a white sky, proceeds through a red blouse to a sign and its wording, and winds around a rhythm of walking, fence posts, bouncing shoulders. "You just can't remember the good times, can you?" and then, "What do you want me to remember, the sun, the moon?" Once the thread is wound tightly or skillfully enough, it is impossible any longer to discriminate the fragments of experience that have been bound together arbitrarily by its winding. This thread is also the one that can be pulled out, in such a way as to cause a whole fabric to come undone.

Skin

No Antonioni film is its story. A number of moments stand out as mysteries, or fragments of mysteries. This is a general problem of cinema, to be sure. Because it can show, the moving picture enunciates a "plot" that is always the whole screen, as much as any figure or point. As Christopher comes out of his tower when this film begins, the "plot" is his emergence, his stride, but also the shape of the door through which he walks, the color of the sky, the breeze nipping at the shrubbery, the stasis of the camera; when Cloe argues with him, it is what she says but also every nuance of gesture she emits, the look in her eyes, what we see that she is not seeing, the way her hair flies around, all the climate of the moment.

Writing of the cloistered medieval garden as "earthly paradise," William Howard Adams notes its suitability for "serving as a spiritual refuge and an escape from besetting fears and doubts that assailed both the body and soul. The monastery garden's function as a setting for the *vita contemplativa* must have called for a certain simplicity and decorum for meditation even though visual evidence of this is scant. There is an air of uncertainty, however, in some of the views we glimpse in the background of portraits where the religious gardens often appear a little sad and foreboding, haunted with a kind of pathos. No one smiles. The Madonna always seems preoccupied" (49).

The Madonna here is preoccupied with retreat, to be sure. We may wonder as to her contemplations as she sits back, almost nude in the dappled light, a song irritating the atmosphere: "You've lost . . . your mind." When Christopher asks her, both perturbed and disenchanted, why they have to "pollute the air with all these fucking words," it is impossible to know whether he is referring to this music or reflecting upon something she said to him before the sequence was made visible to us. Behind her is a huge umbrella, but folded up and lashed so that, generically, it is a neutral phallic presence in her background. The *vita contemplativa* available to Cloe is unmistakably polluted by Christopher's presence, and just as unmistakably, he does not recognize this fact. But the garden encloses and dresses both of them: for the man, as a tissue to be penetrated and moved through; for the woman, as an airy and evergreen presence that both evokes and intimates, provides clues.

We tail them in his Maserati as it creeps over the rough ground toward a beach, our camera eye directly behind it and moving forward at the same speed. Christopher is garbed in sleek and pricey armor, midnight blue. The shirt Cloe has on is rust red, made of woven string, light, even supple, like a bloody tissue in a way. Its very open neck and permeable quality leave her torso blushing but visible. She has a siena brown drawstring skirt of mid-calf length, also supple and airy. Lift sandals. As the camera glides behind the car, these two are not visible inside, so that the polished vehicle becomes a creature itself, a kind of intelligent, prowling robot. When Christopher visits Linda, he prowls through her apartment and her life with the same kind of relentless, not-too-eager, curiosity. Perhaps he is armored because the world aggresses upon him, although here near the sea the world seems pacific, placid, passive. He is sheathed, at any rate, and has spent a fortune—whose fortune?—to guard and encapsulate himself. We must imagine that at the beginning of this film, when these two chewed at one another, the man had long been hiding in such protective shielding: waiting for him to denude himself, Cloe has given up patience.

Her clothing, meanwhile, bespeaks the same class privilege: design that focuses on expressing the purities of surface and line rather than on decoratively covering the shame of the body, and that is fabulously costly. Too, her clothing has a leafy, almost living softness, and we may easily believe that when she dresses she is pulling on a skin, an envelope that is cellular, changing, responsive, and open to the air. It is technically possible to see through Cloe's clothing, but one finds greater aesthetic pleasure in regarding it as a cover. What this may cause us to recall is that the body itself is open to the same kind of inspection: we can surmise the organic structure inside—the bones, the flush of circulation—if only we surmount the intoxicating obstacle of the flesh. The flesh is overwhelming.

After they lunch at the restaurant, Cloe and Christopher stand on a little makeshift pier, while he stares off at that second tower. "This mud is disgusting and I get caught in it every time," she whines. He is sanctimonious: she is always looking for purity and ending up in shit. He just loves all this mud. "You love it? Then you stay in it!" says she with finality, turning and striding off toward the camera. The confrontational dialogue, blunt, snappy, without rhythm or decoration, is affronting to the viewer, who can no longer avoid noting the distaste with which these two regard one another (typically in cinema, even loathing is beautiful). She has rinsed her feet in the water and now must stoop to pull on her shoes, so once again we are treated to the sight of her working to cover herself. As she bends over, a foot keeps missing a shoe, and so she must repeat. (Again, we wince.) The camera rests calmly while Cloe works to lay surfaces upon herself, or place agency between herself and the world. We track backward as she walks purposively away, her steps laborious and heavy in the soft ground, and then we follow as she glides past and disappears offscreen next to two bright green dinghies docked in green water that bears the Pre-Raphaelite reflection of myriad green rushes and grasses. The contradiction in Cloe is that the filth of nature appalls her, while at the same time she can separate from nature only through awkwardness and strain. In social situations, she is nude for all intents and purposes; yet the sophistication of her garb forbids anyone from pointing this out.

Origin

Who are these two people and where did they come from? We are to surmise that they were avid lovers, that their affair is on the verge of concluding. "Now that everything's out in the open," Antonioni wrote in his story "The Silence," prefiguring this, "now that they're being honest, they have nothing more to say to each other. A story of husband and wife who have nothing more to say to each other. Just once to shoot not their conversation but their silences, their silent words. Silence is a negative dimension of speech" (*Tiber* 25). Do they own this tower in which they are living, or have they rented or borrowed it? It is cold, defining centuries but not attitudes. Its garden, the chairs, a towel spread upon the chaise—all this has the quality of a human trace, but the tower is less a place than a marker of place. Have they just arrived, or been waiting for ages for their argument—this film—to begin? In their interaction, their sharp voices, we can hear two things: the tedium that characterizes a loss of enchantment, yet also a kind of formality that suggests they have only recently met, or do not recognize one another in an enveloping emotional darkness (that belies the dappled sunlight filling the garden). At the restaurant—no more than a beach shack—Antonioni keeps his camera outside, peering into the plate glass windows on the surface of which the ocean is reflected in dazzling sunshine: as Cloe and Christopher arrive and walk up to their table, they appear to emerge from the waves, children of Poseidon.

Yes, imagine that this man and woman are creatures of the sea, call them sea gods, and that they have emerged to play on dry land for a measure of time. Such a reading is enabled by the startling fact that almost every shot in the first part of the film, and many of the shots in the conclusion, show water bordering the territory in which the action is set: not merely water, but green water. The stilted formality of the conversation now makes a little more sense, seems to have a slightly textual quality. If they are not sea gods, then as people they somehow represent the spirit of sea gods, a fierce independence of both the world and one another, a dignified openness to movement and experience. It is evident with Christopher that he is hungry for sexual tribute, because at one point he strides away from Cloe, barking that she isn't giving him any. With Linda, his sexual hunger and impatience are more than apparent, and yet, for all their rollicking in bed (he has learned that if he joins her there, she will tell him her name), the desire that passes between them seems utterly perfunctory, this rather emphasized by the extraordinary length of the lovemaking sequence. Christopher worships form and formula, knows what he is supposed to want, seeks it to his own peril.

How does Linda come to be riding her horse on that beach? We have no idea. To be living in the second tower? We cannot guess. She had an experience with a saxophonist, now she is alone. Empty of conversation, Linda seems to have neither recollection nor anticipation. After making love to her, Christopher kisses her toes and whispers, "*Ciao,*" as if there were no tomorrow.

Twin Towers

Standing with Cloe at the water's edge, while she complains about the filth of the mud, Christopher gazes off at the second tower. It is something of a ziggurat against the pallid, inviting sky. In the restaurant, he had asked Cloe who the girl with the horse was. The girl who lives in the second tower. A delta with two towers, two identical towers. In each tower, a girl. The man moves from tower to tower. At Linda's, he climbs up the stairs as though heading to be sacrificed. Cloe's tower is inside a cloistered garden, Linda's is at the water, near a small forest.

On the roof of Linda's tower, Christopher slowly makes a circuit, scanning the horizon in either boredom or complacency. He looks without caring that he is looking. (No other tower is to be seen.) Is he, perhaps, thinking of himself as Stephen Dedalus?

> Where was his boyhood now? Where was the soul that had hung back from her destiny, to brood alone upon the shame of her wounds and in her house of squalor and subterfuge to queen it in faded cerements and in wreaths that withered at the touch? Or where was he?
>
> He was alone. He was unheeded, happy and near to the wild heart of life. He was alone and young and wilful and wildhearted, alone amid a waste of wild air and brackish waters and the sea-harvest of shells and tangle and veiled grey sunlight and gayclad lightclad figures of children and girls and voices childish and girlish in the air. (Joyce 145)

And Cloe and Linda are remarkably similar in appearance, so much so that when we see Linda stepping alongside the green stream that borders her tower, then reaching up into a monster prickly pear to withdraw a piece of driftwood, we think, "Is this Cloe again?" Are the "two" girls in the "two" towers in "reality" two sides of one girl? And why must Christopher visit both towers, and possess both women, except that for him, territory exists to be inhabited, structures to be invaded, towers to be climbed, sacrifices to be burnt, temporality to be devoured? In Linda's quarters, he is uncurious. She has a framed work of art that appears to be made of flower petals—fuchsia, golden, orange, scarlet—and the camera zooms in to glance at it and pulls away, as though it constitutes nothing more than a momentary attraction for the hungry eye. Perhaps for Christopher, Linda was an attraction of the moment. He desired her at the restaurant when he saw her on her horse. When she stepped inside to fetch some apples. When Cloe informed him that she was the girl who lives in the second tower.

There are only two desires Christopher expresses patently in the film (his sexual hunger with Linda, whatever it is, is merely toyed with in the extended foreplay sequence, then finally implied as Antonioni fades out when the intercourse begins). First, that he be allowed to progress: his every gesture, every step, every utterance is a way of departing, moving on, setting himself for the next challenge, scouting territories, using people for the energies they can donate to fuel him; secondly, that he reach, specifically, the pinnacle of Linda's tower, gain a point of view. Movement and perspective: the old story. He wants to apprehend and appreciate territory, and to urgently move through it. As for Cloe and Linda, the former seems happy to lie in the sun, the latter to ride her horse by the waves. The two towers constitute polarities between which the man must find his place and his pathway, and neither is a world, or the home of a princess, important to him as such. He is only "a mature man, a man who no longer has the patience and unconsciousness that love requires, who no longer has the language of love" (Antonioni, *Tiber* 149).

II

So much can happen to steal away language. Language, not vocabulary. Words and phrases can become outdated, as advertising and its principal clients, the young, contract and chisel them. The press of modernity can accelerate our jitteriness, confound our trajectories, so that we cannot find one another, so that one's mouth may no longer be oriented toward another's ear: the urban babel from a million lips. Desire can be stunned and then eroded, frayed, diminished or dissolved; or else can manifest itself without warning, so that one is stupefied, tongue-tied, by its appearance. There is a magnificent moment in Doug Liman's *The Bourne Identity* (2002), for example, as Jason Bourne (Matt Damon) and his new friend Marie Kreutzer (Franka Potente), racing through Europe to save their lives, work quietly in the bathroom of a cheap hotel to change her look. He dyes her red hair black, then uses a pair of shears delicately to make a whole new cut, as, unsure who this man is (with whose fate she has agreed to tie hers) and why he is in flight for his life, she quietly, patiently yields. It is a tiny bathroom. Without warning, as they gain footing there, they are very close, touching, noticing that they are touching. In a flash their mouths are together, and then she is lifting away his olive green tank top. Her eyes look into him, and his give her permission: two fates in one shot, two sources of expression localized in the organs of the head, "witness enough to our allegiance to the detached head as a symbol of what we think we are and what we're up to" (Davenport, *Objects* 50). To have forgotten the language of love is perhaps to float above such situations, to be distant from the body of the other, or from embodiment altogether.

Evidently Christopher has withdrawn from the situation of love, the situation in which he could see Cloe truly and plainly for the reality of her experience. Noting his extreme purposiveness, that in every situation he possesses, expresses, and strives to fulfill motive, and the superficiality of his responsiveness, one might suddenly see how businesslike Christopher is, then perhaps calculate the importance of his driving a Maserati, of the fact that every statement Cloe makes to him is weighed, assayed, evaluated according to a schema we do not see. We are given virtually no information about Christopher. A knot of engagements and manipulations is at once clearly behind and around him and also elided from our view. Where Jason Bourne, who in Marie's view has committed acts of stunning violence, takes shears upon her with a rigorous concentration and a smooth gentleness, even art, Christopher never shows this capacity for tender concern. There is something sad about him, so young and yet pushed away from love speech.

III

Each gesture is an event—one might even say, a drama—in itself. The stage on which this drama takes place is the World Theater which opens up toward heaven.

—Walter Benjamin, "Franz Kafka"

Sex

Kafka, reports Benjamin in a lengthy and convoluted paean, writes on K.'s sex: "K. constantly had the feeling that he was losing his way or that he had wandered farther than anyone had ever wandered before, to a place where even the air had nothing in common with his native air, where all this strangeness might choke one, *yet a place so insanely enchanting that one could not help but go on and lose oneself even further*" (115, emphasis mine).

One could not help but go on. This is the voyage into a passage where the boundaries between interiority and exteriority are confounded, where the surfaces against which one must move are (it seems) endlessly and wonderfully interconversant with the expanding and contracting visceral secret. Every great text addresses this conversation, the slipperiness of its syntax and the arcane purity of its vocabulary. Pleasure is the regulating principle, which is to say that endlessness and saturation, permeability and dissatisfaction dominate: dissatisfaction which presses into a blossom of possibility.

For hundreds of years, moral entrepreneurs have invoked the same deliriously endless, but apparently also pernicious, journey of possibility and power in writing about masturbation. "No other antisocial act, not even other antisocial sexual acts that captured the attention of doctors and moralists, occasioned the chorus of revulsion that met any mention of masturbation," writes Thomas Laqueur of these notably canting critiques, "The act was outside the pale of not just this or that but any possible moral order" (222). Samuel Auguste David Tissot, for example, urged just after the first decade of the eighteenth century that the act "secretly undermines without those who are its victims thinking of its malignancy" and further opined upon the wily captivations of self-love that, "Nothing can be more ensnaring" (qtd. in Laqueur 223–4). Indeed it could be said, as regards the unpopulated spaces in which typically it was practised and their association with a propertied class, that "the battle against masturbation was one of the main engagements in the long war fought to ensure the right kind and just measure of bourgeois privacy" (226).

Christopher comes peeping at Linda's tower, the "second" tower, where after a walk by the river she finds him. Linda walks Christopher up a long flight of stone steps to her door—which waits at a distinct height from which the estuary is visible, and also the adjacent forest, a stand of trees noteworthy in its measured greenness—then teases him inside her parlor, a rectangle decorated with pictures, and leads him up to her roof; but quickly announces that she is cold and races downstairs again only to mount a second, interior staircase—all carpentered of finely tailored cedar—to her bedroom: a vortical move—up a staircase into the ziggurat, then, up a second staircase to a roof and a vista, down a staircase toward a warmth, up a staircase into a privacy, all in a turning urgency that opens a tract. This is not a voyage to a terminus, this is a voyage that continues. "I've always wondered," wrote Antonioni, "whether it's always right to provide an ending for stories" (188). Linda is on the bed, kicking off her designer jeans. She is thinking of his presence and his absence: that he is above her head, yet also that he is not here with her.

In a long sequence now, she carefully masturbates . . . while we, behind our camera down on the coverlet, watch with surgical care: the groping, the twisting, the arching, the moaning, the discovery, the rediscovery, standing up, looking down at us with eyes wet and out of focus, fingers hungry, hunger etching itself upon the pink plate of the flesh.

Is this preparation for him? Or rejection? Or has he invoked a sexuality that is entirely independent, encouraged a language that is complex and pure even if isolated? That her finger, probing arrhythmically, desperately, seems insufficient does not mark her act as incomplete or unsatisfying but instead signals hope and sureness. Antonioni does not move away from her gestures, as though he is invading a privacy (a privacy: the idea of masturbation; or this actress's knowledge of masturbation, since now before the lens it is an act she is committing upon herself), but instead lingers to watch, as though this act is no prelude but a fulfillment of need at a real moment, and thus a statement true and simple. ("There are various ways of getting certain expressions from actors, and it is of no interest to know whether or not there is a corresponding mood behind these expressions," Antonioni told Billard [49].) Two of the secrets Linda knows, Montaigne taught: that "from the regular routine treachery of men nowadays there necessarily results what experience already shows us: to escape us, women turn in on themselves and have recourse to themselves or to other women"; and that "where love is concerned—a subject which is mainly connected with sight and touch—you can achieve something without the witty graces but nothing without the bodily ones" (255; 256). She is caught up, at any rate, in a stunning labyrinth of secrecy, whose walls folding in upon themselves never cease to hide or beckon.

Welled within herself, Linda traces and invokes a long history of private experience as it blossoms into a twenty-first century efflorescence that includes esoterica, cell phones, muttering, phantasmal meditation—all of which are on view in this film. In the seventeenth century, writes Laqueur, private experience was allied with the quintessence of social value: "Some private vices were said to translate to public goods; this was the basis of one of the earliest and greatest defenses of the marketplace. Some private reading was a road to self-knowledge and also to the knowledge of others. . . . This was the world that witnessed the creation and burgeoning of the modern autobiography. The realm of the private was the basis for civil society in which individual interests negotiated and contained each other. In other words, privacy and secrecy also had all sorts of positive associations as sites of truth and as foundations of a real self" (226).

However, and at the same time, "It was in contrast to this affirmation that *the* private vice assumed such importance. It was the negative of all this, the paradigmatic emblem of solipsistic privacy or secrecy of the wrong sort. Masturbation represented socially inappropriate or uncontrolled privacy" (226). Nowadays, masturbation in one form or another is virtually everywhere: the daydreamer driving down the road, the student doodling or texting in the classroom. In his celebration of Bradbury's futuristic *Fahrenheit 451,* François Truffaut conceived a monorail on which commuters sat silently, dreamily fondling themselves after their day at work.

Christopher enters. "What," asks he, "would happen if I joined you there?" And she replies, "I would tell you my name." He has shown no interest at all in knowing her name; to us, her name, like Cloe's, is the least interesting thing about her.

They make love, it need hardly be said, perfunctorily, quite as perfunctorily as I am telling you this, and also like specimens under observation, whose turning and self-consciousness, whose calculations as to the placement of the hand, are as much for the sake of normal appearances as pleasure. Because the perfunctory quality of their action is its raison d'être and its wholeness at this moment, it seems evident that it should happen. And so it does—rather like an exercise at the barre. Afterwords, the male says thank you, sweetly enough yet without sincerity, and kisses the female's foot (as though she is Sheherezade), backs off, vanishes. It has been, all in all, a remarkable enough sequence. Christopher deposits no trace, and brings no spirit of presence. The man has lost his interest in the woman, but is with her because some arcane formula requires it. Later, on the beach, running some horses, Cloe will use her cell phone to contact him in Paris. His disembodied voice at the other end of the line has more passion and vibration than his heated body with Linda on that bed. Women are here. Men are there.

Body

The view of the surrounding countryside from the top of Linda's tower: a green woods, a stretch of water, a far shore, a slow-gurgling river, as we move slowly across and around, never stretching our muscles, the waters blue or blue-green, the shores sandy, the sky open—quite as though feeling a body, the camera's own body and thus our body, too, every orifice and surface, feeling for possession and without hope—long entrancing desperate distances, regularities and unmatched vistas, brave but meaningless transitions. Of bodily consciousness and bodily vision, Vivian Sobchack reminds us that "there seems to be an inverse ratio between *seeing* our bodies and *feeling* them" and that "our contemporary image culture (as well as our contemporary theory) has increasingly reified our bodies as manageable matter. We have become fixated on the appearance and objectivity of the visible—and, as a consequence, both images and bodies have lost their other dimensions and values" (179; 181). Further, because we work to master sight and the seen world, and ourselves as visions: "Visual self-possession allows us objective knowledge of ourselves as visible bodies, but we are significantly revealed as distant not only from others but also from our own consciousness and our own substantiality" (188). How strange in the face of this to acknowledge that as Christopher gazes at the littoral he seems already to disappear, to be replaced by our own eager participation; but also that we in our turn vanish in the face of the forest, the water, the far shore, having a distinct sense of presence but also no image of ourselves gazing. We know with a certainty that this, too, is an exquisite masturbation, and that Linda, as she works upon herself, is on the same voyage in and through, without self-regard. Her secret, like ours, is not a fascination with the image of the self but an eclipsing of that image, a meeting of and joining with the world by way of one's own interior—say, a connecting with the world that one has incorporated.

It is this world within the self that Linda is exploring when Christopher is lying with her. So fascinated, so disoriented is she by its turns and vistas that his parting is an utter nonevent.

The body is, of course, an adventure. When in one of his stories a Kafka character says, "I can hardly understand . . . how a young man can decide to ride over to the next village without being afraid that, quite apart from accidents, even the span of a normal life that passes happily may be totally insufficient for such a ride" (qtd. in Benjamin, "Kafka" 135), he points to the great prolixity of internal experience, to the fact of continuing and expansive sensation and reflection. Our reception of the countless details of consciousness—all embodiment—is often accomplished by a kind of summing up or reduction, so that we lose sight of the full shape of feeling and being in place. To say that Christopher interests Linda, then, is merely to adduce his postures and pretenses as ways of sharing her space, to acknowledge that he presents himself as something of an obstruction or outcropping in a territory over which she is already ruler. With Cloe it would have been the same. Without family, and inhabiting one of the two towers more or less independently, each woman is capable of meticulous attention to her living in a space to which her embodiment could precisely and deliciously, if also blindly, conform.

Patrice Petro describes a feature of something earlier and quite different, women's experience in Weimar culture: "the sensory deprivation of household labor, where women were called on to manage an ever more precarious family existence" (61). This condition might, she suspects, have led to women's perceptual acuity and delight in watching cinema. For Weimar women, at any rate, a "kind of heightened sensory experience" could have "simultaneously responded to and compensated for women's experiences of everyday life" (62). Of Cloe and Linda's everyday life we learn almost nothing in this film—although from their forthright disinhibition it does seem evident that they inhabit a world less repressed and far less strictured than would have faced Weimar women. Yet they would also have been inheritors of the kind of "heightened sensory experience" that Petro finds in Weimar culture, with the result that rather than "compensating" for perceptual "deprivation," their detailed notice of themselves, coupled with their appreciation for the surround, may have swelled and intensified as a kind of efflorescence, this to the extent that the body became a subtle and overflowing reservoir of intelligence and sensation. To regard this liberal condition as "solipsistic" has its own political thrust, since each woman has opened for herself the option of a full and sweeping regard of the landscape through which the voyage of the self is undertaken. The body is always its world. Anke Gleber observes that "women's specific use of space has historically been marked by anxieties and limitations that make them go about their daily matters in a more cautious fashion than men, assuming fewer, less expansive spaces to be open to their gaze and presence at any time. Restricted to the home, limited to functional forays into the public, forced to forgo the lure of aimless strolling without a specific purpose or destination, women are unable to indulge their full fascination" (73). This view of the obstruction that has confronted women is thus outdated, even negated, by Cloe and Linda, at least to the extent that they have come to know and feel themselves independently of male prerogatives. The body is the space that substantiates it, and is thus social as much as personal. As she masturbates with Christopher waiting in her wake, Linda owns herself: herself, which is to say, both her figure and her perspective.

Name

When they are sitting in the beach restaurant and the horse rider comes in to beg some apples for her mount, Cloe tells the curious Christopher who she is. "That," says she—and I quote once again, and exactly, what some observers have deemed her *awkward* English—"is the girl who is the girl who lives in the second tower." What a curious way to name someone!

In Cloe's view, Linda is not just the girl who lives in the second tower. She is the girl *who is that girl*. In short, Linda is playing a role. She is staged—and thus a surface. We have license to wonder whether, if Cloe is real, Linda is real in the same way. Or whether Linda exists as a purely imaginative figuration embedded in a narrative construct of Cloe's making. The sequence in the second tower could then become a daydream of Christopher's, *as imagined by* Cloe. The final sequence on the beach, when Cloe and Linda are in one another's "presence," represents a kind of opening of consciousness, or transformation, by means of which Cloe can begin to imagine Linda—that is, someone like Linda—more fully for herself.

Cloe makes an extraordinary leap, then, at the last moments of this last of Antonioni's films. She abandons the real settings in which she lives her life, puts aside her desires or feelings in relation to Christopher, and works to adopt not this man who has invaded her life but the essence of his imagination, as she has imagined it. To be with him—I do not say to love him—she moves beyond him in order to accept as her own not a view of him but a view of his views. The two women on the beach do not touch. Discussing our perception of reality, William James highlights the importance of the tangible: "It is as tangibles . . . that things concern us most; and the other senses, so far as their practical use goes, do but warn us of what tangible things to expect. They are but organs of anticipatory touch" (II: 306). The two women cannot touch, because one of them is an invention, a wraith, a spirit. A kind of invisible proscenium hangs over and between them, in this brilliant sunshine, as the waters lap in.

Shadows

But to return to that beach, one more time:

There is a windy field under purple clouds. Chestnut brown horses are running together, as Cloe takes a cell call in her parked car. It is a man, presumably Christopher, calling from Paris, where he is watching the snow fall. "I'm at the beach," says she, "The horses have run away again. I have to get them back to the house." You want me to be there with you, says he with irritation, and she strides off toward the water, the pale blue water beyond the dry yellow field. He is nowhere to be seen. The horses run past behind her, thrilled in this beautiful place. "It's so damned white here," he moans, "The snow should be calming me down, it's just making me anxious." But everything makes Christopher anxious in one way or another. "Then," says Cloe, with regret or with distaste, "it will be an ideal companion for you today." She turns to the horses offscreen and gives them a good sound whistle: "*Andiamo!*"

But the horses don't want to come. So she heads off toward the windy sands. And now we see Linda arrive in her pickup. She gets out, smiling to herself. A long purple coat, the color of mulberries. The sun streaming through her auburn hair. Birds sing loudly as she walks. The surf sound, the wind. She is on the strand, green waters lapping in, the sun lambent. She has the coat off and is swirling it like a banner. She trails it on the moist sand at water's edge, picks up a piece of driftwood and draws snaky lines. She strips off her clothing: another masturbatory frenzy? Nude, waving the stick, she dances on the sand, steps into the water, backs away until she is lying in the sunlight, under an opened blue beach umbrella. "She seemed like one whom magic had changed into the likeness of a strange and beautiful seabird," as Joyce writes of another such wraith (145). We hover in the air, gazing down at her, at the umbrella, at the sand, her shadow, her coat, her outstretched arms, her lips spread but not smiling, the dense hair in her crotch, her outstretched leg. She breathes in and out, her breasts perfectly round. The water laps in, the far surf, the wind blowing. A shot from the sand, looking out at the water and the promontories of land: Cloe enters, looks around, holds up her hands to heaven.

Is Cloe on the same beach?

(Driving to the beach restaurant, Christopher and Cloe stopped briefly at a quarry. Splashing water sound, birds chirping, a high-pitched soprano incantation. The water jade green, the chiseled rocks an etching by Piranesi. And next to the waterfall in the center of the picture, as the camera zooms in, a pair of girls with long hair, looking our way, their nude bodies glowing with an apricot radiance. The camera is at ground level, gazing up at Cloe and Christopher looking off at these sirens. "How come we've never been here before?" he asks, sincerely. "We haven't been paying much attention," says she. But who are these girls, real and unreal? And why do our observers not seem to see them?)

Cloe throws her arms out, stretches her head back, turns her arms so that her hands dangle like wing tips. Stripped, in close-up, she dances while a non-diegetic female voice sings of "flowing water . . ." Linda's dance was improvised, quasi-sexual, but Cloe's is more formal, postured, sculptural. She has a large tattoo on her flank—a serpent? A Chinese calligraph? Into the water she goes, throwing her arms above her head, arching her back, and leaning all the way backward with her legs stretched apart so that her face is pointed directly up at the sky. She pirouettes a few times and then, seeing something on the beach, stops and walks out of the water. "On and on and on . . ." moans the singing voice. Cloe has discovered Linda. Or "Linda." Linda sleeps. From above we see Cloe's shadow approach the body, then Cloe herself, and the two women are enclosed in the frame, one still sleeping, one watching.

Although this is the point where the film ends, the point, indeed, where Antonioni's filmmaking ends, it is to be presumed that in some manner the two women will meet. Something equivalent to a "meeting" will take place, if Linda is as real to Cloe as Cloe is to Christopher and to us. Antonioni's touch is to close the film while there is distance between the two nude bodies in the neutral, primordial space of the beach. Although they share the diegetic and aesthetic frame, and share some strange wild territory, they do not—in our sight—occupy the same space. Cloe has not only conceived Linda as a phantom *for Christopher,* but has conceived her *in Christopher's absence.* Linda is what Cloe wants to meet at the beach—her muse—and so she has dutifully arrived.

Linda turns her head, sits up. A smile crosses her face. The two shadows become one.

• • •

Il filo pericoloso delle cose (2004), photographed by Marco Pontecorvo in the 1.85: 1 format; 30 m. Released in the United States as *The Dangerous Thread of Things,* April 8, 2005.

The Mystery of Oberwald

He thinks so much of the Queen.

—Michael Fagan's mother

PROLOGUE

At around six o'clock in the morning of Friday, July 9, 1982, Elizabeth Windsor, the present Queen of England, awoke to find Mr. Michael Fagan sitting comfortably at the end of her bed. This unemployed and wounded intruder, a visitor, as it happens, from Ireland, who had intended to kill himself with the Queen at his side but who came to the conclusion when actually confronted with her that "it wasn't a nice thing to do," conversed calmly with Her Majesty about family life, noting that each of them had four children, until—rather belatedly, and more than twelve minutes after she asked for them—authorities arrived (Rogal and Henkoff). Following this episode, security around the royal bedroom was enhanced, Elizabeth II went on with her monarchy at least apparently unfazed, and her "guest" was given his freedom, since, actually, by the laws of England, he had committed no criminal offence.

How a complete stranger was able to gain such easy access to Buckingham Palace grounds; how he found it possible to make his way inside the palace at all; how, indeed, he could have brought himself to a position from which one could directly observe the Queen asleep or could approach her closely enough to engage in polite bedside conversation (not to say more unrestrained action) are all questions that remain essentially unexplained, except to say that the protective force employed by the monarch herself, or provided by the government of

Great Britain on her behalf, was either scathingly insufficient or else inexpert at guarding, or both. As a symbol, after all, the Queen's essential quality is inaccessibility: that she stands (and even reposes) at a conceptual height considerably distanced from her people and the quotidian affairs of state and commerce she tranquilly oversees. She is aloof, she is invisible. If in some respects a person just like all other persons, she is yet at the same time subject to continuing treatments accorded no one else in the nation. She contains and represents all power—or at least such considerable power that her potency is beyond question—and is surrounded, or taken to be surrounded, by minions sincerely and wholeheartedly devoted to her care and to the furtherance of her official ambitions and interests. In November 2007, indeed, in the little city of Lincoln (to which the Queen had once paid a visit), a former member of the Grenadier Guards (bodyguards of the Queen), now employed in city government and giving a little talk, raised his voice in my presence each time Her Majesty's name was mentioned, and uttered the little prayer, "May God give her long life and guidance to stay on the throne forever!"

The Queen, further, tends not to take action herself, but instead commands a retinue of workers who act for her—a man, for instance, who before every formal banquet at Windsor Castle, and wearing special slippers, walks down the center of the great dining table to polish it like Aladdin's lamp. In the case of Michael Fagan, she therefore took no steps herself to evict him, but casually picked up the phone and rang—to no avail, as it turns out—for help. Actions are typically taken for the Queen, in the Queen's name, by those who, exactly by virtue of their endeavor, stipulate openly that they do not possess the power that substantiates what they do, a power that resides wholly with the woman to whose bedchamber one simply does not—we imagine—know the path.

Also:

Two impressions are successfully fostered by a massive publicity front marshaled for the Queen. First, that she spearheads a singular, coherent, smoothly functioning, morally benevolent, and rational organization, "the monarchy," and is bolstered in her every gesture by supporters whose loyalty is perpetually guaranteed. Secondly, that she is at heart a person no different than all others, thus susceptible to perfectly human petty jealousies and affectations, humors and yearnings, this conventionality properly leading the Beatles to chant, "Her Majesty's a pretty nice girl" and the populace at large to take it in stride when the lady goes riding, walks her corgis, chats in reception lines about world events, or blushingly reaches out to touch famous entertainers when they come nearby (Elton John was pressed to jitterbug with her once, he announced to James Lipton on "Inside the Actors Studio" ["Sir Elton John"]). It was the Queen's "humanity" that caused Londoners to so sadly disapprove when she failed to "properly" mourn the death of her daughter-in-law in 1997 (all this tidily, if imaginatively, described in Stephen Frears's *The Queen* [2006]). And it is the coherence of the monarchy that provides reason for seeing in the royal household a single unbroken public relations façade, or for suspecting that there are no significant fault lines inside the palace itself. When the Queen makes an utterance, it is as though all of her aides on every level line up and chant, "So say we all."

The Queen is an innocent, at any rate. We do not imagine her ever to have been directly responsible for death: we do not watch her paraded in the streets and remark that (between her coronation and the abolition of capital punishment in Britain in 1973) she assented to executions, that deaths were systematically produced in response to some articulation of her will. No genteel official, we imagine, ever murmured, "In the name of the Queen I take your life" before throwing a trap door. She is not a killer. She is "mum."

So it is that we do not trouble to consider whether any sane person might seriously think to kill her or give her discomfort (Mr. Michael Fagan could not possibly have intended any harm to the Queen's person), or that any palace faction might conspire and collaborate to wrest power from her hands. We do not conceive of liveried servants whispering behind the Queen's back (even though, of course, sometimes, in order to do their business, it might reasonably fall upon them to do so), or ladies-in-waiting repeating every word that they hear in the royal bedchamber to malevolent outsiders bent on humiliating the regime. At worst, we can see how it is sometimes necessary in palace life that servants be sworn to secrecy in order that after retiring from their positions they do not publicize stories that might have the technical effect of embarrassing or compromising the seamless face of monarchical power. But plotting against the person of royalty is not a modern gesture. It belongs to the era of high Romanticism, in which passions are taken seriously and power is seen as a characteristic of personality. Aiming one's weapon at the throne is the stuff of *The Man in the Iron Mask*.

Nor, as outsiders to royal life, do we tend to imagine—of the Queen of England or any other queen—what with anyone else would seem so possible, that she might take a visitor into her privacy for her own entertainment and behind the eyes of her watchful retinue. As to emotions, queens must every day make judgments of a serious kind regarding national interest—indeed international interest—and so they are not, we surmise, subject to unpredictable flights of fancy or irrationality, not abject daydreamers. The misbehaving, malevolent, even murderous queen may swiftly spring to our imagination *fictionally,* but as to reality, reality is the home of queens who are sober, wise, protected, protective, and whole; or else dithering and self-absorbed; but in any event, neither monstrous nor keepers of monstrosity.

Therefore, for someone unaccustomed, *being with* the Queen in everyday private space would be a thoroughly transforming experience.

WITH THUNDER

She can't count on anything, not even accident. For there are lives without accident.

—Balzac

Around ten months before the Fagan incident, Antonioni premiered *The Mystery of Oberwald.* "It's a movie," wrote Vincent Canby, "that probably wouldn't last five minutes in front of an audience in control of its wits." Here, as at Buckingham Palace, a royal bedchamber is penetrated, but within a notably different context and with notably different results. The interloper gains a wholly different kind of "freedom," from a queen who is anything but calm in the face of his appearance. The film has been called "dazzling" and "important" (unlabeled clipping), "experimental" and "sober" (Griffiths). It is surely one of the filmmaker's most loquacious and romantic works, disarmingly loquacious, indeed, given the express tendency of Antonioni's characters to be introspective and taciturn (as he himself frequently was—but occasionally was not!). "I think people talk too much," he told an interviewer in 1969, "that's the truth of the matter. I do. I don't believe in words. People use too many words and usually wrongly. I am sure that in the distant future people will talk much less and in a more essential way" (Samuels 86). The film is virtually operatic in its use of setting, its development of characterization, and its extraordinary—and extraordinarily authentic—opulence. It is a film that works its way past our defenses, in a typically Antonionian modesty but also through an explicit seduction, whereby the skin of our divorce from nature is struck repetitively, like that of a drum.

The sense of an atmosphere full of charge is presented immediately, with a tense scene that takes place as a thunderstorm looms. We are in the precincts of Oberwald, one of a group of royal castle retreats high in the Tyrol, late in the nineteenth century, at night, and it is spring. Night in springtime—that extraordinarily rich and mysterious green destination, as once again the world comes to life. Soldiers are frantically making their way down the slopes of the forest, and a desperate fugitive (Franco Branciaroli) is running from them to save his life. In one remarkable shot, he steps across a patch of ground next to a little stream, where the earth is blanketed by moon-silver snails, curling out of their shells and shown in closeup as his foot tramps down upon them. We move swiftly, even brutally, to the interior of the castle.

As the wind howls without, and dark branches shudder in the darkness, imperious, ambitious Edith de Berg (Elisabetta Pozzi) and taciturn, observant Felix Willenstein (Luigi Diberti), the Queen's lady-in-waiting and equerry—and a pair of former lovers—are scurrying around the royal chambers in vituperative argument. As the storm brews, rain washes in, and fires are to be lit in the grates. The windows may not be closed. The Queen (Monica Vitti) loves storms, loves fires burning, loves the touch of the wind, and tonight is her special night, the anniversary of the death by murder of her young husband the King, whose mother the Archduchess strives to control the country from behind the throne. ("That," says the Queen in a later scene, referring to this kind of clandestine control, "is politics.") The Queen will never have her windows shut, to block out the glory of the storm. In spirit at least, she is youthful and rebellious, loved—or so she presumes—by her people just as much as she is feared by her court, because she has a penchant for overturning conventions. Although the Queen loathes the Archduchess (who never, even for an instant, appears in the film), she must tolerate Edith de Berg, who is the old lady's confidante, an asp who betrays the Queen's every breath to this invisible and cupidinous power. Also under the Archduchess's finger is the unctuous Count Foehn (Paolo Bonacelli), chief of police and a toady of the first order.

It becomes apparent subtly and disturbingly that the Queen has long, and silently, been in mourning. More, that upon the King's sudden death, she "buried herself," as she puts it, in her castles. She has been too long absent from court life, thinks the Archduchess, and too self-indulgently; the Queen's retreat to Oberwald and Krantz, one after another—and in random order, so that no one will ever know exactly where she is—has given Edith de Berg's patroness the space she has needed for insinuating herself into the real workings of court power. The Queen is still hiding behind her veil, still feeling pangs of love for the man who was torn from her so long ago and after so fleeting a union: he was crowned, and within hours he had been slain. Worse, as she later confesses, they had raised her to be a queen, forbidding even that she should learn how to spell, and then she met Frédéric, and everything changed.

Having dismissed Edith and Willenstein and settled at table for a private and heartfelt anniversary dinner with the ghost of this lost husband, the Queen is suddenly startled, gazing up to his full-length portrait, to see nothing less than the body of her husband tumble forward from behind the canvas and collapse on the floor . . .

The intruder, wounded, has been hiding and has fainted, but he bears so remarkable a likeness to the dead king that the two men might indeed be one. The picture has come alive! Death has been undone by love (the preeminent tenet of Romanticism)! The spirit of the King has been waiting silently upon this canvas for this singular moment in which to liberate himself, still almost a boy. The Queen rouses the young man, brings him to table, bandages his leg, attempts a conversation, but, terrified or delirious, he will not say a word. It is as though he has not fully been born from the paint in which he was frozen, or as though he knows no language. (Perhaps when he was raised no one would teach him to speak.) She tells him that she knows he is there to kill her, and that if he has not succeeded at his task within three days, she will kill him. It is apparent that he intrigues, even entices, her. He has the darkest curls, and stands with the greatest poise (as though his blood is royal). She appoints him to replace the detested Edith as her personal reader, and sends him off with her mute servant Tony to be shown his bed. The next morning he is considerably relieved, and tells her the story of his life, how he lived in the mountains, came down to the city which was full of corruption, and fell in with people who convinced him to kill the Queen; yet it is perfectly clear he has at least changed his mind, and has no spirit of violence left in him for this engaging, even affectionate woman.

This is a queen who has long lost love, and forbidden herself to imagine it. And this is a man who has only dreamed of queens, adorned them in his wildest imagination, and withheld himself upon a mountain from the active pleasures of knowing life down below.

To say more: it is evident that when he looks into her face and admits he was instructed "to kill the Queen," this woman is very far from "the Queen" he had in mind. "The Queen" can be only a disembodied form, an aegis. This woman is too alive, too present, too sociable, too unable to tear her eyes away from his face to be "the Queen" who must die. But attraction goes both ways.

Sebastian—this is his name—has his own ideas and his own life, he assures her, and the idea that he is an assassin is just her myth: he supposes that perhaps she "died" when her husband was murdered and now wishes to "die" again. He is a poet, and she recognizes him as the author of a lengthy antimonarchical diatribe that was circulated at the court—a piece of work she rather admired for its forthrightness and beauty—admired, indeed, and memorized. As the hours pass, the two fall increasingly under one another's spell, and soon become lovers, the Queen possibly accepting Sebastian as a reincarnation of her husband and even admitting to him, in a tryst in the fields outside the castle—the limey green fields in which the wind blows the high grass—that he has fulfilled his command and "killed the Queen." He has "killed her too much," indeed. The "Queen," in short, a figurehead and tool of the court bureaucracy, has evaporated—this is *her* talking—so that the person who had embodied her might emerge. (An intriguing and relatively modern proposition: royalty as occupation.) The Queen admits that she has an anarchic spirit, the spirit of youth that always revolts against the present. This is a delicious moment: it is as though two actors who have committed to playing complementary roles go into a particularly intensive rehearsal with one another and immediately discover that the roles are, in truth, nothing, have fallen away; that it is as persons, not *figurae,* that they respond to one another, and that they are in love. And, of course, all love is this way, in the sense that the framework through which we experience an encounter suddenly melts away, leaving something purer and more original in its place: the phantom beings we are, before and beyond the roles we play.

With the malignant Foehn ignorant of his presence at the Queen's side, Sebastian plans with her that she will emerge from her cloister, take power in the court, dismiss Foehn, reduce the Archduchess, and finally be reunited with him. But the haughty Edith signals Foehn that the fugitive is hiding inside the castle—a threat to the court's ability to control and manipulate the Queen—and Foehn seduces Sebastian into a conversation in which he makes it plain that he plans to arrest and kill him. Sebastian confronts the Queen, who has only begun to understand that a trap is closing around her, and then secretly ingests poison that she has been keeping expressly for herself. Now she taunts and insults him in his dying moments, to the point where his fury is released and he shoots her in the heart. Dying, she draws him close and confesses her love for him, admitting she had to put on an act in order to bring him to the point where he could finish her. In a quiet passageway inside the castle the two lovers die together, their *Liebestod* witnessed by a platoon of armed soldiers as, silently, the film ends.

IN SPRINGTIME

Someone once said that words, more than anything else, serve to hide our thoughts.
—Antonioni

"Well, you know, it's not one of my films," Antonioni told Seymour Chatman, "I just directed it. And I tried to do my best" ("Interview" 159). Vitti had proposed that they do Cocteau's *La voix humaine* together but, Rossellini having done a version with Anna Magnani, Antonioni felt it "might seem like a kind of confrontation," and so, since they "had Cocteau in hand," they went for *L'Aigle à deux têtes,* which would be "easier to do" (159). Because the film was to be produced for RAI, the Italian national television network, an opportunity arose to make use of electronic technology for the shooting and editing. Antonioni saw this as particularly exciting, not only because one could see the rehearsal in a television monitor and make changes spontaneously but also, and principally, because the television camera could effectuate an easy and felicitous modulation of color in the middle of a shot, or at any time, and with address to any object in the frame more or less independently. "[Color] can change everything for you," he told Bert Cardullo, "even the faces of the actors. The subtle use of different shades of light and dark is possible, but it's a complicated technical process on TV. What is fascinating about it is that you can make corrections afterwards, even violent ones" ("Interview" 153). And the television cameras, he found, "offer a very free working method," a chance to bring to the screen a sense of "the reality that counts. My reality" (Bachmann, "Interview" 125). The colors obtained in television could be saturated in a different way than was possible with film, and they could fluctuate without it being necessary to strike and reset the lighting. With every scene of *The Mystery of Oberwald,* then, the images could be "more abstract" (Chatman, "Interview" 159). Color modulation might be used for telling a story over and above the narration being recounted in accord with the script, notwithstanding that the technology had hardly been perfected and that transferring the video images to film would require that Antonioni travel to California to supervise the kinescoping (Cardullo, "Interview" 153). The videotape had a mere 625 lines of information, rather than the 1025 lines available soon after, so the images, projected in VHS or DVD format today, seem somewhat less striking than intended (Tomasulo 167).

Antonioni's approach to the Cocteau story was simple enough:

> It's a kind of melodrama, a very strong drama between a queen and an anarchist. It also contains some ideological reference to our contemporary scene in Italy: this anarchist could be compared to a terrorist, though the connection is rather slender. But I found it diverting to tell a kind of story which is so different from my own stories. I have never shot very dramatic scenes, but in this film I had to do so. That didn't frighten me because in this strong scene the emotions are very precise. They are not full of nuance or withheld; they are not ambiguous. (Chatman, "Interview" 159)

The "emotions are very precise" most notably in the love scene, a ramble through the hilly woods outside the castle in which the Queen and Sebastian reveal their true selves to one another. (I mention *true selves* without the ironic scare quotes so frequently employed in contemporary evaluative thought. This film is clearly nothing if not a romance, and in thinking about a romance to put oneself off from the presumptions and perfumes of the form is disingenuous.) The scene gives a distinct opportunity for seeing how color effects add a layer of information that transforms the drama.

We look down on the pair as they stand among tall grasses studded with wildflowers, and he tells her that he doesn't have a mother anymore. He had hidden some papers with a peasant woman who is his godmother, and he had to go and burn them. The tall grasses wave hither and yon as he explains. That the surround is burgeoning with the early effects of spring reflects upon him, too, because he seems just born, a tender shoot, with an intelligence both articulate and stuttering; the Queen is not in the springtime of her life, and this fact is marked all the more strongly because Sebastian is surrounded by soft green leaves the color of a monarch butterfly's chrysalis. Now Antonioni cuts to a medium close shot of the heavy green branches of a rich fruit tree, with bulbous pale yellow blossoms all over it. The camera pans and we discover our two figures approaching, the Queen asking whether, earlier, when she had hidden him in a chamber off the library and entertained Count Foehn, he had been able to see the Count's face. "Yes," says he, lifting a branch away from his own face as he walks, while she waits next to the trunk of the tree. She says she is grateful to him for keeping silent and he says he used all his strength to resist coming out and strangling the man (interesting that with pompous types like Foehn the impulse is, precisely, strangulation). To illustrate, he seizes a dry branch and snaps it viciously in two. We look down onto Sebastian through the branches, with some of the leaves, jagged like sawblades, prominent in the frame. She says that Foehn would hardly have been surprised to know about the two of them, that for Foehn, "The Queen considers herself a poem and him a poet." The camera is zooming into her face framed against the old trunk, with blossoms and leaves all around. She fingers one of the blossoms in her hand. What was he planning to do after dispensing with his documents? "To kill the Queen," says he in a perfectly honest voice, but also in a peculiar way that permits the words to float away from him with a meaning that is entirely their own. There is no hint of violence in him. The sun is brilliant on the grass, and he is looking straight into her eyes. She smiles now, wipes the tawny blossom against her lips, and steps away from the tree trunk; a floor of blue, pink, and magenta blossoms appears amid the greenery behind her. She is wearing a dress of loden green satin, trimmed with violet lace. She turns to gaze at him from among the heavy branches. "The newspapers would have said, 'The Queen falls victim to a savage attempt on her life.' " He would have been put to death, with the Archduchess and Foehn watching in mourning clothes. "There would be funeral services, bells ringing," and a Regent would be appointed quite officially. Life in the court would continue, with the Archduchess in command but really Foehn governing from behind.

As we hear this fatalistic, but also cynical and revealing speech, a speech intended to position the Queen's consciousness at the cusp of the modern era, since it deconstructs power and the apparatus of publicity that power thrives upon, music slowly wells up extradiegetically, the passionately lyrical and slowly gathering "Von Den Hinterweltlern" movement from Richard Strauss's *Also Sprach Zarathustra,* Op. 30. In brief flashes henceforward in the scene, as the vivid sunshine breaks through the bright and overcast sky, the palate of colors swiftly warms—a rosy tone comes into the Queen's cheeks, the leaves are emeraldine, the surrounding blossoms are candied—and just as swiftly cools again, as the sun disappears. He slowly turns his head in close-up, the music filling out. As she takes his hand, a branch heavy with blossoms obscures their faces.

Is it difficult for the postmodern sensibility to appreciate the lushness of filmmaking like this? The woman and the young man are filled with desire, and the fluctuation of colors behind and around them, which accompanies their utterances syllable by syllable, is meant at once to depict and heighten the agonies of their hunger for one another. After the sexual revolution, imported to the screen in the mid-1960s (not a little because of Antonioni), sexuality has almost nothing to do with desire.

He touches her waist, she his face.

We watch from behind him as she kisses his neck and holds this new husband brought back from eternity, one of the *Hinterweltlern,* the men who went before. "You killed the Queen more than you wanted to." As the yearning phrases of the music painfully continue, mounting, reaching, always finding Alps upon Alps, he kisses her face tenderly. Behind her are colored wildflowers. "I thought only of love. . . . I was going to become a woman, but I couldn't. . . . I buried myself in my castles. Then you arrived and upset this balance." The camera pans along the ground across an array of blue and pink and yellow flowers. "I want the castle to stay the way it is now, as if it were under a spell." A spell: we recollect, perhaps, an earlier moment, Sebastian's arrival night swelling and transmogrifying into morning, with the castle on its hilltop slowly emerging out of the darkness and hovering upon the dove gray catafalque of dawn. The camera tracks up to the castle, barely visible among the trees of the hillside orchard, and now the color shifts so that the sky, the castle, the overhanging leaves are all shot with vivid green, the green of early potentiality, of hope, of meditation, the hungry green that will never be fulfilled.

The shifting of the Queen away from her official mask and toward her authentic humanity, which is that of a young woman eager for love, is reflected in the shift toward saturated, sunny colors. Because this technique of color manipulation is available, Antonioni can play out this scene in which the Queen explains to Sebastian that he has captured her heart in such a way that we can directly see the vivid subjective effect he is having on her. She is being transformed by his presence. Something hidden inside is blossoming, and she feels herself coming alive the way she did when she met Frédéric. To say all this is one thing. To focus on her face—the "extremely expressive" face of Monica Vitti (*Film Culture* 40)—as she awakens is even more. But to have the light infusing the wildflowers and leaves, to be able to "paint" the flowers one by one on the ground, and finally to swathe the castle and its environs with the eagerness of green, is to raise the viewer's desire in a way commensurate with the Queen's. One must not be prudish to see this film.

The symphonic music helps us grasp that *The Mystery of Oberwald* is a symphonic exposition upon contrasts: the Queen with her aching memories and Sebastian with his pressing quotidian duties; the hewn wooden architecture of Oberwald and the constantly shifting, lush natural surround; the sweetness and openness of the Queen and the brutal secrecy of her lady-in-waiting; the talky liaisons between Edith and Willenstein, the Queen and Edith, the Queen and Sebastian, Sebastian and Foehn, and the Queen and Foehn, as contrasted against the muteness of Tony, who sees and understands everything, and that of the forest, which is primeval; the Queen's imagination and sense of feeling—that is, royalty as experienced by she who embodies it—as set against the unfeeling and exigent pressures of the court, the outside world, public opinion; the tempest outside and the tempest in Sebastian's spirit and the Queen's; the profound landscape of desire that the Queen inhabits, to which she introduces Sebastian, and the mask of propriety that overlays and represses everything inside the castle, not to mention the chilling product of passion and desire that is death; Sebastian's urgent poetry and the dry legal claims of Foehn; the omnipresence of the Archduchess's will and her physical absence; the physical embodiment of Sebastian and the phantom of the King, of whom he seems an exact copy. And a final conflict, even paradox: that the Queen wishes for love with Sebastian, a rebirth of her relation with the King, and yet, suzerain of Oberwald, she is as unable to save her lover from his fate as to save herself from her own imagination.

"The electronic system is highly stimulating," claimed Antonioni, "When you approach it, it seems like a game" (Griffiths 30). Since the film was to be shown first on television, each shot had to be framed within two rectangles, one for the broadcast and a second for the eventual transfer to film. Keith Griffiths remarks on the loss of Antonioni's trademark "virtuous camera movements" and on the "carefully constructed" images, the colors and color shifts which evoke the fusion of "peasant and nature" that the impressionist Camille Pissarro had hoped for (30). Grasses, flowers, curtains, and complexions change color as we stare at them, or radiant white light suffuses a persona as time passes, or the blood of slaughtered chickens thickens and deepens in color as their limbs cease twitching. An exterior shot, writes Griffiths, "zooms to the carcass of a shot deer. The image transforms to the deep black red of death" (30). The maker of this film is certainly not the Antonioni who told Jean-Luc Godard, in 1964, "I try to give things and landscapes their correct color on location, so that I don't have to touch them up in the developing room" (296). Even the inside of Oberwald has been radically desaturated, so that the wood paneling seems a fawn's pelt; the tapestries modest and old and suggestive, like scholars; and the books in their orderly shelves all worn and reposeful in their pristine bindings, like so many sleeping owls.

MONTAGNARDS

Two aspects of Sebastian's presentation should be highlighted. His startling resemblance to the dead king lends him the aspect of a ghost, and so for the Queen his every utterance and every silence signal an unearthly, perhaps transcendent, meaning. He is always a figure who is both here and not here, both alive and dead, and thus at once a manifestation (an intruder) and an apparition (a projection). She can never be certain about him, or deny the depth of her uncontrollable attraction. But at the same time—and this is the second point—since as a queen she has little truck with commoners, she is confined not only inside a chamber but on a certain dimension with him. To the extent that he appears before her as the shade of her dead husband he is close to her heart and her thoughts; but when he convincingly presents himself as a poet of the people he becomes removed and strange. The shifting colors made possible through the technique of the television camera, the constantly variant kaleidoscope which is the Queen's world, thus logically reflect a state of affairs in which identifications shift all around her, and she can never be quite definite about the man she is with.

When the Queen has repeatedly questioned him, and lectured to him about how he is her Fate, Sebastian finally bursts with a kind of sweet rage, indicating that he actually had a life before she found him fainting in her chamber. He had been raised, says he, in the mountains, and came down to the city where the pervasive sense of court intrigue oppressed him. We are looking at him from behind as he stares off at the Queen's face, with the camera low on his back; and his body is at the left side of the screen, like a theatrical proscenium. Directly ahead of us as we gaze, to Sebastian's left, is a large, open, framed window through which it is possible to see the mountains of which he speaks. The interior of the library chamber where this conversation is taking place has already been shown: it is paneled in softly worn, pallid wood, its walls covered entirely with books, and its floor is beautifully parqueted. Soft woody hues fill it, and the Queen is wholly suited to the place in her moss green velvet dress. There is thus a fashionable and warm-toned quality to the room and its effects, but the mountains we see outside are a crisp and cool greeny blue, flecked with acid purple. Through color effects, then,

Antonioni separates this exterior world from the domain of the palace, Sebastian's past from his present, and the call of his nature from the political maneuvers the Queen is undertaking with his assistance.

Antonioni had himself been a montagnard for a time. During the German occupation of Rome that followed upon the collapse of Mussolini's regime in 1943, he worked as a translator because "cinema didn't exist." "But then I became involved with the Action party and the Germans looked for me. I escaped to the Abruzzi hills" (Billard 63). At least for a time, before he was pursued there, the mountain hideaway must have seemed like a paradise simply in that it was a release from constraint and impossibility. Here, early in his career, Antonioni discovered the schism between organized social life—dictatorship of one sort or another—and the liberty that accompanies flight. The break with social constraint is a central motive in his filmmaking. "There isn't a school in Italy still, not a law court without its crucifix," he told Pierre Billard, "We have Christ in our houses, and hence the problem of conscience, a problem fed to us as children that afterward we have no end of trouble getting rid of. All the characters in my films are fighting these problems, needing freedom, trying to find a way to cut themselves loose, but failing to rid themselves of conscience, a sense of sin, the whole bag of tricks" (83). Television was mountains, in a way: "You can paint your images. You can change the colors. Since the colors are electronic, this is easy, as it is for a painter. . . ." (Bachmann, "Interview" 125).

If the Queen, pinioned by her power and her love, stands for Antonioni himself, if her constant desire represents his own hunger to be loosed from certain horrifying restraints, then what is it about his existence that confines this filmmaker and how exactly does the Queen's predicament reflect his own? His technique of filming was to open himself maximally to the inspiration of the moment, and so he would frequently make only marginal use of a script, would be more interested in the sound of a line of dialogue coming out of an actor's mouth than in the grammar of the text, would need the freedom to change the form or color of the scene, would need the camera to discover filmic truths as they were happening. He preferred "arriving at the moment of shooting, absolutely without preparation, virginal" (Labarthe 8), and would systematically demand about half an hour's time by himself on the set, totally undisturbed, before making a shot, in order to examine, meditate, reflect, and invent (Manceaux 18), this because "the best results are obtained by the 'collision' that takes place between the environment in which the scene is to be shot and my own particular state of mind at that specific moment" (*Film Culture* 27). What is unloaded in this method? The filmmaker's entire carapace, the identity he is forced to carry that affiliates him with the social mechanism and positions him in a status hierarchy, and the person he must enact as husband, lover, historian, philosopher. The very fact that he is making a film must also dissolve, must be replaced by a pure sensitivity to the unfolding world before the camera, which somehow meets his state of need and reflection at a moment in time. The act of being next to the camera, for Antonioni, is one of constant surrender, an abandonment of a certain imposed self in order to discover and manifest something that only the moment can know.

The Queen had this same alarming and overwhelming sense, this freedom—which is also a challenge to receptiveness and honesty—when her husband revealed himself to her and infused her with love, but then in a brutal agony was torn from her. For years she retreated into dark echoes of pain, then slowly began to feel herself in nature again, to wish for storms, to want the windows open, so that she became ready to go off on the hunt for experience, cognizant that invisibly, inexorably her minions were cloistering her and blocking experience off. She felt her position as increasingly heavy, really obstructed, and saw that every propriety was a move in a closed game which had to end with impotence or cunning. Given all this history, when Sebastian falls out from behind the portrait of Frédéric, it is a miracle. But what must seem more miraculous still is that the Queen, ready to receive his visitation, opens herself to true dialogue, casts off as relatively ephemeral the ugly and quotidian fact he shares with her, that he has come to be her assassin. When he protests that she is too caught up in his myth, too convinced that assassination is the whole of his self and world, his youth prevents him from noticing that she has already divined this; she has already seen past his surface and realizes that he represents something shocking and unfolding, some bold birthing of time itself.

MYSTERY OF OBERWALD

The magic happens from listening and bending towards each other, to make one.

—Bill Charlap

Why, however, when all is said and done, should it be a *mystery* that we discover in Oberwald—a mystery and not a problem, battle, revelation, discovery, rebirth, tragedy? What is the secret rite underpinning what we see here?

It is hard not to recall the strange and mysterious tale of Ludwig II, King of Bavaria. Eldest son of Maximilian II, heir to a lavish fortune and a mountain kingdom, effete, etiolated—said some—by passion for the arts, a principal benefactor of Richard Wagner, who wrote the Ring Cycle in his honor, a recluse with a prodigious fantasy life, he had five dream castles, some in the mountains (Neuschwanstein, Hohenschwangau), and flitted from one to another in rigid secrecy so that he could stay away from the mundane world of court intrigue. He stood well over six feet tall and was an Olympic swimmer. Yet by 1886 he had become what many in his court called "paranoid," and he was sent to Castle Berg where a psychiatrist, Gudden, was to diagnose him officially. Late in the evening of June 13, 1886, the two men were found floating dead, near the shore of the Starnbergersee. How Ludwig died has never been proven. In that he was a powerful swimmer yet was found drowned, one may speak of "mysterious" circumstances, as though facts that might produce a rational explanation had not, for any of a number of possible reasons, seen the light. It is not hard to grasp that the soldiers who come upon the bodies of the Queen and her poet in the final shot of *The Mystery of Oberwald* might find the situation similarly inexplicable, and that after the time which has occupied our attention here, rumor might circulate in the Queen's realm as to the manner and drama of her death. The demise of the Queen is, ultimately, a "mystery of Oberwald."

Yet this is scarcely a "mystery" for us, since we have been let into its staging area, and have seen the impossible love grow and reach its apotheosis. What of the "mystery" of the Queen's true self? Where is her moral and experiential center, given that although she has formal power to command the court she is nevertheless almost trembling with happiness when in the orchard she announces to Sebastian that he has succeeded in "killing the Queen" and in fact has "killed her too much"? This Queen rejects her own monarchy; she sees the role she plays—but not her person—as meriting the incessant deference that is directed at her, deference and also hatred, leading to Tony's unquestionable loyalty on one hand and the murderous plot against her life on the other. Under or behind the performance, she is human: her dreams, her sense of fulfillment, her sense of loss, all these are personal and also communal, shared with any young women who have wanted, and lost, love. That monarchy is enacted upon a stage and prepared in a staging area is a proposition that would be bluntly rejected by the court bureaucracy, which becomes stabilized upon the public image of a queen whose rule is guaranteed by purity of blood rather than charm or legal convention.

This is what Weber called "traditional authority" (Gerth and Mills 296–7), and it is a form substantiated through myriad acts and attitudes of the court as formalized institution. Just as she tells Sebastian, this Queen is as much an anarchist as he is.

The bald fact of her anarchy is no mystery, but the complex shifting that she must enact between the royal façade and the feelingful woman, between power and personality, is. "She's very nice, but she's a woman, and that means she's an actress," Cocteau used to say (Steegmuller 463). As, through his electronic manipulations, Antonioni presents a picture in which the colorations subtly and suddenly change, flicker, or divide—in the Queen's audience with Foehn, he is all purple and blue and she is all in much warmer colors, this in a split two-shot—he also conveys the perpetual (and perpetually inconclusive) vacillation between her formal and personal attitudes, between the state-sanctioned postures and the needful expressions that would trammel the state. So, another "mystery of Oberwald" is the Queen's fluctuating experience, its rhythm, its sign.

Sebastian is the third, perhaps the most potent, mystery: not the fact that he is captivated by the Queen's personality, or that he begins to love her; not that he is intimidated by Foehn and finally takes his own life for despair in his love; not that he is deceived by the Queen's imposture in the finale and shoots her; but that in all of this he should persist in doubling for the dead Frédéric. The dramatic idea is that the Queen should be so convinced of the similarity that at first she believes her dead husband has magically come back to life. In the play, this is assisted by the theatrical device of costuming the dead king as a montagnard in the portrait that hangs in the Queen's chamber (Cocteau 33), so that when Sebastian leaps onto the balcony and presents himself in the window frame, albeit soaked through and with unruly hair and worn thin, because he also wears the outfit of a montagnard he is "*exactement semblable au portrait du roi*" (Cocteau 35)—a duplicate of the king's picture. Antonioni can use a different technique, since his camera will give a close view of the portrait and a closer view of the young man: he employs the same actor to achieve the portrait, which is done not by painting but by photography. Although the clothing of the poet does not match that of the King, their hair, their cheekbones, their eyes, their lips are identical. Sebastian, then, looks exactly like . . . a picture.

Not like the King, but like his portrait. Is the portrait not a kind of puppet, and Sebastian with it, a kind of "alchemical product of the fusion of its creator's thought processes with the material at hand"? (Nelson 59). Invoked here is the theme of repetition, since the portrait itself is borrowed from the image of the King in life and now the look of Sebastian is borrowed from the portrait. Calvino says of faces: "I thought: 'You reach a moment in life when, among the people you have known, the dead outnumber the living. And the mind refuses to accept more faces, more expressions: on every new face you encounter, it prints the old forms, for each one it finds the most suitable mask' " (95). To look at a face and see in it what Calvino did is to meld visual experience with memory, even to transform what one sees into a phantom from the past. In musical terms, one might speak of the "recollection of a theme," even, as one listener hears it, a "saccharine" theme (Youmans 246). To see is to travel into the past; even more, into the past as a forest, since in his *Zarathustra,* to which Strauss's tone poem looks back, Nietzsche had punned *Hinterweltlern* with *Hinterwäldlern,* the men of the past with the men of the forest. In the love scene in Antonioni's film, as Sebastian is shown in portrait listening attentively to the Queen's every pregnant syllable, we begin to discover him as a reflection of earlier men, forestial men (he is making love to her among the fruit trees). His every gesture and expression, once he is thus defined, throw light back onto Frédéric the King, the man who came before. The Queen's love for him is a recapitulation of an earlier love, a love reborn—much as the flowers and blossoms are reborn in the spring. By conflating cycles of rebirth, the myth of the dying and reviving god (discussed by Frazer), the forestial clime, the magical aeries of Bavaria, the mysterious deaths and therefore echoes of Ludwig II and his protégé Wagner, thus the Wagnerian operatic cycle with its own echoing mythic concerns, as well as the sociology of the court and the trials of love against convention and social form, Antonioni directly raises the issue of the originality of our experience, and therefore of our role in history and the pervasive haunting thrust of the past. As to the past: the past entire, with its whole mystery, *mysterion,* the secret presence of the divine. All of this film, its every moment, moves backward (and this is why there is no hope). And the "mystery of Oberwald" is that in our faces we carry traces of other faces that have gone.

TRACES

I want my characters to suggest the background in themselves.
—Antonioni

But as to traces, an interesting problem. It is only in present being that we have memory of before, or that we experience something again, retrospectively, and thus conceive of what we call a "past." To perceive *again* is to interrupt a currency that would otherwise continue to absorb us. I see a man walk toward me down a sidewalk, swaying a little with each footstep. As his feet touch the pavement, I try to recollect what he looked like only a moment before, when his feet were touching the pavement a few steps further back. To the extent that I can reconstruct that vision I must be blind to what is happening now. ("Now" . . . "then": a scaffolding that facilitates description.) Because it is always only "now" that my memories happen, they are alive in my present, interrupting it: through memory the past comes alive again. The past is present and alive for us perceptually, to the degree that we struggle to perceive it against the competing flow of perceptions that perpetual change presents to us. How painful it is to retrieve perceptions from only a few moments ago, since these visible fluctuations of our current surround seem to travel away from us at a very great velocity while other fluctuations from long ago seem to have halted or to pose in a gallery of experience. Déjà vu is often a casting back of experience from the immediate (very proximate) past to a further remove, as though a long lost memory is suddenly revivified.

By convention, we take the portrait of the King to be a faithful representation, and using it as a measure, we adjudge the young Sebastian to be a twin of the dead monarch. The monarch portrayed in the hanging photograph has been long gone, and his image seems to stand permanently as an icon. Each successive image of the current Sebastian seems to flit past, with the effect that it is difficult to "remember" his appearance from a few moments ago; slightly easier to grasp one from a previous scene; and easiest to see him back at the beginning of the film, standing next to this portrait, which itself stands rather determinately next to an invisible King whose presence is almost perfectly determinate.

Writing about the accretions and excesses made normal by modernity, Mary Ann Doane notes an "increasing understanding of temporality as assault, acceleration, speed" and comments on the emergence of time as a "problem intimately linked to the theorization of modernity as trauma or shock" (33). It was in musical scores and written texts, she says, that time had been preserved beforehand (34), and we can take this to mean that the ghosts of the past could exist for us in present moments through words and music, through literature and the symphonic oeuvre—in both of which, notably, repetitive phrasing is an explicit feature of composition and scoring convention. (Reading through John Cage's *Notations,* it is fascinating to see how after the 1950s, time in musical representation came more and more to be space.) The motion picture made possible a different and overwhelming temporality—yet overwhelming in a thoroughly fresh and beneficial way, even though Doane does show a certain anxiety, following Kracauer, wondering a little nervously, "what taxonomic principle can *govern* the breakdown and ordering of a 'flood' or a 'blizzard'?" (33, emphasis mine). In a typical motion picture of the early sound era, there would have been an uninterrupted flow of something like 145,440 discreet images (I choose Mark Sandrich's *Top Hat* [1935]), and by the mid-1950s even this barrage or banquet had expanded so that viewers would sit enraptured as something like 221,760 pictures flew past their eyes (*A Star Is Born* [1956]). Certainly, persistence of vision made us see images onscreen more or less in terms of shots: we did not discriminate individual frames. The sense of a flow of images tended to be linked to editing patterns and to the coherence of the shot, regardless of the photographic technique through which a shot was made. Films of the 1930s contained roughly three or four hundred shots, each of which would play out for fifteen seconds or longer. By the early years of the twenty-first century we were habituated to watching three or four hundred shots go by in as little as five screen minutes (in, say, *The Bourne Supremacy* [2004]).

It is one of Doane's arguments about time and modernity that the extreme condensation of images produced through cinema was experienced latently; that modernity sent us a Kracauerian "blizzard" that we took entirely for granted as we watched. But this multiplication of sights we were taking for granted, as cinema expanded and centralized itself in our cultural consciousness, was also a phantom experience. Unbeknownst to viewers, through the agency of their direct perception, images from the recent past were hovering and remanifesting themselves as images of the flitting present. (We were remembering as well as seeing.) Furthermore, the ongoingness of film determined that each perceptual instant was related to images that had gone (even hours) before, through an unbroken chain of images—unbroken, regardless of the editing. Cinema's continual unfolding means that the past is continually reappearing as the present and that every present glimpse is also a reexperience of the past.

Watching *The Mystery of Oberwald* we do not necessarily bear such considerations in mind, although we might. Yet these are the considerations on the "table," and our very disattention forms part of the complex that has moved Antonioni in his making of the film. The invocation of the King's rehabilitation through Sebastian, the idea that the young man is a kind of ghost figure representing the King, opens a clear pathway to such thinking, whether we engage in it or not. Although no standard portrait or figuration is given of the Queen's ancestry or past, we may also imagine that she, too, is a ghost of what was, and in much the same way. Who, indeed, is not? In this film, then, each dramatic moment seems palpably linked to previous ones in a musical way, exactly as each character seems continually to be trying to trace the past in a present moment: the aggressive de Berg observing her Queen like some sort of police witness, keeping records of each expression and utterance against a secret file that constitutes a bureaucratic history; the Archduchess, plotting with an unflagging memory of her son and his utility to her as through him she planned to command the court; the mute Tony, with a loyal memory of all the injustices his Queen has suffered; and so on. While the surface structure of the film, as Antonioni admitted, was melodrama, the film itself is considerably more. "More than anything, I hate melodrama," he once said to Cardullo, "Melodrama is the easiest thing in the world to do—the scene of the drunken whore or the brutal, shouting father—and it is the cheapest thing to do, too. And so not worth doing. Far more difficult, more complicated, and thus more artistically challenging is to make a film that reflects the true rhythms of life" (146). In Sebastian's resemblance to the King, stressed and restressed here through photographic, casting, and editing effects, is an evocation of those "true rhythms" in which the past reverberates now, and in which this moment will last and reverberate tomorrow.

PERSUASION

Aus der eigenen Asche und Gluth kam es mir, dieses Gespenst.
[Out of mine own ashes and glow it came unto me, that phantom.]
—Nietzsche, "Backworldsmen"

Central in *The Mystery of Oberwald* is the Queen's obsession with the dead Frédéric, whom we both do and do not see. That with him she experienced the first flush of love; that this love was unfulfilled; that swiftly upon his coronation he was torn from her; that he was torn by vicious and sadistic plotters who sought to control his court and were happy to alienate his queen; that she cannot get him out of her mind; that she lives every day with a portrait of him in which he lingers like a ghost; that now a young man running at night through the royal forest—and might not the King run through his own forest at night?—is pursued by precisely the same forces, the army, controlled by the malevolent Count Foehn, that attacked the King; that the young man in this way both symbolizes the lost

King and reconstitutes him in present time; that this young man secretes himself in the Queen's chamber, behind the portrait of his look-alike; that at a critical moment he tumbles into her view with no warning, although, without him knowing it, she has been fixating upon exactly his image and praying for exactly his return for years: all this deposits a thick perfume of insatiable want and burning curiosity, a perfume that clings to the thread that separates the world of the living from the world of those who have gone before.

Optical fascination with spiritual manifestation goes back to prehistory: for example, the Old Testament describes Moses as requiring visible signs of God's power in Egypt. "It seemed to me as if I had sight of Paradise, of Hell and of wand'ring Spirits and Phantoms," wrote Charles Patin of a magic lantern show in 1696, "so that altho' I know myself to be endu'd with some measure of Resoluteness, yet at that time I would willingly have given one half to save the other" (qtd. in Mannoni 60). In particular, there has been an intensive querying of the possibility of life beyond the material world as we know it, especially with Philidor's projections during the French Revolution ("I will bring before you all the illustrious dead, all those whose memory is dear to you," he proclaimed [Mannoni 144]) and Robertson's in Paris after it. January 20, 1798, Robertson (as Étienne-Gaspard Robert was known) showed "apparitions of Spectres, Phantoms and Ghosts, such as they must have appeared or could appear in any time, in any place and among any people" at the Pavillon in the Rue de l'Échiquier (Mannoni 150). After 1840, when spiritualism became organized and popular both in the United States and in Europe—and at the time, too, that photography was in its infancy—a new urgency came to the prospect of seeing the world in all its manifestations. If through the agency of a medium, lantern show, or phantasmagoria, communication were possible to some extent between the living and the dead, or at least if presentation of the dead in phantom form could stun the consciousness of the living, could not a system of imagery systematically make visible those who had not lingered among us? Could photography possibly see *beyond?*

Now, of course, we wonder whether through the magical agency of cinema a similar discourse might be engendered between the *here* and the *there*. To give just one current example, after his shocking death in March 2008, Heath Ledger was almost immediately rumored by fans and onlookers to be not merely posthumously appearing but "coming back to life" as the Joker in Christopher Nolan's *Batman: The Dark Knight*. David Williams rhapsodized in the London *Telegraph* that Internet fans were "immortalizing" him, and Tom Leonard reported to the same paper from New York that Terry Gilliam was planning to digitally "recreate" him for *The Imaginarium of Dr. Parnassus.* Fans circulated a hot electronic discourse about Ledger "receiving" an Oscar for his performance in the Batman film, and one demurrer suggested, "Ledger returns from the grave says '***** the rest of the movies' takes an Oscar and returns to the dead" (RobotLeAwesome).

Clément Chéroux notes that ever since the late 1840s and 1850s, "by proclaiming the possibility of communicating with the dead, several practitioners began interpreting photographic phantoms as real ones" (45–46; my translation). Photographic phantoms had been detected for years upon insufficiently washed collodion plates intended for reuse. According to Chéroux, two strains of photography developed: one intended explicitly for entertainment purposes, as in the Eugène Thiébault publicity photographs of the magician Henri Robin, "who caused specters to appear every night in his fantasmagoric spectacles on the Boulevard du Temple" (46; my translation); and another, owing to a strictly scientific mandate that had been imposed upon French photography in the spirit of Allan Kardec, devoted to establishing phantoms as not only verisimilitudinous but also *real* manifestations, within pictorial imagery, of the residents of the spiritual world. One of the leading spirit photographers, Édouard Isidore Buguet, was arrested (at 2 P.M., April 22, 1875) and brought to trial (along with two others) for fraud: "It is *persuasion* to which they attempted to give birth," claimed the prosecutor, "and *that* is the fact that I submit for your consideration" (50; emphasis original, translation mine). So, a principal effect of spirit photography was a division of the gaze, between playful admiration and decreasingly hesitant belief, between the ability to advertise public thrills and the ability to convince audiences that they were truly witnessing the dead hovering among the living. Finally, concludes Chéroux, citing Max Milner's observation that photography was able to play on belief and doubt at one and the same time, "*Les fantômes vont par paires. Le spectre de la mort accompagne celui de la dérision comme son ombre. Ils nous hantent à deux.*" ("Phantoms come two at a time. The specter of death accompanies the specter of derision like a shadow. They haunt us together") (53; translation mine.)

In her way, the Queen is caught upon the twin prongs of this dualism, since she both believes and disbelieves in a reincarnation. It is clear enough when she tolerates Sebastian's presence during the rainstorm, when she hides him, when she permits him to overhear her audience with Foehn, and when she appoints him her personal reader that he is for her only a peasant poet from the mountains who has written an engaging little diatribe, good looking, able to serve her ends as she makes plans to play the court intrigue against itself: in short, the perfect entertainment for a limited period of time. He is a graphic image of Death, a reconstitution, and as such he brings the frivolous pleasure of curiosity and wonder about what cannot truly be understood. When, however, he makes bold to reproach her for thinking of him only as an assassin, when he tells her he has a mind and plans of his own, when in the meadows and glades around the castle he permits her to discover in him the passions that have been smoldering since their first meeting, he becomes a real man with whom she can fall in love—and, falling in love, walk in open partnership. That she can relate to him in this real way, though he is the double of the dead King, means she can be with the King again when she is with Sebastian, or that Sebastian is indeed a king, and quite as real as Frédéric must have been for the Queen when first they loved. For this commitment, what is needed is conviction, not mere pleasure, and in fostering both pleasure and conviction at once, the ghostly Sebastian becomes a kind of duplication, a "specter of death accompanied by the specter of derision." Victoria Nelson muses, "It is difficult for us now to picture a time when the independent territory of *imagine*—a realm neither material nor transcendental, and completely distinct from that of *believe*—was not freely available" (58).

As we watch the film, we enjoy and calculate this twinning through our own wonderment and belief, and then through our doubting that Sebastian is the man he resembles so completely. (Why might the King, discovering an attempt upon his life, not somehow have escaped into the mountains? In saying that she saw him stabbed near the heart, can the Queen perhaps be inventing a horror from which to withdraw, a horror that in its ugliness masks off the even more chilling memory that out of fear or caution he left her alone with his enemies, alone to rule in her abject and trusting innocence a coterie of devils who would do anything for power?) We note the resemblance of the two men periodically; and then we forget about it, and concentrate on Sebastian's individuality and warmth, his hunger, his fear. He is, and at the same time is not, the King. Alternately, he *is* the King, but only metaphorically; and then through metaphor he *is the King,* in present fact.

Fascination with the idea of communicating across the boundary between life and death, which entranced the spiritualists and which is reflected in the Queen's relation with Sebastian in this film, is less overwhelming, perhaps, than the simultaneous presence and absence of death in human affairs that the film constantly invokes. In the orchard as she unveils her soul in love, the Queen is addressing both a man and a ghost. In 1943, Hitchcock had invoked this paradox, somewhat comically. In *Shadow of a Doubt,* a hardworking bank clerk, Joe Newton (Henry Travers), chats every night after dinner with his neighborly chum Herbie Hawkins (Hume Cronyn), a milquetoast who is caught up in an ongoing search for the perfect way to commit a murder. One night, Herbie has a confidence to share. The coffee he just gave Joe over at his house, he says gleefully, was spiked with baking soda—could you taste it? Because it could as well have had poison! "I *didn't* taste the *soda!*" urges Joe, meaning that the additive was weak and nobody could have tasted it while poison, by contrast, would be more apparent and nobody would be fooled. Herbie vehemently disagrees. If Joe didn't taste the soda, he most certainly wouldn't have tasted the poison. And then he says, with a smirk of triumph, "For all you knew, you might just as well be dead now."

It is typical in Hitchcock that a line of dialogue might carry the load of a double meaning. *Knew* is both indicative and subjunctive. If Herbie had put poison in the coffee, Joe would be dead now, because *he didn't know* while drinking that there was a problem. But simultaneously Herbie is saying to Joe: given the limitations of your knowledge, you might be dead now just as well as you might be alive. Anyone, that is, might "know" himself to be dead now, as much as he "knows" himself to be alive. It is fascinating to think that we do not actually have a way to be certain that we are alive, except that reason offers us the formula which links what we call experience to what we call life. We seem to see, to move, to sense, to dream, and thus take ourselves as "living" beings; and normally a presumption like this works quite sufficiently to bring us through any eventuality. Yet, *we have no apparatus for really knowing.* In that we do not really *know* death, do not grasp or understand it, we certainly also do not know whether it is part of our present constitution. With Herbie and Joe, the consideration of life and death is undertaken not by esteemed philosophers in some remote tower but by ordinary working-class people in a small town as part of routine casual small talk, small talk, indeed, in which they are convinced quite another level of discourse obtains. The truth of our dance with life and death is a vulgar truth, an everyday truth, a truth befitting small talk just as much as rigorous philosophical argument. It is like the air, evanescent and mysterious but also simple and omnipresent.

The simplicity, and thus elegance, of the ghostly presence that Sebastian represents for the beleaguered Queen—that he is here now, but also a reflection of someone who has not been here for a long time—is made emphatic by the strange juxtaposition of his commonness with her regality, his dignified peasant self-assurance with her august intonations, his rude experience of life expressed through poetry with her elevated, even effete sensibilities. Sebastian is virile and very strong: but for all he knows he might be dead. The Queen is effusive in her grief, demanding, quick-tempered, and passionate, but she, too, might be dead for all she knows. Thus our lives are played out in the shadows of a grand mystery, no matter how sparkling the blossoms in the trees.

• • •

Il mistero di Oberwald (1980), photographed by Luciano Tovoli in the 1.37: 1 aspect ratio in PAL video, with collaboration on color and electronic effects by Franc De Leonardis, then kinescoped and projected in a Kodacolor positive print; 123 m. Shown at the New York Film Festival, September 30, 1981.

Zabriskie Point

Over the desert reigned a vast silence as of a house in order.

—Antoine de Saint-Éxupery, "Port Étienne"

TOPOS

In the desert, the horse drinks first.

—*The Barbarian* (Sam Wood, 1933)

The Mojave. A two-lane blacktop, midday. Tanned, optimistic, and tolerant, a young woman who has been freelancing as a secretarial assistant to the chief executive of the mammoth Sunny Dunes real estate development company in Los Angeles has "borrowed" a vintage slate-gray Chevrolet (belonging to some spacey young man who has crashed in her apartment), and is driving off to meet her mogul (her mogul/lover) at his hilltop residence in the desert near Phoenix. Head there directly she does not, but takes an extended detour, searching for the sleepy little town of Ballister where, rumor has it, meditation is terrific. At one spot by the side of the road, she pauses to fill a tin cup from a large yellow steel drum, and here we get: a rare glimpse of water in this film. WATER FOR RADIATORS ONLY is printed at eyeview: we can read the words at leisure as, crouching in her loden cotton tunic and love beads, Daria (Daria Halprin) patiently fills up.

Twice more, and only twice more, we will see water, but each time water distinctly unobtainable, at the executive's home (an architectural masterpiece that the script describes as "perched high on a mountain of egg-shaped rocks"). Some women are sunbathing beside a turquoise pool, yet the pool seems utterly pictorial, forbidding, a source not so much of water as of the look of water. At around this time, David Hockney was apotheosizing this sacred vision. And, dripping down some granite boulders that face a shaded flagstone walkway into the house, a stream of water bespeaks salvation, respite, the pleasure of the oasis. Standing against these cooling rocks, however, Daria wants no drink, though she lets the water trickle over her face and soak her dress.

On the voyages to and from the sublimely beautiful Zabriskie Point that are described in this film; and, with a single exception, in the world of the film itself, it is the automobile that drinks, not the people, although the setting is relentlessly sunny, arid, bleached, and desiccating and we can imagine thirst everywhere. (For readers who do not know the desert climate of Arizona, California, or Nevada, the air in the summer and fall seems to gently and incessantly sip moisture from one's pores, so that one is almost always parched. It was a technical problem with this film to maintain the look and feel of this bleaching heat, since it was shot over the long period from September 9, 1968 through May 9, 1969 but in order to depict a narrative that occupies only a single day [Rubin].) The exception is Ballister, nothing if not a ghost town, where the days of yesteryear have been eclipsed by an unseen resident guru who works there with disturbed children. (Daria Halprin recalls that this ghost town was "truly in the middle of nowhere" [personal communication].) Aside from him, the place and its inhabitants could be living vestiges of the early twentieth century. One old cowpoke sits meditatively at a bar, alternating between a peaceable cigarette and a tall glass of beer; a middle-aged and heavyset ranch hand sips from a glass of buttermilk; and a Native American is being served a cup of coffee by a proprietor who seems all sagacity, all patience, all desert wind. We see these three drinkers within seconds of one another, and they are marginal even to this very brief scene, but drinking they unmistakably are. Their drinking can be taken to signal the repose and satisfaction, if not the memory, of a much earlier California than Daria and her mobile generation know; the California of paradisiacal dreams, to which streams of immigrants hopefully flowed (including the men who would make the movies).

For Daria, Southern California is another place altogether, a high-tech paradise that resulted from decades of development beginning in the earliest years of the twentieth century: a place where real estate speculation is normative, and where a relatively arid climate has been mastered through artificial delivery of water, in order that a lush garden community can spread from the San Fernando Valley southward beyond Long Beach and

Irvine. Writes Mike Davis, "The vast citrus forests that once surrounded Los Angeles, as well as cities like Riverside and Anaheim, have been transformed into pink stucco death valleys full of bored teenagers and desperate housewives. . . . Throughout the foothills, meanwhile, free-range McMansions—often castellated in unconscious self-caricature—occupy rugged ocean-view peaks surrounded by what foresters grimly refer to as 'diesel stands' of dying pine and old brush" ("Diary"). Sunny Dunes occupies a "McSkyscraper" that is all sleekness and modernity (although in Los Angeles, a building doesn't have to be very tall to scrape the sky!). The exterior and lobby were shot at Beneficial Plaza, on Wilshire Boulevard between Oxford and Serrano, erected in 1967 by Skidmore, Owings, and Merrill; the scenes in the executive suite were done in a makeshift structure erected on the roof of what was then the Mobil Oil Building, formerly the General Petroleum Building, at Wilshire and South Flower, built by Wurdeman and Becket (see Chatman and Duncan 120–121), the head of Mobil at the time being "a cultured man" who wanted to help (Starr, personal communication).

The population of this urban zone, as Davis is quick to point out, was largely formed of "new settlers" with "nervous eastern imaginations": "The railroad publicists and the chamber of commerce promoters repackaged the Los Angeles region as 'Our Mediterranean! Our Italy!' For more than a century, this Mediterranean metaphor has been sprinkled like a cheap perfume over hundreds of instant subdivisions, creating a faux landscape celebrating a fictional history from which original Indian and Mexican ancestors have been expunged" (*Ecology* 11–12).

Central to the development of the modern California, the California not of sleepy missions and fragrant orange groves but of two-lane blacktops and freeways, turquoise pools nestling in the rocky crags of the desert, and business concerns like Sunny Dunes, was a pronounced and long-lived pattern of exploitation and corruption, involving the transfer to the Los Angeles area of water from Owens Valley, 250 miles to its north. "In the Los Angeles Basin of 1,400,000 acres of habitable land (6% of the state's total)," wrote Carey McWilliams in 1946 in what has come generally to be regarded as the most influential critical history of the area, "reside 45% of the inhabitants of California. But this same basin has only .06% of the natural stream flow of water in the state. Water is the life-blood of Southern California. Turn off the flow of water that now reaches the region from such remote sources as Owens Valley and the Colorado River and the whole region would be bankrupt" (183). In 1924, seeing their properties drying up and dying as their water was systematically siphoned away southward to Los Angeles, residents of Owens Valley—principally orchard owners and farmers—blew up parts of the California Aqueduct and fought the city over its right to consume this water. But, McWilliams reports, the Los Angeles power structure was hardly vulnerable or naïve and "the sponsors of the Owens Valley project . . . knew how to cope with such stubbornness. The resistance in the valley had been financed by two pioneer bankers who, by manipulating their books in violation of the state banking act, were able to carry delinquent mortgages. Waiting until these leaders had become deeply involved, the powers-that-be then had them indicted and sentenced to San Quentin Prison. Having broken the resistance movement, the City of Los Angeles then proceeded, in 1931, to buy up most of the remaining lands in the valley" (190).

Nor was the average resident of Los Angeles in any direct way involved. McWilliams asserts emphatically that as late as the mid-1940s, most Angelenos had no idea about what Morrow Mayo (in his 1933 book *Los Angeles*) called the "colossal swindle" that was carried out upon the citizens of the city by William Mulholland, the supervising engineer of the project, and the craven capitalists who connived to divert Owens Valley water in order to irrigate thousands of acres of land they had acquired for next to nothing in the San Fernando Valley between Burbank and Tarzana. In Los Angeles, as it seemed, water simply appeared.

By the end of the 1960s, as we see from *Zabriskie Point,* the blissful ignorance that had been engendered by the seemingly natural presence of water in this desert clime was converted to what McWilliams called an "impression of impermanence" that continued to suffuse Southern California:

> Although Southern Californians do not understand the semi-arid environment in which they live, they are haunted by a vague and nameless fear of future disaster. . . . "There is something disturbing about this corner of America," wrote J.B. Priestley, "a sinister suggestion of transience. There is a quality, hostile to men in the very earth and air here. As if we were not meant to make our homes in this oddly enervating sunshine. . . . California will be a silent desert again. It is all as impermanent and brittle as a reel of film. (199)

And even eighteen years after *Zabriskie Point* (and fourteen after Roman Polanski's *Chinatown,* which depicted the water diversion scandal as a symptom of a more diffuse moral rot that was already infecting the

Los Angeles scene), Joan Didion echoed the same observations, and with more acerbity:

> What it turned out to be was a five-two, followed by a dozen smaller aftershocks, and it had knocked out four of the six circuit breakers at the A. D. Edmonston pumping plant on the California Aqueduct, temporarily shutting down the flow of Northern California water over the Tehachapi range and cutting off half of Southern California's water supply for the weekend. This was all within the range not only of the predictable but of the normal. . . . A five-two earthquake is not, in California, where the movements people remember tend to have Richter numbers well over six, a major event, and the probability of earthquakes like this one had in fact been built into the Aqueduct: the decision to pump the water nineteen hundred feet over the Tehachapi was made precisely because the Aqueduct's engineers rejected the idea of tunneling through an area so geologically complex, periodically wrenched by opposing displacements along the San Andreas and the Garlock, that it has been called California's structural knot. ("Days" 147)

Wolfgang Schivelbusch observes that "All political systems have showcase projects through which they present themselves to the world and expect their aims, method, and ideals to be judged" (*Deals* 138). The lush Southern California created by the northern waters—"Today the entire area from Santa Barbara to San Diego is an irrigated paradise. Water gurgles from irrigation pumps, water rushes along irrigation laterals and canals, and costly sprinkling systems spray a seemingly inexhaustible supply of water on elaborate lawns and gardens" (McWilliams 183)—was nothing if not such a project, openly visible to all the world for its efficiency, its profitability, and its physical glory.

Not surprisingly for a project in which Sam Shepard was an early creative force, *Zabriskie Point* posits an eerie and intoxicating mythical territory at once self-sufficiently elaborate and apocalyptically barren, what one writer called "a land of the deluded and the self-deluding" (Lingenfelter 1). As Daria squats at the roadside water tank, her designer tunic and casual adornments reflect back upon the swank, air-conditioned, modernist office environment of Sunny Dunes where she did temporary work and was picked up as a personal assistant by the chief executive: the Sunny Dunes universe was built upon the assumption of fertility and magnificence, and in it water existed automatically (and invisibly) to satisfy the needs of a burgeoning capitalism. But at the same time the water tank in the desert, simple and limited—WATER FOR RADIATORS ONLY—speaks to the fundamental dearth of a vital resource, to the aridity of the terrain all around, and to the fragility of the modernist human enterprise in the context of the spreading, bleached, and hostile—although shockingly beautiful—desert. If a few years later in *Chinatown* the water problem would be enunciated and played out through the mounting drama, here it passes beyond speech into the hard, shapely figure of the desert landscape and the hard, shapely manufacture that is urban civilization in sunny Southern California. Water, itself physically invisible in almost all of this film, is by implication everywhere and in everything we see, just beneath the surface, or, notably, not. Water is the pretext and presumption of the story, since it is the pretext and presumption of the place.

Beverly Walker, brought into the production team as publicist while the sequences at Zabriskie Point were being shot, remembers flying to the location after sunset. "The desert at night looks like the ocean. I woke up in the morning and there I was, in Death Valley. A mind-blowing experience." The script, she affirms, was originally not a political but an environmental story: "The desecration of the desert for the greater glory of a city like L.A., where people have their sprinklers going night and day: that was the core story of *Zabriskie Point,* that Sam Shepard developed with Antonioni. And I'm sure it was based on Antonioni's ideas. He came over here and they gave him this long, long tour of the country, and from an impressionistic point of view that's what hit him between the eyes, this despoliation of the landscape, and that meant a lot to Antonioni but you never hear it talked about: *land.*" Walker still recalls one of the first things Antonioni said to her. "All of this desert happened so that people in L.A. could have a drink of water" (personal communication).

ENCOUNTER

And suddenly I felt free, my mind was lifting up, up, up in flight. . . .
Nothing could touch my peace.
—Sam Shepard, *Operation Sidewinder*

Already something of a concubine in a hypermoral utopia, the carefree Daria meets a strange young man as she drives through the desert. It is clear already that she is altogether a creature of the modern world, with her crystalline green eyes always trained on some horizon, her casual and provisional attitude to working relationships, her artful and thoroughly brushed ponytail trailing down past her waist as a self-conscious lure, and her penchant for movement and changes of scene. She always has a plan, an idea that precedes an experience. The boy,

Mark (Mark Frechette), has a much more primitive approach to life, reacting in situations on the basis of impulse and sensation rather than according to prior arrangements, and his articulations of thought seem loose and fragmentary, not worked out according to a bridging (and necessarily class-based) philosophy. He suddenly descends from the sky, in a candy pink Cessna that dives and swoops, tracks, glides, circles, and dives again. "A recurring leitmotif in Antonioni," said producer Harrison Starr, "is that bandit sexuality coming from strange places" (personal conversation).

In his flight, Mark has not been on the hunt, at least not for a girl with whom it would perhaps be pleasurable to spend a boring afternoon in the desert. What he searches for, as he peers out of the plane at the skimming undulations of ground below and the blue, blue vault above, is an "anything," the smallest flicker of modulation or transparency that might constitute "happening," "meaning," or even "promise." He is alive to the moment but not traveling through it in order to achieve presence somewhere else. With no flight path (metaphorically or literally), his is a direction without a vector. This isn't boredom, it's the rudiment of science, the attitude that opens the senses toward the world and hungrily incorporates every possible nuance of experience, every datum, every transformed and transforming embodiment of light.

The plane drones away. Closing the hood of her car after putting in the water, Daria looks up, squinting, then drives off toward some purple-mountained majesty—a majesty that Antonioni, at one point, had thought to change. Production designer Dean Tavoularis was in Barstow with his painter, Roger Dietz, engaged by the filmmaker in conversation about those distant "lavender gray" mountains. "Can you make those red, from there . . . to there?" Antonioni asked. Tavoularis said to Dietz, "What about a crop-duster?":

> I checked around and there was a bi-plane, kind of à la *North by Northwest*. And I said, "Get as much red powder sent from L.A., from Hollywood, as you can," and Roger put the red powder in the big bins for the chemicals they would normally use, and I instructed the pilot. Watching through binoculars, from where the camera would be, as the plane made several passes over the mountains, I noticed no particular change. "Do it again," I said. Again, no change. Then, "What about liquid? Can we get another plane that has a liquid system instead of powder? And can you get red dye instead of red powder? Rust red dye?" So we did that with another plane. I watched again with the binoculars. . . . I did try. I made a valiant effort. I explained to Michelangelo, and I had a couple of photographs to prove it. I don't think he expected that the mountains would ever change. Just wanted to see somebody step up

> to it, wanted to see somebody try. That was the important thing. That's what a master is. Life isn't about winning, it's about trying.

"What an extraordinary person he was!" (Tavoularis, personal communication). But now, as absent-mindedly she chews her gum, the plane makes a pass just above Daria's rooftop, so close, indeed, that she covers her head and ducks. "Jesus Christ, what the hell was that!? Fuck!!" We see him—from a position outside his cockpit and beneath his wing—gazing down; his eyeline passes the hot pink "Lilly 7" inscribed on the fuselage; he sports a broad smile of engagement. With his next pass, it becomes more than evident that Antonioni is thinking of that celebrated Hitchcock sequence, Daria's charcoal gray car standing in for Roger O. Thornhill in his swank, charcoal gray suit in that broadly open (desert-like), hence unprotected, surround.

As the pilot skims along the highway not ten feet off the road, then swoops up over the car, she has a look somewhere between irritation and curiosity. Antonioni arranges for his camera to swoop upwards as the plane climbs into the blue, so that we can share the boy's sense of exhilaration. His body, his feeling, his presence are united in an airy dance. He can go anywhere, through any route, with no obstructions, and always with a bird's-eye view of the social world below, thus, without the binding constraint of social responsibility. (In truth, there was considerably less freedom than met the moviegoer's eye. On a practice run setting up one of these shots, at 9:10 a.m. on November 11, 1968, the pilot, Jim Wilbanks, had to swoop so low to get the desired effect, with Antonioni and cinematographer Alfio Contini strapped inside, that the plane's nose wheel smashed the car's windshield and fell off. Of the two planes in regular use by the production, he had forgotten that he was flying the one without retractable gear [Walker, personal communication]. Assistant Director Bob Rubin, who was in the car with Halprin and script supervisor Bonnie Prendergast, suffered serious facial lacerations [Walker, "Leviathan"; Rubin, personal communication], while Wilbanks, for his part, had to circle until the fuel ran out before attempting a landing [Chatman and Duncan 123].)

From Mark's airborne perspective, we see Daria's car crawling along the road, holding assiduously to its position in lane, a perfect little cipher of order, linearity, and obedience. He is descending and angling in on the road now (as we occupy his position at the controls and stare through the window), apparently ready to use the highway as a landing strip. With the motor droning and the desert flashing pinkly past, he zeroes in on the dotted white line: but suddenly an object is coming nearer . . . nearer . . . and it is the car, which whizzes past beneath. We cut to Daria, eyes wide open at the wheel. Now she knows it is a game and has caught the excitement. He makes yet another pass. "Shee! What the hell was that!" She stops and gets out, shading her face from the sun and looking up for him, but he has become a bird, wheeling away quietly in the distance. She goes into the sand and lies down, covers her head. He swoops above her, not six feet up. She throws sand after him. In the sand she is scrawling something unintelligible, except there is an "!" at the end. He reaches behind him, seizes a red shirt, tosses it down to her. Soon she is rolling along again, with the Youngbloods' "Sugar Babe" blasting on her radio. Looking off the road, she sees with a little smile that his plane has landed in a flat. She drives off to meet him.

No doubt this is courtship, and an especially beautiful variety since the partners to the procedure don't know one another in any but the most superficial way. Daria's first impulse in the face of Mark's avian gestures is self-protection and outrage, and it is inconceivable to her that he is an innocent. For his part, Mark can see little beyond the kind of uptight and obedient behavior that her driving evidences. He needs gas, however, so she agrees to drive him to get some, and on their journey they come without warning upon Zabriskie Point.

IN MY END IS MY BEGINNING

We must do what the gods did in the beginning.
—(*Satapatha Brahmana* VII.2.1.4)

"From the look-out," reads an early treatment Antonioni wrote in Rome, "the great desert valley stretches out to the horizon. It is mustard yellow and undulates. A sort of primaeval desert which still keeps the form of its origins, the bed of an ancient sea. The fantastic landscape is shot through with a radiant light. A violent, cosmic emotional impact. There is a large stone with an inscription and we see that this is the lowest point of land in America: 270 feet below sea level" (August 1967 Treatment 10). *Playboy* reported that in reality the place wasn't colorful enough: "Antonioni spent thousands of dollars actually dyeing the desert, even the lizards, various shades of pink and green." On set, however, Antonioni told Marsha Kinder that in *Zabriskie Point* he doesn't change colors; "I try to exploit the colours that I have" (29). The vision at Zabriskie Point is certainly breathtaking, and suggests the end of the world.

The end of the world, the beginning of the world; a world that is not a world: "strange . . . strange," Hiro Narita (who shot some background footage for Antonioni) told me, "almost like a yellow sulphur wasteland" (personal conversation), language falling off in the face of this expansive frozen sea of yellow dunes and rusty rock crests, ashfalls and saline muds and gravels, borate, mudstone, and siltstone, golden arches, a dried-up river bed, the hillsides covered with a soft and enveloping dust, long stretches of bleached stone, fossilized camel, horse, mastodon tracks, soft sediments that "erode into lovely forms: smoothly rounded hills with deep creases in their flanks. There is a chocolate-colored cap layer that runs through these 'badlands,' sometimes tilted, sometimes sprinkled over the golden shales just enough to let them show through" (Hyde 109).

Black lava from three-million-year-old eruptions. The river bed reflects only the memory of a river, only the thought of a river: everything here is arid, the land of the Fisher King. A thousand ochres are lit up by the unyielding sun blazing upon the sediments of what, five million years ago, was what today we call Furnace Creek Lake. In that ancient past, an alien geology: what is dry land was under water. Running down to the riverbed, meandering on the dusty steppes, rolling on the ground, Mark and Daria discourse of death, of themselves, of anything and also of nothing, since language can carry us beyond the moment of articulation into plots and passageways that these two are careful to avoid. Each syllable is for the present, and so the present moment is intensified, warmed, deepened. With every ambiguous word, time seems to have stopped.

If this is not another planet, our two young protagonists are at an unfathomable distance from Western civilization, the rippling flag, the police vehicle, the preaching revolutionary, the snack stop, the meat factory. "Supposedly carefree," wrote the publicist, "supposedly a city-boy experiencing the wonder of the desert, of nature primeval, for the first time . . . he whooped and hollered" (Walker, "Leviathan").

Critic and conservationist Nancy Newhall writes that late in the nineteenth century, when early explorations were made there, Death Valley was still "remote, two hundred dry and torturous miles from anything that could be called a road. . . . Rumors drifting back told of an awful pit, undarkened by so much as a shadow of a hawk, where no life could exist—or, one variant ran, only the most repulsive life—snakes, scorpions, carrion crows; of terrible heat and poison springs surrounded by bleaching skeletons; of corpses uncannily preserved for eternity by the salt flats. Mountains of any ore you liked floated about in the heat. Death Valley became for Americans a folklore hell" (9).

Mark goes into one of these "mountains" and emerges from the dark mouth of a cave clutching a piece of borate, half-opaque and milky, which he holds up in front of Daria's face. "Phenomena that anywhere else would be objects of pilgrimage are here lost in the immensities" (Newhall 17). Mark is surely searching to be lost this way—no, not searching: willing. He does not desire to leave a world behind, but he would as soon do so—nothing seems to stick to him. Yet his "folklore hell" is back in Los Angeles: here, the desert is a perfection of cleanliness, the sky an open question. The heat is the fire that purifies. What John Burks calls Mark's "anarcho-radicalism" has evaporated (36), and all his thought now is for an eternal present.

Queried about his flight in the plane, he says he "had to get off the ground," which is to say, away from binding attachments to a fixed and hopeless, not to say demeaning and constraining, world. Daria's method of flight is getting stoned. She dares to smoke a joint and offers him some, but he is living with people who are on a "reality trip," which means, to her, that "they can't imagine things." Is there a ring of regret in her voice when she says this? No. The sun is high in the sky and seems permanently fixed there, a beacon and a blaze in whose reach the far past is reborn at the moment when the world was conceived, a moment before life; and where also the end of the human journey has been found, the emptiness that is the destination of all wanderings. The massive rippled valley, the long undulations of rock golden and russet and gray, the atmosphere of dust and stillness all constitute a dream state, in which it is possible to concentrate one's attention and perceive with great articulateness the smallest details of harmonized and unrelenting circumstance. Mark is no fool, but he has not been marked by an education—his clothing is a second skin, not a covering, and his thoughts are as naked as he. He left college because of "extra-curricular activities: stealing hardcover books instead of paperbacks, making phone calls on the chancellor's stolen credit card number, whistling in class . . . and bringing illegal things onto campus like a dog, a bike, a woman . . . . They finally kicked me out after I broke into the dean's office and reprogrammed the computer. I made all the engineers take art courses. Once I changed my color but it didn't work, so I changed back." With more discipline he might have been an organizer, a mover of others, but Mark cannot trouble himself to take up causes.

Daria muses about how peaceful the place is. "It's dead," says he, quietly:

> DARIA: OK, it's dead. So let's play a death game. You start at one end of the valley and I'll start at the other, and we'll see who can kill the most. We'll start on lizards and snakes, and then move up to mice and rabbits. At the end, we'll count up how many deaths we've had and the winner can kill the loser.
>
> MARK: I don't want to play any games at all.

Mark is not free, however, and the hesitation in his footsteps, the way he pulls his lips back when he thinks, show that he knows this. "Pretend your thoughts are like plants, what do you see?" she wants to know, and he replies, "I see sort of a jungle." Even resting with her, he is in some kind of tension, struggling to get away not from this place, this moment, but from something in himself, something that was troubling him long before this film began.

In "getting off the ground," what has Mark left below? Fealties, repressions, arrangements, navigation. He is just here, with Daria, not particularly having planned to find the lookout over Manly Beacon (that "lighthouse in a desolate sea, wrapped in unearthly stillness" [August 1967 Treatment 11]). They stepped up to a precipice, were caught by the strange horizon. It can be said that the broader culture that Mark has escaped is an unfriendly one to youth, a military-industrial state in which the armed force of the police is ready on a moment's notice to serve the needs of high capital. The city is an agglomeration of proud egotisms, in which Mark and his generation are trapped in protest and exclusion. Agents of power are either intelligent but utterly aloof, retreated into self-aggrandizement and the delights of a pleasure dome, or else crass and uncomprehending, the sorts of men who do not merit the power they wield except by virtue of the fact that brutally, they seized it. And the vast reaches of nature are hourly being consumed by hungry developers, descendents of the men who pushed for the aqueduct. How far away is civilization and its police force, even here?

Mark and Daria are shouting and twisting in the sand, kicking up dust, somersaulting, laughing. Like children, some might say, but not like children: like young adults free of the burdens of duty. "So anyway . . ." sings Daria, with a kind of meaningless eagerness. "So, anyway . . ." Then,

"'Soanyway' ought to be one word, the name of some place, or a river. Soanyway River." They kiss:

> MARK: Would you like to go with me?
>
> DARIA: Where?
>
> MARK: Wherever I'm going?
>
> DARIA: Are you really asking?
>
> MARK: Is that your real answer?

Jerry Garcia's "Love Scene," a long, meandering solo guitar riff, is coming up on the soundtrack. "The music is so suggestive," said the 1967 treatment, "that the sense of panic that shook them when they first looked down into the depths of that primaeval sea is gone. The atmosphere lulls them, softly, softly" (12). He undresses her. Slowly, endlessly they make love (in the 1967 treatment, what was called for was "a long love making on the yellow earth of the desert, under a sun which is now blazing with heat and light" [15]). Dozens of other young people materialize on the hills, tumbling, rolling, catching at one another, bathed in dust and sunlight, clothed and nude, embracing and rolling, twos and threes, nearby and far off, the music trickling, the sunlight unyielding, the dusty bodies striving and unwinding, the bodies multiplying, couples dotting the horizon. In Chicago, Antonioni had seen "the National Guard charging against some youths who were demonstrating in front of the building where the Democratic Convention was being held" and this "contributed to changing the whole course of the film" (Cottino-Jones 320), but he knew, too, as he had told Pierre Billard, that "in California's 'love-in' parties, there is an atmosphere of absolute calm, tranquility. That, too, is a form of protest, a way of being committed. It shows that violence is not the only means of persuasion" (55). (The primary figures in the love scene are members of Joseph Chaikin's Open Theater: "They didn't use the word; they used the *sound* of the word . . . always attempting to involve the audience in the *experience* of the action and not the *idea* of the drama" [Cardullo, "Film Is Life" 149].) The treatment was explicit about this, if also more aggrandized: "As far as it is possible to see across the desert there are hundreds, thousands of boys and girls, only boys and girls, all making love. They lie side by side, without shame, as though nothing were more natural. And not only boys with girls, but boys lie with boys, and girls with girls. There is no hint of vulgarity, or erotic frenzy. Others dance, some sing—all beneath the mildest sun which barely casts shadows across the earth" (13). And even that couldn't come close to what Antonioni had originally wanted, according to one observer: "When Antonioni first discovered Death Valley's Zabriskie Point, he said: 'I want to see 20,000 hippies out there making love, as far as you can see.' National Parks Ranger captain: 'The answer to that is a flat no.' Harrison Starr, a man in his 30's and probably the closest Hollywood can come to a sympathetic producer for a man like Antonioni, said later: 'Well, you can imagine how hard it was to talk to the Rangers after that' " (Bensky). At one point, Antonioni had imagined a rock concert in the desert instead, possibly with the Stones and the Beatles. Bryan Gindoff reports how executives at MGM showed him the way out of that impossibility: "With the aid of a wall map and a compass, a giant circle was drawn with LA in the center; it looked like one of those things that tell you how far away you should be when the bomb hits. As best as I could make out, Hawaii and Heber, Utah, both looked safe. Anywhere in between, the cataclysm amounted to twenty thousand people times $29.15 a day plus meals and penalties and overtime; it was more than I could multiply in my head" (3).

And yet, as Daria Halprin recollected to me, no matter "how outrageous and provocative the scene was to stage and shoot . . . the scenes were amazing visually, but perhaps even more importantly, I think Michelangelo captured the 'free love' message, intersecting with raw beauty of natural landscape and human body with great subtlety and regard" (personal communication). One particular feature of the sequence which contributes powerfully to the communication of this "message" is the intercutting between Mark and Daria wrapped in lovemaking and the medium-long and long shots of the myriad others crawling, coiling, writhing in the sand: the personal becomes the communal, the self is blissfully lost.

By August 1968, the script for the scene indicated a cataclysmic event, one which would suggest not merely a crowd or even mob but an entire generation devoted to the act of lovemaking as though the earth collaborated to support them in this conviction. Homoerotic encounters are especially called for (although barely appear in the released film):

> SCENE 96
>
> Beside Daria and Mark are another couple making love. They too are young and their love-making is tranquil and warm. A little further off another couple are laughing and joking: the phase that goes before love. Then they kiss and stretch out on the earth.

SCENE 97

More couples suddenly appear on the hills around. Gradually the couples become more numerous.

SCENE 98

Strewn across the desert *from horizon to horizon* there are thousands of young boys and girls all making love. There is not only love between both sexes, but also between boys with other boys, and girls with girls. (August 1968 Script 77; italic mine)

The desert lovemaking sequence—in which it was planned to use Chaikin's actors as a nucleus and arrange two hundred carefully chosen extras around them—was an adaptation of the culminating passages of the Open Theater's performance, "The Serpent," which featured "bodies intertwining, mingling, and in convoluted crescendo, spiraling to the sky" (Gindoff 4). Shooting it was problematic on many counts, not least of which was the producer's feeling that Right-wing forces were out there trying to stop the film and that "the studio was very sorry they got involved" (Walker, "Interview"); not to mention the fact that the caterers had not been warned to provide enough water for two hundred extras. It was plenty hot. Further, writes Gindoff, "The ground was hard; it hurt to roll over." Walker reports that "since real sand hurts if you roll around in it, hundreds of pounds of synthetic sand were trucked in. Gigantic wind machines were laboriously lugged down the slopes; gauze facial masks were provided. . . . With their faces obscured by white gauze, director and crew resembled voyeuristic medical technicians, watching blue-jeaned and shorts-clad 'earthlings' groping each other while 'sand' was blown into their faces" ("Leviathan"). The rehearsals, in which the Open Theater actors had worked with the uninitiated extras (all hired in Las Vegas) to open them up and get them to shed inhibitions, now seemed to backfire, since the desert was "so different from the comfortable dark carpeted rooms that everyone had gotten used to" (Gindoff 5). It didn't work. "Michelangelo knew instantly that it was a mistake," said Walker, "people making love in the desert. He only did one take of the master scene. It didn't look the way he imagined it, didn't have the look of something almost primeval" (personal communication). In fact, he had confided to Marsha Kinder that the scene "was just an idea, but I never saw this idea as something real. I didn't have the image, I couldn't find the key to doing it, I saw lots of love-ins in America—with groups playing and people smoking or dancing or doing nothing, just lying on the ground. But I was looking for something different—something which was more related to the special character of Zabriskie Point, and I couldn't find this relationship" (28). Just as Antonioni had suspected, "the canyon was a giant womb that needed twenty thousand bodies to be sated" (Gindoff 6). But "it had within it thousands of 'sub-wombs'—ridges, frills, cavities, crevices—all perfect repositories for scattered couples. No coherent nucleus could exist; and ultimately the 'Love Scene' became an orchestration of individual lovers, no more able to get it together en masse than the revolutionaries at the beginning of the film" (6). A month after shooting stopped, MGM was charged with having violated the Mann Act in transporting innocents across state lines for the purpose of filming "scenes of nudity and copulation" ("Mann Act Charge"); subsequent reports suggested "that the hearing was 'politically inspired' in an attempt to thwart the release of the picture, said to be anti-American. 'If this picture ever is shown in this country,' said one courtroom observer, 'they'll hang Michelangelo Antonioni . . . in effigy on every street corner in America' " ("Justice Dept.").

The love party may have struck some viewers as unconventional, but it was hardly as bleak and unforgiving as the vision Antonioni had in store. Ultimately excised was an apocalyptic finale to the sequence, that would foreshadow the violent end of the film and apotheosize the struggle of this young generation against forces malevolent and overwhelming:

> SCENE 99
>
> After a bit, a light breeze springs up. Then it blows harder and harder. All the boys and girls have to quit their love-making. They stand up. The wind is blowing so hard now they have trouble even standing up. Great gusts of dust blow into their faces so they can hardly breathe. They struggle away through the dust, towards any shelter they can find—hand in hand. They have their arms around one another as they push ahead. The hot desert wind is a force of nature, destructive as a whiplash—a screaming curtain of black dust against which the young couples are seen battling desperately, as they appear now and then in the distance. (August 1968 Script 78)

To leave the grid of social organization, as we see these bodies doing at Zabriskie Point, is to enter a general body, to writhe hungrily as all humans writhe. The less order, the more unity. "The world will find it easier to believe that we are all mad than to believe that the psychoanalysts are not," wrote Norman O. Brown in the year the film was shot, "And further, it does not seem to be the case that the psychoanalytical mode of reaching the unconscious has superannuated the poetic, or artistic, mode of attaining the same objective" (*Life* 312). And then: "The 'magical' body which the poet seeks is the 'subtle' or 'spiritual' or 'translucent' body of occidental mysticism, and, in psychoanalysis, the polymorphously perverse body of childhood" (313). In Antonioni's sequence, body is finally land, land is body; heat is dust; sound is rhythm; and the thrust of individuality is multiplicity. In the lovemaking, like each of us, Mark and Daria sense that they have ceased being themselves, that they are part of something vast and historical and old, called life. Mircea Eliade writes of how after cataclysms, "even the disappearance of an entire humanity (deluge, flood, submersion of a continent, and so on), . . . a new humanity is born from a pair of survivors" (87).

NO WORDS

In the air the flying man's heart beat more powerfully. His temperature rose. His sensation became more vivid and more discriminate, his intelligence more agile and penetrating. He experienced a more intense pleasure or pain in all that happened to him.

—Olaf Stapledon, *Last and First Men*

Just as Daria is not driving her own car into the desert, Mark is not flying his own plane. These are two willful types, who have taken advantage of vehicles in their path. With Daria, there is a sense of careless urgency in her appropriation, perhaps bourgeois self-involvement, as though the ownership of an automobile is only a mundane matter, beneath the consideration of a girl with well-brushed hair. With Mark, an aroma of criminality may well seem to surround him, if only because his behavior is unkempt, on the margins of the civil order It is a thoroughly bourgeois sensibility—Daria's sensibility—that would view Mark this way, and Antonioni has cast him and sketched his behavior and social relations precisely to provoke the easy comfort of a sensibility such as hers. At any rate, Mark has borrowed his pink plane.

At the small Hawthorne Municipal Airport (at Crenshaw and El Segundo Boulevards, just east of LAX), where executives are delivered in Learjets, he has found it, nestled among other small craft, the door ajar and the key inside (a signal of one rich owner's complacency if nothing else). "Just a little scenic flight," he tells a technician nearby. "Why the pink plane?" William Arrowsmith wondered rhetorically. "It matches all those rosy pinks of the desert. We can say, if we like, that the director has himself chosen the colors because they suit his chromatic and thematic purpose. But he *shows* us Mark choosing the pink plane and in this way tells us something of Mark's state of mind, his desire to escape the city whose colors are blazing, aniline primaries" (131). Surely too, the filmmaker is throwing the epithet "pinko," applied to him frequently in America, in the audience's face. The plane takes off easily and skims over suburban Los Angeles before heading out to the freedom of the desert and leaving behind a smog-blanketed nest of freeways—John Burks sniped in *Rolling Stone,* "Antonioni has constructed his movie of so many lame metaphors and bad puns that it's staggering" (37). In Mark's hands, the controls seem natural, as though he is an experienced pilot, all the while the expressions of joy and innocence on his face give clear indication that he has never done this before and is just winging it. On this clear day, one can see forever.

In Mark's case, escape from Los Angeles has been a natural, unreflected matter, just like getting off the ground, as though by magic. Hanging around a student protest meeting at the University of Southern California, he found the revolutionary leader Angela Davis and many other speakers doctrinaire and tedious: in a jam-packed room, Mark is sufficiently alienated from the half dozen young people bravely articulating their political positions with eyes shining—he's probably no registered student himself, perhaps the roommate of one—to find the posturing pretentious and empty, the rambling rhetoric ultimately self-serving and impotent. He stands up boldly. "I'm willing to die!" All eyes turn to him. "—Just not of boredom." He walks out. Later, appearing at a detention center to find one of his roommates, who with dozens of others has been arrested picketing the administration building, he is himself detained. And not long afterward he purchases a gun, then shows up on campus in time to see egregious police brutality enacted upon unarmed students in the name of the Law—which is to say, a social order dominated by the rich and powerful, if not, as Mark Neocleous suggests, by the police institution itself, which has "been central not just to the repression of the working class and reproduction of order, but to the *fabrication of order* . . . policing should be thought of as at the centre of the construction of a new form of order . . . increasingly a *bourgeois* order" (xii; 20). It's pandemonium, the police equipped with tear gas and shotguns. *Playboy* opined somewhat blindly, "That cops are pigs and that affluence is evil are revolutionary tenets accepted at face value by Antonioni" ("Untitled"). The filmmaker had been "incautious," indeed, telling *Rolling Stone* (in March 1969), "It's incredible the kind of power police have in America. When I was in Chicago, some kids were singing in a park and the cops took them away to jail. Why? They were only singing. . . . In Los Angeles, the cop is everywhere. They arrest you if you say 'fuck.' Everyone is afraid of the police" (qtd. in Walker, "Leviathan"). Stanley Kauffmann was more forgiving yet hardly less negative, calculating that the "political gesture of this film may not be much more than a kind of personal therapy. It may be an attempt to exorcise a guilt for having been politically quiescent in his recent work, just as the whole film may be an attempt to exorcise a guilt about being middle-aged" ("Zabriskie" 31). One young unarmed black man is shotgunned in the chest. Mark has his pistol out and is prepared to shoot the murderous cop, but in fact he hesitates, and in this moment the killer is killed by a gunshot from another direction. The thought of murder, however, is enough to shock him, and from guilt or sudden awareness that this is truly a mortal space, he flees.

Antonioni had explicitly addressed political violence in a "Note" to the treatment that could hardly have been more forthright:

> The story touches upon a very serious theme: negroes. Perhaps it would be more accurate to say that the problem is glanced over. First of all because it is directly dealt with only in one sequence; also because it deals with events which are shown from an entirely objective view point, with no political implications, since they do not interest me; and finally because the value given to the images of the revolt, will be emphatically spectacular: the spectacle of violence, the most characteristic of the period we live in.
>
> I have thought it best to open the film with scenes which might be considered savage, not so much because they are likely to appeal to the audience (though that would be a good enough reason for the producers), but because this opening sequence should be made to counter weight the other imaginary sequence in the desert, where everything breathes peace and serenity.
>
> According to the most important American sociologists and psychologists, like Friedenberg, Goodman or Lorenz and many others, this is the tendency of the young today: non violence.
>
> There are 41 million young men and women in the United States. This film is addressed to them.

His plan, secure in his mind as a stranger with a distinct view of culture, politics, trauma, and racialization in the United States (he was well aware of the 1965 Watts riots in Los Angeles), had originally been to shoot the bulk of the film in South-central L.A., and to deal explicitly with African American young people on the cusp of significant racial violence. At Watts, Antonioni "first learned that a refrigerator was a revolutionary object, being loaded with desire" (Arrowsmith 137). Strands of this theme perdure in some of the campus action, and in the involvement of Black Panther leaders (including Kathleen Cleaver) in small parts of the film. But on reaching Los Angeles, Antonioni brought on the extremely young Bob Rubin as assistant director, a position that for European filmmakers was central to production and tenable only by someone a filmmaker implicitly trusted, since the responsibility of making the connections and arrangements on set to get the filmmaker's vision onto the screen would in large part fall to this person. Rubin had been born and raised in L.A., indeed in Beverly Hills, and had attended Beverly Hills High School and the University of California, Los Angeles. His attitude was that "to be a pawn of the producer and not an assistant to the director is a big mistake . . . we should not fight a director and tell him something can't be done" (Kasindorf 31). Antonioni, he thought rather swiftly, "didn't quite get it. He knew about the Watts riots. He thought that was what it was all about. I said, 'Look, I want you to spend some time . . .' We went to UCLA. '*This* is where the problems are. *This* is where they're going to be.' We spent some time walking around UCLA and that's how we segued from riots in the streets" (personal communication). The issue of politically involved, angry young white children of the bourgeoisie hadn't previously really struck the filmmaker, but now it did. And now a denser and more troubling vision of the American scene began to develop in the film.

Two of these forty-one million young men and women were Daria Halprin and Mark Frechette, both twenty when shooting commenced. She was a child of Marin County, the daughter of the best-known landscape architect in the country and a choreographer who had put people onstage nude at New York's Town Hall. As a college student she had seen Antonioni's films, and brought that impression of his work with her to this set. As a dancer, "the nonverbal and visual approach M.A. took actually wasn't so foreign to me" (personal communication). Frechette came from a broken home in the East, "the progeny of an Irish-American mother and French-Canadian father . . . reared a Catholic and apparently . . . chafing under Catholicism's strictures" (Walker, "Leviathan"), and was now tightly bound in a Roxbury, Massachusetts commune called Fort Hill, run by musician and self-styled guru Mel Lyman. Frechette had been adopted (as he craved to be) by Lyman once he secured the role in this film (he "liked to think of himself as an extension of Mel's will" [Giuliano 26]): instructed to publicize the radicals' activities, he would bring copies of Lyman's *American Avatar* "to the producer, the director, the reactionary Southern California crew, and always, always, to every journalist that visited the set, tirelessly explaining over and over again the importance of non-violence. Everyone indulged him" (Walker "Set"). News of this young man's psychiatric history had preceded him to the production—"He had a ton of raw talent. But he was also a very confused young man . . . he did have a hard time, before, during and after the film" (Halprin, in personal communication)—and he quickly became a publicist's nightmare because of his persistent proselytizing and his tendency to fly off the handle. One of the articles he would have placed before Antonioni's eyes, early in 1969, was "I'll never forget the day my father took me aside . . ." by Mel Lyman and Wayne Hansen. It began:

> I'll never forget the day my father took me aside, the way he always did when he had something to say to me that was of importance to him. We sat down on the back steps, he fumbled around a little bit, pulled out a cigarette, and said, "You know, son, a college education is a valuable thing, and you should start thinking about it now, because I'll never have the money to send you to a good college, but they do have scholarships now, they didn't have so many when I was your age, and if you work hard at your studies, it's possible you can get one. So give it some thought."
>
> I gave it some thought, about thirty seconds worth, then I finished mowing the lawn and went off to throw firecrackers at toy soldiers in a sandpile. What a gas, sand flying all over the place, bodies falling, just like a real war in miniature.

This, interestingly, came long after the initial screen treatments for the film had been written, based on material by Sam Shepard, in which a bomber squadron finally makes an assault sortie on America per se; and months after Antonioni had attended, and reacted with shock and dismay to the anti-youth police violence at, the 1968 Democratic National Convention in Chicago (Narita, "Memories")—"What I saw there—the behavior of the police, the spirit of the young people—impressed me as deeply as anything else I had seen in America" (Cardullo, "Film Is Life" 149–50); but before the college riot scenes were shot, at Contra Costa College near San Francisco, with their focus on the brutal police killing of a "negro" and the active (and well-paid) participation of the Black Panthers. According to Rubin, Frechette was "a bad environment for Daria" and, pointedly, "incorrigible . . . not supportive of the production, . . . not helpful to Antonioni or to the film." Trying to get the young man onto the set was a daily nightmare, since he "always had something better to be doing" (personal communication). This, when he had been plucked from a street corner in Roxbury and given the opportunity to work with one of the world's master filmmakers, and for good money (sixty thousand dollars, which he put back into the Lyman commune). In many ways both on- and off-camera, then, Frechette was the epitome of the angry young man of the 1960s, a boy with the kind of authority problems that would make him go rigid in the presence of the police. And the police were almost as central to the film as the water we hardly see.

Throughout the work, the police presence is carefully documented by Antonioni as not only brutal but also ignorant, base, and inimical to education, culture, and social harmony. Pauline Kael somewhat churlishly observed that "the evil police have been cast from the same mold as the old Hollywood Nazis" ("Beauty" 96), as though the depictions do not ring authentically enough for her; but when she screened this film she was fifty, and writing for the most prestigious literary publication in the East, which is to say, a card-carrying member of the Establishment. When Daria makes her first entrance to the massive, marble-lobbied sanctum of the Sunny Dunes Corporation, a space lit with a sickly green reflected light, she encounters a security guard in full uniform seated at a forbidding console larded with closed-circuit surveillance monitors ("Such a unique thing at the time: unheard-of. Antonioni was fascinated by that" [Rubin, personal communication]). Rather than being neutral or civil, the expression on this man's face shows intense resentment at the mere sight of this beautiful girl who walks with a happy, self-fulfilled gait. His face is twisted in reaction to her evident youth, his eyes sharp with suspicion and hostility, until the chief executive appears from one of the elevators, at which point he becomes mawkishly obedient, the perfect exemplar of an authoritarian submissive. At the detention center, the police are mindlessly bureaucratic, serving the need of an overarching surveillance system to keep records of every civil "misdeed": one man standing at the grille has his eyeglasses taken away from him. "Associate Professor of History," he replies forthrightly when asked his occupation, but the officer taking his information says that's too long, and types into the record, "clerk." And arrested by the blue meanies, Mark gives his name as Karl Marx; we see an officer typing "Marx. C-a-r-l . . . ." The police come and go from this place with a smooth efficiency and blasé carelessness, unconcerned about the fact that they have wounded many of their prisoners and done nothing to secure medical attention for them. When Mark and one of his friends go to get some guns (to a location on Ventura Boulevard in the Valley), they find themselves in a kind of systematized hunting preserve, a shop offering every imaginable instrument of death to any client with sufficient funds. Not wanting to wait several days for official certification, they claim they have to "protect their women," thus invoking what Murray Forman notes as "the ongoing public debates about handguns, their availability and circulation, and, in the U.S., the powerful influence of constitutional Second Amendment rights," which led to a state of affairs in which some states "actually eased their existing gun laws or squelched bills that would constrain gun access and instate more aggressive safety measures" (50). The police were major purveyors of gun violence in America at the time. At this shop, indeed, some cops are on their way out as Mark walks in, presumably having bought ammunition: they sport big-time shotguns, and stride off with the confidence that comes with having the power to aggress upon anyone who stands in the way. No doubt these agents are off to hunt for "dangerous" college kids. Much later, at Zabriskie Point, a patrolman comes upon Daria and Mark as they prepare to depart, and Mark hides in a bright red outhouse while Daria talks the man off. The boy has his gun in hand again, and is on the verge of murdering the cop, whose routine drive-by (reprised from Hitchcock's *Psycho* [1960]) has been an ugly intrusion into a dusty dreamworld.

When Mark brings the plane back to Hawthorne, we have been well prepared for a grisly denouement. The police, an intrusive and destructive force apotheosized by a malevolent pack of helmeted gun-wielding uniformed men in squad cars, take over the runway space, force the shy little aircraft into a tight box, and hail bullets on the confused pilot. By this time, Mark and Daria have painted slogans on the fuselage and breasts on the wings, and have covered the roof of the pink machine with a green jungle; at the moment of Mark's death the camera circles above, gazing down at the pink manifestation covered with insouciant calls for peace, as it sits inertly inside a ring of police cars on the green, green grass that borders the hard, hard runway.

In this casual way, Antonioni establishes an intrinsic relation between death, even violent death, and the superficial beauties of consumerist culture, yet also between nonexistence and the fully blossoming spirit of youth. As painting, the décor of the plane is immature and energetic, direct and uncensored, willful, charged, vibrant, spiritual, and confrontational. At the same time, through its police the military-industrial system shows itself to be coordinated, rational, intentful, precise, anti-introceptive, tactical, and relentless. In dramaturgical terms, the plane has been painted precisely in order that this antinomy can be established visually at this critical moment, since in its ordinary state a plane upon a runway constitutes one basis of a conventional vision of social order. Planes stand on runways. This machine has to become more than an airplane, more than a mechanical device that costs money to build; that is owned by a rich person; that is hijacked by a carefree young sport; that is technically capable of elevating him so that he can look down upon the earth. It must also be a native spirit, a giant bird, and its flight patterns must mimic the boy's emotional state and physical awkwardness. As the Cessna swoops down toward Hawthorne Field, then, it is both purposive—in its steady descent—and nervous. That the plane is "silly" to look at—an old man in the desert has painted a toothy grin with a tongue protruding behind the propeller, and the kids have inscribed "Freecome," and "NO WORDS" on the sides—perhaps conflicts with its flowery charm; but certainly also antagonizes precisely the sentiment in viewers, that they can share with the security guard at Sunny Dunes, of resistance to, even fear of, the young.

"FAILURES"

When the film was released in 1970, public attitudes toward youth culture were for the most part strident and negative, not to say condescending and dismissive—precisely the reaction that was offered at the time by most "serious" critics to the film itself (and that continues to be offered by people looking back: "There's a weirdly persistent tradition of American film studios hiring foreign directors to make essentially anti-American movies" [Begg]). "Antonioni has no feeling for young people," wrote Roger Ebert in the *Chicago Sun-Times,* "In his European films, he allowed his characters to behave mostly as adults. In *Zabriskie Point* we get kids who fall in love and act like kids (running up and down sand dunes, etc.) and the sight is even more depressing than adults doing it. He has tried to make a serious movie and hasn't even achieved a beach-party level of insight" ("Zabriskie Point"). Ebert (a whopping twenty-nine when the film came out) is looking seriously for a movie about something else.

More generally, and assuming a point of view fundamentally sympathetic to that of the police and the bourgeois interests that control them, critics saw little in *Zabriskie Point* but Antonioni failing. Stanley Kauffmann led the charge with the indictment that "Michelangelo Antonioni, one of the finest artists in film history, has made a mistake . . . this film does not seem to me even a good tourist's notebook" (20). In *The New Yorker,* Pauline Kael turned her thumbs down, calling the film "a rather pathetic mess" and snidely finding in the filmmaker's central usage of

Death Valley "the perfect Antonioni location, because his infatuation with desolation has become his defining characteristic. He wore out his material in his Italian films, and he has not renewed himself. . . . In *Zabriskie Point* . . . he has rigged an America that is *nothing but* a justification for violent destruction" ("Beauty" 95).

Time's reviewer complained that the film lacks "even . . . superficial vigor" and that Zabriskie Point, "one of the lowest points" in the United States "occupies a similar position in Antonioni's career" ("Void Between" 47). "It is possible that the experience of America overwhelmed Antonioni and he was incapable of translating the chaos into a coherent cinematic statement," wrote Richard Goldstein in the *New York Times,* after first mockingly reporting on the filmmaker's six-week preparatory voyage through the country:

> What a trip that must have been: cross-country in his fiat accompli, stopping only for a vanilla shake in Abilene and a chili dog in San Berdoo. Holding open auditions for a leading man at the Electric Circus. Meeting real Black people and politely asking where the next race riot was being held. Getting into cinegroupies. Giving out interviews and saying things like "———ethics." Bringing dozens of people out into the air-brushed desert for an orgy while the sheriff waves the Mann Act in his face. Then flying back to Rome to be alone with his movieola, only to be haunted by a stream of executive commands: take the skywriting out; no pubic hair; cut the orgy; just kidding, paisan—leave it in.

No artist can show everything. But what Antonioni is faulted for leaving out, one has to suspect, is what learned observers like Goldstein would apparently feel more comfortable if they could see: yet one more paean to the supposed liberating classlessness of American society. From such a critical perspective of general denial, Antonioni's color appears charming but purely decorative and inutile. In his affable pink concoction, dropping down out of the sky, Mark represents, if not "hippies" per se, then the "flower culture" (or the flowering of culture), to which young people in the late 1960s were trying—in vain, it now appears—to direct us.

Early in the film, we are carefully prepared for this dichotomy between natural and artificial coloration, this tension between the desert glory of Zabriskie Point and the punishing utilitarian business world of Sunny Dunes—a jarring contrast that the critical establishment, by and large, either failed to appreciate or did not see. "Enjoy the full relaxation of outdoor living," a neutral voice intones, and we see that Sunny Dunes executives, cigarettes fuming in their mouths, are studying some proposed television spots. The screen is filled with the suntanned face of a woman in repose—not real, but a plastic doll. She wears pink lipstick and plastic sunglasses, and the play of sunlight is shiny upon her plastic face. We zoom back and find others—all plastic—in bathing suits. "Bask in the desert sun by your own private pool." A red, blue, and white beach ball goes spinning into the lap of a plastic blonde in a green, white, and yellow bathing suit. At a "tennis court" laid out in front of rusty desert hill formations, a young "man" and "woman" bat a ball back and forth beside a neatly clipped sunny green "hedge." "Drink fresh mountain water from oaken buckets. Breath the unpolluted air." A plastic quail veers in an azure sky studded with puffy clouds. The camera pulls back to show a "father" and "son" hunting below, "in the wide open spaces": the kid is dressed as a cowboy, with a pair of six-guns in holsters and his hands ready to draw, a look of blank ferocity on his plastic face and his dark plastic eyes gleaming with focus. "You might even bag a mountain lion"—we see a stuffed mountain lion and the "father," in his green lumberjack shirt, pointing his shotgun. Half bored, skeptical, discerning, judgmental, the executives sit in their gray silk suits to study all this. They look bedraggled, imprisoned as all office workers are, and so it seems that it is to them, not to an intended television audience, that the voice now beckons, "Get out in the sun, in your own private garden!" A "man" in a multicolored shirt and white cowboy hat is sprinkling some shrubs, the water from his hose raining directly into the lens (yet another nod to *Psycho*). "Forge a life of your own, like the pioneers who molded the west." We see one of the executives in closeup: a balding man whose dark moustache and thick glasses betoken his rationality, his sedentary life, his devotion to bean counting—anything but one of those real pioneers who struggled to survive in the Mojave or Death Valley, prospector Jim Martin, for instance, lugging out a huge piece of silver in 1862 and inspiring a hunt for precious metals. Now "mom," in a fuchsia dress and gay pink apron, watches over redheaded "baby" in his stroller in the modern "kitchen," where sliced and unsliced oranges, ripe and explosively colored à la Cézanne sit on an island countertop next to a cake iced blushy pink and some glass bowls of fruit cocktail; outside the picture window stands "dad" with his hose. When we hear about the "fully equipped Sunny Dunes kitchen" a zoom-out close-up shows that the toddler is actually screaming at the top of his "lungs" (emitting no sound) and that "mom's" face is slathered with makeup, her strawberry blonde "hair" swept daringly into a pair of cheeky curls that match the twin six-guns earlier. We duck down to see two gleaming aluminum pans full of lusty red "bacon" and sunshine yellow "eggs" on mom's spanking new "stove." In this sequence, while the operatives of the corporation are distinctively colorless, the fabular world of their enterprise, gussied up for mass-market media sales, has the bold, saturated, ostensibly unequivocal colors made possible by the introduction of plastics into the consumer market in the 1950s. This is the color of a sequestered environment, produced through commercially processed dyes that borrow from nature but transform natural chemistry in order to seduce the always mobile human eye in an environment of total transformation, provisionality, rhetorical shifting, and bargain-hunting. By comparison, the vistas at Zabriskie Point seem sepulchral. Now for golf, the apotheosis of nonsense in a desert: putting to his heart's content on a special Sunny Dunes "green" is a tanned mannekin (of military build) dressed all in eggyolk yellow, the sky as blue as lapis behind him. The camera swoops down to follow his ball as it runs happily into the cup and his caddy, a red-headed "boy" sporting a huge "grin," deftly lifts the scarlet flag.

Antonioni's genius is to set this critique of America's militant capitalism as a quasi-cartoon Norman Rockwellesque image-within-the-image, and to show the critical faces of business types as they evaluate its possibilities for use as advertising. By plasticizing the depiction of "success," "luxury," and "leisure" in America—that is to say, the products and experience of the controlling class—he is able to demur against accusations that he is critiquing a country in which he's a stranger. Yet at the same time he can be stunningly on point, and reflect the executives' cold and distanced calculation as they see their own world parodied (yet react to the images as if they are straight). The eagerness of the "father" teaching his "son" how to be a cowboy with innocent avian victims, for instance; the triumphant pose of the "mother" in her splendid kitchen; the "fresh air" that is in fact neither fresh nor air; the false colorations all gaily beckoning and celebrating a way of life disconnected from real social connection—all this is hardly myth, and is the focus of numerous cultural criticisms published by American sociologists and cultural critics at the time (exactly the writers Antonioni had named); yet here it gains force by materialization and concretization. The images and their dummy content speak bluntly, and thus with amplification.

Class and its structural conditions are everywhere in this film: the chief executive's splashy office fortress atop his building, with the floor-to-ceiling picture windows giving onto a rippling American flag half as big as a battleship (still flying at this writing) and a splendid view of the "black gold" art deco Richfield Tower (next door to the Mobil Oil

Building, at 555 South Flower Street; built by Stiles O. Clements, 1930; demolished 1969), and with wall screens giving in rotation the time in various cities around the world; the lowly resentment of that Cerberus in the lobby below; the tedium on the executives' faces as in the desert outside Phoenix they plan their puissant futures; the mindless robot efficiency of the police as they protect these lords and their interests; the blatant aggression of advertisement, with its empty lies, its spectacular promises, its hooks for catching at the innermost fears of common people; the civil distrust that permeates the culture even in the face of colossal bounty and productivity: that near the airport and starving, Mark cannot manage to get a sandwich with a few meager pieces of salami and some overripe tomato on the promise of returning with money. "'Well, a foreigner like Ant Oneeonee cares more about these things than we do,' I heard one critic say to another as we filed out through the lobby doors," concludes Goldstein, "And I agree." Even the critical establishment, by 1970, has bought into the capitalist ethic. Establishment cinema of the 1950s and 1960s had offered fat-cat capitalists as essentially adorable romantic types who only happened to exploit people on the way up. Antonioni flips this arrangement, positing his chief executive as part of an essentially exploitative system, and giving him only a marginal romantic attachment that plays no role in the development of the story. Conventional studio-system screen hunks—Frank Sinatra, Dean Martin, Cary Grant, Paul Newman—were all handsome, debonair, and attractive *first,* and bourgeois only by implication. In *Written on the Wind* (1956), the character who has the most money, Robert Keith, is transmuted into an impotent and fragile patriarch; his son (Robert Stack), who stands to inherit, and whose financial capacities are unlimited, is openly seen as an exploiter and dominator, but he is also a reprobate and a wreck, not the love interest in the film. Rock Hudson, who is shown as the man of every woman's dreams, has no money to speak of. In *Zabriskie Point,* Rod Taylor's executive, who at least takes himself to be a love interest (and, presumably, is one in moments that we do not see), is mainly shown controlling his company, a fistful of landgrabbers and thieves ready to refashion the desert for their private gain, not preening in front of a mirror or shining in the limelight. Given this remarkably candid vision of class and power, whether or not Antonioni airbrushed the desert that he photographed is relatively insignificant.

The great and central theme of *Zabriskie Point* is neither the resilience and arrogance of the corporate elite nor the dreaminess and zest of the young taken for itself as an object of study or celebration, but instead a certain morbid ressentiment that characterizes American society and that through his lens Antonioni has been able to pinpoint and characterize. *Ressentiment* had been defined by Nietzsche in 1887 in his *Genealogy of Morals* as a basically reactive response to the world, a way of saying "no" to the not-self, a mode intrinsic to slave morality (22). In 1912, Max Scheler articulated a fuller statement about this condition and its relation to modern life, seeing it, in Manfred Frings's description, as "an incurable, persistent feeling of hating and despising which occurs in certain individuals and groups. It takes its root in equally incurable *impotencies* or weaknesses that those subjects constantly suffer from" (5). When a tendency toward valuation of persons or things relative to one another is accompanied by impotence, wrote Scheler,

> Then the oppressive sense of inferiority which always goes with the "common" attitude cannot lead to active behavior. Yet the painful tension demands relief. This is afforded by the specific *value delusion of ressentiment.* To relieve the tension, the common man seeks a feeling of superiority or equality, and he attains his purpose by an illusory *devaluation* of the other man's qualities or by a specific "blindness" to these qualities. But secondly—and here lies the main achievement of *ressentiment*—he falsifies the *values themselves* which could bestow excellence on any possible objects of comparison. (34)

An "inescapable consequence of exploitation," ressentiment is seen by Edgar Z. Friedenberg, an important American social critic of the late 1960s (and one of the thinkers Antonioni had been reading), as "a free-floating disposition to visit upon others the bitterness that accumulates from one's own subordination and existential guilt at allowing oneself to be used by other people for their own purposes, while one's own life rusts away unnoticed" (*Disposal* xi). Rebellion can reduce ressentiment sharply; acquiescence makes it worse. For Friedenberg, the America of the late 1960s, which is the state described by Antonioni in this film, is a place rife with ressentiment, where a mass electorate can find it "much easier to accept atrocities than public generosity"; thus, the casual intermixing of scenes showing the bourgeois managers at Sunny Dunes enjoying their self projections in the animated advertisement and scenes showing stunning police brutality on campus. "Most citizens," writes Friedenberg, "despise the very idea of idiosyncratic and personal self-expression as the very essence of privilege, and expect the bitter disciplines of adult life to stamp such tendencies out"; further, they are happy enough to support police who are "the visible and ceremonial expression of the ressentiment felt by the frustrated law-abiding citizen including, especially, themselves" (xiv).

Around the perimeters of *Zabriskie Point* are normal civilians going about their normal jobs in California, people who do not question the social order or the repressive functions that prune off dissidents and idiosyncratics. Exploited workers accept the conditions of their exploitation, and turn with rabid ressentiment against Mark because he refuses such acquiescence. And it is more than clear in the film that he is only one of many such resisters, a boy with a flightier fancy than many, perhaps, whose imagination is less creative than Daria's while also being in tune with her. But it is unmistakable that Antonioni is seeing and saying that the serious adults of this America have no time or consideration for the young, and thus, in a vital way, for themselves and their own spirit. The young are to be exploited, or sequestered in educational institutions for their own good—"What is learned in high school, or for that matter anywhere at all, depends far less on what is taught than on what one actually experiences in the place" (Friedenberg, *Coming* 40)—but not respected and tolerated as equal members of society. "There are techniques for keeping body and soul together in an inhospitable wilderness," writes Friedenberg, "This kind of scouting is appropriate to and an integral part of adolescence. A boy who has never experienced it, at least vicariously by sympathy and affection for the kind of boy who has, may never become quite a man. But, what is more to the present point, the society that prefers the kind of man who has never examined the meaning of his life against the context in which he lives is bound to believe that it has a youth problem" (*Coming* 25).

Zabriskie Point clearly shows such a society; but what is more to this point, the critics who loathed or deprecated the film and saw in it only a failed attempt to come to terms with America, themselves lack sympathy for Mark and what he represents, and are therefore, ultimately, in offering their critiques, assenting to that society in all its meanness. Recently, for example, Mimi White deplores that Antonioni's characters seem to be "consciously playing at being revolutionary or establishment figures. They all seem to sleep-walk through the film, in a laconic, stoned out stupor" (43). In 1968 and 1969, to be stoned for many was to be very far from stupor. Mark and Daria plainly assert that to be "stoned out"—or cast out—is to be vitally alive, and that far from hallucination, what they experience throughout this narrative is a feelingful, often tender presence in an environment that systematically works to shun and destroy them.

A CONDITION OF COMPLETE SIMPLICITY

In what way were we trapped? where, our mistake? what, where, how, when, what way, might all these things have been different, if only we had done otherwise?

—James Agee, *Let Us Now Praise Famous Men*

For all its moral hideousness, late 1960s America reveals to Antonioni, and he to it, a striking physical beauty that implies the promise of something better. We consistently see young people onscreen as purposeful, generous, collaborative, gentle even in their plotting against the establishment; people carried away by dreams and by belief in possibilities that lie beyond the cold horizons of the economic prosperity being celebrated by the rich and powerful. As to the past—typified by the short sequence at the bar/café in Ballister—it has almost vanished (appropriate for a culture that reveres movement forward and denigrates its own history) yet what traces remain are sweet, poised, soft in their wornness, beckoning, virtuous.

The bar scene, played by, among others, Paul Fix—an icon of the American screen who had appeared in *Johnny Guitar, El Dorado, Nevada Smith, The Sons of Katie Elder, Shenandoah, The Outrage, To Kill a Mockingbird, Night Passage, Giant, The Bad Seed, Island in the Sky, Red River,* and 210 other films—is backed on the soundtrack by Patti Page, the top popular female vocalist of the 1950s, singing her No. 1 hit (and one of the great popular hits of all time), Redd Stewart and Pee Wee King's "Tennessee Waltz" (usage of which the State of Tennessee, regarding it as something of an anthem, fought to deny Antonioni). This is a song with a hypnotic and elegiac tone, the plaint of a lone woman seeking a lover lost in the past. It beautifully evokes Daria's loneliness—for all her self-possession and tranquility, she seems without real connections, diminished in a vast landscape—and also Antonioni's heartfelt regard for a culture both popular and authentic that was never, truly, his and that therefore beckoned and enchanted him with unbearable force.

And in the midst of it all, with an old timer sipping beer at a padded bar in a room full of suspended thoughts, and with Patti Page singing in harmony with herself, and with Johnny Wilson, "middleweight champion of the world," toothless and amicable and set upon by the alluring sylph that was Daria, we find one of those shots that transforms cinema. Daria's friend James Patterson from the city is working in Ballister with a pack of lost children, and finding them she asks where he can be found; but the little boys gather round her in a way that is not quite overtly threatening but also not quite sufficiently innocent, and therefore, in its way, terrifying, so she runs to her car and drives off. But the camera . . . the camera lingers just outside that bar, where the letters POOL ROOM are painted on the window. The old timer sits with his beer and his cigarette, a man who seems always to have been there. (When the company arrived, as Dean Tavoularis and Bob Rubin recollect, they found that bar precisely as it is seen in the film, with the old man sitting there just like that. "Ask him why he's here," Antonioni prodded. "What do you mean?" said Tavoularis. "Ask him why he lives here." Tavoularis complied and asked the question. "I don't know any better," said the man, framing what seemed at the time a perfect answer [Tavoularis, personal communication].) Patti: "I remember the night and the Tennessee waltz/Now I know just how much I have lost . . ." And that camera sashays in, *right through the window,* focusing on the old timer with the smoke crisply oozing from his lips, and then pulling back a little. Right through the window. (This magical shot, what seems to me a reflection of Hitchcock's *Vertigo,* was done with a forward zoom/reverse dolly combination [Rubin, personal communication], a little homage, and the cigarette back-lit to emphasize the smoke.) In cinema, there is always no boundary for the camera, which is to say, the camera exists in cinematic space the way we exist in dream space. But the freedom of the camera is almost never so directly or so effortlessly stated as here. This freedom to move and to see is precisely the freedom that Mark and Daria, each in a different way, desire and feel hungry for in a country that preaches "freedom" but affords almost none. Antonioni's camera has it in its camera blood.

"Those desolate towns," Beverly Walker reflected to me, "Part of the reason this town had been made desolate is that all the energy, the water, had been drained away toward Las Vegas and L.A. . . . All these people sitting around these dead towns with nothing to do. These were real substantive visual statements" (personal communication). But after New Years 1969, there was a five-week hiatus in the shooting (for script work and location hunting), and Sam Shepard, whose vision this arid, lingering California was, left the company. Fred Gardner, a student and member of the militant Students for a Democratic Society, and Clare Peploe, Antonioni's companion and translator, contributed the student confrontations. The company was eagerly seeking college locations, but, according to Walker, "Several colleges did not want the film on campus, did not want the attention—the *kind* of attention—it would bring. It's hard to over-emphasize what an incendiary period this was. . . . The movement against anything politically radical—tie-dyed clothing, beards, etc. had already begun and was gaining steam" (personal communication). Harrison Starr was beset by people murmuring, "You're communists." It was, he says, "the far-Right Republican set of mind. The film business had so much internecine warfare on that basis. This was a counterculture film, obviously, and they just couldn't understand" (personal communication). And Tavoularis recollected a chilling personal story that reveals the extent to which the Right-wing fears about this film had spread beyond the production itself. He was in Calgary, working on his next project, *Little Big Man,* when one night, in the middle of a winter storm, at three o'clock in the morning, there was a banging on his door:

> Two guys, F.B.I. agents, with raincoats, dark blue suits, and hats. They came in, I had my robe on. I said, "What is this?" They said, "What's your name?" and they asked me questions about *Zabriskie Point,* and especially about that scene in the desert. . . . the transportation of these people, as they say, "across state lines for immoral purposes" . . . I realized these guys'd had a couple of drinks. They came from L.A. They flew from L.A. to Calgary, . . . they had come and knocked on my door, made a report to justify the trip, and went home. But there were these questions about that love scene, the mime scene.
>
> For about ten years after that, every time I traveled out of the country and re-entered, I would always be held up: shuffle me to the side, search my bags, open all my bags, and it would take hours. Once I was coming to America from Europe and I didn't want to go to New York so a friend said, "Go from London to Boston, it's easier." So I did that, but it was worse, it was hours. I finally said to the guy who was searching my clothes, my books, opening letters, "Why're you doing this every time? I know there's a red flag on my passport and every time I come into the country I'm put aside and searched. Why?" He nodded to one side of the room. There was a guy standing there. He had to do his job. And then, bang, I fell off the list, I never had to do that again. But I thought about those two agents, what it cost to send two guys from L.A. up to Calgary. Those were the days, paranoia in America. (personal communication)

Another sequence of great beauty—but urban and modernist, not bucolic and pastoral—occurs very early in the film, when Mark is driving one of his roommates to a sit-in at the USC administration building. Before gliding into the palm-lined streets of Beverly Hills (a section of Los Angeles not at all near USC except in the fictive geography mounted for the film), they pass through a cityscape that is left over from the optimistic postwar boom of the 1950s: faded but evocative colorations, softened geometries, eagerly self-referential billboards attest to an age of high commercialism devoted to intensive visual appeal. In the twittering marketplace, every angle is opened to the possibilities of attraction and allure. Here, the cinematography by Alfio Contini works through compositions that recall the earlier work of Walker Evans *(American Photographs)* and the contemporary, more ironic work of Lee Friedlander, but with a vibrancy of color derived from the abstract expressionists. The sequence begins with a Holstein cow staring out at the viewer from the side of a robin's egg blue panel truck that is moving leftward offscreen. The beast stands on a little green island of grass, at once contented and provocative. As the truck pulls away, we are confronted with a full-screen mural, its coloration and painting style derived from comic books: a farmer standing at the back of a faded red feed hauler loaded up with squashes and turnips is frozen in the act of throwing these goodies overboard into a vast green field bordered by forest growth. A jump to a close shot gives details of his serious mustachioed face, his broad-brimmed hat, the red bandana around his neck, and, through the painter's use of highlight and shadow on the man's arms, thighs, and back, the musculature bravely devoted to work under the unrelenting sun. Cut to a continuation of the mural, camera slowly moving to the right, as we see thousands of dark gray pigs scuttling in the field, presumably toward the feed they are being offered, then a trompe l'oeil two-storey barn-red wooden factory, with chickens and a pig visiting its roof, power lines running alongside it, and blue cloud-studded sky at the far end as the camera now picks up Mark's red truck zooming toward us up the street. By the end of the shot, the real Los Angeles street containing the mural is as visible as the mural is, with a cloud-studded blue sky and real power lines, shadows of which had constituted the "power lines" in the painted image. This is Farmer John's Meats on Soto Street between East Vernon Street and Bandini Way in the Vernon section of South Los Angeles, one of the big pork producers in California, supplier of "Dodger dogs" for the Los Angeles Dodgers, and thus a perfect metaphor for the police state. "That was the point there with the visuals," Rubin assured me (personal communication), and indeed, in the succeeding shot Mark and his roommate buzz past a pair of motorcycle cops and give them the finger. The similarity of the sky—slightly more ominous—and the power lines works to link the painted image on the meat plant with the photographed scene, not only to make a play upon the act of imaging a reality through a representational form (the mural is actually painted on a long rectangular building made of cement blocks), but also to link the frenzied consumerist postwar commercial enterprise of the late 1940s and 1950s with present-day operations in the big city. As the truck comes to the corner (of Vernon and Soto) and turns, we can see green and white delivery vehicles for Farmer John's Meats backed into an enshadowed loading bay, utility poles (like crosses) with high tension lines reflected through their shadows on a second mural at right angles to the first, this second one showing a farmhand who has wrestled a black hog by the neck and is holding the beast in the air. The camera zooms in to reveal the frenetic energy on the boy's face, his tousled black hair, his bulbous eyes and grimacing mouth, and the surprise in the animal's eye and its ferocious open dark pink maw studded with white teeth. Is this play, or a prelude to slaughter, or both? As the truck drives along we cut forward to more fields with hilly ranges in the distance, and black and white hogs frolicking, standing to fight, drinking from a stream where a barefoot boy in jeans and a yellow shirt sits upon a stump fishing. The bucolic and fecund rural agricultural America of the nineteenth and early twentieth century is here juxtaposed against the industrialized urbanized transformation that dominates the twentieth century.

The soundtrack now bearing the persistent repetitive noises of factory construction, Mark drives on, both navigationally at home in this world and emotionally withdrawn from it. A massive fiery red BETHLEHEM STEEL CORPORATION LOS ANGELES PLANT billboard. A Ladewig Company Water Meters Valves sign, white and red, in a neo-deco futuristic sweep of metal. Another sign in white and blood red: Danola Ham & Bacon, here the orthography ornate and implying sophistication. Then, brown on white, in bold caps, BROWN BEVIS INDUSTRIAL. A white Pacific Metals Division truck lettered in forest green. Heller Machines. The blue and white rear of a Transcon Freightliners semi, lettered in red, black, and white. As the truck swerves around a corner, a black-and-white sign for Conway Coating Co. (Antonioni would sometimes see a sign he liked, and then the production had to get the permission of several counties to move it temporarily [Walker, personal communication]. Some billboards were constructed for the production by Tavoularis and, according to the producer, "it wasn't cheap. MGM, who were so desirous of seeing us fail, made sure that we paid top dollar and did them absolutely not as movie props but according to all of the rules of a major outdoor sign" [Starr, personal communication].) Speeding past flickering scrap yards, all rusty and multiform. Then an urban panorama: massed traffic photographed in telephoto on a road lined with tall utility poles and billboards, a creamy yellow office building complex from the 1930s. In all of this, the past remains, not so much alive in the present as transformed and reconstituted, with a rush of humanity moving forward to its purposes and Mark simultaneously lost and not lost in the midst of it. Finally, the palm-lined blue sky of Beverly Hills (North Beverly drive, heading southbound toward Sunset Boulevard) looks precisely like a mural painting of itself, with the stereotypical overarching high palms and the twinkling exotic greenery on all sides.

Given the beauty of the color in this film, and given its centrality—the harsh and clashing urban blotches, the tender and elegiac rural scapes, the fruity yet sunworn flesh—it is something of a riddle why, with its negative ready for printing in the late fall of 1969, a time when Technicolor was still going very strong in Hollywood as the top-of-the-line color facility, this film was turned over to Metrocolor for positive printing. Technicolor's demise as a dye-transfer color laboratory was still five years in the future (even with its founder Herbert Kalmus gone, and with the company restructuring under the economizing pressures of first Patrick Frawley and then Harry Saltzman [Haines 132]) and there were numerous technical reasons why a matrix print from them would have been far superior to any positive print that Metrocolor could, however speedily and at whatever comparatively low price, produce. Metrocolor, for example, had begun two years before to print from color reversal internegatives (CRIs), negatives made from the camera negative that, although they reduced wear, were exceedingly grainy. It is not inconceivable that Carlo Ponti had struck a deal with MGM to use their laboratory facilities for his entire three-film contract with Antonioni. Nor that the line producer on the film, Harrison Starr, believed then of Metrocolor as he does today that it was "the best color lab, the easiest to work with, in the west; they were so sophisticated, . . . absolutely first-rate" (personal communication), and that Antonioni allowed himself to be persuaded by these arguments. And it was true enough that as a money-saving plan, Technicolor had by this time started striking as many as eight hundred prints from a single set of matrices (matrices designed to give superior dye-transfers for a maximum of about four hundred prints). More likely as an explanation, however, was the convenience for the *Zabriskie Point* team while doing postproduction at MGM in Culver City of having the Metrocolor lab on the lot and thus easily accessible for dailies and other business. In using Metrocolor, the studio, as distributor, would have been funneling money to itself while simultaneously reducing the reported profit margin on the picture, such as it was (Haines, personal correspondence). One other theory, that the new management taking over MGM at the time would not have wished to make serious investments in a film that might ultimately redound to the credit of its predecessors, is contradicted by a December 1969 report in the *Los Angeles Times* to the effect that the newly installed president and chief executive of MGM, James T. Aubrey, was of the opinion that "Antonioni's a genius." The film had been projected for a loss. "The previous management had panicked," Aubrey explains, "due to adverse publicity and all that talk about the company's violations of the Mann Act," and subsequently the film had been cut by the director, but Aubrey phoned him with the message, "This is a new ballgame. You assemble that film as you conceived it." The executive informed the filmmaker, "I was absolutely stunned—more so than about any film I've ever seen in my life," and Antonioni, apparently, "broke down and cried" (Haber).

The color in this film perfectly captures the spirit and flavor of the times. Because of the Maestro's utter sincerity and passion in filming, because even in his innocence about America he chose always to look it squarely in the eye, the scenes are radiant, and also unforgettable. Nevertheless, *Zabriskie Point* was neither a critical nor a financial success; it never reached the heights that members of the production team fervently hoped for.

POEM OF THE END OF THE WORLD

Dust allowed him a perception of time as a kind of seamless duration in which past and future could not be sundered.

—Carolyn Steedman, *Dust: The Archive and Cultural History*

To be cinematic instead of painterly, a scene requires action. Is it in order to pronounce the revolutionary spirit that Antonioni explodes the executive's hilltop mansion at the end of the film? This is one of the celebrated sequences in the director's oeuvre, unforgettable and pungent. Daria has heard on the radio that Mark is dead. She goes into the aerie with some trepidation and not a lot of energy, passes by that pool where some rather vapid wives of executives are having a rather vapid conversation, moves along a shadowy passageway where that spring water seems to seep downward into a little footpool, gets wet there ("I think Antonioni gave me a nudge and then I took it where I took it," said Halprin [personal communication], "I imagine it as a kind of symbolic attempt to reconnect with a certain quality—the rocks and water vs. the house and men and business going on inside"), losing herself to her thoughts as the water rushes over her dress. She enters the house where the executive tears himself away from meeting with his collaborators, wonders openly where she has been, and tells her to go downstairs to her room and change her clothing. Instead, she walks out. She drives perhaps half a mile down the road, then stops her car and steps out to look back at the house, now jutting out boastfully from the rocks with the sun glaring full in the picture windows that cover its face. Suddenly it blows, a huge fireball with black smoke that floats upward into the blue just as a storm of wooden fragments drops onto the rocks below. The camera tilts up into the fiery mushroom cloud. Then, from further away, the house, placid on its perch, blows up again, fire suddenly racing out of it like an army of demons, with the fragments of wood again tumbling. Now, closer, as we are looking up from one side near the rocks that cover the house, it blows again, dirt and fire and brown smoke besmirching the perfectly blue sky, and the sound of wood and rocks and glass falling. Closer again, as we look up, it blows, the fragments flying near us. From below, even closer, again the house blows. And from directly beneath, again. And now, we hover in space only yards in front of the wooden veranda when the place blows, a windstorm of wooden stakes and spears engulfing us and moving past before the fire can light up the background. And now we are just beneath one corner of the balcony and it blows again, rocks hurtling in our direction like so many asteroids. We have jumped to just below the balcony, where the stone columns hold it up and, bang, it blows, the fire and the rocks. Then again, from immediately in front of the balcony we are included in the fire as the house blows, the screen going orange with the firelight and the fragments of wood and stone tumbling around in the air before our eyes.

Now yet again it blows, the thunderous blowing sound, and in the dark smoke a refrigerator is demolished, twisted shards of chrome floating up. Black smoke against a blue sky, the camera dropping onto the firepit. Then in closeup, the flames, crimson and orange and brown and yellow, and a secondary explosion with a sharp blast, flaming wood, rocks, flames, the ferocious hungry licking of flames around the stonework at the base of the house, and licking the fallen rafters, and as the camera flashpans to the right, a blue perfect sky, like water in a great aquarium. To the music of Pink Floyd, objects exploding and floating in the blue, deck chairs, tables, towels, a beach ball twisting, a table with parasol, a rack of clothing, bikinis, hot lime green, tangerine, maple pink, a television set with yellow flowers all smithereens of glass, flotsam of suburban life buzzing and flickering in Brownian motion, a fish, a book, a cucumber, a lobster, Campbell's soup, a 33⅓ rpm recording, an olive, a box of Kellogg's Special K, a raw steak, carrots, a chicken turning and turning as in outer space—the great chicken explorer—clothing torn in shreds all red and purple and white, flowers, pages from a letter or a manuscript, fabric white and beige and red, a loaf of Wonder Bread, a tomato with its peel slightly shriveled, turning and turning and turning in the peaceful blue, books, a library, a bottle, more books, books like anemones, a wall of books demolished, pulverized, atomized, the pages torn and flipping, a shelf twisting and twisting and twisting and twisting and—

And suddenly in silence Daria stops staring, the sun is setting red on her face, she has a smile of concentration, she gets into her car and drives away as Roy Orbison sings "Dawn comes up so young,/Dreams begin so young . . ." The actress had not been happy with Antonioni's non-guidance during the shoot, one reporter claimed, and finally, here in this climactic shot, felt "she couldn't cry for Mark because Antonioni had not made her feel Mark's death" (Giuliano).

The August 1968 script had been far more uncompromising and even bellicose in its finale:

> 130. EXT. ROAD NEAR COUNTRY HOUSE
> She stops again on the long straight road that cuts the desert in two. Slowly, as though lost in thought, she gets out of the car and turns to look back at the house high up in the rocks.
>
> 131. After a few moments, she hears the increasing roar of a squadron of bombers. The volume becomes deafening. Daria never takes her eyes from the house. The air is filled with explosions and shattering screeches.
>
> 132. The airplanes flash in the sunset light and the bombs rain down like harmless objects until the moment they hit the ground.
>
> 133. Tremendous, overwhealming [sic] explosions.
>
> 134. EXT. ROAD NEAR COUNTRY HOUSE—DAY
> The house is blown to splinters, to dust, and the bodies of the businessmen and their wives are blasted one hundred, two hundred yards away.
>
> 135. We recognize the remains of one of the women from the swimming pool, her lovely face still smiling frozen in death.
>
> 136. EXT. AMERICA—DAY

> But the bombs are not only falling there. They are falling all over America. On factories, army barracks, skyscrapers, beautiful houses with drives and gardens in parkland, ghettos, humble houses on the outskirts or way out in the desert. Napalm bombs or ones even more terrible, blister the earth wherever they strike and transform the legions of All American corpses into the scarred fragments of monsters. (99–100)

Hiro Narita, who was working covertly with Antonioni in shooting footage for the film, recollected that he had been given "a list from Antonioni of over one hundred images of American life—super markets, factories, highway traffics, oil fields, schools, etc. that were needed" for the effects shots that would simulate the bombings: "Just as I started to shoot them I was told by the producer that Governor Reagan's office strongly objected to that idea. So Antonioni came up with a brilliant solution to the problem, with the ending we see today: the image of a house blowing up in extreme slow motion, including close ups of food and furniture accompanied by the original Pink Floyd score" ("Moments"). This ending required two identical houses, one for shooting the action and an empty duplicate that could be exploded. The action was shot at Carl Hovgard's home, "Bouldereign," off North Cave Creek Road in Carefree, Arizona. For situating the duplicate he would build, Dean Tavoularis "had to find a cropping of rocks where I could put the house so that it would be oriented to north in the same way. . . . I had to fly around in a little airplane, with the door open, and leaning out while someone was holding my belt, and photographing rock croppings and marking the compass readings somehow. In art direction, there's a lot of flying involved, and hanging out of airplanes" (personal communication). In the film as shot and released, we are left with Daria "witnessing" destruction, less grandiose and apocalyptic from a geographical point of view but stunning and completely evocative from a poetic one. "I have always thought of this scene as an act of imagination," Halprin told me (personal communication).

Yet, in the logic of the film itself, why does the house explode at all? Why does this sweet girl have such a fantasy? Is it to make the revolution that Mark and Daria have not made? Or is it to exemplify the powerlessness Daria inherits, that blocks her impulse to action in the world and forces it inward as daydream? Kael's opinion gives an eloquent example of rational calculation operating at cross-purposes to perception and understanding, when she wonders:

> At the end, when America is so lusciously destroyed, is the sequence deliberately beautiful because Antonioni thinks America is so evil that destroying it is a beautiful act or because Antonioni is such an aesthete that, like Musso-

> lini's son Vittorio, who wrote poems about the beauty of the bombs exploding in Ethiopia, he cannot resist the photogenic glories of destruction? . . . It is perhaps a true sign of his aristocratic aesthetics that in the final sequence, when America blows up, there are no bloody bodies, no people at all; only our material objects go up. ("Beauty" 98)

It is not, after all, America that was finally destroyed, but a single symbol of certain arrogant class interests. And the metaphor, if that is what we can say it is, focuses on material objects in part because of the pressures of the Republican administration in California at the time and in part, significantly, because material culture is what America of the 1960s was all about. Further, if what seems evident is not violence but beauty, this is not because Antonioni finds this destruction beautiful in itself but because in it he finds creation. Daria has certainly had an epiphany of political growth, has become able to see clearly the relationship between the particular people from whom she is just happening to be earning some bread and the brutal social order that has destroyed Mark, her new friend. "Isn't it possible that we are, at times, more radical in our minds than in our literal actions?" (Halprin, personal communication). Her interpretation was that her character was a "child of the sixties" in a very different way than Mark was.

But even if Daria wishes to destroy the house in her imagination, a single explosion would suffice. Antonioni had some seventeen camera crews shooting the explosion, so that the footage from a number of points of view could later be edited together into this dance. The central idea that emerges as we see the explosion happening again and again is repetition, and also reversion. What is blown up is instantly reconstituted, a fort-da game of immense consequence and aesthetic force, and the chain of explosions is testament to our investment in joy as we watch. The tranquility changing to vibration; the sudden presence of the hot orange flash and its expansion; the extrusion of the civil property into space through fragmentation and sharp, racing centrifugality; the rain of debris, lazy, happenstance, uncontrollable; and overall, the transformation of architectural form into atomic form, then back again.

Writing about dust and the dustheap of history, the dustmen of London, the turning of things always and eventually to dust, Carolyn Steedman observes finally that dust is "not about rubbish. . . . *It is not about Waste.* Indeed, Dust is the opposite thing to Waste, or at least, the opposite principle to Waste. It is about circularity, the impossibility of things disappearing, or going away, or being gone. Nothing *can be* destroyed.

The fundamental lessons of physiology, of cell-theory, and of neurology were to do with this ceaseless making and unmaking, the movement and transmutation of one thing into another. Nothing goes away" (164). And, indeed, one always has the sense that this sequence of Antonioni's is too short: that his explosions should continue and continue, endlessly continue the cycle of fragmentation and unification. But suddenly we are given Daria's enfevered face. Where does she go now, back to the city, to temping, to smoking her way out? She will not—she cannot—go away. Is she looking for the poem? (Daria Halprin went to live with Mark Frechette in a commune for a while, but he fell in with some violent folk and she left; later she married Dennis Hopper. Frechette, something of a Marxist by reputation, got involved in a bank holdup, was arrested and sent to prison, where at the age of twenty-seven he was found dead one day with a barbell on his throat.) We don't know where she goes, but she goes.

"Everything," said Antonioni, "is true in America. And everything is false" ("With 'Blow-up' "). We pan across the saguaro and toward the dusty pink and orange sky. The great fireball of the sun is setting behind the orange hills, as if all this just happened one day, and all this will happen again.

• • •

Zabriskie Point (1970), photographed by Alfio Contini in the 2.35: 1 format and Eastmancolor with Panavision lenses at Death Valley National Park, Hawthorne (Calif.), Northrop (Calif.), and Los Angeles, and positive-printed by Metrocolor; 110 m. Released in the United States February 9, 1970.

The Passenger

I supposed he was suffering from Korsakov's syndrome: as you may know . . . it is an illness which causes lost memories to be replaced by fantastic inventions.

—W. G. Sebald, *The Emigrants*

He's not your Harry or my Harry. He's Harry.

—Judy Holliday to William Holden about Broderick Crawford, *Born Yesterday* (George Cukor, 1950)

ANOTHER LIFE

On the evening of Wednesday, July 27, 1949, Aldous Huxley, author of *Brave New World, Antic Hay, Point Counter Point,* and *Crome Yellow,* and his wife, Maria, arrived at the home of Igor Stravinsky, composer of *Le Sacre du printemps, Petrouchka, L'Oiseau de feu,* and *Histoire du soldat,* and his wife, Vera, to dine. The composer's friend and assistant Robert Craft was in attendance, and reports the author to have been "even taller than anyone had warned," with "silver-point features, especially the slightly hooked, slightly haughty nose" (10). The trouble for Huxley—he was virtually blind—was that his host and hostess were diminutive in the extreme, manikins, as it were, and had with all reasonability carved for themselves, behind a lemon and a guayava tree in the Hollywood hills at 1260 N. Wetherly Drive, a somewhat elfin cottage, where the giant could not help but seem, as Craft put it, "the wrong size" and "absurdly out of scale. . . . He crouches under the low ceilings, ducks through the doorways, flinches by a chandelier, stoops at table, until we feel as though it may *really* be unsafe for him here, that he *could* actually trap himself in one of the tiny Stravinsky W.C.s and never get out" (10).

Huxley, whose voracious knowledge and ample gesticulations intimidate Stravinsky to no end, is repeatedly "hunching and cringing from the constrictions of Lilliput" (11). How curiously charming it is to read of these two men's trepidations and stumblings with one another, and how profound to consider that as Huxley tries on Stravinsky for size, he discovers a bad fit. The two are nevertheless bonded, and the encounter is repeated on Friday, August 19 at Huxley's mansion. When Stravinsky dies, twenty-two years later, Huxley orates about him. Yet it is manifestly true, and somehow wondrous, that with all his polymathic brilliance; and through the rush of admiration he feels for his friend's astounding creative ability; and even in the face of contradictions between the two of them—Huxley loves banana splits but thinks the movies inane, the typical movie audience full of "semi minus epsilons" and "monstrous oafs," while Stravinsky "would go to any movie, no matter how bad, as frequently as anyone could be found to take him" (15)—H. cannot quite fit into S.'s petite life.

"Ordinary man is at the end of his tether. Only a small, highly adaptable minority of the species can possibly survive," H. G. Wells had written three years before (30); "There is no way out or round or through" (15). Huxley, who often seemed to the admiring Craft and others a man of limitless tastes and surprising wisdoms, had found in the presence of Stravinsky the incapacitating tug of the leash.

OFF THE BEATEN PATH

How shall the murdered man convince his assassin he will not haunt him?

—Malcolm Lowry, *Under the Volcano*

Following in my footsteps will not take you where I have been.

—Buddha

Imagine a man who has come, in an even more substantial way, to the end of his tether. His strengths, duly recognized by all who have met him, do not seem to lead him forward. His accomplishments are underappreciated, or else unrecognized, in the face of a groundswell of admiration for work that has brought him no pleasure and that he does not esteem as very important. Because in his profession he has maintained a deep commitment to pursuing fact, regardless of political consequences, he has achieved a certain casual and even polite arrogance, and he is without friends. If from those he encounters he has respect, he has no love, except in the focus he can bring—thanks to his sharp concentration—to the people whose lives and social arrangements he persistently probes. He has the power to make his observations generally known; and while he sheds light on brutalities that masquerade as etiquette, and evils got up as exigencies; and even though he is energetic and unyielding in his striving to see and to report, still there comes a point when it must seem as though the inexorable, immeasurable flow of events that he has witnessed in his life, and the boundless whim of human sensation and response, are nothing less than an incalculable, interminable ocean, which engulfs and swallows all who work to speak it and which renders every gesture of fidelity vacant and moot. Yet—and this is important—weariness and desperation are a long way off, for he does not cease or retreat or collapse. Instead, a doorway presents itself and our character steps through, into a new field of probabilities. A door opens and, on the spot, he goes through.

In *The Passenger,* we meet a man who is driving through the villages of an unnamed country in Africa. Vigorous and middle-aged (he has a receding hairline, he has come to expect disappointments), comfortable in a Land Rover, with sunglasses and a plaid cotton shirt and safari pants and plenty of cigarettes and some kind of burning question, he stops to converse secretively with squatting natives clothed in dark burnooses—one dark dignified man, pouring tea, gestures for a smoke—and is pointed to a shack in which he meets still others who claim cigarettes and point him back onto the road. Now a young boy, in the passenger seat of the car, gestures the man forward. "*Gauche, gauche,*" pointing. The man decides to teach the boy English: "Left. Left." Suddenly, however—and with a distinct British pop—the boy says "Stop!" gets out, leaves the driver to his own devices. Frustrated (now the opening credits are over), this man who is searching Africa (Jack Nicholson) drives off into the desert, the camera watching his vehicle swoop into frame and curve away in a graceful orbit, not unlike a satellite. He runs off the end of the hard road onto soft mounds of sand, halts. Gets out. Looks up at the blue blue sky and around past the rose pink sands at the rocky hills, all emptiness, all vacancy.

Clearly this is a follower, but whom is he following? Do these individuals with whom he talks have information or not? When they point, there is something offhanded about their gestures: "Note carefully," they seem to say, "but do not understand." The shots that succeed one another in this passage point without stating, indicate without specifying, and lead without seeming to know. Watching this, we are like the protagonist we have fixed upon, seeking an answer to a question we cannot frame yet, since even the question that guides us is more of an answer than we can fathom.

Is it a place our man is looking for, or another man? Now here a man comes. Far in the distance, bobbing upon a camel, and coming closer, closer, closer. As he passes by he turns—his long legs furiously pumping upon the beast's neck—to catch a glimpse of this stranger with his "vehicle." "I am no one to you," his face seems to say, a little superciliously, or at least boasting the success of not being mired in these sands. "I am not for you, I am not the one, I am on my own trajectory." Of course, his peremptory nod might also be a signal . . .

Our man keeps looking up into the hills, and suddenly in a jump we are high in the rocks, at the very focal point of his gaze. Next to us, an African emerges from a thatched structure and looks down into the dune-filled valley where the Land Rover sits. In this subtle and marvelous way, we learn explicitly what was already hinted at in the linguistic interchange between this driver and the boy, namely, that he often does not see what is right in front of him. The thatched home in the rocky hills was there even as he looked past it, and the boy did not need instruction in English although this gentleman—presumably an American—made the assumption that of course he did. The American must have walked up to meet this African in the hills, or the African walked down to fetch him, because after a jump cut we are perched high among some rocks watching the two of them climbing upward toward us on a journey of some evident prolongation. Our driver is wearing a sun hat now and porting some canteens; his guide has rifles. They walk upward into the sun. "How far is it?" asks the follower. "They will tell you when we get there," says the other, rather tersely. "Do they have arms?" "Soon, when we get there."

This is a delicious way of invoking the position of the spectator as he unravels a film, since each moment is a kind of confrontation with strangeness negotiated through surrender to the active, expressive consciousness of an other—the absent (but also present) filmmaker—who is choosing at each instant how explicit to be. How much to say? Every storyteller, for that matter, must make choices of this kind, since at each instant of any and every tale, a disarming and shocking revelation is possible—that illuminates aspects of the moment, the place, the relevant persons—that can be taken to be true and interesting and also irrelevant and distracting. The unwinding of a narrative, or its unwrapping, its unfolding, is thus always a matter for arbitrations in judgment, and the audience is always perforce in the hands of someone unknown, perhaps untrustworthy, unloved, and yet depended upon. Are we taking the right path, will this lead to some fruitful development and conclusion? Not only in narratives but also in journeys this is at each moment always true; and true in the journey of life. What comes next? "Soon, when we get there."

Yet it is all a garden of forking paths, as Borges reminded us. "Centuries of centuries and only in the present do things happen" (45). The plan, the plot, the vector is interrupted, then washed away in the blaring heat. From the top of a hill, the guide and his tourist look down on the desert floor far below, where a military caravan is passing. Too dangerous, far too close. The guide picks up and scrambles away, leaving our man stranded in the high heat without direction, without prospect or purpose. He is soon back at his vehicle, around the tires of which the desert wind has blown the sand so high there is no digging out. "All right!" he bellows into heaven, dropping to his knees, spreading out his arms in a silent crucifixion. "I don't care!" He must walk now in the heat of midday across the desert and back to the town, and we see him emerging into "civilization," which, by comparison with the shifting sands and dark, high, almost unpopulated hills, it must be called. The hotel is whitewashed clay, painted inside with walls of pale and soothing indigo. He orders water and retreats to wash in his spare white room (an entrance through ochre doors in a shadowy indigo hallway). With the shower water running—the camera moving up a whitewashed wall, with a whitewashed electrical cord supporting half a dozen curious black insects; the attendant knocking and coming in with some vodka bottles full of water on a tray; the sound of the trickling water, off-camera, turning this nondescript bunker of the service economy into an oasis—he discovers there is no soap, and sullenly walks out to get some from Robertson, his next-door neighbor.

But Robertson, it becomes too evident as soon as our man enters his room, is dead. The body is splayed upon the bed. The overhead fan running. The body must be turned over. There is a wristwatch, no shirt. He sits next to it, thinking in shadow. We see him from behind, slowly turning on the bed, a pale avocado green door in the distance behind him. From under the bedclothes he draws Robertson's daybook, already opened on the white sheets between the man's spread legs. (The sound of a flute is heard in the distance.) The eyes of the corpse are open and bright, a slight breeze tousles his forelocks. Our man leans over him, staring intently into the dead face. The fan is running. The breeze touches both men's hair. The faces are similar, very similar, too similar. He touches Robertson's hair.

Now he opens the green shutters of the window and leans out to scan the horizon, the small herd of black goats. (The perfunctoriness of life and death.)

Back inside the room, later sometime, a pan from the chambray workshirt tossed on Robertson's chair to his opened suitcase with wallet, belt, passport, folded shirts. In closer shot, a hand reaches in and lifts away the passport, draws it up, opens it. A shot of the body in stillness upon the bed, a travel chess game open and partially started near his stilled right wrist. In close shot, looking at an air ticket. On the outside, in black pen, "MUNICH BOX 58." A hand reaching down into the suitcase and carefully withdrawing a black handgun. From below, we look up at our man as he regards the room, Robertson, whatever is in his offscreen world, with suspicion, wonder, eyes narrowed, face blushing. Now in long shot he paces slowly around the bed and the body, helping himself to one of Robertson's cigarettes. The fan above is running. Picks up the chambray shirt, replaces the cigarettes in the pocket there, exhales and looks up at the fan. The camera follows his gaze, focuses on the spinning blade, pulls slightly away, then moves left and down to where, now dressed in Robertson's shirt, he picks up, then quickly drops, the telephone receiver next to that avocado green door. With a second thought he grabs the receiver again. "I want to inquire about flights." We can hear the desk clerk's accented English: "There are only two flights in the week. The next flight . . . is in three days." He backs out of the room, locking it, and quickly withdraws to his own space.

Again, a shot of a ceiling fan, and the camera dropping to find our protagonist, shirtless, sitting at his table with mucilage and two passports. There is a knock at the door, very distinct, very present. He looks up sharply, pensive suspicion on his face. We hear him say, "Come in," and sense instantly that the knock was in memory, not present experience: his lips are not moving. (Antonioni is guiding us through the labyrinth of time, and so, watching this story of mortality, we directly experience the stuff of mortality.) The man is recalling something from some time before:

"Sorry to barge in like this." A deep, resonant, superior British voice. "I saw your lights on, thought you might like a drink." It is Robertson. (Close shot: fingers with razor blade slicing the photograph out of his passport, delicately, tenderly.) "Oh yes, come in. I saw you on the plane. I'll get some glasses." "My name's Robertson, David Robertson." (Just to confirm for us, so we can be certain we know where we are, whom we are listening to.) "First time I've been in this part of Africa. Do you know it well?" "No, I've never been up here before. I'm a reporter. My name's Locke." (Our first formal introduction.) "Not *David* Locke!"—cooing admiration. And so they meet, or met, and so we meet them in and through the meeting they had once, the meeting from before, recalled now. We are admitted through listening to the recall of a man who met someone, and who was met, and who is even now, while recalling, switching the photographs in their two passports. Delicately, tenderly. Perhaps it strikes us—Antonioni has certainly arranged that it should—that names are incidental in this particular aesthetic universe: Locke we encountered rather fully before knowing him as "Locke," and only now through an act of his recollection do we even learn his name since it is a previous "Locke," a "Locke" of the past who was introducing himself once and is now caught in that act through the agency of a gaze backward through time. Of this Locke, at any rate, we can now learn (from his thinking back to not only what he said but also what his interlocutor responded) that he is a journalist, a celebrated one, "putting material together" for a documentary on Africa, and "finished now or almost finished." (The photograph of Locke is securely out of Locke's passport and in Locke's hands now.) "What more do you need?" says Robertson helpfully. Locke would like to make contact with "the guerrillas."

Quickly, we form the realization that the drive into the desert, the hike up into the hills, was precisely in this quest. The caravan that spooked the guide was military police, also hunting for the guerrillas, and for very different reasons. We are in a police state, where overthrow of the government is some people's passion.

Now, however, it is clear enough that on a chair, a Uher tape recorder is slowly playing—playing, in fact, all that we are hearing and all that Locke is hearing while he works. Locke is not remembering at all, or conjuring this conversation out of his memory; he is listening to amplifications of magnetic signals on a tape that was (perhaps secretly) recorded during an earlier conversation. The voices are not coming from the past, through his recall, but from this very room in the present, by way of the tape and the machine's speaker. Media technology reconfigures time. They've been fighting around here and just arrested some farmers, says Locke, more or less. Robertson's not a journalist too, is he? (Locke turns at his table, looks off-camera, and the camera follows his lead and pans left to the open window.) No, Robertson is here on business, and he's been so many places in the past few years it doesn't make a difference anymore. Robertson strides across the balcony outside the window and Locke joins him. These images are surely his memory, a memory in which the two men play out their conversation on a tiny stage bounded by the proscenium of the window and backed by the "setting" which is the African horizon. Are we able to see Locke and Robertson on the balcony only because Locke is remembering? Or has the camera glided through a membrane and taken us directly back in time, back without the help of Locke, back beyond the space where Locke can go? Have we dissociated ourselves from Locke?

ROBERTSON (gazing off at the desert, and quietly): Beautiful! Don't you think so?

LOCKE: Beautiful . . . I don't know.

ROBERTSON: So still. Kind of . . . Waiting.

LOCKE: You seem unusually poetic for a businessman.

ROBERTSON: Do I? (turns around to face camera; the performer is Chuck Mulvehill, subsequently the producer of *Bound for Glory, Being There, The Milagro Beanfield War, The Godfather III, Mickey Blue Eyes,* and *The Last Samurai*) Doesn't the desert have the same effect on you?

LOCKE: No. (turns around, too) I prefer men to landscapes.

ROBERTSON: There are men who live in the desert.

We have seen that this is true, of course. There are men who live in the desert and men who know how successfully to traverse it; therefore Locke was not listening with particular care to Robertson. In the early moments of the film—which we now know succeeded this conversation in diegetic time—he was not particularly sensitive to men living in the desert, the fact that they lived there, how they lived, although he "prefers men to landscapes." At any rate, Locke now proceeds to change places with Robertson, Robertson who told him that he had "no family, no friends, just a few commitments including a bad heart," Robertson who is a "globetrotter," who will "take life as it comes," who thinks all places "are the same in the end" (Locke doesn't agree: "It's us who remain the same"). Locke changes places with Robertson, dragging the body into his room, dressing it, donning Robertson's clothes, informing the desk clerk: "The gentleman in No. 11, he's dead . . . Locke, David Locke. He was a newspaperman, I think." A door opens, and he walks through.

Through this transforming encounter: the constantly running ceiling fans; the breeze, the casual conversation, the interfluencies between perception and memory; the soft compositions of pale blue, pale green, and white; the almost identical bodies; the face looking down onto the face; the identically-sized and repositioned passport photos; and the calm pans of the camera, the film speaks forcefully to the provisional nature of identity and the substantial nature of being, as though one's name and background, one's profession, one's connections were all a suit that could easily enough be worn or stripped, by the self or by others, even as the body itself has a gravity and resilience whether living or not. "Only in the present do things happen," and further, that pungent, horrifying, edifying sense that "all that really is happening is happening to me" (Borges 45). My acute perception of the insects on the whitewashed ceiling fan wire; or the folded shirts in Robertson's bag; or the razor blade prying up the photographs in the passports; or the little crew of black goats bleating in the scrub; or the water bottles delivered upon the tray by the careful, bronze-dark attendant standing against an ochre door. Reality always acute and fleeting, pointed, pointed here, pointed here where I am standing (where the camera has me standing). When Robertson's life is gone, the array of artifacts surrounding the corpse, each attached to a body of knowledge—"MUNICH BOX 58"—are available for us, exactly as, with anyone, artifacts floating in a set of orbits around an embodiment are generally available for use and reconstitution. Now in a sharp transition that is also nothing but matter-of-fact, we are in the very brightly lit editorial chambers of a huge London metropolitan news organization as a worker goes to the files and withdraws the obituary prepared in advance for "Locke, David." Everything in place? Photographs, yes, check. Life and experience reduced to a dossier, the dossier in a cabinet, the cabinet in a room, the room with a slightly off-kilter Venetian blind and other workers noiselessly, casually going about their calm quotidian business.

This transition to the obituary file is both a movement and an indication. It carries us across time and space, in a kind of essential metaphor; from Africa to London, from the distance and simplicity of a tiny rural village to a busy center of global media production and public awareness. But it also signals an entrance into the public sphere, a broadcasting, and thus deprivatization, of personal experience. What was in its primary instantiation a masquerade, a transfer of objective material under new codes, and an intensive encounter is now become an announcement, a recategorization, an identification, a pronunciation, and a ceremony. That in Africa the corpse of Robertson (become Locke) has been carted off to a nearby Catholic seminary for storage is diminished by the fact of the journalistic reconstitution that now begins, with talk-show testimonials and a local producer set to the task of stitching together a documentary of the "late" David Locke's most stunning work. Locke's transformative actions in the African hotel indicate—because they eventuate in—a process of mediated (and thus, somehow, legal) definition. The death and rebirth are at the core of an information transfer, a message of sufficient weight that major institutions of communication can be invoked to transmit it.

The transfer is also a reembodiment, or a loss of the self. We may easily imagine that David Locke has been addressing the demands of numerous strangers for some time, traveling to meet them, trying to understand them, decoding their subterfuges, translating them for his public, meeting deadlines, kowtowing to producers' requirements, adjusting his thoughts and responses to the limits of journalistic decorum, and all this to such a degree that possibly his inner voice has become stilled, or at least drowned out by the cacophony of demands that modern life has aired in his direction. If he has no further sense of who he is, no ear for his own voice; if the Other has fully adumbrated him; if his intentions and will have systematically been overthrown by his sense of responsibility, then may it not be that the personality of Robertson lying defunct upon the bed has as much attraction for him as his own? It is with a kind of direct, even easy familiarity that he picks up Robertson's chambray shirt, and we can hardly feel surprise when we see him wearing it or notice that he has dressed the dead Robertson in his own shirt and trousers. Language will become a little more difficult, as we see by his stuttering to the desk clerk the name of the man who is dead, but soon enough he will get used to a new name, will study and memorize that passport he has at first constructed as a crutch but will eventually appropriate as his own. What he picks up, of course, in donning Robertson's life, is not Robertson's flesh but Robertson's agenda: the calendar, the prearranged dates, the contacts and business plans as yet unsuspected; expectations—not that he will have as he moves forward in time but—that others, important others, will have of him. Of all this, he is utterly innocent. It could be argued that he is modeled, in this way, after Hitchcock's Roger O. Thornhill in *North by Northwest,* a man who must unavowedly and strictly learn, from (unwittingly pedagogical) others, who he is in life and what is expected of him, and therefore a man who is a signal example of Harold Garfinkel's secret apprentice (see Pomerance, *Eye* 14–23; Garfinkel, *Ethnomethodology* 116 ff).

At the same time, he is now, perhaps more distinctively although no differently than ever he has been, a man confronting the fact that he has no direct access to the otherness of his others. There is a point in the sequence—when Locke's face is positioned a few inches above the dead Robertson's, and we can see the matching aquiline noses and receding brows—when the impossibility of extending knowledge or speculation across the interpersonal gap becomes palpable and sharp. That Robertson's eyes are open allows Locke, and us, to imagine that the corpse is actively looking back, that a message flows from the ghost to the man. But still at this instant, we can detect a form of silence and withdrawal in the corpse, a forbidding gesture that blocks access. And this point therefore intimates what is in some vital way perpetually true between consciousnesses, or between bodies: that each is comfortably trapped within itself, interplaying socially only by means of an artful game of projection that disguises itself among the less unforgiving as translation. There is a sense in which all language is unintelligible, all experience unexchangeable. Even the common codes we build cannot reliably be tested for accuracy or effectiveness, in that we can never transcend our imaginations of understanding. "We translate every situation, every experience, into the same old codes. We condition ourselves," the reporter says. This problem of intersubjectivity will no doubt come to plague the former David Locke, as awkwardly and bravely he takes his first steps in the world as a new man.

A final comment, for the moment, about this sequence of the film devoted to re-embodiment:

It would have been simple enough, and conventional enough, for Antonioni to work his miracle in a more direct way than he does, with Locke arriving in Africa, checking into his hotel, bumping into David Robertson who invites him for a drink. A scene on the balcony with the two men exchanging their views of the world—

> LOCKE: It's obvious they don't trust me. How do you gain their confidence? Do you know?
>
> ROBERTSON: It's like this, Mr. Locke. . . . You work with words—with images—fragile things . . . I come with merchandise, concrete things. They understand me straight away.

—and then Locke goes off into the desert. When he returns, Robertson has died. Locke goes about the process of inserting himself, as it were, into the dead body, or of transferring Robertson to his own embodiment. But Antonioni does not do this.

In the film, the re-embodiment of Locke as Robertson can be effected only through a voyage in time, a voyage stipulated in the screenplay but altered some by Antonioni in the released edit: ". . . he notices the tape recorder again. He goes over to it and switches it to 'rewind.' He holds it for a few moments. Then he stops it and switches to 'playback.' We hear a moment of jumbled voices, a second of silence, and then a guitar solo." The tape recorder: the sound track of the film is itself produced through a tape recorder, undoubtedly a tape recorder just such as the one we see, since the Uher has superior sound reproduction even at extremely slow recording speeds (such as 15/16), a recorder that supplies us with "voices on tape" that are indistinguishable, sonically, from the voices we hear "directly" in the film. It is through this analogy that the knock on the door that sounded so present and real could be made understandable as a recorded knock: *even in its presence and realness it was a recorded knock*. But the tape signals history, a recording made before, and as we see the spools revolving we—and Locke—are transported back in time. For Antonioni, the transfer of identities from body to body, the reestablishment of personhood, is inextricably bound with the movement from the present to the past, from experience to memory. It is the case that Robertson is (and Locke becomes), not a man who lies dead now upon a bed in the next room but, a man who once before stood upon a balcony; a man whose existence is entirely in recollection. The act of transference is thus less a physical motion or interpositioning than an act of the imagination, a traveling within the self—memory is part of the self—and in this way, Locke finds Robertson as part of his own thought. Robertson, even before the transposition, *is already* Locke.

GHOST

> The world of the living remains under the petrifying gaze of melancholia: empty, bereft, filled with people too enervated to live and too cowardly to die.
>
> —Tom Gunning, *The Films of Fritz Lang*

After we see Martin Knight (Ian Hendry), Locke's principal producer for television, expressing his sadness on a televised panel, we withdraw to discover the television that is broadcasting this program situated in a sedate London house, with French doors leading to a large garden. Watching the screen, and sipping some white wine, is a woman with red hair, who keeps shifting her weight from leg to leg. This, we have every reason to suspect (although we will not be informed until later) is Locke's "widow," Rachel (Jenny Runacre). Meandering through the concrete spaces of a mall (the Brunswick Centre, Bloomsbury) is Locke's

"Robertson," wearing a moustache and brown suit. He passes a girl reading on a public bench (Maria Schneider), stops to regard her (and she him), and moves away, while she closes her eyes to recline in the sunlight. As for her: she wears an apple-green linen shirt and has apple-green eyes, dark curly hair, a soft, young face. We are meant to notice all this and to find her interesting, even handsome, but that is all. Back to Robertson (Locke), who is walking the streets around Lansdowne Crescent in Notting Hill, where he comes upon a tall sedate house with white columns, standing back from the sidewalk. No. 4, his house. He climbs the steps and rings the bell.

Rings the bell! Locke's intention is to manifest himself before his wife! If she was part of the tedium of a life he was all too willing to abandon in Africa, if she was even the center of it, still he is considerate enough, and loving enough, to want her in his confidence, and to believe that she can cherish his secrecy. But Rachel is not home (we note with a dark sigh of relief: relief because we desire Locke to have his adventure; dark because this is, after all, a replaying of Nathaniel Hawthorne's provoking, terrifying, engaging story of Wakefield, published originally in 1835, in which a man simply walks away from his family and hides from them for several decades, only and suddenly to return). With his key, he enters. The woodwork in the foyer is painted snow white, the walls covered with William Morris "Willow" paper from Sanderson's, and through the transom we can see lush green leaves being shuffled by a vigorous wind outside. The real leaves and the hand-blocked leaves; a bright green ocean and an optical swirl of design; and with these, the real Locke and the designed Robertson. He enters the sitting room (with that television turned off), spies a sheaf of telegrams next to the telephone, climbs the stairs and enters the master bedroom, which is painted tobacco brown. On the TV show, Knight had said Locke possessed "a talent for observation. He was always looking, always noticing." Now it is clear he is looking at, and noticing, the bedroom in which he lived that discarded life. The cupric green coat tossed on the oxblood red leather chair. He stands in the silence, while the world goes on around him: traffic sounds in the distance, the chirping of a nearer bird. At the end of the bed his obituary in a folded newspaper, flagged with red marker. He picks it up, drops it back in place. This would be how a ghost visited a site, examined the props and artifacts through which, unselfconsciously, a life had once been acted through. "His uncompromising search for the facts was combined with a philosophical detachment," reads the obituary, "and resulted in a consistently penetrating analysis of political trends." A quick race of the eye to other facts, as we hear his footsteps receding: died aged 37 in Saharan Africa, born in London, educated Columbia University, returned to the UK to work for Reuters, married Rachel Hamilton in 1960 . . .

He stands at the tall window in his chocolate brown suit and forest green shirt, hands in pockets. Moves his eyes around, strides out of the room, passing by a note clipped to the door. Camera zooms in a little to see the blue ink on the watermarked paper: "Where were you to-day? Tomorrow afternoon at Ossington Street? Love U Stephen." Now Locke is in his study, a somewhat cramped space, withdrawing a locked wooden box and placing it on a tabletop adjacent Alberto Moravia's *Which Tribe Do You Belong To?* and a postcard of Venice. He unlocks the box, takes a stock certificate and some money, leaves. He puts the house behind him as carefully as he had approached it, keeping a roving eye on the street, then withdraws and examines that air ticket, one of the shards he retrieved in Africa for Robertson's new, second life. We get a close shot. Mr. D. Robertson. Not usable after 09 August 74 (my twenty-eighth birthday, as it happened, and the day of Richard M. Nixon's resignation). Douala—Fort Lamy—Parigi—London—Munich. On the outside once again: MUNICH BOX 58. Robertson, by his own words, is a globetrotter. We do not inquire why for Robertson it was important to pass through London (since Munich can be reached directly from Paris), satisfied that the detour now gives Locke the opportunity he needs to be a ghost in his own house, to inhabit its rooms (its coolish, generally rather large rooms), to appreciate, perhaps for the last time, the charming neighborhood (in which, signally, there are no familiar neighbors). In every glimpse of this escapade we see, much less than the conceptual, verbal universe of David Locke, the concrete objective universe of David Robertson: wallpaper, paint, real estate, decorative accoutrements, the cheap newspaper, the telegrams, the watermarked note, the expensive brown suit, the handsomely planted rose bushes, the bottle of white wine. The books lining Locke's study from floor to ceiling were the fragments he shored against his ruins, his brave utensils, but now they are of no more value than stacked indecipherables. For Walter Benjamin, "The technology of reproduction detaches the reproduced object from the sphere of tradition," puts that object—in this case each volume in Locke's personal library—at an indissoluble distance from what was once a "highly sensitive core, more vulnerable than that of any natural object" ("Work of Art" 254).

Division and distanciation are evident once again in the next sequence, at the Munich Airport's AVIS counter, where Robertson is trying to get a car. All the colors here are for globetrotters, which is to say, vibrant coloring-book greens, yellows, oranges, and reds aimed at informing and directing the displaced international traveler who must situate himself, routinely and forever, in foreign territory. "Where do you want to leave the car?" asks the girl in her red smock, but Robertson, amicably enough, doesn't know. "Where are you going?" "I haven't made up my mind." He is speaking ambiguously, she is not: for Robertson "direction" invokes life choices, futures, a "road" that is not on any map. He is going toward his fate, but he can hardly give this as an answer to an Avis sales clerk. "Yugoslavia," he surrenders, "I'll go to Yugoslavia." She wants more detail. "Dubrovnik?" Yes, Dubrovnik is nice, he'll go there. "How long for?" He makes a little joke, "The rest of my life," but only she is amused, wondering why he doesn't buy a new car. Standing here, he is anybody, everybody, nobody. Circulating through modernity, he leaves no trace.

Or almost. Because when he steps away from the booth (and the shot), the camera lingers on two men who have been watching him and who now get up to follow. One of these is tall, white, bespectacled; the other, an African, is built more squatly, and seems to gaze more languidly. Robertson walks under a bright green "Baggage lockers" sign into a corridor with purple walls. Box 58 contains a cheap black faux-leather portfolio, which he unzips to discover a sheaf of papers: photocopies of machine guns and other weapons. Distractedly reading this, he saunters back into the reception room, and then we see him drive away from the airport. As Locke has become a passenger in the vehicle which is the life—the identity (because of the centrality of performance in modernity, identity *is* life)—of David Robertson (since he is about to meet people who have never met Robertson, his body and Robertson's body are now indistinguishable); as Locke in his Avis car is really a mentality and personality riding a vehicle which is inside another vehicle; we, too, must become passengers and go along for the ride, the ride that is the gradual unfolding of Robertson's new life (Robertson's life lived as Locke would live it). Munich through the front window. A carriage painted white with yellow and red flowers, pulled by a pair of white horses. A placid little street, beside plaster walls painted apple green, between rows of leafy trees, with a passerby slowly hiking up the sidewalk in a vivid kelly green sweater. A *kirche,* the lush graveyard of which is heavily planted with vibrant red impatiens and geraniums. Birds twittering. Robertson steps into the chapel.

As we scan the solemn, even beatific faces of the congregation there, seated between garlands of white carnations, we realize that a wedding is in process. Robertson respectfully backs up at the rear of the whitewashed chapel, and suddenly Antonioni cuts to a view from the altar, showing the (frozen) bride and groom directly in front of the lens, then the congregation, then Robertson far at the back. A wedding: a ritual transformation of identity. Locke has "married" Robertson. As Robertson steps around the back of the room we see that a greenish light is filtering in, that the altar is ornately gilded and set with painted sculptural figures. The ceremony done, the priest and his altar boys (in white and scarlet) lead the congregation back toward the door where Robertson is standing, and we see them all embrace and congratulate the two young lovers. In a cutaway, as the bride fills the screen in her filigreed white gown, orange flames consume a pile of dead leaves in Locke's back garden, while he stands laughing in the face of a disgruntled neighbor. "What the hell do you think you're doing!" cries Rachel, running out in her white silk negligee, "Are you crazy?"

He walks toward the house and looks up. "Rachel, where are you going . . . ?"

And here, we are confronted by a stunning edit (by Antonioni and Franco Arcalli), one of those metamorphoses that typifies both an art and an experience—and that shows how cinema is far from the simple summation of performance, staginess, and camera presence implied by Benjamin when, in distinguishing the "artistic performance" of a stage actor from that of his confrère in the cinema he writes, "The recording apparatus that brings the film actor's performance to the public need not respect the performance as an integral whole" ("Work of Art" 259). As Locke cries out, ". . . where are you going?" there is a jump cut, but at the same time the amplitude of his voice in the sound recording is smoothly diminished, so that in the completion of the cut his words seem to echo in a large chamber far away, the chamber of memory, the chamber of time. Rachel is now standing at the windows of the house, looking out, her back to the camera. Locke's bonfire burned in the height of autumn, but Rachel stands in a summer day, the leaves rich and green outside her windows. She wears a dark plum burgundy velveteen jacket, over which her coppery red hair is brushed to catch the sun. The camera tracks into her head and shoulders, now over silence, and then dips right and down into the decidedly empty yard with its little wrought-iron fence and opened gate. "Where are you going?" can imply an active or a passive drive on Rachel's part: she can be simply turning away from the balcony and into the house, or else leaving him more generally, or going off with someone else (the "Stephen" who wrote that note on the bedroom door?), or "going" somewhere philosophically; or else he can feel that he is being pulled away from her, perhaps irrevocably and without intent, and that, therefore, she is "leaving" his presence. But if the first part of the question is clearly coming from his lips as he stands in the autumnal garden with the leaf blaze going strong, what is the origin of the echo that we hear as we see Rachel at the window? Is Locke/Robertson in the Munich *kirche* recalling this autumnal afternoon with the leaves? Does the echo in Rachel's mind recollect David from before his "death"? The coupling of the sound alteration with the jump cut and the overlapping of one on top of the other produce a conflation, so that all these memories are happening at once, or not at all. "Robertson" in the *kirche* is remembering David Locke-as-was; Locke is remembering his past and his wife; his wife is remembering him; the fire in the leaves is the fire of youth, that now consumes the young newlyweds in the *kirche;* David's "craziness" in lighting that blaze—his forgetting because of his Americanization, although he is British, that in Notting Hill one does not do such things (it is not Guy Fawkes Day)—has also inspired him to light up a new life, to throw a life away, to throw away Rachel without watching where she is "going." The "unique value" of a performance (in Benjamin's words [256]) is not lost or "withered" through the fragmentation implicit in an edit such as this one. In this process a filmic entity appears that is built in part from shards of performance but that as a whole entails a new and unheralded richness. Through the cut, a cinematic moment is made that has a new aura.

The identical feet of Robertson and Locke, at any rate, stand in silence now upon the snowy fragments of carnation that litter the *kirche* floor. He walks (with echoes) to a pew, jacket in hand, and sits. Votive candles burn on the altar before him, and the echoes of new footsteps are heard behind his back. He stares up at the altar, perhaps affected by the ornate beauty. "Mr. Robertson? . . . Mr. Robertson!" Slowly he turns, to meet the gazes of the two men from the airport, who wonder if something went wrong. "We, uh, were expecting you to contact us there." Here begins a long chain of perils that the "secret apprentice," as Garfinkel calls him, must handle with instant aplomb although he has had no specific preparation: questions the answers to which he is expected to know; botched arrangements he supposedly knew how to keep; names he is bound to recognize, and so on. Any slip, and the possibility looms that an identification, a choreography, a life collapse on the instant. "Yes, uh, I'm afraid there was a . . . slight muddle": never deny the obvious truth, and keep that voice low, respectful, sweet, untouched. He is introduced to Mr. Achebe, who speaks with a French inflection and thanks him for having "taken enormous risks for our sake." Now the white man demands to know if he managed to get everything they wanted, whether he has the papers. He is momentarily dumbfounded, but suddenly remembers the little portfolio: Mr. Robertson, after all, can be slightly dotty, even a man with a wobbly recall, as long as he knows how to read a weapons order and supply what he is being paid for. It is imperative for those who must secretly learn how to behave in a situation to mobilize their co-performers into giving needed explication without feeling that in doing this they are being at all abnormal, or even informative. Robertson hands over the papers and says, "You'd better tell me what you think," a direct command to these two gentlemen to give an open reading of the paperwork *as their free consumer opinion* when in fact for him it will be a guidebook to their overall purpose and his role in it. Sitting and reading page after page, Achebe is very helpful when he whispers, "Yes . . . Oh, excellent!" When he remarks with some sadness that it's a "pity about the antiaircraft guns," Robertson can agree, as though the supply problem is quite beyond him. "Our main problem," complains Achebe, "is the military assistance the government is getting from Europe." The white man hands over the first installment of Robertson's fee, indicating that the remainder will be paid in Geneva and that their next meeting will be in Barcelona. "The arrangements for that remain unchanged."

Robertson, plain-faced, has been confronted now with a mechanical process into which he is supposed to fit, although no dates have been provided and he is, it need hardly be emphasized, at a loss for obtaining the weaponry he has just sold. To drive home his precarious position at this moment, since it partakes of the flavor of a danger which will be omnipresent for him through the rest of the film, Antonioni stages a brief conversational moment in which Achebe can confide in him. The soothing roundness of the African's civilized voice hides the secret threat which is launched if Robertson doesn't catch his clues:

ACHEBE: I have heard a lot about you, Mr. Robertson. I realize that you are not like the others, that you believe in our fight. This will be of great assistance to our people. Of course, you realize the present government has agents who will try to interfere with you. In that case, I hope you will try to get in touch with us. We will help in any way we can. Give my regards to Daisy.

ROBERTSON: To whom?

ACHEBE: To Daisy.

Robertson smiles equivocally—who or what is Daisy?—and is soon alone in the hollow of the church as outside a bell clangs. When he looks at the money, he is stupefied to find a small fortune.

DATES

MARCO POLO: It's a wonderful country.
GUARD AT THE PALACE OF KUBLAI KHAN: Yes, it's a country where no one is too unimportant not to be watched.
—*The Adventures of Marco Polo* (Archie Mayo, 1938)

Rachel has come to Martin Knight's editing room to see some black-and-white footage he is splicing together of an interview Locke conducted with the president of an unnamed African country. The questions pertain to a "United Liberation Front," and control of the "northern provinces." The president, a gaunt, middle-aged, bespectacled sort of puppet, sits in a wholly artificial pose of tranquility and domination, gold jewelry upon his wrist, his gaze artfully directed to the great undifferentiated and unidentified No One who constitutes the global audience. The film clip ends. Knight wants to know if he can raise Rachel's enthusiasm for this documentary "portrait" of David, but she has a slightly more cynical view of the man and his work: "Reporters, interviews. David really wasn't so different." She was there when the interview was filmed, and swiftly we cut to the same African scene, in full color, with Locke and his tiny crew setting up among the date palms in the president's garden. Wicker chairs, a small table with juices. "I don't mean to sound disloyal," says she in voiceover, "but he accepted too much." In a flowered green dress, and holding a drink, she is pacing like a caged beast outside the perimeter of the conversational area while he squats obediently in front of the president. "There is no . . . fighting anymore . . ." the African preaches, while Locke turns to watch his wife with suspicion and doubt, "The situation is practically normal." The camera is panning to show the vast presidential compound, servants in white linen, armed guards in scarlet berets. "No opposition. We are a unified nation." Driving away with him in his Land Rover, she says, "You involve yourself in real situations but you've got no real dialogue," a critique (often leveled against the filmmaker) that now shows Locke to be complicit in producing the government's clean publicity image when he was in a position to be more probing, more aggressive, more original. "Those are the rules," says Locke.

At a café in sunny Barcelona, Achebe and his tall white friend are accosted by a gang of paid thugs, who kidnap the African and bring him for a torture session, all this to emphasize that the president, dignified but impure, was lying when he said there was "no opposition." The opposition is systematically being eliminated, and at his command. At a *biergarten,* Robertson opens "his" daybook to see a litany of codes: on Monday 10 September 1973 is written "Melina—3 p.m. Plaza de la Iglesa, S. Ferdinando"; and the next day, in red, "DAISY. 5 p.m.—Osuna. HOTEL DE LA GLORIA." For Sunday 16 September, "call Daisy in Madrid." Back a few pages to Wednesday 5 September: "BARCELONA 12 a.m.:—Parque Comunal—Umbraculo." At a pay phone, while the bartender is filling steins one after another, he announces to Avis that he's not going to Dubrovnik, he's going to Barcelona, "Yes, that's right, for the rest of my life." He peels off the fake moustache and affixes it to a large hanging globe, then, in a temporal jump forward, runs onto the funicular that will transport him over Barcelona harbor. As a foghorn sounds below, he stretches out his arms at the front of the car and "flies" over the harbor, its dark lapis waters flickering with sunlight. This same posture in which he can look down upon the world he sustained over Robertson's corpse.

The Parque Comunal, a roofed colonnade over palms and other greenery, with a gaggle of kids happily playing an arcane game of chase. An old man hobbles toward the bench where Robertson is languishing in royal blue trousers and a robin's egg blue shirt. Pit-pat, pit-pat, come the man's short steps. Pit-pat. He stops at the bench:

ROBERTSON: My name is Robertson. (The man turns, bends down a little.) I've been waiting for someone who hasn't arrived.

OLD MAN (chuckling, pointing off to the kids playing in the brightly dappled sunlight): *Niños.* I've seen so many of them grow up. Other people look at the children and they all imagine a new world. But me, when I watch them I just see the same old tragedy begin all over again. They can't get away from us. It's boring.

ROBERTSON: Where did you learn to speak English?

OLD MAN: You want me to tell you my life?

ROBERTSON (broadly smiling): Yes.

OLD MAN: All right. One day, very far from here . . .

On that line, an exquisite cutaway to something indeed "very far from here," so that the old man's life and the scene we are about to witness are interwoven, just as Robertson's life is interwoven now with Locke's. This is a public execution in Africa, by firing squad, of a man the government wishes to kill, presumably a member of the resistance. The film depicting the event has a cyan tint, as if it is old and faded, as soldiers on horseback marshal a crowd gathering upon a beach to watch the condemned, a tall, large man, led into place, tied to a stake in front of some empty oil drums mounted against the edge of the surf. A cutaway shows the empty wooden casket ready for use. An officer in a scarlet cap reads the warrant as journalists' microphones are held in front of his face. A priest speaks to the man in medium close-up. Three riflemen march to position as the surf washes in rhythmically, line up, aim, and fire, the cameraman zooming in to catch the victim's protruding tongue, bulging eyes. He tries to raise his hands but another shot finishes him. We pull back abruptly as Martin Knight says solicitously, "I'm sorry, I didn't mean to upset you." (We are in the editing suite.) This is presumably more of Locke's footage, being used for the documentary (in fact, it was actual execution footage garnered by Antonioni for usage here). Rachel is just leaving, in a royal blue dress, with the frozen and robin's egg blue image of the executed rebel on Knight's monitor before her. There is a man called Robertson, says she, who stayed at David's hotel. She'd like to talk to him.

She is now dressed again in the green dress with the flowered border that she wore when accompanying Locke to that interview in the presidential compound, but we find her in a flat overlooking the Thames as she speaks with a younger man, presumably her lover, Stephen. A long whitewashed space, with paintings hung salon-style on a wall; casual comfortable furniture; the sun glazing the river. She didn't care at all before, says she, but now that he's dead, in some strange way she does. "If you try hard enough," says the man coming very close, "perhaps you can reinvent him." He means, of course, "through me," but the words hang filthily in the air and cause her to withdraw in consternation. The idea of reinvention has been invoked. It is turning through her thoughts. They kiss, but she rips herself away, leaving him to stand blushing at the sunny window. She is using his blood red telephone to call Martin Knight, but learns the "marvelous" news that he has gone off to the Hotel Oriente in Barcelona, that he may have found Robertson. When she tells the young man, he becomes coy. "Still looking for him?" She takes his face and kisses it warmly. "Yes."

Barcelona, the bird market outside the Hotel Oriente. Robertson emerges, unseen by Knight waiting at a café, sits for a shoe shine; but suddenly he sees Knight in a mirror and flees. We see him enter Antonio Gaudí's masterwork, the Palacio Güell. The rooms are shadowy and dark, set with mahogany banquettes or stained glass windows. Sitting on a bench in one of these spaces and reading attentively is a girl, who turns to stare as, in the doorway, he waits to stare at her. We have seen her before. She has curly dark hair, and a flowered shirt over a differently patterned flowery skirt. He approaches. "What is it, do you know? I came in by accident?" She speaks with a European lilt. "The man who built it was hit by a bus." She gathers her bag and leads him away, into a large chamber they use for concerts. She doesn't understand how he could come in here by accident, so he explains, sweetly enough, that he was escaping from a man who might be following him, a man who might recognize him. "Well," says she enigmatically, "I can't recognize you."

It is clear enough that these two are struck by one another, and also that in some indecipherable way she is several steps ahead of him on whatever arcane path he has been following. When, therefore, she asks with all innocence, in this high chamber which emphatically echoes her voice, "Who are you?" it is possible to dimly suspect that she is already formulating thoughts about this, that in some vague way she may know more than he does. "I used to be somebody else, but I traded him in," says this man, who has also traded in the vehicle he rented for a trip to Dubrovnik for a vehicle that will take him to Barcelona, for the rest of his life. As to herself, she admits, "I'm in Barcelona. I'm talking to someone who might be someone else." This conversation is riddled with the enigma of eroticism, to be sure, but its situation in this dark chamber, the way the two slowly pace around one another like huge cats, the echoing double entendre in everything they say, provide a different kind of harmony, one in which the present quotidian world seems to be rebounding against some hypothetical possibility. She's going to see the other Gaudí buildings, they're all good for hiding in—hide from one's past, one's convictions, or one's obligations, hide from enemies, hide from oneself. She hopes he makes it. "People disappear every day." And then, presto, she disappears, behind a gleaming column.

This comment is an invocation of death, but also of transfiguration. We cannot watch this man for a moment as Robertson without knowing that underneath and "in truth" he is Locke; yet this "truth" is hardly more than a packet of cultural certifications, which have now, thanks to that published obituary, been undone. It is also apparent that his "performance" as Locke was no less contrived and rehearsed, no less habitual. Who was playing David Locke but a man who could also give no clearer answer to the question "Who are you?" than "I used to be somebody else"? And more: if Gaudí's buildings are especially good for hiding in (that is, perfect for our figure), we must wonder why *she* has decided to see all of them. Is this young woman, perhaps, hiding, too?

But any further reflection on these matters is interrupted by a flash of vivid crimson in the local Avis garage. Wearing her trademark "We try harder" button, a dark-haired clerk dressed in matching crimson—so that she disappears into a corporate identity and corporate optical surface—thinks his car should be serviced and will give him a new large one. But, by the way, she has a message for him. It's from a Mr. Knight, who doesn't know Mr. Robertson but wants to get in touch. "He's staying at the Hotel Oriente, the same as you, I think." The camera dollies in. With the massive angular white A of the company's logo behind him, against the vivid red wall, he drops his eyes to read Knight's tidy British schoolboy script in bright blue ink on the Avis memo paper:

> Dear Mr Robertson, We had a mutual friend David Locke about whom I would very much like to talk to you. Grateful if you could get in touch with me as soon as possible at the Hotel Oriente.

"Son of a bitch!" He won't now be needing another car.

Gaudí's ornate and organic concrete block, La Pedrera. Robertson is looking inside for a "*muchacha*" with curly hair. He is directed to the rooftop, a maze of mosaic turrets and walkways. "Hey," comes her voice from off-camera, "Have you decided not to disappear?" He hopes she will help him, and explains that he must find a way to fetch his clothing and get out of town without being seen by a certain man who—"it sounds crazy"—really is following him. He bought a secondhand car. She'll happily oblige, but first, and now that these two have formed a working bond, a secret collaboration, Antonioni pauses to have them look down as upon a sunny balcony a husband and wife carry on a vituperative little spat. "So you want me to get the jewels and secret documents?" says the girl, with a charming and ironic smile. She goes to the hotel and checks him out while, nervously at the bar, Knight watches. He catches up with her outside the hotel. She's in her predominantly pink flowered blouse, he's in a rose pink Oxford cloth shirt.

> KNIGHT: I'm sorry to intrude like this, but I understand that you're a friend of David Robertson.

GIRL: (her face darkening in suspicion): Who?

KNIGHT: David Robertson.

GIRL: Yes, in a way. But who are you?

KNIGHT: Well I've, uh, been trying very hard to find him. I thought perhaps you might know where he was because I gather from the hotel that these are his things.

GIRL: Yes.

KNIGHT: Oh I'm sorry, my name's Martin Knight, I'm a television producer from England. I've come all the way out to talk to him but I can't find him.

GIRL: I see. . . . Well, I'll take you to him.

She persuades him to follow in a taxi, then swiftly loses him in traffic. We may wonder why, if Knight is to be abandoned so peremptorily and if he is to fail in his attempt to find Robertson, it was necessary for the filmmaker to observe this conversation at all. When she has picked Robertson up and they are happily driving out of town, he turns to see her blue bag nestling on the red back seat.

They are in the country now, traversing a long straight road bordered on both sides by matching rows of tall linden trees, the trunks of which are marked with whitewashed bands. The camera tracks backward twenty or so feet in front of the car as it advances, with the flickering leaves and shuddering dapples of sunlight flashing into the distance. A close shot from inside the vehicle shows her dozing in the back, the wind ruffling through her hair. She leans forward. "Can I ask you one question? Only one, always the same. What are you running away from?" In a perfectly calm voice he answers, "Turn your back to the front seat." Sartre described Baudelaire: "It is not enough to say that he resorted to intellectual subterfuges in order to give his life a faded appearance. He deliberately operated a radical conversion; he chose to advance backwards with his face turned towards the past, crouching on the floor of the car which was taking him away with his eyes fixed on the disappearing road" (*Baudelaire* 163).

The camera looks down now from above the hood, as the car continues to race. She is on her knees in the back, with her arms outstretched for a second just as his were in the funicular. From beneath her face, the camera shoots up into the sunlight, past her blowing hair, her broad grin, to the gliding green canopy of the trees. But she is no longer smiling. We cut to her point of view: the road, empty, receding, a point at the end of the focal range becoming smaller and smaller in the canopy of green.

A roadside bodega. They sit on the sunny patio as cars race by. He is telling her his Wakefield story, how everything had dried up for him, how he ran out on his wife, his house, an adopted child. "How did you get away with it?" He says there was an accident. Everybody thought he was dead. He let them think so. "There's no way to explain it, is there." He's a gunrunner, he thinks, and she observes, "Then it depends on which side you're on." As for her, "I'm a tourist, become a bodyguard (she laughs), studying architecture." He wonders what kind of impression she thinks she makes, and she tells him the people think she's all right. "Nothing mysterious. You learn much more packing someone's things." It is curious, and also beautiful, that this girl's self-estimation matches exactly with the viewer's initial response to her. There is a persistent charm in her effortless costume, her casual haircut, the relative lack of makeup, the directness with which she responds to questions. If she personifies youth and vibrancy—a contrast to Locke's oppressive sense that, as he told Robertson in Africa, "No matter how hard we try it seems impossible to get rid of our own habits"—she also intimates a profound wisdom, an alluring and ancient enigma that reduces him.

They arrive at a "very beautiful but over-restored" hotel built "into the walls of an old castle" (Peploe, Wollen, and Antonioni 121), where the old porter pauses to listen through the door after he has closed them in. Evening. Naked upon the bed. Later, in a sunflower yellow robe, she toys with the gun in his bag until he takes it away, as though from a child. She picks up his daybook. "That man"—he is alarmed—"said he was looking for David Robertson?" She has become his secretary, dictating with a soupçon of jealous curiosity. "You've got a date with Merina, at three o'clock on the tenth of September. Don't forget." A cute smile. ". . . And another next day, in a place called Osuna, with Daisy . . . at the Hotel de la Gloria. Very picturesque, perhaps."

Emptily: "I won't be there."

"What a pity. All these girls. Lucy, Merina, Daisy. Daisy again. Daisy seems to be your favorite," with a wondering little smile.

"I think this Daisy is a man."

It is not merely that there are things he will not wish to tell her, and in fact things he will urgently wish not to tell her; but that in all likelihood he does not know what these things are, since evidently he is sailing without a chart and without a great deal of knowledge of how to guide his craft. While Locke had aged and dried out through hard commitment to work, this Robertson is young in his persona, just getting to know the world and its inhabitants. The girl is therefore the older of the two, even if she suspects—she is too smart not to suspect—that a tired adult is lingering beneath the surface of her fresh young lover.

As a student of architecture she can help him construct a new identity. As to his adventure, that he has just finished selling a horde of weapons to a bunch of people fighting some war a long way off, she couldn't be more delighted. Without being obvious, without being romantic, this is the real thing. On what tiny shards of information and ambiguity do we build our conception of the real! Who is she, that she should fall in love with him? Who was he, that he should have thrown his life away? And who is he now, that she may know him?

CIRCULARITY

And we are forced to consider whether it was not life . . . but death, that he took into himself, with each lungful of dust.

—Carolyn Steedman, *Dust*

David Locke is conducting an interview. "Yesterday when we filmed you at the village I understood that you were brought up to be a witch doctor." In a makeshift tent, outside a kind of Dogon structure. A tall and slender man, with a fan. He fans himself, gazing forward, his eyes twin moons. "Isn't it unusual for someone like you to have spent several years in France and Yugoslavia?" A smile, a drop of the head, and the fanning stops. "Has that changed your attitude toward certain tribal customs?" The eyes look up, white and penetrating. "Don't they strike you as false now, and wrong for the tribe?" Locke paces his words with equivalent weight, as though addressing someone who barely understands English (as with the young boy in the credits scene). The man leans forward. "Mr. Locke . . ."

"There are perfectly satisfactory answers to all your questions. But I don't think you understand how little you can learn from them. Your questions are much more revealing about yourself than my answer would be about me. . . . We can have a conversation but only if it is not just what you think is sincere but also what I believe to be honest." He reaches forward and takes the camera, which is whirring, and turns it upon Locke. "You can ask me the same questions as before." Rachel has been watching this on the editing equipment in Knight's studio. He says

Robertson disappeared as though he was frightened about something. They should get in touch with the embassy. Rachel has plans to be there the next day, and in the ambassador's office she is told that Robertson is a gunrunner working with the United Liberation Front under a "difficult" man named Achebe. He gives her Locke's "things." Later on, she goes into the study at home to examine them. The Bolex in its black case lined with crimson, the Uher in its worn brown leather pouch—"Wouldn't it be better if we could just forget old places, forget everything that happens, and just throw it all away day by day," wafts out of it in Locke's worn voice—a notepad, a book—"People will *believe* what I write." She picks up Locke's passport, sits down at the desk as the tape runs out, flips the pages. On the photograph page, David Robertson stares out at her. She stares and sits up, thumbs it, looks more closely, now with desperation and concern.

Robertson and the girl pull up to a vacated whitewashed structure at Plaza de la Iglesa. A modern church and tower against the blue sky, a few tiny kids watching them. She gets out to wait for him, sits in the shadow of an archway. He lights a cigarette and stands in the sun to wait. No one.

Back in Barcelona, Rachel speedily enters a police department. David Locke's past, the life he gathered around him, is now running after him. Rachel knows, or must suspect, that he has become "Robertson," and that Robertson is a hunted man. Though Locke is dead, she is racing to save his life. Try as he might to establish the contexts and boundaries of his life as Robertson, another life is hot on his tail. To be is to flee.

Robertson and the girl are in an orchard, on the green green grass beneath a lush orange tree. He has been dozing, in his green shirt and white pants. She kneels at his side in her pink and white shirt and mauve pants, holding an orange. "What the fuck are you doing here with me?" The wind blows. A dog barks. In the restaurant of a fancy hotel they are finishing lunch. "Do you believe in coincidence?" he asks, "Now I see it all around." A guitarist is playing softly. A waiter comes in to say a policeman is outside, looking for the owner of the white car. He goes out. She turns to watch him, as the camera holds on her seated at this table in this empty place, with the pale apple green cloths on the other tables, the wine glasses, the pink napkins, the ivy growing on the wall. The look on her face is that of someone who is saying goodbye. Outside, she has followed. She translates that the officer is looking for a white convertible with Madrid plates. She will go, it's better. When after a short while she returns, she strides up to his table and sits seriously. "They are looking for David Robertson. There is a woman named Rachel Locke. She thinks he is in danger." The soft, lyrical guitar music. Through the window the sea of green, and some palms, and brilliant sunshine. "In danger of what?"

Robertson and the girl are in the city, a hotel lobby, trying to get a room. But right next to his shoulder he hears a familiar voice on the telephone, Rachel! The two of them run out. Rachel looks out of the phone booth and runs after them. Now the car is racing out of town, careening around corners, making the highway. A rocky hill looms up ahead, with a tunnel passing through. We follow the car as it moves toward the tunnel entrance, but pull off the road as Robertson and the girl disappear ahead. At the lip of the entrance, a large sign painted in red: *GRACIAS POR SU VISITA.* Sirens wail past us as we stop.

We must regard this sign as an indicator that our sojourn as passengers in Robertson's car, attached to his adventure, has ended. From here on, we are free to watch the developments of the film in a detached, even improvisational way. Perhaps this is true for the girl, also. We ride in the back seat now, as they race down the highway. She wears a turquoise shirt patterned with birds. The sirens are nearing. The road curves. A green police car passes them and draws them to the shoulder, but once it stops, Robertson hits the gas and races ahead. Now he has left the road and is driving in scrub, the police having been lost behind. But there is a hole in the pan and the car will soon be dead. The wind is blowing the high grass. They stop near a hilly village at the Bar Fatima to get directions. Back in town, outside the police department, Rachel and an inspector enter a car and drive away with two uniformed officers. At the country bar, Robertson is sanguine. "The police will come soon." She persuades him that escaping to Tangier is not the right move. "Keep the appointment. . . . Robertson made these appointments. He believed in something." She is kneeling in front of him as he sits on the car seat with the door opened. A cock crows. Cars pass. A perfectly typical day, not a special day. Nothing noteworthy going on. The sun shining. "But he's dead." She raises her voice a little. "But you're not." They will meet in Tangier in three days' time. A bus pulls up (the sound of the bus pulling up in the cornfield in *North by Northwest*) and she gets on with some other people, a few older women, a teenaged boy. She waves from the back window, goodbye, see you, goodbye, goodbye. A couple crosses the road nonchalantly, habitually, the way they always cross the road. The bus turns the corner and disappears. If this is not a particularly special moment, it is a particular moment. If this is not a notably auspicious day, it is a day. Borges might have commented that it is a day "without premonitions or symbols" (45), or else that Robertson or Locke, for it is now impossible to discern between them, had in their pursuit or their flight—for it is now impossible to discern between those two possibilities—wandered or headed into a labyrinth that was "infinite, no longer composed of octagonal kiosks and returning paths, but of rivers and provinces and kingdoms. . . . a labyrinth of labyrinths, of one sinuous spreading labyrinth that would encompass the past and the future and in some way involve the stars" (48).

Now he—which he?—is in a whitewashed village, with a black dog and a chubby girl chewing bubble gum, and he sits on the curb against a whitewashed wall under a green venetian blind in his red shirt and nobody comes. Nothing happens while everything is happening. The time passes. The cops have the car now, so he grabs a taxi to the Hotel de la Gloria. A herder leading goats across the road. Some palms. Some telephone wires. Some hills in the distance. A little whitewashed structure, perhaps a bank. A few men and a boy squatting in the shade outside. A large dirt yard, more palms. Inside, colorful postcards near the desk. He gives some knocks with his fist. The patron has a cigarette in his lips. "Thank you, Mr. Robertson. Mrs. Robertson has arrived a few hours ago. . . . We don't need your passport. One is enough." Adjoining rooms. When he opens the door we see her standing at a window, by her reflection in a full-length mirror. An apple green shirt. The flowered skirt. The curly hair.

LOCKE: What can you see?

GIRL: A little boy and an old woman. They are having an argument about which way to go.

This is *them,* of course. Looking out the window again, but with the camera over her shoulder, she tells him what even we can see. The seeing, the telling. To see is somehow empty until the words fill it in. A man scratching his shoulder. A kid throwing stones. And in much the same way, the happenstance of the world is somehow less until it is seen. The man is there, the kid is there, but now in the seeing of them, in that they are framed to be seen, they gain reality. The bleached sky. The vast gravel plaza. Bars on the window. "And dust," she says. "Isn't it funny how things happen."

Dust is what never goes away (Steedman). Locke is not gone; nor, thanks to Locke, is Robertson. Nor is the moment, which seems to stretch into an eternity.

THE PASSENGER

All at once everything—even the moment that he was actually living—seemed to belong to the past.
—Sartre, *Baudelaire*

I say what I can say, not what I want to say.
—Antonioni

If our protagonist is not satisfied with sights and descriptions, we must be. He recounts a tale of a man who had been blind since birth and who had learned to live with contentment in his world. But late in life, being suddenly given his sight thanks to a surgery, he began to see a world of movement and danger everywhere. Things so depressed him that he soon killed himself. Given that we must see, however—that we must see the little landscape pinned to the wall over his head as he recounts this bleak tale—Locke's sad meander is only the prelude to his own finality, his own "inexorable" death (Borges 45). He is lying on the bed. The girl goes out. She tries to pack. She sits. There are birds. A knock. The grille at the window. He stands by the bed, takes a cigarette, sits, lights it, lies back, exhales. Hammering outside.

(. . . And now, in a tour de force penultimate shot—"The idea of doing this classic shot occurred to me at the beginning of the shooting of the film" [*Cinematographer* 134]—lasting close to ten minutes, and made in one single continuous gesture of the camera, over several days, during a windstorm, by the use of a high-tower crane and a gyroscope mount rented from Canada and a break-down set of window bars, and a ceiling-mounted dolly track . . .)

His feet at the end of the bed and the space of the chamber enveloping them, the opened shutters and the grille, a voice screaming in Spanish outside. A man sitting by the wall of a bullring, a little black-and-white dog. A train passing. The camera moving toward the window, slowly, inexorably. A car approaching, turning away—a driving school. The girl walking outside, looking at the window. The camera moving toward the window. Slowly, inexorably. A trumpet fanfare, for the bullring: essence of Spain. A motor being gunned (essence of modernity)—the driving school—the car pulling off. A kid in a red t-shirt running in, throwing something at the old man, turning, running off. *Niños* . . . . The camera moving toward the window. A white car driving in, stopping abruptly. The two thugs getting out (those who took Achebe in Barcelona, and who lounged outside the police station when Rachel Locke went in), one turning and going back to the car, a woman jogging past in red and black, the camera moving toward the window, slowly, inexorably, the car driving off, a sound of doors opening nearby, a door outside, the second thug looking in at the window for a brief second, just checking, just checking, turning, walking away to talk to the girl. "*Vous parlez français?*" The camera moving toward the window. Slowly, inexorably. A motor starting up, mounting, receding. Closer to the window. The girl approaching the old man. A sound of a door opening nearby, behind us. The car driving past the window outside. The trumpet playing, mounting some metaphysical escarpment. Very near the grille. The old man sitting silently with the dog. The girl walking away to the center of the plaza. Very near the grille, very near, then through the grille. Slowly, inexorably. A siren wailing. The girl standing, touching her head. A police car racing into the plaza, circling, kids running up and officers keeping them back. The girl walking to the right, where the driving school car is still waiting, but now driving off. The girl slowly walking, then running forward as a second police car arrives, with Rachel and the inspector. The camera in the plaza turning. Turning a hundred and eighty degrees. At the door of the Hotel de la Gloria. Mr. Robertson? The patron pointing. The camera watching the girl inside now, trying to get into Robertson's room, but the door is locked. The camera sliding over to the next window. Through the grille we see the body on the bed, slumped, tranquil, Chatterton. The police inspector: "Is this David Robertson? Do you recognize him?" Rachel, kneeling at the bedside: "I never knew him." The girl standing at the door, in a kind of shadow. "Do you recognize him?" Quietly, nodding. "Yes."

Now at sunset outside. The driving school car finally moves away, because the excitement is over. The sky is shot with purple and pink. A guitar starts up, the haunting, singing strains of the Catalan folksong "Canco del Llabre," set by John Duarte. The old man is walking away with his dog, they have had their afternoon, darkness is coming. The many-colored glass inside the Hotel de la Gloria is alight.

> Life, like a dome of many-coloured glass,
> Stains the white radiance of Eternity.
> (Shelley, "Adonais")

EVERYTHING YOU ALWAYS WANTED TO KNOW BUT WERE AFRAID TO ASK

Freud says the *unheimlich,* the uncanny, can be understood well by beginning with Jentsch's surmise regarding instances of doubt as to "whether an apparently animate being is really alive; or conversely, whether a lifeless object might not be in fact animate" (qtd. in Freud 132). And Pascal Bonitzer suggests, "The more familiar or banal an object or act is, the greater its capacity to inspire terror" (153). David Locke comes in from steaming in the desert, his convictions evaporated, his intentions leached away, his bravado desalinated, his vision strained, his voice cracked, his memory dissipated: consider whether an apparently animated being is really alive. Or David Robertson laid flat upon his bed, eyes open and green, the wind ruffling his thin hair, his wallet and daybook open for the checking, a man who offers concrete objects, not words, with thousands of dollars in gun orders waiting in a check box at the Munich airport: whether a lifeless object might not be in fact animate. Consider that as Locke works upon Robertson to embalm him: extracting the vital information, locking away the body in false clothing, renaming it: voices are coming back from the past, Locke's voice and Robertson's voice chatting about the horrid conditions in Umbabene, being globetrotters, the airports being the same all over the world. How uncanny is the discovery of the body upon that bed, while the fan turns overhead? Uncanny Locke driving into that village in his Land Rover under the opening credits, being signaled to by Africans who will not speak. Uncanny the man on the camel, prodding, jabbing, prodding, jabbing the creature's neck, turning to stare—Penelope Gilliatt wrote that this man had "a violently trembling leg that doesn't seem to belong to the rest of his body" (118)—uncanny the beast that can traverse the desert and the figure who controls him, the figure who is of a higher order. Uncanny, *unheimlich,* coasting in the rental car behind the white horse-drawn carriage in Munich, the carriage with the huge wheels, street after street. Uncanny the *kirche,* the gilded chapel where guns are sold. "Give my regards to Daisy," uncanny. What are Achebe's "regards"? He cannot mean, "Look at Daisy for me." Uncanny being a ghost in one's own house, and is the house a *heimlich* house? "Rachel—where are you going? . . ." Uncanny Rachel opening that passport, in the darkness, in a white satin robe, and seeing Robertson's photograph next to her husband's name. Uncanny the girl in her flowery dress, perfectly suited—yet too perfectly suited—to her every location. Why is she reading in London, the city of prose? Uncanny the Gaudí buildings, awkward yet magnificent in their awkward, magnificent space, with their echoes. Uncanny running away from one's own past. Uncanny the Time that makes the past, past.

Uncanny, *unheimlich,* being terrified that one's past will catch up, abort the future. Uncanny at the Hotel de la Gloria the trumpet solo for the bullring, *unheimlich* the little driving-school car going back and forth and circling and waiting and going back and forth, and waiting, and waiting. Waiting for what? The sounds of the dog barking, uncanny. *Unheimlich* creeping closer to the window, the barred window, as of a cell, Locke imprisoned in Robertson, Robertson imprisoned in Locke, the two of them fated together. The uncanny is the secrecy of the innermost vesicles of the home, the ultimate hominess, revealed and made unhomely, the story of the man who was blind since birth, the idea that people disappear all the time. Both appearance and disappearance are generally uncanny. Uncanny the green of our green home, the secret of the planet come out into the sun, the green shirt of the woman on the street in Munich, the green shrubs and flowering bushes of the churchyard, the green upon the carnations in the church, Locke-Robertson's green shirt, Robertson's dead green eyes, the green of Africa filtered out as blue walls and ochre door panels, Robertson-Locke lying on the green grass beneath the green orange tree near the Plaza de la Iglesa, the apple-green linen tablecloths in the fancy hotel, the green receding trees on the long straight road, green for life, green for vegetation, green for the slime of death, green for purpose, the green of the African president's garden, green for innocent and callow, the green of Locke's interviewing technique with the witch doctor. The green police car that chases Robertson and the girl out of the city, that runs them through that tunnel. Green is the color of *unheimlichkeit,* since it betokens that which is living but appears dead and that which is dead but appears living.

Does he die at the end because Robertson was fated to die, and his attempt to revive the man could only be short-lived? Or because it was Locke's moment to die, as himself or in disguise as Robertson? Or because with Robertson, finally, Locke felt the incapacitating tug of the leash? Because in Robertson's life, brave vehicle though it may have been, he did not, without hunching and cringing, fit. It seems evident enough that the Hotel de la Gloria, the hostel of glory, is heaven, that however he did it, whoever he was when he got there, he had found his way, or at least an escape from this plaza where the cars zoom and halt, the thugs meander, the man sits with his dog and that trumpeter keeps sounding off his signal that all is ready, all is ready for the event:

> Hopscotch is played with a pebble that you move with the tip of your toe. The things you need: a sidewalk, a pebble, a toe, and a pretty chalk drawing, preferably in colors. On top is Heaven, on the bottom is Earth, it's very hard to get the pebble up to Heaven, you almost always miscalculate and the stone goes off the drawing. But little by little you start to get the knack of how to jump over the different squares (spiral hopscotch, rectangular hopscotch, fantasy hopscotch, not played very often) and then one day you learn how to leave Earth and make the pebble climb up into Heaven . . . , the worst part of it is that precisely at that moment, when practically no one has learned how to make the pebble climb up into Heaven, childhood is over all of a sudden and you're into novels, into the anguish of the senseless divine trajectory, into the speculation about another Heaven that you have to learn to reach too. And since you have come out of childhood . . . you forget that in order to get to Heaven you have to have a pebble and a toe. (Cortázar, *Hopscotch* 214)

The guns are a MacGuffin in this film, if an Italian filmmaker can have a MacGuffin. Our man doesn't supply them, never sees them, has no idea where to find them. Only because Achebe is caught and tortured does justice forbear to fall upon him for taking that money and trading back nothing. He is not, in the end, Robertson at all, the man who has concrete things instead of words, because, like Hamlet, all he ever has is words.

As to the girl, who was reading on that bench in London and whom he finds exploring Gaudí in Barcelona: she is Daisy Robertson, of course. "Mrs. Robertson came a few hours ago. *We don't need your passport, one will do.*" And she has known for some time that he is hiding inside her husband's shell. Martin Knight told her on the pavement outside the Oriente, when they were both so pink, and for emphasis the camera looked up at their shockingly frank pinkness against the shuddering green of the park across the road. She bears no malice, "Isn't it funny how things happen." In the end, both Rachel and Daisy tell the abject truth. Rachel, asked if this is David Robertson, replies that she didn't know "him." She never met Robertson; and now it is evident that she never really met David Locke either: his deepest secrets, his most *heimlich* and *unheimlich* parts (which are, says Freud, the same) she cannot identify. And Daisy says "Yes," because she did know David Robertson and she also knew this one, as well as he could be known, as well as ever she needed to know him, and who knows anything better than that?

As the sun goes down, both women will head off not really to grieve. *Gracias por su visita.*

. . .

Professione: reporter (1975), photographed by Luciano Tovoli in the 1.85:1 format in Eastmancolor, at London locations (Notting Hill and Russell Square), Spanish locations (Almería, Barcelona, Málaga, Sevilla, and the Côte d'Azur), Fort Polignac (Algeria), and Munich; 126 m. Released in the United States as *The Passenger,* April 9, 1975.

Blow-Up

I don't know, I didn't see.

—The photographer, in *Blow-Up*

All my life, as far as I can remember, I have been more interested in what things look like than in what they are. So much we cannot afford to see, since every sighting is a hiatus, a loss of progression, and since the eye cannot appreciate the fullness of the visual field. The eye sees—can only see—what it chooses to see, what it desires (this in the light of whatever shines to illuminate), and can only see now, at this moment in history, while down the street a *clochard* is folding a newspaper. And on and on.

Antonioni's *Blow-Up* is taken from a short story by the Argentinian novelist Julio Cortázar (born 1914 in Brussels; died 1984 in Paris, where he had been living for some years). In the mid-1960s he made a huge name for himself internationally with *Hopscotch,* which followed an earlier and stunning novel, *The Winners.* Originally entitled "Las Babas del Diablo" ("The Devil's Drool"), the piece that is the basis for this film was translated into French as "Les fils de la vierge" ("Virgin's Spittle") and then finally, by Paul Blackburn, into English as "Blow-Up." It concerns perception and vulnerability, and begins with a narrator's doubt and blockage: exactly, perhaps, the doubt and blockage that challenge any sensitive interpreter who, receptive enough to the depths of a racing experience, is confronted or daunted with the need to spell it out: "It'll never be known how this has to be told, . . ." That. Since every event has its own nature and its own structure, both before and beyond what we think to impose upon it, and since things are exigent. Easy enough, always, the urge to tell something, but what is it, finally, that must be said? "It'll never be known how this has to be told, in the first person or in the second, using the third person plural or continually inventing modes that will serve for nothing. If one might say: I will see the moon rose, or: we hurt me at the back of my eyes, and especially: you the blond woman was the clouds that race before my your his our yours their faces. What the hell" ("Blow Up").

The peregrination from this spot, this instant, these molecules, to an outcome in a future; or to the past, the many pasts—or into subjunctivity since other possibilities could have taken shape, or still could—and the skipping around because the mind will not settle long upon anything before feeling that hunger to move again. Elaine Scarry notes the "high ratio of intensity to extension . . . already at work in the flower" (56). Concentrate on anything, a tiny gecko on a drainpipe, and soon with a flicker the mind jumps off to a puddle of green slime or a packet of cigarettes, a sleek town car, an old man dusting antiques, the streets of London.

A young photographer, so the story goes, more or less weary of his fashion work, more or less weary of London, goes off one (Saturday?—film does not share our calendar) morning and finds a beautiful, secluded park where he shoots pigeons, tennis courts, the wind blowing through the trees. (A creature in a little brown fedora is marching around stabbing stray pieces of paper with a stick, and there are round plots of roses that bring to mind both T.S. Eliot's "Burnt Norton," since they have the look "of flowers that are looked at," and Dashiell Hammett's *Red Harvest,* since they are "sitting very still, as if to call attention to how still they [are] sitting" [138]) A gray sky, neither hopeless nor offering. A man and woman are climbing up a hill, and he bounces off to follow them into an upper grove where on a long green lawn—spectacular!—bordered by tall windblown trees and near a giant bush they embrace and perhaps argue, he cannot hear. In a lonely moment, what can a man argue about with a woman? Snip, he works at them as the wind blows, snip, snip, shooting and winding that film, crouching, squatting, leaning, hiding. "Wind-swayed branches," a very early script directed, "Here everything is green, even the pair of lovers strolling about" (Script for *Story of a Man and Woman*). Everything is green—a beautiful circumlocution of a physical and philosophical problem, since, as C.L. Hardin points out, "We are not entitled to say that physical objects have determinate colors *simpliciter.* Given a particular observer in a particular adaptational state and particular standard conditions, a color can be assigned to an object as precisely as the observer's perceptual condition warrants, but we cannot expect the assignment to remain the same when the set of conditions or the observer's adaptational state is changed" (81).

But everything is green. Is she holding the man, is she reaching for him? Are they afraid to be here, in this apparently empty Arcadian place where all the forces of mortality hover and swell, and alone (they do not yet see the photographer)? He's shifting position, moving forward from behind a little tree. Snip, snap. She's looking around, frozen, terrified. Detecting him, she comes running: "You can't photograph here! We want to be left in peace!" He can do as he pleases, it's a public place, and it's not his fault there's no peace, but if she comes round to his flat he'll give her the film (this after she lunges with her teeth upon his hand like a rabid dog). She goes back to find the lover, who has now vanished. Snip, snap, the bush. Snap, the woman standing there, then running off, over a hillock, down, away. The photographer takes himself home. Next door at his friend the abstract painter's, he sees a completed canvas lying on the floor, all colored dots dropped, as it were, at random. The painter confides that it becomes fascinating as soon as you have something to hang onto—like finding a clue in a detective story.

What is it to find a clue in a detective story? As the author's point is to ongoingly engage the reader, the form must be constructed in such a way that finding a clue gives no particular illumination at all. Illumination is reserved for the narrational deus ex machina who appears in the final moments to explicate, in that well-worn matter-of-fact way, what has hitherto been inexplicable. You find something to hang onto when you find a clue, but only temporarily. Hanging on is not having or joining.

The girl from the park shows up and, at his invitation, smokes a little pot with the photographer as he stalls before deciding whether to give her the film she so desperately seeks. They prepare for an idyll together that—oddly enough for Antonioni, who virtually never resists filming an idyll—we won't see, since it is decisively interrupted by a commercial introjection, the delivery of a propeller he has earlier (and on a whim) bought at an antiquary. (More than anything, it is heavy and propels nothing.) The boy and girl, shirtless and ineffably smooth now, banter for a moment about where such a thing could go: a conversation of two or three lines that is at once an address to the profound aesthetic question of the placement of objects in space and also nothing, a perfect ort. But look at the time, she must run! She takes her leave, and as she goes he watches, the way he might observe any object receding from view. He makes prints of what was shot in the park—and presto!—discovers something bizarre and life-changing in one of them. All along, this young man has been self-possessed, brazenly dispassionate, unfeeling about his world, but by film's end, because of what he has seen and not seen, he becomes what we can only call a human being. Or (and at film's end this becomes an important "or"), he becomes what we wish him to become.

Some viewers thought the film Hitchcockian, some found it offensive, some were puzzled, some electrified. In one of his very early film reviews Roger Ebert reported that "it is all the thing now to try to figure out what in hell Antonioni was up to, and at cocktail parties 'Blow-Up' is analyzed scene by scene, almost shot by shot, and even the Hollywood people, even the studio PR men, are going to see it. It is a dazzling accomplishment, they agree. Rarely has color been put on film with more skill" ("Interview"). The usually stiff Stanley Kauffmann, thinking it showed "a remarkable ability to absorb and redeploy the essences of a foreign city without getting either prettily or grimly picturesque," admitted he "would be content to see one film a year as good as *Blow-Up*—from Antonioni or anyone else" for the rest of his life (74, 77).

Along with his habitual writing partner Tonino Guerra and the British playwright Edward Bond, Antonioni adapted this piece—originally set on Paris's Île Saint-Louis—for a London locale, where he filmed in 1966 with a cast including David Hemmings and Vanessa Redgrave (both relatively unknown), Sarah Miles, John Castle, Peter Bowles, and the celebrated international model, Countess Veruschka von Lehndorff. Produced by Carlo Ponti for under two million dollars as the first of a contracted trio of English-language films (the other two were *The Passenger* and *Zabriskie Point*), and released by MGM in the midwinter and early spring of 1967—not to art theaters in North America but to first-run theaters, thus becoming the first European import to compete openly with Hollywood fare on American screens—*Blow-Up* had netted more than twenty million dollars worldwide by the end of the decade and has taken in more than six million dollars in video rentals in addition. Its sexual frankness drove one of the final nails into the coffin of the Production Code. Its visual allure—making use of an especially vibrant look (even though, like the other two Ponti projects, it was processed at Metrocolor)—and its hiply casual use of London locales and "mod" action (drug use and partying), not to say the obliqueness of the narrative and its shocking lack of closure, all reflected the typical elevation of the modern everyday that was to be found in philosophically informed European film, and awestruck American audiences. (I saw it in the Midwest in March 1967 at a theater not one single seat of which was empty, and in which, as the end credits rolled, there was stunned silence.)

It is immaterial to an analysis of Antonioni's method and effects to dwell at exceeding length on the transformations he effected from his source materials: rather like Hitchcock working with literary sources to which he felt no compulsion to be faithful, he sees in literary works the necessary skeletons upon which he can build his films. In Cortázar's original story, for example, there is no gun and no killing, but the photographer, who is also active in recalling all this for us, shoots some pictures of a woman with a pretty young boy and speculates to himself what sorts of adventures these two might get up to: "the teasing kisses, the woman mildly repelling the hands which were trying to undress her, like in novels, on a bed that would have a lilac-colored comforter, on the other hand she taking off his clothes, plainly mother and son under a milky yellow light, and everything would end up as usual" (123). When the woman catches the photographer at work, at any rate, and disputes his right to take pictures in public, the young kid takes off, "disappearing like a gossamer filament of angel-spit in the morning air" (125). Later, however, looking at his blowups, the photographer sees that a man in a parked car nearby wasn't as peripheral to the scene as he'd thought: "The real boss was waiting there, smiling petulantly, already certain of the business; he was not the first to send a woman in the vanguard, to bring him the prisoners manacled with flowers" (129). And then he begins to see a clear future, one of those "extensions" beyond "intensity," in which the boy, caught in the trap, "was going to say yes, . . . the proposition carried money with it or a gimmick, and I couldn't yell for him to run, or even open the road to him again with a new photo, a small and almost meek intervention which would ruin the framework of drool and perfume" (130). What Antonioni retains of this is the mystery of the photograph that contains multiple meanings, the photographer hungry to photograph, the idea of the sexual setup, the contrast between one apparently blissful eventuality and another that can be taken to be darker. He makes a shift "from the presumption of homosexuality to the fact of murder" (Kauffmann 72), yet retains that comforting bed of lilac purple, as we shall see. A bed for defloration of sorts, a bed for alternation. A bed for truth, and for despair.

CULMINATION

'Tis a consummation
Devoutly to be wished.
—*Hamlet* III.1.1756–57.

Blow-Up begins twice.

After the opening credits sequence, in which the idea is repeatedly expressed, through mirror words superimposed upon a field of grass, that our knowledge of the world is but a reflection of ourselves, we are in a hollow, white, neomodern, urban cavern, the forecourt of a group of imposing but utterly vacated skyscrapers. This was shot at the London headquarters of *The Economist,* just off St. James's Street between Jermyn and Ryder Streets, a spacious plaza with a trio of buildings in the "new brutalist" style by Alison and Peter Smithson, erected in 1964 and clad with Portland stone. With raucous noise, a Jeep full of masquers blazes in, circles around, and leads us through the streets of London. Students during Rag Week, many British observers agree; yet these folk seem too old, too sad, too resigned for that. Spurts of arrogant hilarity (not joy), protest (against nothing in particular), celebration (of, perhaps, emptiness)—it is difficult to be sure of the motive of these (young or not so young) people, who wear garish black and white or black and red costumes, each different, each functioning more as a skin than a cover, with faces reconstituted in white paint (Julian and Claude Chagrin and their mime troupe). The Jeep finds its way into a park, sailing along a dark paved road past empty tennis courts, with the incomprehensible gaggle of voices continuing its alien transmission in the otherwise tranquil air.

The second beginning:

A group of destitute men who have spent the night in a Camberwell doss-house are emerging into the day. (Catterall and Wells suggest this place was "nicknamed the 'Spike' after the protruding metal spikes overhanging the building" [29], but as Orwell makes clear, virtually all doss-houses from the earliest days of the twentieth century were referred to by the men who were forced to inhabit them as "spikes" [*Down and Out*].) Because they are all dressed in not very well fitting hand-me-downs, gray, brown, tweedy, and unrelievedly dull, and because the bricks of the buildings between which they walk with sullen gait are besmirched with grime, we might imagine them a crowd of miners (but not the stalwart Welsh miners of *How Green Was My Valley*). They also replicate, in a quick homage, the workers emerging from the Lumière factory in Lyon, who were the subjects of one of the first projected film (1895). One of these men separates out, in a dark sort of pea coat with dirty carrot red hair. He stops to chat under a huge parabolic railway arch at "Consort Road" and then, checking around him to see that none of the others is watching, slips into a licorice green Rolls Royce Silver Cloud and drives off. This is our protagonist, a young photographer (Pauline Kael calls the Antonioni who filmed him a "tourist in the city of youth") who has been secretly shooting these figures who are "naked, in company with . . . other nudes," like the shades described by Luigi Pirandello in his novel, *Shoot!* (14–15).

At a cozy table in a cozy Sloane Square bistro, the artist shows his pictures to his agent Ron (Peter Bowles)—the photographs, somewhat contrasty, and thus subject to a palpable gravity, are actually by the celebrated English photojournalist, Don McCullin—contents of a book he's making, for which, he announces, with a little more excitement than usual, he's found something completely different, peaceful, for the ending. "It'll be better that way." Gazing at these decrepit burghers, at their coal black, demeaning little world—"The old men are nothing but skin and bone. All have sagging muscles, and the wretched look of men who do not get a square meal from one end of the year to the other" (Orwell, "Day" 7)—we may think again of the park, the wind blowing greenly through those sedate trees in that "fantastic primordial place" with "its own microclimate" where "in freezing November you can stand in certain parts of it and feel a great warmth emanating from the earth" (Catterall and Wells 30, 31); think again of a man and woman leaning in silence against gravity; and also, because he is no party to their hot moment, see this eager photographer slyly snapping shots as he creeps closer and closer, an observing guard who keeps watch over the moment and to whose uncommittedly engaged but also constantly adjudicative eyes this little performance is being played out.

For surely this tryst is as much a performance as is mounted—as must be mounted—by any of us in our consciousness that we are visible in the world. No matter the gulp of hesitation, the itch of desire, the gelid fear, the questioning impulse to explore that the man or the woman might feel, they have contrived to see to it that every button is properly done up, every stitch of clothing fits, every angle of posture is commensurate with what strangers could recognize as a stance, the choice of locale is logical, the mutual gazes are from that old textbook. "Lovers," we say on the instant, because they have the look of lovers who are looked at. And to be fulfilled in respect of this, to be offered culmination, looked at they must be, not only by us, through the transparent puissance of Antonioni's camera, and therefore in a way of which we can afford to be utterly unaware, but also and mordantly by a young man who has his own passions and fears—he must, he is a young man—and who in snaking closer and closer to this primal couple tastes the truth of their moment by noting its every aspect and every phrase. As he sees it, we see ourselves seeing it. And for this reason, to stylize the encounter and eliminate as much as possible the myriad antierotic objections viewers might bring to this forced observation, the filmmaker designs the lovers in chiaroscuro, and swiftly: she in a short medium gray skirt and black, gray, and white-checked shirt with medium-length rusty hair stylishly brushed; he in a gray suit with salt-and-pepper hair, tall, lanky, a Giacometti clown dressed up for a noontime business lunch. They must seem to hover in space before our eyes, their every breath a statement.

And the greenness of that green park:

It is true, as has been said many times over, that in his color films Antonioni often paints the locations, and here, yes, he did have the green grass painted green, maybe to recapture, as Baudelaire has it, "*le vert paradis des amours enfantines,*" where "*tout ce que l'on aime est digne d'être aimé*" ("Moesta et errabunda"). At any rate, "Antonioni eliminated colors that were contradictory," Assheton Gorton told me (personal communication). Now, what color green do we choose when we paint things green? The green of bullfrogs, of barns, the green of the pine, of spring shoots, the sucrose green of the swag dangling behind the cupid in Boucher's "La toilette de Vénus" (1751), or the dark licorice green of the forest in his "Pensent-ils au raisin?" (1747)? That Antonioni redid the grass is not frivolous, but indicates that as an artist he is composing his frame with an eye to a range of formal values, and that the saturation, intensity, and hue of a coloration as registered upon a film stock constitute an important formal value to him. The greenness of the park is hyperrealistic, overwhelming, the green of a malaise, the green of a "delicious solitude," and of course Andrew Marvell's green thought in a green shade:

> No white nor red was ever seen
> So amorous as this lovely green.

"They wrote the script into the locations" (Gorton, "Interview"). In Daoist lore, writes Victoria Finlay, "the green but hazy mountains symbolized the pureness of nature" (285), but this is also a Romantic conceit, since the greenness of the mountains, of anything natural, fades and revives. Finlay also notes that greenness is a "reminder of the illusion of nature" (286), of the fact that nature, like men, puts on a look. If the lovers in this park are posturing (or aware of their postures), if that man embracing that woman realizes that "his *truth* does not consist in what he can know of himself, but . . . it is hidden in the large, terrible yet gentle eyes which are turned towards him" (Sartre, *Baudelaire* 52), so, in its way, does the park itself seem to sense that it is being regarded, that its efflorescence seduces and stabilizes a picturing. And even that is a green thought. A green thought is both a fresh thought and one that will dry and change. But there is more to the color green and the green park.

What is staggering about greenness is its essential inhumanity, that it comes upon us from without, to press and tickle and challenge, a product of verdigris and vinegar—as in the case of the bride's dress in Van Eyck's "The Arnolfini Marriage," "symbolic of fertility and gardens" and also made of "a manufactured substance that is born from the corruption of pure metal" (Finlay 298)—no less than of chlorophyll; that it is not only an indicator of life, or death, as the case may be (Napoléon may truly have been poisoned on St. Helena by an atmosphere containing arsenic, that green invader [Finlay 290ff]), but also a momentary challenge, even an outrage, since it is a contradiction, at once penetrating and intoxicating, of water and blood and flesh, a mover of phantasy, a repository for eroticism without being erotic, an eternal question. Shakespeare pointed to a green memory, a green girl, green Neptune, green sickness, the "green mantle of the standing pool" (*Lear* III.iv.1926), a green estate, a "wither'd branch, that's only green at top" (*Pericles* II.ii.780), and an eye of green (*Tempest* II.i.758), among his hundreds of greens.

As to the park, it has the capacity to give the impression of not having been created, of springing to reality. When we think of a green shade, we perform the magic of invoking coloration where there is no light, inventing a space that is interior and yet topological, a space illuminated (because green can exist only as illumination) by spirit rather than radiation. In greenery are the animal world that we do not fully know, danger, the unpredictable, the hungry, the capricious, the sedate. In all of Antonioni, there is no space more haunting or more sedate, more charged or more aggressive *as a space,* than the park in which the photographer finds these lovers. And the hiss of the wind through the dark margining trees is memorable decades after seeing the film, even in the face of the undeniable fact that the wind can come and go in everyday life without leaving a trace.

Outside the bistro where he and his agent are looking at the photographs, a stranger is trying to rifle through the photographer's car, so he races out, checks to see that his camera is safely locked away in the glove compartment, and drives quickly to his studio: develop and print the new negatives as quickly as possible. When he arrives, it turns out the woman from the park has followed him. Gingerly, tense, she fills his space, pacing around like a trapped great cat. He tries to be sociable, says he'll give her what she wants "later." She removes her shirt, since it is clearly sex a fellow like this is after, although patently he isn't. He goes by way of a catwalk (built for the film) into his darkroom (built for the film) and fishes out a stray roll for her. A little thank-you kiss, the *idea* of a kiss. A bigger kiss from him, a kiss emphatic. Yet in both cases, a kiss perfunctory, obvious, unimpassioned. "You've got it," says he, as she poses against his lavender seamless, "There aren't many girls who know how to stand like that." Indeed, she is a *Vogue* cover if ever there was one, one knee puckered out, hips relaxed, eyes glaring. This isn't personal attraction, but something greater: professional fascination. She is the model he has been longing for, the answer to the mindless "birds" who fall asleep on their feet while he tries to photograph them or to spacey Veruschka, doped half unconscious and bored with life as he shoots her against a black drop with an arched cascade of pink and lavender ostrich feathers and she dreams of being in Paris. "Even with beautiful girls, you look at them and that's that." Karl Miller reflects that the journalist Francis Wyndham had published "The Modelmakers" in the *Sunday Times* on May 10, 1964, a piece containing some of the germs of this mise-en-scène. For him, what Wyndham described—and later briefed Antonioni upon—was a world "governed by wealth, sex, a romantic allegiance to the style (rather than the income) of the working class, by fashions, precedents, and the exercise of power through taste and illusion. . . . 'David Bailey makes love daily.' . . . A record plays throughout the session, and 'the only thing between you and the girl is the camera' . . . . Something phallic seems implied, yet there is an impulse . . . to forget the camera altogether and to concentrate, or meditate, on the chemical thing instead" ("Dilemma").

A "chemical thing" of a different order was going on in that park. The shots that our young hero prints and tacks up sopping wet, once the girl has gone, are black-and-white 16″ × 20″ images; he's placed them in sequence against a heavy wooden beam. The two figures tugging against one another, with the fence and trees behind them and gleamy splotches of studio light reflected against the paper sky to give the effect of breaks among dark clouds. With a pan to the right, the man kissing the girl, his back to the camera, dark trees measuring the distance between them and from them to the camera. Back to the left, with a little zoom in, the two in their queer linkage: she tugging like a devoted mule, he drawing back a little, thinking what? "Work harder" or "I don't want to go there." Back to the right with more of a zoom now, that clinch, the darkness of the trees, the long extension of the little fence and the low trees behind it, the utter solitariness of this meeting. Now Antonioni's camera has crossed the axis and is behind this image. We can gaze through it as the photographer gets up from his couch and strides forward to peer more carefully, the dark shadow of his head obscuring the part of the picture where the lovers are. Parker Tyler has written perceptively of the role of the camera in mounting detective activity onscreen in Robert Montgomery's *The Lady in the Lake,* a film in many ways strategically related to *Blow-Up* because it also puts the subjectivity of the "detective" before us as he hunts. Our photographer is surely aware that "every cameraman . . . is a detective. Every cameraman is responsible for the ultimate meanings of the imagery he records" (73):

> Somebody, sooner or later, was bound to think of this highly charged device. . . . the detective is played by the camera eye as substantive for a man's body and, of course, his eyes. The camera's movements, that is, indicate the open-eyed passage of the detective's body through space wherever he pursues his clues. . . . The value of the extra tension provided is obvious: the spectator technically is identified with the detective, and so *we* feel—comfortably or uncomfortably as the case may be—his peculiar responsibility to solve the crime. (70)

We watch from behind his back as he takes one more look at the two images: more to do, more to do. The camera lingers on the pictures, the long horizontal wooden beam at the top of the frame, an angular beam descending behind the prints at sixty degrees—nice, rich wood, what happens eventually to trees. The sound of footsteps receding down the catwalk to the darkroom.

Then footsteps approaching again, as he enters the frame and tacks a third image to the right, where the beam meets the wall. A tight shot on the clinch, the man burying his head in her hair, she gazing off-right, with one arm holding the center of his back and the other resting comfortably on his shoulder, her eyes as dark as night. In whatever way the trees' green has been transmogrified in the photography, so, too, have these eyes been silvered, flattened, made into terribly accurate memories. As he leans against the wall to stare, we cut into a close shot of the two subjects, head and shoulders. Her lips are parted. Her nose, aquiline, points off in the direction of her gaze. The man is completely distracted. The photographer gazes again (all of what is happening is the movement of the pair in the park but also the movement of the photographer watching them now to see how he had watched them then), shifts left, touches the couple in that clinch shot, runs his finger off-right a little to follow her direction of gaze, but there's . . . nothing. He walks off to the side and puts some jazz on the phonograph: a one-minute-ten-second cue called "Thomas Studies Photographs" by Herbie Hancock. (In early scripts, the photographer is called Thomas, but nobody speaks a name for him in the film.) From the glass coffee table, where it's lying between a large hunk of pink quartz and a bowl of decorative blue porcelain balls, he gathers up a magnifying glass and approaches that clinch shot once more. Something in the grass between the couple and the fence? Or near the couple? He leans in closer. Quickly darting behind the picture he grasps a white grease pencil and uses the magnifying loop to outline a rectangle in the shot, near the fence. A framing to isolate and elevate. Removes the picture, walks off.

Tacked on a stretch of whitewashed wall adjacent the other three images, a blowup of the rectangle, with the fence now enormous and grainy filling the bottom half and flickers of light looming above. He examines it, then looks at the close-up of the woman staring off. The camera follows her line of gaze back to this blowup, where behind the fence there floats, perhaps, in some of the highlight, a face. And perhaps not. Back to the close-up with a little zoom in, the shrinking of the woman against the man; is it fear? Back to the blowup, now zooming all the way in, with highlights undulating in waves and that lumpy essence ponderously waiting, taking on personality. He backs off a few steps, folds his arms, points.

Back in the darkroom, under amber light. A dozen or so 5″×7″s are stretched on a tabletop in front of him, and he's marking one with a grease pencil. Tap tap tap on the counter, the tattoo of intelligence in heat. He marks another. Back in the living area, we look down on that whitewash as he steps up and tacks in a vertical shot of the girl racing toward him, one arm raised in front of her face to block his view, panic shooting out of her eyes. Adjacent to that, the girl and the man again.

She's turned away from him, seen from another angle. The camera cuts in as we look at that solo shot of her running forward, the gray skirt pulling over her knees, her lips parted, wind through her hair. Pan right and zoom: She stands with the man, his hand catching her elbow, his weary face buried in her hair once again. She is staring directly into the lens, hostile, defensive, frozen. Lips icy, body stiff. One more picture to the right of this, with another little zoom: the man staring off with his hands in his pockets, the girl posing with her hand at her mouth, her eyes pinioned at some point behind us. Then right again, with a vertical image tacked on a second beam: the man alone, hands loosely at his side, face resigned, shadow on his cheeks, the dark dark trees aching behind him. The photographer, with his dapper blue-and-white checked shirt and his tousled rusty hair is standing next to this, now quickly swiveling around to point his crystal blue eyes off-camera left, really in the same direction that the man in the photograph is looking. He seems to realize something, but realization is so difficult to display in cinema, which is all realization. Leans over with his fists on his couch, defeated. She gave him a number, so he yanks up the phone and dials it. KNightsbridge 1239. Of course it's a false trail. In frustration, back to the images. He moves past the advancing girl and stares at that blowup, exhaling. There's something to be seen there, something as yet unseen, and he's seeing it, or trying to, his head precisely covering the center of the photograph in the cinematic frame. Now, with real purpose, he backs off and runs down to the darkroom, where he blows up the shot even further. We see him lift it out of its bath, the water deliciously trickling as it drips down and he stares at this new-made treasure in his amber hands. The fenceposts now gigantic. In the middle of the shot, behind the fenceposts . . . . He leans close, then dunks it again. Now we are back outside as he emerges and puts the shot up in the place of the advancing girl, who moves to the far right end of the sequence. Hands on hips, he stands in repose to gaze at his work.

In a kind of semicircle he has positioned the shots in what must inevitably turn out to be an order of advancement. As he walks his consciousness from one to the next, the pictures will seem to tell a story, will enter history. The girl tugging the man up the hill to the upper park clearing. In a macro-zoom, we see that her head is down, her body playing at being forceful, while her lover plays at being recalcitrant to heighten the pleasure. The sound of the wind blowing through the trees. The clinch with the long dark foliage at left, the wind swelling. The close-up of the clinch, the girl staring off, the wind swelling. The clinch from behind, the wind blowing, as we track rightward along the line of her gaze to a spot behind the fence where there is something like a tiny white face. The contrasty blowup showing mouth now, and nose, and two eyes, and the sound of the wind blowing.

And a hand clasping a pistol equipped with a silencer . . . pointing left to where the couple are.

Then the shot of the troubled embrace, the man's back to the pistol, the woman turned to gaze into the camera in shock. The wind blowing loudly (asking us again and again, "Do you see?"). The man with his hands in his pockets and the woman touching her lips, realizing something, staring toward the photographer. The man alone, remonstrating, "Come on, let's go." A macro–close-up of that female face, fingers wrapped around the mouth, eyes open in horror. The woman racing toward the camera, arm upraised. A final very long shot showing the whole park clearing, the undulating fence at right, the dark trees at left, a thicket far in the center distance with the woman standing beside it. A blowup of her figure, looking away. Another long shot, and she is gone. The photographer looks around with a little smile, grabs his phone, dials a number. He has moved now to lean against the wall next to a window outside which the wind is ruffling through some trees, as though in mockery.

"Ron? . . . Something fantastic's happened. Those photographs in the park: fantastic! Somebody was trying to kill somebody else! I saved his life!"

But:

OMNI ANIMAL POST COITUM TRISTE EST

Symbols resemble in all directions.

—Roger Brown

A distraction at the door. Two teenaged girls (Jane Birkin, Gillian Hills), eager to be photographed by the great man. Flustered, not without a little irritation, yet bemused by their puppy awkwardness, he tells them to go up and make coffee: nice little azure-and-white striped Norfolk pottery mugs. They start trying on dresses from his collection, boldly colored and designed in a kind of pre-Marimekko style, angles, lines, triangles, squares in hottest neon blue, yellow, magenta, pansy green. As he comes upon them a little tussle breaks out, and soon enough the two start tearing the clothing off one another, aided by him. They dash into the living area and one of them yanks down his purple seamless—that very expensive, perfectly dyed roll of background paper—until it is a rumpled beast spread on the floor (Cortázar's lilac comforter revivified). They all three work to tear one another's clothing off, in a sequence legendary for its heralding of full-frontal nudity and its challenge to the Motion Picture Producers and Distributors of America's Production Code, which had been rigidly guarding American cinema since 1934. (As Vincent Canby noted, this was "the first film to be denied a seal of approval by the recently liberalized Production Code" and therefore "the first test of the flexibility of the new code.") "We notice . . . certain directions which call for nudity in various forms and stages," wrote the censor, Geoffrey Shurlock, to his contact at MGM at the end of March 1966, decrying intimations of pornography in a typically preachy tone: "As you know, nudity is prohibited under the Code, and we could not approve it. . . . We notice that the story calls for [the photographer] to have a sex relationship between two teenagers. This indication which occurs on pages 24 and 256, would not be approvable under the Code" (Shurlock to Vogel, March 30, 1966). Four weeks later, the situation had not materially changed as regards the sexual intentions of the young photographer: "There still remains the unacceptable suggestion that Thomas has a sex affair with two models who come in to his place to be photographed. Such a suggestion would not only be offensive in itself, but is complicated by the fact that the girls are described as teenagers, thus heightening the degree of offensiveness" (Shurlock to Vogel, April 27, 1966). (Age in use here as an implicit measuring rod for offensiveness.) To the two girls it seems evident enough that the photographer's wiliness is sufficient to grant him escape from anybody at any time—he's an epitome of slick, modern professionalism—so they work at double-teaming him in order to get an advantage. Soon he is hot and hungry, blushing like a peony. They are squealing in high pitch, animals in extremis. "The scene with the girls is so barren of any actual libidinous desire that it is more like a wild, hysterical frolic among a bunch of kids. In fact, it is my opinion that it is a sort of juvenile fantasy that occurs to this restless fellow after he has been pestered by the girls and is in need of a little physical relaxation," wrote the rather moralistic Bosley Crowther as he expressed astonishment at the Code censorship in this case. At least one of the "kids" was rather straight-laced, indeed: Jane Birkin admitted in 1993, "I was a very traditional, married 19-year-old when my husband, John Barry, dared me that I couldn't take my clothes off with the light on. So I did. Then when it came out there was such a fuss" ("Through a Lens"). And the business wasn't physically relaxing: "You might have thought what a wonderfully erotic experience I was having," Hemmings wrote in his autobiography, as though to say it was anything but (19–20). So convincing was the sequence, however, that even projectionists were taken in: "Cinema staffs were warned yesterday to stop stealing the sexy bits from Vanessa Redgrave's controversial film, *Blow-Up*. It is claimed that they have been snipping out nude scenes and keeping them for their own amusement" ("Blow-Up," *Daily Mail*).

That Shurlock, as exemplar of its moral standards, and the Code itself were out of tune with the moral fashion of the times, and that in consequence of this and other forces, the Code was in its final days, was made explicitly evident in an early January 1967 communication from William E. Wimer, director of the Office for Audio-Visual of the Stewardship Council, United Church of Christ (shared with Shurlock by its recipient, Haven Falconer):

> As I reflected on some of the implications of BLOWUP it occurred to me that this would be the evocative type of film which our people ought to see. I realize because of the nude scenes in the film, there are some risks involved. However, I think some of the philosophic issues inherent in the film are worthy of consideration, and I also feel the church needs to face up to the question of nudity and contemporary filmmaking. Do you think there is a possibility of our securing this film for use at United Church Assembly? (Scott to Shurlock)

The status of *Blow-Up* in relation to the Production Code was by no means crystal clear. In mid-November 1966, Shurlock and his assistant had flown to New York to review the film for MGM and had requested two cuts, which were made satisfactorily within ten days. While the film was now eligible for a certificate, Shurlock and his partner J.A. Vizzard were asked in early December to go to Culver City to discuss the cuts with Antonioni, "who was not satisfied and refused to accept them." MGM had rights to the final cut, but was "acceding to Antonioni's wishes" ("Code Issue" 1), probably because they wanted to appear respectful of his work (Schreiber to Shurlock, November 9, 1966). Because the filmmaker ultimately refused to cooperate, MGM's affiliate Premier Productions released the picture without a Code seal, "under the banner 'Carlo Ponti Presents' " (" 'Blow-Up' Poses Code Issue" 4). In release form, some of the cuts requested were apparently made because Premier requested a re-review on January 27; but then withdrew their request (Yellow Paper). In order to make certain that "there would be no question as to the form in which MGM was presenting the picture for approval," Haven Falconer gave assurances that the version being screened for the MPAA in New York and that being shown in theaters differed only in the scene involving the painter and his "wife" in bed but were otherwise the same, "including the full scenes of the two young girls" (Hetzel, "Memorandum").

A vision of the sex itself, if not of the preparations for it, was left entirely to the viewer's pictorial talents. There's a jump cut forward in time, with a slow pan that reveals the folds of the seamless, a kind of brittle cocoon, and the two girls, fully dressed again, pulling on the young man's shoes. He sits up from his dreamy postcoital slumber, a look of distance and coolness in his burning eyes as he stares past his maenads (who struggle to garb his corpse) at something in that sacred space behind the camera, something off, untouched, and unrealized. Now he stands up and we observe the smooth, naked part of him, Apollo with eyes pinioned off-left. "His evanescent resemblances to the young Roman god Mercury, Robert Mitchum, the early Dorian Gray, a fallen angel, a serious cherub—all of them faintly tinged with the sinister—delay immediate recognition," a Hollywood reporter wrote describing Hemmings (Ager). One of the girls (Birkin), helping him on with his shirt, leaves her hand hanging out, a portrait of loss, but everything now revolves around the fact that he is fixated on one of those photographs, then on a blowup beside it: the woman lingering at the outgrowth of bush near the back of the clearing, just before she disappears. The girls have been waiting in silence, but he throws them out, submitting again to the siren call of his muse and now, released of his charge, entirely without hope. They slip on their red shoes, their blue shoes, and exit like sentries, while he, disconsolate, exhausted, wracked by some inner agony, stumbles down to his darkroom, pausing to work something out, to think, to put fragments together into something less fragmentary—our old game. In a tiny studio space he tacks up a blown-up print of the bush and the grass all round, positions some lights at angles from the sides, and using a 4″ × 5″ view camera makes a nice, fat, healthy 8-second exposure (which is to say, an exposure with a small aperture, to gain every possible clarity of focus and revelation). The print out of its bath, slimy as a child's fingerpainting, dragged down and clipped to a support in his living area, the young man squatting in front of it so that we cannot see. No music through any of this, just the quiet working sounds of him stepping around, his view camera's shutter snapping open and then closed, the print dripping. Now he backs away and see we can: black black splotches and white white highlights arranged in what can be taken for a body flat upon the ground. As the camera tracks below the photograph to the blowup from which it was manufactured, pinned just beneath it, we see the grass running out to the bush, and behind the bush, now undeniably, nothing less than a corpse.

Back to the rephotographed blowup, the puzzle of forms and secrets, and then to the young man, his face drawn and frightened. It is night on the street with the antique shop outside the park. He drives up and parks. Utter silence, a wall painted red as drying blood against the darkness.

The park's upper regions are abutted by a tall neon advertising sign mounted on a high platform, barely visible in the photographer's first approach to the area, on the morning when he shoots the couple, but far more distinct, even intimidating, when he returns now at night. The sign glows with a hot turquoise light, casting a pall onto the green grass—the emerald and metallic green grass, seen this way—that instantly but only briefly invokes its opposite color, blood red, the color of life now vanished from this place. John Freccero is moved to think of this park as Arcady, the locale where Death "is, too," as Guercino suggested in his painting "Et in arcadia ego" (1618–22). For Freccero, the greenness of this place is all deathly:

> According to our mythology, it was after the fall in the garden of Eden, that sexuality first entered the world and with it entered death. According to the Church Fathers, the act whereby a man asserted his manhood was the same act whereby he entered the cycle of generation and corruption that indicated, unmistakably, how transient his life would be, how soon he would have to make way on the generational line for his own children and those of others. For various reasons, we no longer perceive the connection between sexuality and death with the same immediacy. (124)

The sign itself: slanted to the right, as in italic, a capital F with its central arm extended as the roof of a trapezoidal O; and then what can be construed as a Greek lambda, Λ. F-O-L, acoustically, if you like, but visually *FOΛ*. Given that it seems to be a word—seems because, even in the face of the eminent design, we can discern language ciphers, letters—we hunt for its significance. We ask ourselves whether a concept or truth is being epitomized on this sign, and thus whether light is being shed in the park by means of intelligible data: perhaps we are to see the body "in the light of" what this "word" means. "It was not meant to be anything," said Assheton Gorton, "It had to be like a Paul Klee" (personal communication). It is not a word in any known language. It is the form of a word, signifying the idea of a word, without actually being a word. It has the look of language. It says nothing (like so many Antonionian characters), yet at the same time enunciates "saying." In the same way, the greenness of the park is unmistakable as coloration, as pronunciation, without actually conveying a signal or standing for something else. If greenness in general suggests or stands for nature, the greenness of trees, the greenness of the grass; then what can we say the greenness of trees or the grass stands for or suggests? The depths of selfness, presence, confection, solidity, retreat. Or the Great Force? An inwardness, but not of the body; an inwardness of the mind. The green shade.

He strides into the park and passes underneath the prickly unintelligible light of that neon sign, *FOA*, which makes the leaves of a bush glimmer electrically. In the upper park—Cox's Mount, it's called—stepping quietly, hesitantly, with our camera inches from his face, his jacket dark green as mossy water, his pants diamond white in the night light, and then he runs toward the bush, tracing across the emerald lawn. The vague sound of distant traffic. He is very far from the camera, still stepping onward. Then we jump forward in space so that he is approaching us, the thick green grass spongy as an endometrium but heavy in its greenness, perfunctory and profound in its greenness, and we pan a little as he moves with his shadow long and green upon the green grass, and now in an unprepared cut (that gives us the defense we must want) we are behind his head stepping in his wake. He will see it first, then, will know it before we do, has already seen it, is already seeing it, stepping forward. There, lit by *FOA* light, patient and responsive as only the dead can be, the man from this morning. Since this dead man has never been identified, has no station, we can think of the body as not only *this man's body* but, more profoundly, *The Body*. The photographer approaches in that sickly confirmation. The bush twittering beside, all green. Kneeling slowly, as at a tomb, reaching out to gently touch the face, but quickly pulling away. Did the hand actually connect? (Stanley Kauffmann thinks it did, but touching is not photographic.) In its green knowledge, its green sight, the corpse could surely tell.

Gray suit. Gray face. Gray hair. We look up into the photographer's face, staring down with regret. He shakes his head a little to say "no," but to whom, about what? No, I couldn't save you? No, it's all leading to this? (Edie Wasserman at Jule Styne's funeral: "It's about time.") No, you won't speak to me? Now the corpse in a splendid utterly silent portrait shot: neat black tie (as for funerals, a Hitchcockian joke), wing-tipped collar, the eyes wide open watching, keeping guard. Watching for what, the living . . . ? Watching *FOA*, transcribing *FOA*, memorizing *FOA*. "The green make-up was uncomfortable," said Ronan O'Casey, "as was holding my breath for that long take" (personal communication). Or else, sucking in the conversation of the leaves. The lips parted, like Cordelia's. "There is no feeling for family," Antonioni marveled to Rex Reed, "No religion. Most people of the new generation are dreamers. LSD and mescaline are better for them than love."

Now we pull back to see the photographer slowly rising. The body remains politely at attention, but horizontal: hands rigid at the sides in perfect deference. As he stands, the photographer hears a single snap from behind his back, behind our back, that ineffable *behind* that is neither the camera's place nor that of any identifiable creature but that provokes us always; the repository of a gaze, the point of view of an inspection and surveilling that we cannot fathom. He who watches over all action is back there, behind the audience gazing, behind those who gaze at the audience gazing and those who gaze at them. Is it the snap of a shutter, because the photographer is himself being photographed with his subject? The sound of the cocking of a pistol, because the photographer is next—participating by becoming a target himself? The snap of a match striking, or even the memory of this? In the March 16, 1966 treatment, the young man sees the body by the light of a match he has struck (26). Or the snap of a twig? What it sounds like is precisely the snap of a twig, an explanation for which comes from Géza Róheim, writing of an ancient Koryak practice: in the presence of a corpse a line must be drawn, so twigs are broken off a nearby bush and strewn around to represent "a dense forest which was supposed to surround the burning place" of the body. Having done this ritual, the mourner makes a significant gesture: "Before leaving the pyre he drew with his stick a line on the snow, jumped across it and shook himself" (165). Perhaps the sound of the snapping twig here is to bring our consciousness back to such primitive moments, moments we do not consciously remember, and to signify that here the grass beneath the corpse is already, in its way, a forest that cuts him off from the world of the living. The park is the territory of the dead.

The young man runs out, at any rate, confirmed, terrified, educated, brought to the brink. Death is so simple, so plain. And inconceivable: since these eyes are open and must be seeing what they stare at with a disenchanted hunger. The mouth is ready to speak, what will it say?

This man stood and moved, pulled back against his girl, held her hair around his head, put his hands in his pockets, waited and frowned. He climbed the hill, he desired. He must only be sleeping.

As the word "green" does not befit the things that wear it, the word "death" does not befit the dead. We tell ourselves, looking at the corpse, that for this man time has stopped. And our words come back to haunt us, because in his presence, now, here upon this green, time has for us just been born.

Home again, our photographer goes to visit his neighbors, who are having sex, mournfully, hungrily, the girl with darting eyes—the scene from which Antonioni agreed to lose a few seconds. During orgasm, or what we can imagine to be her orgasm, she stares at the photographer. Does she fancy him? Is she thinking of him rhythmically while the painter penetrates her again and again? Moments later she comes up to his flat, clad in a dress made all of blood-red string. The studio has been utterly ransacked. All the photographs are gone but one: the macro-blowup from the photographed photograph, the shot that shows the lumpy indiscriminate form of a body or else . . . nothing. He tells her the story. "Who killed him?" His voice weary, stale, flat, and unprofitable: "I don't know, I didn't see." He wants to know if she's ever thought of leaving the painter. "I don't think so." He gets into his car to find Ron, the agent, at a party somewhere in Chelsea—find Ron, show him the body, Ron will know what to do, Ron always knows what to do. But on Regent Street, near Robinson & Cleaver's, he sees the girl from the park staring into a vitrine. Is it really her? He looks again, but like a very phantom she's disappeared into thin air. Poor Roger Ebert, knowing this vanishing is uncanny, tried to pinpoint her move. At the 1998 Virginia Festival of American Film in Charlottesville, he says, "we ran the sequence a frame at a time and could not discover the method of her disappearance; presumably she steps into a doorway, but we watched her legs, and they seemed somehow to attach themselves to another body" ("Blow-Up"). He wanders into an after-hours club where the Yardbirds are singing, lanky Jeff Beck having trouble with an amp, finally stomping on his electric guitar and tossing it to the crowd. Lucky "bride" to be, our man yanks it out of the air, races with it onto the sidewalk outside, trailed by a pack of souvenir hounds. But once he's alone, panting, the object ceases to have value, becomes only a thing. He drops it and moves on. Ron is discovered in a townhouse, with joints stuffed between the fingers of both hands. The young protégé is led to a back room where the vapors of the East will overpower him. "We've got to get a shot of it," the young man protests as

Ron leads him to the debauch. "I'm not a photographer," says Ron. With delicious speed the morning comes, and he retreats to the park, but now the sky is as pale as a pearl and the body, or the imagined body as some viewers insisted (and still insist), is gone.

ARCADY

How lush and lusty the grass looks! how green!
—The Tempest II.i.55–6

That intoxicating park. The designer Assheton Gorton thought he'd looked at three hundred parks before finding this one (qtd. in Tuson 106), and Antonioni was exceedingly enthused about it, coming to fetch him very early one morning so they could go scout it (personal communication). Exquisite yawning rectangle of green, unblemished unspotted green, undefiled green, proud green, resonant green, the green of truth, of ultimate truths, the green of remorse and vegetable love, of pathos and puerility, the green of innocence, the green of everything that is outside civilization. A green we aspire to and fear. Therefore, a green that enunciates mortality, a final green. Vivian Sobchack delightfully reads Jean-Paul Sartre's recounting of the confrontation of Antoine Roquentin with a chestnut tree in a park on a quiet Sunday:

> The awful contingency of brute materiality and unspeakable immanence are transformed for him into the awesome "grace" of the world's merely being there in all its expansive fullness. All things—subjects and objects alike—are embraced and comprehended by their mutual enfoldedness in the objective world's profane illumination and the subjective unity of his look. . . .
>
> This Sunday world is blessed, however, in no transcendental sense; rather, it has grace in the fullness of its precise, dense, and universal objectivity. Roquentin moves about it (and, more important, within it) describing all its contours, all its universal burgeoning, and all the qualities of light that make its being visible. (307)

The photographer is similarly *within* this envelope of green. A green we cannot quite look at, must look away from. A glancing green. A green that in its darkest darknesses—among those shuddering trees—makes us tremble, hesitate, reflect, wonder, doubt, doubt ourselves, doubt our possibilities, doubt facts. "Feelings must take the form of colors" (Pirandello 44). A green that stares us in the face. "You stand there and astonishing fables tempt you" (Sinclair 348).

How shall this be told, here and now, or there when it happened but I am remembering? Watching a motion picture, we are always trapped in the present. Was there a body in the park, to be seen or to be conjured? No way to be sure, without, of course, rewinding the spools, "Here I end this reel. Box—*(pause)*—three, spool—*(pause)*—five. *(Pause.)* Perhaps my best years are gone. When there was a chance of happiness. But I wouldn't want them back. Not with the fire in me now" (Beckett 28). Spools which are the memories of . . . what? Events or perceptions of events? Of all Antonioni's films, this is the most equivocal, the film, in truth, without a beginning, even though it has two beginnings, the film in which everything happening is also an impression of a happening, the film with a protagonist who can never be certain how this has to be told. Committed to his camera and its world, he has formed an airtight epistemology: knowledge is sight. But at night in the park, he did not bring the camera, did not bring his sight, and so he cannot know. When he had the camera, in daylight, all he could photograph was an indiscriminate aggregation of blobs, a tendency toward unity but not a unity itself; a projection, a hypothesis. The body was always a hypothesis. Even the man and woman in the park kissing, tugging, arguing, staring: tendencies toward unity but not unities themselves. Mortalities in passage. Inhabitants of the green world. And as they stood and moved, were they thinking of grapes? While they were kissing, were they thinking of love?

Knowledge is sight, sight knowledge: he has penetrated the Camberwell Detention Center and gained knowledge of the lives of the poor (as Orwell and Mayhew did before him). He has come to know the painter's imagination and style. He has known Veruschka, her fluid sexual grace, her emptiness. The models in the fashion shoot, posing and stuttering against gray glass screens, he knows their ennui. The girl from the park standing proudly against his seamless, he knows her spirit, her defiance, her panic. But by the light of that neon sign, what can he know? A kind of vigil haunts this film, as the photographer dedicates himself to keeping watch over the world in order to know and be part of it. By that sign's light, does he see the stone roll away from the mouth of the sepulcher?

THE ACT OF SIGHT

I think that I know how to look, if it's something I know, and also that every looking oozes with mendacity.

—Cortázar, "Blow-Up"

Cortázar's photographer is Roberto Michel, who stays at 11, rue Monsieur-le-Prince (a curving very narrow little street near Saint Sulpice, with a few quaint shops and much silence, a passable café). "One of the many ways of contesting level-zero," thinks he, "and one of the best, is to take photographs, an activity in which one should start becoming an adept very early in life, teach it to children since it requires discipline, aesthetic education, a good eye and steady fingers." These are the tools of the photographer's discipline, the methods of his surveillance. As Hemmings portrays the occupation, photography is entirely athletic, requiring a man to crouch and run, hide, leap, lean, always reconfiguring, twisting and focusing, snatching glimpses of the light and deciding on f-stops. In the park it is a dance he performs, first chasing pigeons, then grabbing hold of that fateful couple and striding after their ghosts. To see every possible point of vantage, to position oneself and make of one's body a tripod, to know the camera as one knows one's hand, flicking through the aperture settings without looking, knowing how long and at what range to permit that device to suck in the light of the world; and, crucial, how much light. To recognize that the photographer "always worked as a permutation of his personal way of seeing the world" (117), that is, to know that it wasn't the camera seeing, it was the self, that the camera had become a part of the self, or that the self had extended outward into gears and polished glass, into spools and celluloid wound as tightly as spirit. A *permutation* of a personal way of seeing, since every shot changes things. On Regent Street at night, when he halts his car and sees the girl staring into that vitrine, a little sign above her head brightly reads, in the omniscient third person singular, "PERMUTIT."

Four notes about the array of photographs that our eager, nameless protagonist spreads out upon his beams:

1. It is quite impossible not to detect that as they aggregate and confront him, are stared at, ensnare his attention in their surfaces and in the spaces between, the images become a movie.

Typically, of course, any frame of any film is a photograph representing 1/24th of a second of real time. Very like a still camera, the movie camera slices time into fragments that are discontinuous one from another. (The camera operator who narrates Pirandello's *Shoot!* observes, "Already my eyes and my ears, too, from force of habit, are beginning to see and hear everything in the guise of this rapid, quivering, ticking mechanical reproduction" [8].) Between any one frame and the next we leap willingly, since the size of the filmic fragments feels so very insubstantial, and since we cannot with the naked eye perceive what may lie in the voids between cells cut so finely. Persistence of vision is partly the desire to extend a frame so as to negate the nothingness that terminates it, but also an incapacity to see. When things are very small, disregard them, plus or minus. To see film—to see this sequence—is to have the still images changed in front of the eyes in such a way that the impression of movement is produced. Because the photographer moves so very slowly between frames and because each frame is so alluring in itself, a greater effort of will is required for making the narrative leaps. This effort is aided by the sound effect of the wind blowing steadily as we shift from shot to shot, a sound that calls up the photographer's building eagerness to proceed with commitment and excitement: as we identify with him, we assume the attitude of his body and intelligence in seeing the pictures consecutively, "over his shoulder."

More important than the fact that *Blow-Up* is "about" this movement between images to create a sense of fluid "reality," or the cinematic effect, is that an intense dramatization occurs through the fragmentation. Each still image seems to have its history and project, each gesture seems to be leading somewhere and coming from somewhere, and in this way the frames, one by one, have contingency. Since each image gains a certain dramaturgical weight, or thrust, it is logical that Antonioni's camera should now and then dolly into a shot or track across it, simulating the action of the viewer's mind—the movement of engagement—as it tastes the delicious history and futurity of each moment.

Since any viewer must proceed through a group of photographs in some order, an order that for the viewer is experientially absolute, it can be said that photographs hung next to one another are always sequential, and further that since the photographer can make only one image at a time, any collection of images always also constitutes a sequence of a biographical kind. To examine a contact sheet, for example, is to see a record of existential action (as I learned from Dave Heath). In this sequence we are delightfully confounded between two kinds of sequentiality that compete for the photographer/observer's attention: the sequence of images in the order that he shot them (the order of history), and the sequence of images in the order that he wishes to see them (the order of desire). He is both recorder and composer. A matter unresolved in the film is the relationship between the two orders. We watch this scene by taking the viewing order to be a faithful enough representation of what went on, but actually what it represents is the sequential building of the photographer's hunger as he looks at (surveils) the scene. Every looking oozes with mendacity.

2. In filmmaking generally, and to the relief of the viewing audience who pretend to vanish into thin air in order that the camera may stand in for them, characters do not look at the lens. Further: the lens, the camera, the viewer—all are not regarded, or more precisely, all are regarded as though they have no weight and no significance, no interest and no shape. We may say the viewer wishes to hide as he spies the cinematic world (as the photographer, at the beginning of his escapade in the park, hides so as not to be seen photographing). In this sense, the viewer assumes a voyeuristic stance, a stance oddly linked to erotic excitement and one in which intensity matches our closeness to getting caught, our subjection to that eye of the screen that can unclothe, unmask, and undeceive us (see Dixon). But a more general condition is the desire for invisibility altogether, a condition in which happily one cannot be seen, but also in which the greatest fear is success: that one will pass through the (cinematic) universe without notice and without contact. At the conclusion of Jack Arnold's brilliant *The Incredible Shrinking Man* (1957), for instance, this is the fear that the protagonist's condition awakens in the viewing audience: not that one will be caught or stripped, but that one will never be noticed. That one will exist, but in such a way that one's existence is entirely immaterial. If we do not wish for exactly this condition, nevertheless our awareness of how close we are to it, when the figures of the screen bypass us time after time, brings a chilling gasp.

So, then, the image of the young woman racing toward the photographer—toward us—yelling, "Stop!": her hand covers her face because he is now shooting at close range and she considers this compromising. But her dark eyes, fixed on the device that is "attacking" her—"You've no right! This is a public place!"—accord us a profound gravity through their gaze. We are here, looking, with "no right," perhaps too much here and thus more important than we thought ourselves to be. This moment is Antonioni's way of directly implicating us in the gaze that frames and forms the film. *Blow-Up* is every bit of it something that exists because we are looking, something that we *know* because we are looking. Further: while normally we see without being particularly conscious of seeing (being conscious, instead, of *what* we are seeing), here our attention is directed to the specific act with which we are engaged, the act of sight. All of this film—all of film, the director seems to be saying—is offered to us to look at. And in watching this, we engage in a ceremony of looking, a personal way of seeing the world. If the woman in the park has been caught in a fragmentary wafer of a second, the frame (the photograph) extends that moment just as much as the film camera's pause permits it to.

3. It is obvious, and yet at the same time almost a secret, that the photographs calling up the scene in the park, calling up the jittery and anxious scene in that thickly colored emerald green park, are black and white. Far from indicating through the prolixity of their illumination a distance from the reality that engendered them, the tones of the photographs perform a different, strange function: since the man and woman are dressed entirely in black, white, and gray, they partake of the nature of black-and-white photographs. There is a profound sense in which the photographs represent them fully. It is only through the agency of the photographs that they become truly themselves. Through the photographs on his wall the photographer learns who these two "really" are to one another, because he "knows how to look." This is one curious feature of the photographs as material realities. "Film color masked the black and white axis of brilliance," Cavell wrote (91).

Another feature is ironic. The greenness of the park seems evident in the photographs still, entirely present in its absence, quite as though in memory the saturated and round green of the park's surface lingers as a formal trace, a trace we fill in. The truth of the green is in the viewer's imagination, yet also in the film. What, we must wonder, is the relation of the screen image—in particular, the green of the park—to the viewer's thought? *Blow-Up* could not have been shot in black and white, because the photographs would have receded into the film. And if the photographs had been shot in color, the film would have receded into them. The park must be in color in order to be seen: the lovers spending their afternoon there must be in black and white.

Because the lovers resemble figures in a photograph, even when first we meet them, it seems reasonable to suggest they are ghostly from the start. Were they really there, or did the photographer just need desperately to imagine something "peaceful" for the end of his book (his book that is never published, but that is always going to be published)? I mean to pose this question optically and philosophically, not narratively: narratively it is clear that they are present, and that the man is killed by someone lingering in the bushes. But narrative is the least of our concerns.

(It is worth saying we tend to have the feeling, because of the panic on the woman's face, the panic and the surprise, the surprise and the lack of surprise, that she has engineered this assassination for some reason. Tugging the man forward. Positioning him. Checking the bushes [when he can't notice] to be sure it's all a good alignment. Running off for a jiffy [to the photographer] as a perfect cover. Racing to the studio to reclaim those evidentiary images, the ones that can send her to prison for life. And so on. I will return to this problem.)

4. That hisssssssing sound! Is it not the voice of the wind that blows our consciousness from moment to moment, from event to event, Einstein's ether wind? The wind that is omnipresent in the universe, and according to which we measure not only space but time? It speaks to the photographer, whispers the inspiration that he should look twice, stare, stand up, use that grease pencil, keep looking, keep looking. The wind that blows change, that blows mortality. Action according to the wind, death according to the wind, approach and departure according to the wind, seduction according to the wind. But this wind is outside of time, because even when the photographer slices time into his little wafers, that wind perdures. We could say, "Desire according to this wind," but in this film, except that the photographer desires to see, there is no desire. The man and woman in the park desired once, before. The painter and his girl wait to desire, because he must paint. The painter's girl would like to desire the photographer, but that's a dead end. The photographer and his models: desire is fictitious, performed, to arouse in them a glow. They are beneath importance to him, like Jeff Beck's guitar neck that he must possess and retain just until it is his, at which point its totemic value bottoms out.

In this reduction of animated stuff to pure objectification, a simple mortality.

INNOCENTS

You are the most unsubstantiated phantom of the twentieth century.
—David Rothman to Ronan O'Casey

In the earliest treatments for the film, not only is the biological status of the man in the park up for question—has he vanished or is he dead on the ground?—but so is the nature of his relationship to the girl. Originally envisioned was something considerably more elaborate than what we see in the release print, and the man, far from being the girl's steady lover, was rather an interloper on the scene. Her actual boyfriend, having discovered that she had taken a lover on the side, would have tailed the two of them around London, secreted himself in the park, and murdered the new man in cold-blooded rage. Far from being in on the killing, the girl herself—in early treatments she was called Jane—is victimized by it, thrown into a panic of grief and loss.

Consider these passages from pages 3 and 4 of a March 16, 1966 treatment for a film to be called *The Shot:*

> Jane comes out of an Espresso bar and gets into a car beside a distinguished looking elderly man. The car drives off. Another car follows it, driven by a man of thirty: his face is tense and hard.
>
> The car with Jane and the elderly gentleman is a dark green Alvis. It is still trailed by the other car, a gun-metal Rover. The eyes of its driver are glued onto the Alvis. Jane appears to be glancing occasionally at the mirror as if to see whether the Rover is following them. The elderly man driving the Alvis looks positively pleased to have such a lovely young girl at his side.

In a lengthy interview with me, Ronan O'Casey, who played the man in the park, reminisced that his role, that of Sarah Miles, and that of the boyfriend hiding behind the bushes were all severely cut in the final production. The producer had rented a "beautiful silver Jag" in which he was to have driven Redgrave's character "up to Carnaby Street. Never shot." Redgrave and O'Casey

> thought there were going to be all the scenes . . . driving through London. . . . Her boyfriend was supposed to come and wait for me and kill me. . . . Vanessa and I talked about it, what we were going to do in the car, and I drove it a couple of times, because I'd never driven an automatic, in case I'd made a mistake. She said that she had a chat with [Antonioni] in Italian (that I didn't understand) and afterward she said, "I think what he said to me was that it was my desire to kiss you firmly and sexually and then step away and I would be the last experience that you would ever have. . . . My last memory would be of kissing her. (O'Casey)

In the released film, however, there is a delicious edge to the Redgrave performance that lends credibility to our reading her as being involved in the killing, ready to dispense with the older lover. One scene with the Alvis is retained, where she and her thief boyfriend are chasing the photographer to find his home base. When the studio is found to have been ransacked, we have no trouble imagining that the killer did it; or that smirking, he held the final macro-blowup in his hands fully aware that its lumps of light and shadow would be inadequate as proof. He keeps the images that have some evidentiary value and this one he politely hides near the floor, so that it can be discovered and tantalize the young photographer forever, a dirty joke.

Hemmings—a genius casting move—conveys precisely the boundless energy and untrammeled spirit of those who are too young to get it. O'Casey remembers him as "very inexperienced"; the young actor "really did not know what he was up to . . . the gravitas. The weight of the movie. It was over his head, it was just another film. He had no idea, no idea. I did. Vanessa did." Originally (and as reported in the *Daily Mail* February 21, 1966), the role of the photographer had been designed for Terence Stamp, who was convinced that Antonioni "wrote *Blow-Up* for me. He changed his screenplay from an Italian fashion photographer in Milano to a kind of a David Bailey portrayed by Terence Stamp in London" (Catterall and Wells 27). The girl in the park was to have been Jean Shrimpton (Stamp's girlfriend at the time). But Antonioni decided upon a "virtual unknown"—as Hemmings was considered, although he had done seventeen films and a number of television shows before this—perhaps because, as Ali Catterall and Simon Wells suggest, "Stamp and Shrimpton—Pluto and Aphrodite in looks and temperament—would have blown the vision out of all proportion. The director's next choice of leads worked so well precisely because their relative newness to the screen allowed them to assume impenetrable mask-like visages through most of the movie" (27). More likely, however, given his working style, Antonioni simply preferred Hemmings's look, even though on first meeting he opined, "You look wrong, you're too young" (28). There is scarce reason for believing that Hemmings was an absolute innocent, and indeed good reason for crediting him with genuine sensitivity and intelligence. O'Casey tells a story of how he and Hemmings passed a break between shots in the park:

> The edge of this park looks over railway lines. There are trains. Every little semi-detached house has a beautiful little garden. English are not shopkeepers, they're gardeners. I looked at it and said to David, "There's so much soul in that. You have a little patch of ground. You make it into a little beautiful place. It's very touching. It's kind of like going down a mine with miners and hearing them on a Sunday playing in a brass band. It's the soul."
>
> Veruschka came up. "Vat are yu looking at? These are poor people. It's disgusting!"
>
> "Fuck off!"
>
> She was after him very big but that was the end of that little romance. No soul. ("Interview")

LONDON FALLING DOWN

I nearly went crazy there.
—Antonioni to Rex Reed, regarding London

Insofar as all fiction is a ghost story, it is hardly strange to think that Antonioni has here built a ghost city in which to set his tale. What makes so many other ghost stories tangibly thin is that they are set in apparently, or at least perfunctorily, real territories, in which contexts the apparitional stands out as a kind of excess (that instigates embarrassment). Here, however, the setting is carefully shot to mask the various (unquestioned) "realities" that confront us when we move through space: the contiguities of places, the range of natural and artificial colorations, the distances through which a city extends, the casual activity that backgrounds action. In *Blow-Up,* London is used as a location but the "London" of the story is contorted, misshapen, reconstituted as a wholly fabular, oneiric city space in which normal relations and proportions are continually misrepresented.

Take, for example, the geography of the main shooting sites, actually and as they are made to appear in the film. The photographer inhabits a studio on a tiny street, drives off with his camera in tow, passes a stretch of concrete blocks and turns into a byway near a park. In the park a woman runs off behind a bush at the rear of a shot. Earlier, before heading for his studio, the photographer hung out with some beggars near Consort Road. At one point—having swung by London Wall within a stone's throw of Milton's grave and of the spot where the German firebombing of World War II began—he takes a small detour for lunch with his agent in a charming little bistro on a quiet side street, then quickly drives back to his studio, which isn't very far away. Through all of this, we have the feeling of a neighborhood London, a practical London, not London of the tourist trade—Buckingham Palace, Piccadilly Circus, Westminster, the Thames embankment. While obviously spaces must be contracted in film, or "travel time" between locations be curtailed in order that dramatic necessities be addressed forthrightly and without delays, it remains clear that with this film rather extraordinary spatial ellipses have been effected: many urban locations out of reach of one another have been abutted in a transposed space. In a way, we oscillate back and forth between two spatial cores, the radiant park and the photographer's studio and business world. At the outskirts of the narrow ellipse that binds these, we can find Consort Road, the roadways leading to the park, Regent Street where the girl is spotted—and in an alley off which the photographer locates the Ricky Tick Club—the sedate little bistro, and so on. We need never have a sense of the photographer actually migrating from one neighborhood to a distant other, or even leaving central London, and I can recall, in fact, that when first I saw this film, never having visited London, I worked hard to imagine that city along the lines suggested by the film, where the mysterious and beautiful park lingered somewhere not so far from the center of the city, nor so far from a tiny byway where the photographer's esoteric little studio was hidden.

The "map" on which we position the events of this film must be overlaid upon an entirely unmatching configuration of urban space, however. Beginning just off St. James's Street, Piccadilly, the film abruptly cuts to the railway overpass at the conjunction of Consort and Copeland Roads in Peckham, several miles away through twisting roads in Vauxhall and Camberwell. It takes an hour to drive it. Almost as far off in the other direction is the photographer's arty abode—in fact the studio of John Cowan at 49 Princes Place, Holland Park. A few tiny blocks away, on the narrow little Pottery Lane, is No. 77, the exterior that was used for the studio door, this on a street which exits to the north. The photographer is not shown making turns, but driving away from his studio he would have to change direction to head toward the Thames and south London: there is no contiguity between Notting Hill (where one finds Holland Park) and Peckham, or between Notting Hill and the districts of Woolwich through which the photographer proceeds on his way to the park. Maryon Park itself is in Charlton, a village east of Greenwich and more than an hour's drive from Notting Hill at the best of times. Iain Sinclair, a London wanderer, confesses, "It didn't connect with an area of London that I knew" (347). Nor is the park itself configured in such a way that a visitor could walk to the end of Cox's Mount and continue until she disappeared from the view of a camera like our photographer's, near the walkway that leads off to Kinveachy Gardens. The charming little bistro is located just off Sloane Square, at very considerable distance from the park, the photographer's studio, and other locations in central London where shots were made. Guards in bearskin hats are seen to parade along Culford Gardens (a longish march from the palace). Appearing in St. James's Street, various other central London streets, and the park, the whitefaced mimes establish continuities between otherwise disparate spaces.

As to the range of natural and artificial colorations and designs, Antonioni felt free here, as in his other color films, to make adjustments wherever his eye demanded. Walls were painted in Woolwich and on Tamar Street outside the park, and paint was applied inside the park, as well, both to the fencing and to the grass, thirty square yards of which were painted green ("Exhibitor's Manual"). "Everyone talks of the wonderful grass and the wonderful trees," Antonioni said to Rex Reed, "but I painted the grass with green paint and I painted the streets and the buildings with white paint. I even painted the tree trunks. Everything. Since this is not a novel, but a short story, I wanted a subdued unity of tone. I got effects you cannot get in the laboratories." The neon sign was erected, one hundred feet high, not only serving "to make a pleasing Antonioni-type composition for the camera but provid[ing] the lighting cameraman with a light source for two weeks of night shooting" ("Exhibitor's Manual"). The white houses margining the park were formed in a bizarre, legally required gesture: "The tenants of a terrace of 30 houses in the background of the park refused to permit their properties to be painted snow-white. However, they gave permission for a 200-foot-long by 30-foot-high scaffolding to be erected in their collective back gardens, on which was built the façade of 30 snow-white houses!" Kathleen Purcell's grocery shop outside the park was altered temporarily, "filled with truckloads of old tables and chairs, stuffed animals, pots and old iron utensils and converted to a junk shop" ("Exhibitor's Manual")—a transformation that particularly pleased the art director (Tuson 107). Roadways were painted black, both in and around the park: "Antonioni had decided the roads weren't black enough. All paint shops in the area were emptied of their stocks, which were then poured into brand new garbage cans and applied to the road by six men with sweeping brushes," this process causing "houses lining the road [to] stand out in vivid relief" ("Exhibitor's Manual"). Thirty-five blackish pigeons were dyed ink-black (Haden-Guest). About this aestheticization, Antonioni declared, "Color in my films is now almost as important as the actors" ("Exhibitor's Manual").

Much as we struggle to map the film's narrative space into the actual space of London, we also struggle to map the fictive space into the indeterminate space of our own experience—some conflation of geography and imagination. Antonioni himself said, "I am always aware that there are two worlds facing each other—the real world and the visual world. When they impact, there's a kind of osmosis" (Hall). *Blow-Up* wasn't real altogether, Antonioni insisted to Marsha Kinder: "It wasn't really London, it was something *like* London" (29). And to Francis Wyndham: "Perhaps Londoners won't like it, as they see their city in another way. It could be set in Paris or New York without losing truth" (Wyndham). Entering a film, buying its propositions and assumptions, is always a matter of bringing a personal space, in which we understand the world, into alignment with a foreign compass. With *Blow-Up,* we oscillate between the sensation of knowing what kind of place we are in and the acute sensation of being lost.

"A SADLY UNFORTUNATE PERSON"

We are all socially promiscuous. . . . We are all available to whatever happens to come along. We do not exercise choice in our lives.

—David Hemmings to Roger Ebert

Much of the discussion about *Blow-Up,* reported Stanley Kauffmann about criticism and banter that followed the film after its release in the United States, "reflected modes of thought inculcated by the American academic mind, particularly in English departments. Almost everywhere there were people who wanted to discuss at length whether the murder in *Blow-Up* really happened or was an illusion" (71). Much critical discussion, too, revolved around the protagonist as essentially bogus and hollow. How disaffected he was! How cool, unsociable, alienated, self-absorbed, slovenly, narcissistic, and abusive. Bosley Crowther: "The ultimate statement of this picture about a London photographer who is so used to looking for shocks and sensations that he can't recognize truth or love is that anyone brought to this condition by the go-go environment in which he lives is a sadly unfortunate person" ("Eye"). In *The New Yorker,* Brendan Gill was more vituperative still: "The hero of 'Blow-Up' is a young fashion photographer—one of those lank London braves, sprung from the lower depths, whose caste signs are birdnest hair, blue jeans, expensive cars, and an almost total lack of feeling. For this zombie-like creature, well played by David Hemmings, the cameras he carries are not merely his livelihood but who he is and all he is; with their help, his days and nights are passed in a trance of profitable professional voyeurism" (62). In her book *On Photography,* Susan Sontag could not be far behind: "Photography has the unappealing reputation of being the most realistic, therefore facile, of the mimetic arts" (51). Yet photographs are more engaging, more mysterious, more moving than these lines of attack suggest. Every photograph is an extension of the past, but also—because the eye is not always able to see—an extension of reality into the territory about which, fashionably, we speculate and confabulate: images perhaps seem an insult to our dreams but also provoke them.

More than simply riddling its critics, this film provoked them to rashness and extremity. Richard Schickel, in a swoon, found Antonioni "one of the few sober artists attending the long hallucinogenic party that a significant portion of our culture has been staging for the past decade" (93). The *Motion Picture Herald* took pains to insert "(?)" whenever the word "story" was mentioned, and was preorgasmic, if also prurient, in relating the sex:

> In one scene, as two teenage girls are wallowing with a man on the floor in long sheets of colored paper, there is a fleeting shot of pubic hair. In another, a young man and woman are caught in act of copulation. There is another sequence of nudity as a femme strips to the waist in a willingness to go to the pad. No holds are barred, in the foreign manner, particularly in the scenes of the young femmes when first they're in bright-hued leotards, then they're not. Seldom has action been limned in such frankness outside of stag reels. ("Blow-Up")

Pauline Kael was a paragon of snideness: "It has some of the *Marienbad* appeal: a friend phones for your opinion and when you tell him you didn't much care for it, he says, 'You'd better see it again. I was at a swinging party the other night and it's all anybody talked about!'" ("Tourist" 30). Some three thousand words of colorblind sotto voce diatribe she writes, without a single mention of the park or what we see there. London's Penelope Gilliatt found it "effete and capricious" ("Foreign View").

Seymour Chatman, often an Antonioni loyalist, commits a seriatim misreading, it seems to me, when he writes, "The protagonist can't, it seems, finish anything. His photo book is incomplete, his marriage a failure (if he even is married—the dialogue leaves us in doubt), his fashion work dissatisfies him, and throughout his detective inquiry, he keeps getting side-tracked, by impulsive acquisition (the propeller), by sex, by drugs, by forgetting his camera when he needs it most, and so on" (Chatman and Duncan 111). The photo book *was* incomplete, but now he has completed it (and it's not for us, so why do we care?). As to the outraged propriety at the photographer not *even* being married: in the mid-1960s, marriage was no hegemony for the young, and the photographer is demonstrating no lack of piety. That his fashion work disappoints him or displeases him—it tires him, as do the models he must deal with all day to produce it. But this is no indictment; the models are also tired, and tiring in their tiredness. As to getting sidetracked: sex,

Antonioni said to Rex Reed, was the only thing that amused him, so from what (relatively uptight) point of view can one offer the photographer's sexuality as a *distraction?* His sexual engagement in this film is the wellspring of his perception and realization.

That he forgets his camera when he needs it most? This is not untrue, but also not helpful. Antonioni's first object here, and in all his films, is the attention of his audience. If the photographer had his camera at night in the park, he could get a shot of the corpse. But because at this critical juncture he lacks it, *we* get the shot instead. Necessary at this moment is that *we* take over the photographer's point of view.

One does have the sense that the photographer is caught up in the action of a pursuit without ever having the satisfaction of making a full discovery: yet nobody ever finishes things, truly, in this life. That is what mortality and engagement are all about: we are not required to finish the task, but neither are we free to desist from starting it. That Antonioni so brilliantly positions us to watch all these lines of action stimulated and enjoined, but without definitive conclusion—or with the only conclusion possible, an abrupt cessation—is not a critical flaw, it is a philosophical and critical triumph.

And that propeller:

Peter Brunette usefully offers a commentary that is not unreasonable: "After he has purchased a huge, unwieldy airplane propeller in an antique shop, the photographer himself indulges in a bit of aesthetic commentary when he borrows from Kant (without attribution!) to explain that he bought it because it is beautiful and that it is beautiful precisely because it is useless" (119).But this does not touch upon our vision of the thing itself (the propeller is purchased not for the photographer but for us). The propeller is the source of that wind we hear in the park (that is, the propeller is the source of wind, and one wind cannot be distinguished from another), and so, now that it has found its way into the hero's lair, we will be able to hear the wind there, too: when the photographs are printed and assembled.

UNNECESSARY CLOTHING

All the impressions that he formed . . . were derived exclusively, perhaps, from the light which he shed.

—Pirandello, *Shoot!*

In my end is my beginning. The film, for all its brilliance and saturation, for all its heat and wonder and moony darkness, is a thing that moves around us, not merely in that frames are eclipsed by the shutter but also in that the more one sees *Blow-Up,* the more visions seem to swell and dissipate in memory without enchainment. That neon sign, the girls trying on those dresses, the whitefaced raggers, Veruschka being "really" in Paris, the green corpse, the neighbor in her red string dress, the blue porcelain balls on the coffee table, the photographs, the photographs, the photographs. The center of this film, since it is a collection of moving fragments: what is that? The photographer's arrogant callowness turned reflective? The palpability of the body in life and death? Time and its riddles? The mystery of FOA . . . It'll never be known how this has to be told. Or: "If the likely inaccuracy can be seen beforehand, it becomes possible again to look; perhaps it suffices to choose between looking and the reality looked at, to strip things of all their unnecessary clothing" (Cortázar, "Blow-Up" 119).

The center is at the end.

Consider:

The miracle and pain of death is disappearance, and at the end of the film the body is gone. The neon sign stands high, impotent to charge any object by the sad light of day. Hardly surprised, the photographer retreats to the lower park, where the mimes who opened the film have arrived to close it, cheering, whooping, screaming, saying everything and nothing as in their Jeep they scootle through the long lower precincts on the blackened orbital. They stop and run to the courts for a crucial game that will test all their powers, a "lovely commedia dell'arte tennis match . . . sheer fun and beauty" (Barnes). Puff, poof, we can imagine the sounds the ball makes hitting those racquets, the racquets of the strange people in black and red stripes with white all over their faces.

But no sound. No racquets. No ball.

Great seriousness, and overwhelming concentration—there it is!—up, high up, over my head, back, back. The photographer stands with his fingers laced through the fencing, thinking these folk mad, alien, comical, insignificant, yet also compelling. Indeed, the more preposterous, the more compelling. Poof, paff, although we hear nothing.

To know because one has been told, because one has heard, is to be intrinsically social and also historical, linked back to previous moments of telling, receiving through vibration. The rhythm of talk—all rhythm—is the cycling of the stars, the beat of the seasons, the tattoo of time. But to know because one sees, to be able to say, "There it is!": this removes us from time—or from time as echo and record. To know because one sees is a greater desire fulfilled, the desire to link and unite and change. More, then, than allowing us to be historical and social, seeing makes us present. And of all colors, the one that is hardest to remember, the one we must see again and again and invent every time we see it, the one whose memory in a black-and-white photograph is in truth only a race through memory, a hunt, is green. All colors but green we can fix in the mind, but green races away, leaving only its suggestion, so that to know the green world we must see it, and see it over again. To know because one has heard is to be conscious, to be responsible, to be faithful, to be inscribed. But to know because one has seen is to be alive.

In the vault of silence, one clown hits the ball way way way up. Up . . . and over. They all turn and watch "it" disappear into the grass, and the photographer turns, too. Down it comes and hits and rolls. And rolls.

Yet, not only the photographer. The camera turns and follows along the grass, tracking away. Tracking, tracking. The grass rolls past, and we follow. In the center of the frame, always attended by the surveilling camera, the ball that is not a ball, the event that we make into an event. The camera slows and stops. The photographer stares over our way, to where we have come with that ball. The players all watch, portraits of fixation, and point sadly, judging, waiting for his moral commitment. Would you mind, please? He stalls: this is preposterous. These are only clowns, only goofing around. Out there is nothing, no reason to move. Yet they are trapped inside the court/cage, and if he doesn't go to help, who will? Seconds tick by. He looks again. Then he takes a few steps, breaks into a walk, then a loping run, to the point upon which we have been fixating, the ball in the grass, watching it, giving it his energy, his life moment. He bends and in one utterly graceful gesture seizes the ball and hefts it, tosses it for himself in order to feel the ineffable weight of its "being." "He looks like a man who has glimpsed for the first time something of what St. Paul may have meant by 'the things which are not seen'—a man suddenly made aware that there is more to life than what the senses can perceive or the camera record," wrote *Time* ("Things"); but also he looks like a man who has seen what it is to look. What one should do with one's eyes.

He throws it, this globe, this *ding an sich,* this metaphor, high and over, up, up, through the clouds, so that it goes all the way to heaven. The mimes are happy as children and continue their devoted game, and from his distance he stands and watches in absolute tranquility, with new eyes that are not always expecting a revelation. But now, yes, poof, poof, puff, poof, the ball can be heard.

An object, after all, is that which we agree upon. Our agreement makes an object. There is no reality that is not a game of sorts, a collection of gestures, an agreement of orientations and scrambles. We can know because we see. But even what we cannot see is there. We can know by belief. And then we can "see."

Finally we must wonder, is the photographer a witness to this game or the counter in it, the ball batted here and there, up and down, back and forth, by the random pressures of modern life (see Massumi 74–75)? As with tennis balls, with shuttlecocks:

> "Shuttlecocks!"
>
> And she repeated the word "shuttlecocks" three times. I know what was passing in her mind, if she can be said to have a mind, for Leonora has told me that, once, the poor girl said she felt like a shuttlecock being tossed backwards and forwards between the violent personalities of Edward and his wife. Leonora, she said, was always trying to deliver her over to Edward, and Edward tacitly and silently forced her back again. And the odd thing was that Edward himself considered that those two women used *him* like a shuttlecock. Or, rather, he said that they sent him backwards and forwards like a blooming parcel that someone didn't want to pay the postage on. And Leonora also imagined that Edward and Nancy picked her up and threw her down as suited their purely vagrant moods. So there you have the pretty picture. (Ford 226–227)

The pretty picture which is: both multiple viewpoints and passivity, objective consciousness and speed, modern haphazardness and artful intent, finally the use and abuse of persons in the name of action. How surprising can it be if this photographer is himself a "shuttlecock," or a tennis ball, the tennis ball in, and not an observer to, this game, and that finally he should suffer the distinctive fate?

We are high above, gazing down at the green field on which the photographer stands far below, a tiny figurine. And then—

He is gone.

The glory of fiction is a sacred emptiness. There never was a photographer, not really. And that is what this film is about: the intimation or offering that is pure hypothesis, the incitement to see, not the thing seen. No park, no models, no camera, no lovers, no Jeep, no clowns, no city, no world. Only that we agreed to believe we saw, only that we were convinced in our belief. The ball flipped up and down in the palm of that hand: a green thought in a green shade. And now where he was standing on the grass, that fading grass, is a tiny point, a point that expands and changes form, approaches us, and masters our consciousness, taking the shape (today) of words: THE END.

But since this "end" is an opening to memory, it is also, and in truth, a beginning.

. . .

Blow-Up (1966), photographed by Carlo di Palma in the 1.85: 1 format in Eastmancolor, at MGM British Studios, Borehamwood, London and at London locations including Maryon Park, Sloane Square, Notting Hill, and Peckham; 111 m. Released in the United States December 18, 1966.

Works Cited and Consulted

BFI	Library of the British Film Institute, London
HER	Margaret Herrick Library, Academy of Motion Picture Arts and Sciences, Beverly Hills
USC	Cinema Television Library, University of Southern California, Los Angeles

Adams, William Howard. *Nature Perfected: Gardens Through History.* New York: Abbeville, 1991.

Adamson, James. *Sketches of Our Information as to Rail-Roads.* Newcastle: Constable, 1826.

Agee, James. *Agee on Film: Reviews and Comments by James Agee.* Boston: Beacon Press, 1964.

Agee, James, and Walker Evans. *Let Us Now Praise Famous Men.* New York: Ballantine, 1966.

Ager, Cecelia. "Antonioni Hero in Hollywood," *New York Times* (February 5, 1967), D11.

American Cinematographer. "An Interview with Michelangelo Antonioni," in Bert Cardullo, ed. *Interviews,* 131–137.

Anonymous. Unlabeled clipping on *The Oberwald Mystery. Mystery of Oberwald* Clipping File, MGM Collection (USC).

Antonioni, Michelangelo. *That Bowling Alley on the Tiber.* Trans. William Arrowsmith. New York: Oxford University Press, 1986.

———. *Unfinished Business.* Ed. Carlo di Carlo and Giorgio Tinazzi. Trans. Andrew Taylor. New York: Marsilio, 1998.

Arrowsmith, William. *Antonioni: The Poet of Images.* New York: Oxford University Press, 1995.

Atkinson, Michael. "Antonioni Snoozes; Arnold Stretches; Greed is Good Again," *The Village Voice* (November 30, 1999). Online at www.villagevoice.com/film/9948,atkinson,10524,20.html. Accessed September 6, 2007.

Bachmann, Gideon. "Antonioni after China: Art versus Science," in Bert Cardullo, ed. *Interviews,* 121–130.

———. "A Love of Today: An Interview with Michelangelo Antonioni," in Bert Cardullo, ed. *Interviews,* 169–174.

Ball, Philip. *Bright Earth: Art and the Invention of Color.* Chicago: University of Chicago Press, 2001.

Barker, Wayne. *Brain Storms: A Study of Human Spontaneity.* New York: Grove Press, 1968.

Barnes, Clive. "'The Homecoming' and 'Blow-Up': Strange Ballets," *New York Times* (February 12, 1967), 118.

Barthes, Roland. "Cher Antonioni," *Cahiers du cinéma* 311 (May 1980), reprinted in *Deux grands modernes,* a special edition of *Cahiers,* 2007, 85–87.

Baudelaire, Charles. *Paris Spleen.* New York: New Directions, 1970.

Becker, Howard S. *Outsiders: Studies in the Sociology of Deviance.* New York: Free Press of Glencoe, 1963.

Beckett, Samuel. *Krapp's Last Tape and Other Dramatic Pieces.* New York: Evergreen, 1960.

Begg, Ken. "Review of *Zabriskie Point*" (December 31, 2007). Online at http:/jabootu.net/?p=1313. Accessed August 10, 2010.

Benjamin, Walter. "Franz Kafka," in Hannah Arendt, ed. *Illuminations: Essays and Reflections.* New York: Schocken, 1969, 111–140.

———. "The Storyteller," in Hannah Arendt, ed. *Illuminations: Essays and Reflections.* New York: Schocken, 1969, 83–109.

———. "Capitalism as Religion," in Marcus Bullock and Michael W. Jennings, ed. *Selected Writings* Vol. 1, 1913–1926. Cambridge MA: Harvard University Press, 1996, 288–291.

———. "Notes for a Study of the Beauty of Colored Illustrations in Children's Books," in Marcus Bullock and Michael W. Jennings, eds. *Selected Writings* Vol. 1, 1913–1926. Cambridge MA: Harvard University Press, 1996, 264–266.

———. "Moscow," in Michael W. Jennings, Howard Eiland, and Gary Smith, eds. *Selected Writings* Vol. 2, 1927–1934. Trans. Rodney Livingstone and Others. Cambridge MA: Harvard University Press, 1999, 22–46.

———. "The Work of Art in the Age of its Technological Reproducibility (Third Version)," in Michael W. Jennings, Howard Eiland, and Gary Smith, eds. *Selected Writings* Vol. 4, 1938–1940. Trans. Edmund Jephcott and Others. Cambridge MA: Harvard University Press, 2003, 251–283.

Bensky, Lawrence M. "Antonioni Comes to the Point," *New York Times* (December 15, 1968), D23.

Bergala, Alain. "Deux questions (graves) à quelques films en compétition," *Cahiers du cinéma* 338 (July-August, 1982), 5–10.

Berman, Marshall. *All That Is Solid Melts Into Air: The Experience of Modernity.* New York: Penguin, 1988.

Billard, Pierre. "An Interview with Michelangelo Antonioni," in Bert Cardullo, ed. *Interviews,* 46–69.
Billington, David P. *The Tower and the Bridge.* New York: Basic Books, 1983.
Boccioni, Umberto et al. "Futurist Painting: Technical Manifesto," in Charles Harrison and Paul Wood, eds. *Art in Theory: 1900–1990,* Oxford and Cambridge: Blackwell, 1992, 149–152.
Bonitzer, Pascal. "*Notorious,*" in Slavoj Žižek, ed. *Everything You Always Wanted to Know about Lacan (But Were Afraid to Ask Hitchcock),* London: Verso, 1992, 151–154.
Bordwell, David. "Authorship and Narration in Art Cinema," in Virginia Wright Wexman, ed. *Film and Authorship,* New Brunswick NJ: Rutgers University Press, 2003, 42–29.
Borges, Jorge Luis. *Labyrinths: Selected Stories and Other Writings.* Harmondsworth, Middlesex: Penguin, 1970.
Brown, Norman O. *Life Against Death: The Psychoanalytical Meaning of History.* Middletown CT: Wesleyan University Press, 1959.
———. *Love's Body.* New York: Random House, 1966.
Brown, Roger. *Words and Things: An Introduction to Language.* New York: The Free Press, 1958.
Brunette, Peter. *The Films of Michelangelo Antonioni.* New York: Cambridge University Press, 1998.
Burks, John. "Fourteen Points to Zabriskie," *Rolling Stone* 53 (March 7, 1970), 36–39.
Calvino, Italo. *Invisible Cities.* Trans. William Weaver. New York: Harcourt Brace Jovanovich, 1974.
Camus, Albert. *Lyrical and Critical Essays.* Ed. Philip Thody. Trans. Ellen Conroy Kennedy. New York: Knopf, 1968.
Canby, Vincent. "'Blow-Up' May Get New Code Review," *New York Times* (February 7, 1967), 33.
———. "Antonioni's 'Mystery of Oberwald': A Doomed Queen," *The New York Times* (September 30, 1981), C23.
———. "Antonioni's Mystery 'Identification of a Woman,'" *The New York Times* (September 30, 1982), C18.
Caramel, Luciano, and Alberto Longatti. *Antonio Sant'Elia: The Complete Works.* New York: Rizzoli, 1988.
Cardullo, Bert. "Film Is Life: An Interview with Michelangelo Antonioni," in Bert Cardullo, ed. *Interviews,* 138–154.
Cardullo, Bert, ed. *Michelangelo Antonioni Interviews,* Jackson: University Press of Mississippi, 2008.
Catterall, Ali, and Simon Wells. *Your Face Here: British Cult Movies Since the Sixties.* London: Fourth Estate, 2001.
Cavell, Stanley. *The World Viewed: Reflections on the Ontology of Film.* Enlarged edn. Cambridge MA: Harvard University Press, 1979.
Chatman, Seymour. *Antonioni: Or, The Surface of the World.* Berkeley: University of California Press, 1985.
———. "Antonioni in 1980: An Interview," in Bert Cardullo, ed. *Interviews,* 155–161.

Chatman, Seymour, and Paul Duncan, eds. *Michelangelo Antonioni: The Complete Films*. Köln and London: Taschen, 2004.

Chéroux, Clément. "La Dialectique des spectres: La photographie spirite entre récréation et conviction," in Clément Chéroux, Andreas Fischer, Pierre Apraxine, Denis Canguilhem, and Sophie Schmit, *Le Troisième oeil: La photographie et l'occulte,* Paris: Gallimard, 2004, 45–55.

Chocano, Carina. "Three obscure objects of desire," *Los Angeles Times* (April 8, 2005), Constance McCormick Collection, USC.

Cocteau, Jean. *L'aigle à deux têtes*. Paris: Gallimard, 1973.

Conley, Tom. "Getting Lost on the Waterways of *L'Atalante*," in Murray Pomerance, ed. *Cinema and Modernity*. New Brunswick NJ: Rutgers University Press, 2006, 253–272.

Cortázar, Julio. *Hopscotch*. New York: Pantheon, 1966.

———. "Blow-Up," in *The End of the Game and Other Stories*, Trans. Paul Blackburn. New York: Pantheon, 1967, 114–31. Originally published as "Las babas del diablo" in *Las Armas secretas* (1958); translated into French as "Les fils de la vierge" in *Les Armes secrètes* (1963).

———. "The Daily Daily," in *Cronopios and Famas,* Trans. Paul Blackburn. New York: Pantheon, 1969, 67.

Cottino-Jones, Marga, ed. *Michelangelo Antonioni: The Architecture of Vision*. Chicago: University of Chicago Press, 1996.

Craft, Robert. "With Aldous Huxley," *Encounter* XXV: 5 (November 1965), 10–16.

Crary, Jonathan. *Suspensions of Perception: Attention, Spectacle, and Modern Culture*. Cambridge MA: MIT Press, 2000.

Crowther, Bosley. "*Red Desert*: Newest Antonioni Film Shown at Beekman," *New York Times* (February 9, 1965), 43.

———. "'Blow-Up' Arrives at Coronet," *New York Times* (December 19, 1966), 52.

———. "In the Eye of the Beholder," *New York Times* (January 8, 1967), 93.

Daney, Serge, and Serge Toubiana. "La Méthode de Michelangelo Antonioni," *Cahiers du cinéma* 342 (December 1982), 5–7, 61–65.

Davenport, Guy. *The Hunter Gracchus and Other Papers on Literature and Art*. Washington DC: Counterpoint, 1996.

———. *Objects on a Table: Harmonious Disarray in Art and Literature*. Washington DC: Counterpoint, 1998.

Davis, Mike. *City of Quartz: Excavating the Future in Los Angeles*. New York: Vintage, 1992.

———. *Ecology of Fear: Los Angeles and the Imagination of Disaster*. New York: Vintage, 1998.

———. "Diary," *London Review of Books* (November 15, 2007), 31.

Davis, Natalie Zeman. *The Return of Martin Guerre*. Cambridge MA: Harvard University Press, 1983.

De Quincy, Thomas. *The Collected Writings*. Ed. David Masson. London: A. and C. Black, 1897.

de Saint-Éxupery, Antoine. "Port Étienne," in Wayne Grady, ed. *Deserts*. Vancouver: Greystone Books, 2008, 15–19.

di Carlo, Carlo, ed. *Michelangelo Antonioni*. Rome: Cinecittà Holding, n.d.
Dickens, Charles. *Hard Times for These Times*. Harmondsworth: Penguin, 1977.
Didion, Joan. "Los Angeles Days" (1988), in *After Henry*. New York: Simon and Schuster, 1992, 145–173.
———. "Times Mirror Square" (1989), in *After Henry*. New York: Simon and Schuster, 1992, 220–250.
Dimendberg, Edward. *Film Noir and the Spaces of Modernity*. Cambridge MA: Harvard University Press, 2004.
Dixon, Wheeler Winston. *It Looks At You: The Returned Gaze of Cinema*. Albany: State University of New York Press, 1995.
Doane, Mary Ann. *The Emergence of Cinematic Time: Modernity, Contingency, the Archive*. Cambridge MA: Harvard University Press, 2002.
Duranty, Louis Émile Edmond. "The New Painting: Concerning the Group of Artists Exhibiting at the Durand-Ruel Galleries," in *The New Painting: Impressionism 1874–1886*, catalog of an exhibition at the Fine Arts Museums of San Francisco and the National Gallery of Art, Washington. Geneva: Burton, 1986, 37–49.
Durrell, Lawrence. *Justine*. London: Faber & Faber, 1963.
Ebert, Roger. "Interview with David Hemmings," *Chicago Sun-Times* (February 26, 1967). Online at http://rogerebert.suntimes.com/apps/pbcs.dll/article?AID = /19670226/PEOPLE/702260301/. Accessed December 2, 2008.
———. "Zabriskie Point," *Chicago Sun-Times* (January 1, 1970). Online at http://rogerebert.suntimes.com/apps/pbcs.d11/article?AID=/19700101/REVIEWS/1010322/. Accessed August 10, 2010.
———. "Blow-Up," *Chicago Sun-Times* (November 8, 1998). Online at http://rogerebert.suntimes.com/apps/pbcs.dll/article?AID = /19981108/REVIEWS08/401010304/1023. Accessed December 3, 2008.
Elder, R. Bruce. "Antonioni's Tragic Vision," *Canadian Journal of Film Studies* 1: 2 (1991), 1–34.
Eliade, Mircea. *The Myth of the Eternal Return*. Princeton: Princeton University Press, 1954.
Fara, Patricia. *An Entertainment for Angels: Electricity in the Enlightenment*. Duxford, Cambridge: Icon Books, 2003.
Fiedler, Leslie A. *Love and Death in the American Novel*. New York: Criterion, 1960.
Film Culture. "A Talk with Michelangelo Antonioni on His Work," in Bert Cardullo, ed. *Interviews*, 21–45.
Finlay, Victoria. *Colour: Travels Through the Paintbox*. London: Sceptre, 2002.
Ford, Ford Madox. *The Good Soldier*. London: Penguin, 1946.
Forman, Murray. "Getting the Gun: The Cinematic Representation of Handgun Acquisition," in Murray Pomerance and John Sakeris, eds. *Bang Bang, Shoot Shoot!: Essays on Guns and Popular Culture*, 2nd Edition, Boston: Pearson Education, 2000, 49–61.
Foucault, Michel. *The History of Sexuality. Volume I: An Introduction*. Trans. Robert Hurley. New York: Pantheon, 1978.
Freccero, John. "BLOW-UP: From the Word to the Image," in Roy Huss, ed., *Focus*, 116–128.

Freud, Sigmund. "The Uncanny," in *On Creativity and the Unconscious: Papers on the Psychology of Art, Literature, Love, Religion,* Sel. Benjamin Nelson, New York: Harper & Row, 1958, 122–161.
Friedenberg, Edgar Z. *Coming of Age in America: Growth and Acquiescence.* New York: Vintage, 1965.
———. *The Disposal of Liberty and Other Industrial Wastes.* Garden City, NY: Doubleday Anchor, 1976.
Gage, John. *Color and Culture: Practice and Meaning from Antiquity to Abstraction.* Boston: Little, Brown, 1993.
———. *Color and Meaning: Art, Science, and Symbolism.* Berkeley: University of California Press, 1999.
Gandy, Matthew. "Landscapes of Deliquescence in Michelangelo Antonioni's *Red Desert,*" *Transactions of the Institute of British Geographers* 28: 2 (2003), 218–237.
Garfinkel, Harold. *Studies in Ethnomethodology.* London: Polity Press, 1984.
Gerth, Hans and C. Wright Mills, eds. *From Max Weber: Essays in Sociology.* New York: Oxford University Press, 1968.
Gill, Brendan. "Ways of Winning," *The New Yorker* (December 31, 1966), 60–62.
Gilliatt, Penelope. "About Reprieve," *The New Yorker* (April 14, 1975), 112–119.
Gindoff, Bryan. "Thalberg Didn't Look Happy: Or, with Antonioni at Zabriskie Point," *Film Quarterly* 24: 1 (Autumn 1970), 3–6.
Giuliano, Charles. "Massacre of the Innocents," *Boston After Dark* (March 25, 1970), 26.
Gleber, Anke. "Female Flanerie and the *Symphony of the City,*" in Katharina von Ankum, ed. *Women in the Metropolis: Gender and Modernity in Weimar Culture,* Berkeley: University of California Press, 1997, 67–88.
Godard, Jean-Luc. "The Night, the Eclipse, the Dawn (Interview with Michelangelo Antonioni)," *Cahiers du cinéma* 160 (November 1964), reprinted in Marga Cottino-Jones, ed. *Antonioni,* 287–297.
Goffman, Erving. *Asylums.* Garden City NY: Doubleday, 1964.
———. *Relations in Public: Microstudies of the Public Order.* New York: Basic Books, 1971.
———. *Frame Analysis: An Essay on the Organization of Experience.* Cambridge MA: Harvard University Press, 1974.
Goldstein, Richard. "Did Antonioni Miss the 'Point'?," *New York Times* (February 22, 1970), D15, D17.
Goodman, Paul. *Speaking and Language: Defence of Poetry.* New York: Random House, 1971.
Griffiths, Keith. "Antonioni's Technological Mysteries," *Framework* 15/16/17 (Summer 1981), 29–31.
Gumbrecht, Hans Ulrich. *In 1926: Living at the Edge of Time.* Cambridge MA: Harvard University Press, 1997.
Gunning, Tom. "The Exterior as *Intérieur:* Benjamin's Optical Detective," *Boundary 2* 30: 1 (Spring 2003), 105–130.

Hahn, Hazel, "Boulevard culture and advertising as spectacle in nineteenth-century Paris," in Alexander Cowan and Jill Steward, eds. *The City and the Senses: Urban Culture Since 1500,* Aldershot: Ashgate, 2007, 156–175.
Haines, Richard W. *Technicolor Movies: The History of Dye Transfer Printing.* Jefferson NC: McFarland, 1993.
Hall, William. "Antonioni the master says: I'm not an ogre," *Evening News* (November 27, 1973).
Hammett, Dashiell. *Red Harvest.* New York: Vintage, 1972.
Hardin, C.L. *Color for Philosophers: Unweaving the Rainbow.* Indianapolis: Hackett, 1988.
Harris, Marvin. *Cows, Pigs, Wars and Witches: The Riddles of Culture.* New York: Vintage, 1975.
Hawthorne, Nathaniel. "Wakefield," in *Selected Tales and Sketches*, 3rd ed. New York: Holt, Rinehart and Winston, 1970, 164–73.
Healy, Seán Desmond. *Boredom, Self and Culture.* Toronto: Associated University Presses, 1984.
Hemmings, David. *Blow-Up and Other Exaggerations.* London: Robson, 2004.
Higgins, Scott. *Harnessing the Technicolor Rainbow: Color Design in the 1930s.* Austin: University of Texas Press, 2007.
Hofstadter, Richard J. *Anti-Intellectualism in American Life.* New York: Vintage, 1963.
Holden, Stephen. "*Beyond the Clouds:* Transformed by Obsession, Heart, Mind and Soul," *New York Times* (September 28, 1996). Online at www.movies.nytimes.com/movie/review?res = 9C05EFDE123CF93BA1575AC0A9609582. Accessed September 18, 2007.
Huss, Roy, ed. *Focus on Blow-Up.* Englewood Cliffs NJ: Prentice-Hall, 1971.
Hyde, Philip. *Drylands: The Deserts of North America.* New York: Park Lane, 1990.
James, William. *Principles of Psychology.* New York: Dover, 1950.
Jay, Martin. *Downcast Eyes: The Denigration of Vision in Twentieth-Century French Thought.* Berkeley: University of California Press, 1994.
Joyce, James. *A Portrait of the Artist as a Young Man.* New York: Penguin, 1999.
"Justice Dept. Gets 'Zabriskie,'" *The Hollywood Reporter* CCVI 29 (June 20, 1969).
Kael, Pauline. "Tourist in the City of Youth," *The New Republic* (February 11, 1967), 30–35.
———. "The Beauty of Destruction," *The New Yorker* (February 21, 1970), 95–99.
Kandinsky, Wassily. *Concerning the Spiritual in Art, and Painting in Particular.* 1912. Reprint, New York: Wittenborn, 1966.
Kasindorf, Martin. "Symposium: What Makes a Good Assistant Director," *Action* (May-June 1973), 30–35.
Kauffmann, Stanley. "A Year with BLOW-UP: Some Notes," in Roy Huss, ed. *Focus*, 70–77.
———. "Zabriskie Point," *The New Republic* 162 (March 14, 1970), 20–31.

Kelly, William. "*Identification of a Woman*," *Film Quarterly* 37: 3 (Spring 1984), 37–43.

Kemp, Philip. "Eros," *Sight & Sound* 10: 56 (October 2006), 58.

Kinder, Marsha. "Zabriskie Point," *Sight and Sound* 38: 1 (Winter 1968/69), 26–30.

Labarthe, André S. "A Conversation with Michelangelo Antonioni," in Bert Cardullo, ed. *Interviews,* 3–10.

Laqueur, Thomas W. *Solitary Sex: A Cultural History of Masturbation.* New York: Zone, 2003.

Latimesblogs.latimes.com/thedailymirror/

Leonard, Tom. "Heath Ledger 'may be digitally recreated'." Online at http://www.telegraph.co.uk/news/worldnews/1576958/Heath-Ledger-'may-be-digitally-recreated'.html. Accessed July 11, 2008.

Levin, Gail. *Synchromism and American Color Abstraction 1910–1925.* New York: George Braziller, 1978.

Lingenfelter, Richard E. *Death Valley & the Amargosa: A Land of Illusion.* Berkeley: University of California Press, 1986.

Lyman, Mel, and Wayne Hansen. "I'll never forget the day my father took me aside . . . ," *American Avatar* 3 (1969), 18–19. Online at www.trussel.com/lyman/never.htm. Accessed December 18, 2008.

Manceaux, Michelle. "An Interview with Antonioni," in Bert Cardullo, ed. *Interviews,* 11–20.

"Mann Act Charge on MGM Pic," *The Hollywood Reporter* CCVI 11 (May 26, 1969).

Mannoni, Laurent. *The Great Art of Light and Shadow.* Exeter: University of Exeter Press, 2000.

Marcuse, Herbert. *Eros and Civilization: A Philosophical Inquiry into Freud.* New York: Vintage, 1961. First published 1955.

Marx, Karl. *The Manifesto of the Communist Party,* Part I, reprinted in C. Wright Mills, ed. *Images,* 102–113.

Massumi, Brian. *Parables for the Virtual: Movement, Affect, Sensation.* Durham: Duke University Press, 2002.

Mayhew, Henry. *London Labour and the London Poor.* Sel. Victor Neuburg. Harmondsworth: Penguin, 1985.

Mayo, Morrow. *Los Angeles.* New York: Alfred A. Knopf, 1933.

McWilliams, Carey. *Southern California Country: An Island on the Land.* New York: Duell, Sloan & Pearce, 1946.

Meyerowitz, Joel. *Cape Light.* New York: Bulfinch, 2002.

Miller, Stephen. *Conversation: A History of a Declining Art.* New Haven: Yale University Press, 2006.

Mills, C. Wright, ed. *Images of Man: The Classic Tradition in Sociological Thinking,* New York: Braziller, 1967.

Molli, Jeanne. "Antonioni's Tinted 'Red Desert,' " *The New York Times* (March 29, 1964), X8.

Montaigne, Michel de. *The Essays: A Selection,* Trans. M.A. Screech. London: Penguin, 2004.

Mosca, Gaetano. "The Ruling Class," in C. Wright Mills, ed. *Images,* 192–232.

Narita, Hiro. "Moments, Memories and Master," *American Society of Cinematographers Newsletter* 4: 1 Issue 13 (April 2007).

Nelson, Victoria. *The Secret Life of Puppets.* Cambridge MA: Harvard University Press, 2001.

Neocleous, Mark. *The Fabrication of Social Order: Critical Theory of Police Power.* London: Pluto, 2000.

Newhall, Nancy. "Death Valley," in Ansel Adams, Nancy Newhall, and Ruth Kirk, *Death Valley,* Redwood City: 5 Associates, 1954, 7–18.

Nietzsche, Friedrich. *On the Genealogy of Morals: A Polemic.* Oxford: Oxford University Press, 1999.

O'Brian, Dave. "The Sorry Life & Death of Mark Frechette," *Rolling Stone* 199 (November 6, 1975), 32.

O'Grady, Gerald L. Talk on *The Red Desert.* School of Image Arts, Ryerson University, January 23, 2008.

Ortega y Gasset, José. *The Revolt of the Masses.* New York: Norton, 1964. First published 1932.

———. "On Point of View in the Arts," in *The Dehumanization of Art and Other Essays on Art, Culture, and Literature.* Princeton: Princeton University Press, 1972, 107–130.

Orwell, George. *Down and Out in Paris and London.* New York: Harcourt, 1950. First published 1933.

———. *The Road to Wigan Pier.* London: Penguin, 1986. First published 1937.

———. "A Day in the Life of a Tramp," in Peter Davison, ed. *Orwell's England.* London: Penguin, 2001, 2–9. First published 1927.

Panofsky, Erwin. *Meaning in the Visual Arts.* Garden City NY: Doubleday Anchor, 1955.

Peploe, Mark, Peter Wollen, and Michelangelo Antonioni. *The Passenger.* New York: Grove Press, 1975.

Perez, Gilberto. "The Point of View of a Stranger," in *The Material Ghost,* Baltimore: Johns Hopkins University Press, 1998, 367–416.

Petro, Patrice. "Perceptions of Difference: Woman as Spectator and Spectacle," in Katharina von Ankum, ed. *Women in the Metropolis: Gender and Modernity in Weimar Culture,* Berkeley: University of California Press, 1997, 41–66.

Phillips, Adam. *On Kissing, Tickling, and Being Bored: Psychoanalytic Essays on the Unexamined Life.* Cambridge MA: Harvard University Press, 1994.

Pike, E. Royston. *Human Documents of the Victorian Golden Age.* London: George Allen and Unwin, 1974.

Pirandello, Luigi. *Shoot!* Trans. C.K. Scott Moncrieff. Chicago: University of Chicago Press, 2005. First published 1926.

Poe, Edgar Allan. "The Man of the Crowd," in *Selected Tales,* Ed. David Van Leer, Oxford: Oxford University Press, 1998, 84–91.

Pomerance, Murray. "Recuperation and *Rear Window.*" *Senses of Cinema* 29 (November-December 2003). Online at www.sensesofcinema.com.

———. *An Eye for Hitchcock.* New Brunswick: Rutgers University Press, 2004.

———. "A Modern Gesture: Perpetual Motion and Screen Suspense," *Film International* 5: 5 (Issue 29, Fall 2007), 42–53.

———. "Notes on Some Limits of Technicolor: The Antonioni Case," *Senses of Cinema* 53 (Winter 2010). Online at www.sensesofcinema.com.

Powers, John. "Antonioni's Magnificent Impasse," *Film Comment* 36: 4 (July/August 2000), 52.

Prédal, René. *Michelangelo Antonioni ou la vigilance du désir.* Paris: Éditions du Cerf, 1991.

Rancière, Jacques. *The Future of the Image.* Trans. Gregory Elliott. London: Verso, 2007.

Reed, Rex. "Antonioni: After the 'Blow-Up,' a Close-Up," *New York Times* (January 1, 1967), 63.

Riffel, Mélanie, and Sophie Rouart. *Toile de Jouy: Printed Textiles in the Classic French Style.* London: Thames & Hudson, 2003.

Rifkin, Ned. *Antonioni's Visual Language.* Ann Arbor: UMI Research Press, 1982.

Robertson, Peggy. "An Oral History with Peggy Robertson," Interviewed by Barbara Hall. Oral History Program, Margaret Herrick Library, Academy of Motion Picture Arts and Sciences, Beverly Hills, 2002.

RobotLeAwesome, "Ledger returns from the grave says '***** the rest of the movies' takes an Oscar and returns to the dead." Online communication to digg.com, at http://digg.com/movies/Give_Heath_Ledger_an_Oscar. Accessed July 11, 2008.

Rogal, Kim, and Ronald Henkoff, "Intruder at the Palace," *Newsweek* (July 26, 1982), 38–39.

Rohdie, Sam. *Antonioni.* London: BFI, 1990.

Róheim, Géza. *The Gates of the Dream.* New York: International Universities Press, 1970.

Rooney, David. "Eros," *Daily Variety* (October 27, 2004), 42, USC.

Rosenbaum, Jonathan. "Return to Beauty," *Chicago Reader* (n.d.). Online at www.chicagoreader.com/movies/archives/2000/0400/000407.html. Accessed September 6, 2007.

Ryave, A. Lincoln, and James N. Schenkein. "Notes on the Art of Walking," in Roy Turner, ed. *Ethnomethodology,* Harmondsworth: Penguin, 1975, 265–278.

Samuels, Charles Thomas. "Interview with Michelangelo Antonioni," in Bert Cardullo, ed. *Interviews,* 79–103.

Sartre, Jean-Paul. *Baudelaire.* Trans. Martin Turnell. New York: New Directions, 1967.

———. "Masturbation (1952)," in *Modern Times: Selected Non-Fiction.* Ed. Geoffrey Wall and Trans. Robin Buss, London: Penguin, 2000, 115–124.

Scarry, Elaine. *Dreaming by the Book.* Princeton: Princeton University Press, 1999.

Schama, Simon. *A History of Britain: The Fate of Empire 1776–2000.* Toronto: McClelland and Stewart, 2000.

Scheler, Max. *Man's Place in Nature.* Trans. Hans Meyerhoff. New York: Noonday, 1962.

———. *Ressentiment.* Trans. Lewis B. Coser and William W. Holdheim, with an Introduction by Manfred S. Frings. Milwaukee: Marquette University Press, 2003.

Schickel, Richard. "Blow-Up," in *Second Sight: Notes on Some Movies 1965–1970*, New York: Simon & Schuster, 1972, 91–93.

Schivelbusch, Wolfgang. *The Railway Journey: The Industrialization of Time and Space in the 19th Century*. Berkeley: University of California Press, 1986.

———. *Three New Deals: Reflections on Roosevelt's America, Mussolini's Italy, and Hitler's Germany, 1933–1939*. New York: Picador, 2006.

Scott, A.O. "Sex, Sex, Sex, Seen Through Experienced Cinematic Eyes," *New York Times* (April 8, 2005), *Eros* Clipping File, MGM Collection, USC.

Sebald, Winfried Georg. *The Emigrants*. Trans. Michael Hulse. New York: New Directions, 1997.

———. *Austerlitz*. New York: Vintage, 2001.

Setlowe, Rick. "Frisco Fest Buffs Hushedly Pious Welcome for Plot-Killer Antonioni," *Variety* (November 6, 1968).

Shelley, Mary. *Frankenstein or the Modern Prometheus*. London: Penguin, 1992.

Shepard Sam. *Operation Sidewinder*, in *Four Two-Act Plays*. New York: Urizen, 1980. First published 1970.

Simmel, Georg. "Sociology of the Senses: Visual Interaction," in Robert E. Park and Ernest W. Burgess, eds. *Introduction to the Science of Sociology*, Chicago: University of Chicago Press, 1969, 356–361. First published 1921.

Simon, John. "*The Passenger* will please refrain . . . ," *Esquire* (July 1975), 16+.

Sinclair, Iain. *Lights Out for the Territory: 9 Excursions in the Secret History of London*. London: Penguin, 2003.

"Sir Elton John on 'Inside the Actors Studio,' " October 16, 2005.

Sobchack, Vivian. *Carnal Thoughts: Embodiment and Moving Image Culture*. Berkeley: University of California Press, 2004.

Sontag, Susan. *On Photography*. New York: Farrar, Straus & Giroux, 1977.

———. *At the Same Time: Essays and Speeches*. Ed. Paolo Dilonardo and Anne Jump. New York: Farrar, Straus & Giroux, 2007.

Spacks, Patricia Meyer. *Boredom: The Literary History of a State of Mind*. Chicago: University of Chicago Press, 1996.

Starobinski, Jean. *The Invention of Liberty, 1700–1789*. Trans. Bernard C. Swift. Geneva: Skira, 1964.

Steedman, Carolyn. *Dust: The Archive and Cultural History*. New Brunswick NJ: Rutgers University Press, 2002.

Steegmuller, Francis. *Cocteau: A Biography*. London: Constable, 1986.

Stiller, Andrew. *Handbook of Instrumentation*. Berkeley: University of California Press, 1985.

"The Things Which Are Not Seen," *Time* (December 30, 1966). Online at www.time.com/time/printut/0,8816,901936,00.html. Accessed December 11, 2007.

Thomson, Richard. *Seurat*. Oxford: Phaidon, 1985.

Tolkien, J.R.R. *The Lord of the Rings: The Return of the King*. London: HarperCollins, 1992.

Tomasulo, Frank P. "Life Is Inconclusive: A Conversation with Michelangelo Antonioni," in Bert Cardullo, ed. *Interviews*, 162–168.

Tuson, Elizabeth-Marie. "Consumerism, the Swinging Sixties and Assheton Gorton," *Journal of British Cinema and Television* 2: 1 (2005), 100–116.

Tyler, Parker. *The Shadow of an Airplane Climbs the Empire State Building: A World Theory of Film*. Garden City NY: Doubleday, 1972.

Untitled review of *Zabriskie Point, Playboy* (May 8, 1970), 34, 36.

"The Void Between," *Time* (February 23, 1970), 47.

Walker, Beverly. "Frechette of Fort Hill: Robbing the Bank for Mel: On the Set of *Zabriskie Point,*" *The Real Paper* (September 12, 1973).

———. "Michelangelo and the Leviathan: The Making of *Zabriskie Point,*" *Film Comment* 28: 5 (September 1992), 36–49.

Wells, H. G. *Mind at the End of Its Tether.* New York: Didier, 1946.

Wenders, Wim. *My Time with Antonioni.* Trans. Michael Hofmann. London: Faber & Faber, 2000.

White, Mimi. "1970: Movies and the Movement," in Lester D. Friedman, ed. *American Cinema of the 1970s: Themes and Variations,* New Brunswick NJ: Rutgers University Press, 2007, 24–47.

Williams, David. "Heath Ledger immortalised by internet fans." Online at http://www.telegraph.co.uk/news/worldnews/1576957/Heath-Ledger-immortalised-by-internet-fans.html. Accessed July 11, 2008.

Williams, James S. "The Rhythms of Life: An Appreciation of Michelangelo Antonioni, Extreme Aesthete of the Real," *Film Quarterly,* 62: 1 (Fall 2008), 46–57.

Williams, Tennessee. *The Night of the Iguana.* New York: New Directions, 1962.

Winstein, Bruce. "Introduction to Antonioni's *Identification of a Woman.*" Online at www.dvdbeaver.com/film/articles/identificatin_of_a_woman.htm. Accessed December 10, 2008.

Winter, Richard. *Still Bored in a Culture of Entertainment.* Downers Grove IL: InterVarsity Press, 2002.

"With 'Blow-Up' Behind, Antonioni Mulls U.S. As Locale for His Next Pic," *Variety* (June 21, 1967).

Wittgenstein, Ludwig. *Tractatus Logico-Philosophicus.* Trans. D.F. Pears and B.F. McGuinness. London: Routledge & Kegan Paul, 1969.

Youmans, Charles. "The Twentieth-Century Symphonies of Richard Strauss," *The Musical Quarterly* 84: 2 (2000), 238–258.

• • •

Antonioni, Michelangelo. "Note to the Treatment of *Zabriskie Point,*" *Zabriskie Point* file, HER.

August 1967 Treatment for *Zabriskie Point. Zabriskie Point* file, HER.

August 1968 Script for *Zabriskie Point. Zabriskie Point* file, HER.

"Blow-Up," *Daily Mail* (January 6, 1967), *Blow-Up* file, BFI.

"Blow-Up," *Motion Picture Herald* (April 19, 1967), *Blow-Up* file, HER.

"'Blow-Up' Poses Code Issue," *Variety* (December 14, 1966), 1, 4, *Blow-Up* file, HER.

Byrge, Duane. "Beyond the Clouds," *Hollywood Reporter* (October 23, 1995), *Beyond the Clouds* Clipping File, MGM Collection, USC.

Crowther, Bosley. Review of *The Red Desert, The New York Times* (February 9, 1965), *Red Desert* Clipping File, HER.
Exhibitor's Manual for *Blow-Up. Blow-Up* Clipping File, MGM Collection, USC.
Feeney, F.X. "The Body Never Lies," *L.A. Weekly* (December 3–9, 1999), *Beyond the Clouds* Clipping File, MGM Collection, USC.
Gilliatt, Penelope, "London Life—A Foreign View," *The Observer* (March 19, 1967), *Blow-Up* file, BFI.
Gorton, Assheton. Interview, London, February 21, 2009.
Guerin, Ann. "A Many-hued Ado about Nothing," *Life* (March 5, 1965), *Red Desert* Clipping File, HER.
Guest, Don. Interview. December 19, 2008.
Haber, Joyce. "'Zabriskie Point' Rescured by Aubrey," *Los Angeles Times* (December 2, 1969), *Zabriskie Point* file, USC.
Haden-Guest, Anthony. "The Man Who Painted Woolwich Black," *Weekend Telegraph* (September 23, 1967), *Blow-Up* file, BFI.
Hetzel, Ralph. Memorandum regarding discussion with Haven Falconer, January 31, 1967, *Blow-Up* file, HER.
Kael, Pauline. "So Off-Beat We Lose the Beat," *New Republic* (November 5, 1966), *Red Desert* Clipping File, HER.
"The Maestro." "Word of Mouth," November 19, 1999. *Red Desert* Clipping File, HER.
Miller, Karl. "A Sunday Dilemma: Getaway People and Ghetto People," *Sunday Times* (December 14, 1969), *Blow-Up* file, BFI.
O'Casey, Ronan. Conversation with Murray Pomerance. November 2007.
Red Desert Press Kit. USC.
Robertson, Peggy. Letter to Giulio Ascarelli, Universal International Films, Rome, April 8, 1965, regarding *The Red Desert,* HER.
Rubin, Bob. Interview. December 18, 2008.
Sarris, Andrew. "Foolish Notions About Narrative," *Village Voice* XXVII: 42 (October 19, 1982), 49. *Identification of a Woman* Clipping File, MGM Collection, USC.
Schreiber, Sidney. Inter-office memorandum to Geoffrey Shurlock, November 9, 1966, regarding *Blow-Up* and the Code seal, *Blow-Up* file, HER.
Scott, Barbara. Inter-office memorandum to Geoffrey Shurlock, January 20, 1967, directing him to an attached memo from Haven Falconer, *Blow-Up* file, HER.
Script for *Story of a Man and Woman on a Fine Autumn Morning (Bye Bye, Love)* [subsequently *Blow-Up*], copied March 10, 1966, *Blow-Up* file, HER.
Shurlock, Geoffrey M. Letter to Robert Vogel, Metro-Goldwyn-Mayer Inc., regarding sex scenes in *Blow-Up,* March 30, 1966, *Blow-Up* file, HER.
———. Letter to Robert Vogel, Metro-Goldwyn-Mayer Inc., regarding sex scenes in *Blow-Up,* April 27, 1966, *Blow-Up* file, HER.
———. Letter to Michael Linden, November 23, 1966, regarding SMA advertisements for *Blow-Up, Blow-Up* file, HER.
Starr, Harrison. Interview. December 17, 2008.
Tavoularis, Dean. Interview. December 17, 2008.

"Through a Lens Backward," *Independent* (April 21, 1993), *Blow-Up* file, BFI.
Treatment for *The Shot,* March 16, 1966, *Blow-Up* file, HER.
Untitled clipping from *The Village Voice* regarding *The Red Desert* re-release in 1990, *Red Desert* Clipping File, HER.
Untitled clipping from UCLA Archive regarding *The Red Desert,* February 20, 1993, *Red Desert* Clipping File, HER.
Walker, Beverly. Interview, Los Angeles, October 18, 2008.
Winstein, Bruce. Interview. December 17, 2008.
Wyndham, Francis. "Antonioni's London," *Sun-Times* (March 3, 1967), BFI.
Yellow Paper on *Blow-Up, Blow-Up* file, HER.
"Zabriskie Point," *Variety* (May 8, 1970), *Zabriskie Point* clipping file, MGM Collection, USC.

Index